BOOT AND SADDLES:

Military Leaders of the American West

BOOTS AND SADDLES:

MILITARY LEADERS OF THE AMERICAN WEST

THOMAS D. PHILLIPS

CAXTON PRESS
Caldwell, Idaho
2015

ISBN 978-087004-591-2

Library of Congress Cataloging-in-Publication Data

Phillips, Thomas D.
  Boots and saddles : military leaders of the American West / by Thomas D. Phillips.
    pages cm
  Includes bibliographical references.
  ISBN 978-0-87004-591-2
  1. Indians of North America--Wars--1866-1895--Biography. 2. United States. Army--Officers--Biography. 3. Generals--United States--Biography. 4. Scouts (Reconnaissance)--West (U.S.)--Biography. I. Title. II. Title: Military leaders of the American West.

F592.C33P55 2015
355.0092'2--dc23
[B]

2014048015

Cover
By Jim D. Nelson
www.jdnelsonportraits.com

Lithographed and bound in the United States of America

CAXTON PRESS
Caldwell, Idaho
189069

TABLE OF CONTENTS

Maps

PREFACE

The Indian wars of the American West were fought across an immense landscape remarkable for its varied geography and climate and for the cultures of the Native peoples who inhabited it. The wars were waged by a surprisingly small military force. During the 25-year period following the Civil War, the U.S. Army typically numbered little more than 25,000 officers and men. Those few soldiers manned the nation's 150 forts, posts, camps, arsenals, and armories; guarded 6,000 miles of frontier and coastline; escorted wagon trains, stage coaches, and survey parties; shielded the construction of railroads, trails, and bridges; protected settlers and settlements; scouted; and, when called upon, fought Indians. During the full course of the Indian wars, they were called to do that more than a thousand times.

While identical sets of circumstances seldom existed, several frequently recurring conditions served as triggers for many of the wars. These factors varied in intensity from region to region and conflict to conflict. Foremost among them were the westward migration of the nation's growing population – a journey that took thousands of emigrants across Native regions; the discovery of gold or silver on historically Native or treaty land; and the rapid destruction of the continent's two great bison herds.

The government's attempts to address the "Indian problem" by relocating the tribes or moving them to reservations were often resisted by the free-roaming and fiercely independent tribal groups. The Natives who signed treaties and moved to agencies sometimes faced an additional irritant: government functionaries did not always supply the annuities promised in treaty provisions.

Indeed, treaty violations (sometimes in response to incidents perpetrated by the other party) were not unknown on either side. Native actions most often took the form of thefts of livestock and killing raids on homesteads, settlements, outposts, and emigrant travelers.

The conflicts on the Great Plains and in the West and Southwest would present the U.S. Army with a different form of warfare than its officers and men had experienced during the Civil War. They would face difficult opponents – superb horsemen infused with a warrior culture that sprang from incessant warfare with rival tribes.

The conflict area along and inside the nation's western frontiers spanned approximately 1,815,640 square miles – more than half the land mass of the lower continental United States. All or parts of 17 present-day states now shape the immense territory.

The landscape inside that area is as varied as any on the planet. Snow-capped mountains rise from flat, grassy plains with horizons so immense that they almost invariably drew comment in pioneer diaries. Fast, sparkling-clear streams rush down those mountains, stark in contrast to the sluggish, muddy creeks that meander back and forth across the prairies. Some of America's great rivers trace the High Plains, West, and Northwest. In the Southwest single water holes, often quite small, dictated travel routes, influenced the planning of campaigns, and, as adversaries sought access or control, formed sites for ferocious combat.

In the North and Northwest, ample moisture nourished lush stands of timber, offering promise of fuel and shelter. On the "Staked Plains" of Texas and elsewhere in the Southwest, travelers found ground so parched that a single mesquite tree or yucca plant often formed the central feature of a landscape. Seemingly strewn at random, gorges and canyons of monumental size provided hiding places, hindered travel and – then as now – inspired awe.

Like the terrain, climactic conditions across the enormous theater of operations could hardly have been more extreme. Troopers who braved wintertime low temperatures of minus 40 degrees on the High Plains of Montana and Dakota also faced baking, near-suffocating heat on the deserts of the Southwest.

The disparate conditions of climate and terrain had profound effects on military activities. Planning, equipment, clothing, and logistical considerations were all influenced by extremes of weather and landscape.

Events in this book focus mainly on the three-decade period beginning in 1855. In September of that year, General William S. Harney defeated a large band of Oglala and Brule Sioux near present-day Lewellen, Nebraska. The Battle of the Blue Water, as the fight became known, culminated the government's first military expedition against the Plains Indians. Harney's victory was decisive and succeeded in halting raids along the overland trail for much of the next decade.

Conditions began to change beginning in 1862 with the Sioux uprising in Minnesota and then in a more pronounced way following the massacre of Cheyenne tribesmen at Sand Creek, Colorado, in November 1864. Native restlessness coincided with the end of the Civil War, an event which for a time allowed the government to focus greater attention on the burgeoning problem. The two decades following the end of the war in 1865 saw conflict spread across the central Plains, the West, and Pacific Northwest, as well as through West Texas and the American Southwest. Geronimo's surrender in 1886 with his last remaining band of Apaches is generally regarded as the closing episode in the series of wars fought by the United States Army against organized, free-roaming groups of Native warriors. In contrast, the tragedy at Wounded Knee in 1890 was an isolated encounter resulting from a terribly mishandled confrontation.

At the time the conflicts were most intense, the Native population in the area from the central Plains to the Pacific Coast probably numbered 225,000 – 250,000. Not all were nomadic or hostile. Those that were, however, made formidable adversaries. Tenacious and aggressive, Native warriors formed what may have been "the finest light cavalry in history." The war chiefs were familiar with terrain features and water sources across an immense region that often had yet to see a white surveyor or a rudimentary depiction on a map.

To confront the challenge posed by the hostile tribes and carry out the government's policies, military leaders had access to an Army that even in the immediate aftermath of the Civil War was never large and whose effective strength in the West was further drained by the commitment of sizable numbers of soldiers to Reconstruction duty in the South. It was a daunting task at which some excelled and others failed utterly.

In physical stature and personality, the military leaders who waged war in the West were as varied as the terrain on which they fought. William S. Harney and John I. Gregg towered 6 feet 4 inches in height. Frank North and several others were well over 6 feet. The most diminutive, Philip H. Sheridan, stood barely 5 feet 4 inches tall.

Some, like Nelson Miles, were glib, vocal, and articulate; others, like George Crook, gruff and taciturn. A few, like Ranald Mackenzie, anguished over public speaking and avoided it whenever it was possible to do so.

Miles, Crook, and others such as Wesley Merritt and Eugene A. Carr – who personally ministered to his soldiers during a cholera epidemic – were well-liked by their men. Ranald Mackenzie's soldiers recognized his brilliance and appreciated the fact that he kept them alive, but sometimes chafed under his harsh discipline and the high standards he set for them. In the words of his major biographer, "they never loved him, none of his soldiers ever would, but they would follow him anywhere."

George Armstrong Custer, while expressing pride in his men, seldom interacted with them, preferring instead the company of a small cadre of 7th Cavalry officers or his Native scouts. A few officers, like Thomas Moonlight, were so inept in the field or careless in their handling of their troopers as to provoke near-mutinies. Many, but by no means all, were West Point graduates. Whatever their source of commission, their abilities ranged from exceptional to abysmal.

There were notable differences in the commanders' attitudes toward their Indian adversaries as well. Crook and others studied, understood, and respected the Native culture. Indeed, it was Crook who helped orchestrate the proceedings that led to the court case regarding the Ponca chief Standing Bear. The court's decision that Native Americans are persons within the meaning of the law and "have the right of *habeas corpus*" was a seminal event in the history of the United States.

At the polar extreme was John Chivington, an avowed racist who spoke of wading in Indian blood and openly advocated exterminating the Native tribes. Somewhere in between were the views of Philip Sheridan and others who, without expressing a moral judgment, understood the dilemma faced by the tribes and the reasons that compelled them to fight. Sheridan, though, believed that a clash of cultures was inevitable. Wars, in his opinion, were unavoidable and waging them as harshly as possible would hasten their conclusion.

Although the flamboyant George Armstrong Custer continues to fascinate historians and the public more than a century and a quarter after the Little Bighorn, the names and contributions of many of the officers who led forces in the wars of the West are generally less well recalled. Even the accomplishments of Philip H. Sheridan – who guided military operations across much of the region for more than two decades and, as much as any single individual, shaped the outcome of America's western saga – are eclipsed in the public's memory by his exploits during the Civil War.

Indeed, nearly all of the commanders who led forces in the American West were veterans of that conflict. Perhaps because the nation had only recently emerged from that cataclysm, to that generation the conflicts against the hostile tribes may have seemed less consequential, and less memorable, in comparison. To those who came later, the wars remained eclipsed by the clash that tore the nation apart and were then subsumed in the larger saga of America's westward expansion. Then too, the conflicts were fought over an extended time period, against numerous sets of adversaries in a variety of locations. Though major battles sometimes occurred, the majority of encounters were smaller unit actions – though no less bloody as a consequence.

Those considerations have muted the nation's recollections of the events of that period and of the people who participated in them. More so than with almost all of our nation's conflicts, the military leaders who fought the wars of the American West have remained in the shadows of history. This book is an attempt to bring them into the light so their stories may surprise, instruct, or inspire the present generation and those that will follow.

NOTES

Officer Ranks The officers who fought the battles and led the campaigns in the American West were veterans of the Civil War. Almost all of them held at least two ranks: a permanent, official rank in the Regular Army and a brevet rank – a nominal promotion to a higher grade without commensurate pay or specific authority given as recognition for service or actions during the war. The permanent rank was always lower than the brevet rank. The brevet rank was intended to be temporary, although many officers continued to be addressed by the higher brevet rank as a courtesy. Thus, Custer, a lieutenant colonel in the Regular Army, was typically referred to as "General" – a carryover from the brevet major general rank he achieved during the war.

The rank situation was sometimes further confused by the fact that officers could hold brevets and actual, full ranks for service in both the Regular Army and the United States Volunteers. It was therefore possible to hold as many as four ranks simultaneously. For example, Ranald Mackenzie – who held commissions in both the Regular Army and the U.S. Volunteers – was a brevet major general of volunteers, an actual, full brigadier general of volunteers, a brevet brigadier general in the Regular Army, and an actual Regular Army captain.

I have tried to acquaint the reader with the actual and brevet ranks held by the officer whose story is being told. In the narrative discussion, when necessary to specify the officer's rank, I have attempted to consistently use the rank by which he was most commonly addressed at the time.

Army Structure and Terms Although larger campaigns and expeditions sometimes involved 2,000 – 3,000 soldiers, the majority of the Army's clashes with Native tribes involved formations often of company size or smaller. While the nominal size of companies at this time was about 100 soldiers, the Army was in fact chronically undermanned. Infantry companies often numbered only about 40 enlisted men. Cavalry companies quite frequently had no more than 50.

From smallest to largest, the post-war Army was organized in companies, battalions, (generally two to seven companies), regiments/brigades (three or more battalions), and divisions (three or more brigades). In recent years, the term 'brigade' has come increasingly to identify the Army's operational units above the battalion level. During the Civil War and the wars with the Indians, such units were identified as 'regiments.'

'Cavalry troop' is a generic term typically given to a small force of horse soldiers. In the United States military the term is usually associated with platoon- or company-sized units. When necessary, I have used it synonymously with 'company' to improve readability and avoid repetition.

The term 'dragoon' originally referred to mounted infantry and was then subsequently associated with light cavalry forces. In 1861, the United States Army re-designated its existing dragoon units as cavalry regiments.

Regional Divisions Throughout the period of the Indian wars in the West, the United States Army portioned the continental United States into an arrangement of regional commands, each responsible for a defined geographic region. The largest of these regional establishments were called 'divisions'; e.g., the Division of the Missouri. Divisions were divided into smaller entities called 'departments.' Departments were further sub-divided into 'districts.' On occasion, districts were further apportioned into 'sub-districts.' District commands were normally assigned to colonels. Departments and divisions were typically commanded by one- or two-star generals. The Division of the Missouri, the largest and most active of the administrative formations was, beginning with William T. Sherman and followed by Philip H. Sheridan, led by a three-star general.

Division boundaries were occasionally shifted to accommodate changing conditions. During the beginning of Sheridan's tenure as commander of the Division of the Missouri, the division consisted of the Department of Arkansas, Department of the Missouri (Colorado, Kansas, New Mexico, and Indian Territory); Department of the Platte (Iowa, Nebraska, and the territories of Wyoming, Utah, and a portion of eastern Idaho); and the Department of Dakota (Minnesota and the territories of Montana and Dakota). The Department of Arkansas was soon dropped from the division's area of responsibility. When Texas was readmitted to the Union, a new department – the Department of Texas – consisting of Texas and Indian Territory – was added.

Military Installations Military installations were labeled 'camps' if their intended occupancy was to be temporary (even if for an extended duration), and 'forts' if the facilities were designated to be permanent. Those labels were sometimes changed. For example, the historic post in the Nebraska Panhandle was officially Camp Robinson for the first four years of its existence before being re-designated as a fort in 1878. 'Post' is a more generic term associated with military establishments of all types.

Casualties When figures are known or contemporaneous estimates exist, casualties for each encounter are cited in the narrative comments that describe the battle. Estimates for Indian losses are in many cases uncertain and sometimes vary widely when described in after-action correspondence.

There should be no mistaking the intensity of the combat, however. Even though many of the encounters were small in terms of numbers of combatants, losses were significant as a portion of the forces engaged.

Although the numbers vary slightly by source, all bespeak of the scope, duration, and severity of the fighting. One notable study concluded that "between 1865 and 1891 the U.S. Army conducted 13 campaigns against (Native tribes), engaging them in 1,067 separate actions … Army casualties (were tallied) as 948 killed and 1,058 wounded. Meanwhile, Native American casualties in those battles have been estimated at 4,371 killed, 1,279 wounded, and 10,318 captured."

Another historian found that "during the twenty-five-year period that followed the Civil War, 923 officers and enlisted men died, and 1,061 suffered wounds. Army records estimate 5,519 Indians killed and wounded. Also engaged were white civilians, 461 of whom died in these battles and 116 of whom were wounded. General Sheridan reported that the proportions of casualties to troops engaged on the Great Plains in 1876-1877 were greater than those of the Civil War or the Russo-Turkish war then being fought. It was an intense, dramatic confrontation, played out on a great, varied landscape."

References Space limitations in a book of this scope preclude the listing of a bibliography in the traditional sense. Many of the officers who led forces in the American West acquired their first significant military experience during the Civil War. Their records during that conflict – how they performed under fire, their style of leadership, successes and failures, and their growth as combat leaders – offer useful insights into the nature of their later service in the West. In 1996, a study placed the "total number of Civil War books at more than 50,000" of which 1,100 are labeled as "essential"). In the nearly two decades since then the numbers have continued to grow exponentially.

The same considerations apply regarding material on the American West. When information is incorporated (as it must be) on military-specific events, general history, Native tribes, and geography, the reference pool becomes immense in size. Thus, the dilemma for the author is not in finding material but in selecting appropriate references from the tens of dozens of available sources.

In lieu of a traditional bibliography, I have compiled individual reference lists, each focusing on a specific leader. These condensed lists may also serve as recommended readings for those interested in adding further to their understanding of the officers who led forces during this unique time in the nation's history. With the exception of a few older histories, most of the cited references are readily available.

Similarly, traditional footnoting would have required the numbering of every third or fourth sentence and added further scores of pages to the text.

All of the material in the book is extracted from the bibliographical lists specific to each leader. Therefore, in the interests of space and readability, I have confined reference notes to directly quoted material.

Spelling Names of tribal groups and Native men and women are sometimes rendered differently depending on the source. The name of one of the major tribes of the Sioux nation, for example, is spelled at least three ways in major texts: Oglala, Ogallala, and Ogalallah. In this and other cases, I have chosen the version that appears most frequently in recent scholarship. Interestingly, there even exists somewhat of a historic divergence in the spelling of the most famous of all Indian battles in the American West; i.e., Little Big Horn vs. Little Bighorn. I have followed the conventions of authors of recent major works on the subject, Nathaniel Philbrick (*The Last Stand*) and James Donovan (*A Terrible Glory*) as well as the *New York Public Library American History Desk Reference* and used Little Bighorn.

Maps The maps of battle sites and locations of forts displayed in this book are specific to the Indian wars era. While other major engagements and historic installations are also shown, I have included several in each category that, although perhaps lesser known, are most directly associated with the officers whose stories are told in these pages.

Acknowledgements I owe special thanks to the staff at the U.S. Army History and Education Center at Carlisle, Pennsylvania, for their patience and assistance in researching and answering my many questions particularly regarding the careers of Patrick Connor and John Pope. Our nation is indeed fortunate to have such a marvelous facility manned by highly gifted and dedicated military historians. Thanks also to Jeanne Kern for her exceptional insights on frontier history, skillful editing, and wise counsel.

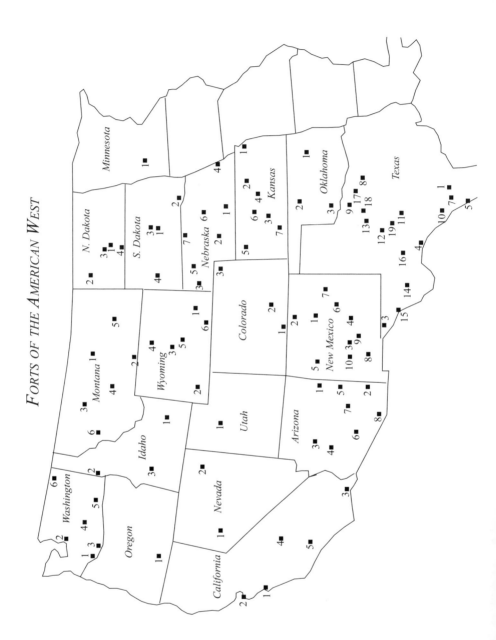

Arizona
1. Fort Defiance (1851)
2. Fort Bowie (1862)
3. Fort Verde (1865)
4. Fort McDowell (1865)
5. Fort Apache (1869)
6. Fort Lowell (1873)
7. Fort Thomas (1876)
8. Fort Huachuca (1877)

California
1. Presidio of Monterey (1846)
2. Presidio of San Francisco (1846)
3. Fort Yuma (1851)
4. Fort Miller (1851)
5. Fort Tejon (1854)

Colorado
1. Fort Garland (1858)
2. Fort Lyon (1860) *Formerly Fort Wise
3. Fort Sedgwick (1864)

Idaho
1. Fort Hall (1863) * A civilian post had existed since 1834
2. Fort Lapwai (1862)
3. Fort Boise (1863)

Kansas
1. Fort Leavenworth (1827)
2. Fort Riley (1853)
3. Fort Larned (1859)
4. Fort Harker (1862)
5. Fort Wallace (1865)
6. Fort Hayes (1865)
7. Fort Dodge (1865)

Minnesota
1. Fort Ridgely (1853)

Montana
1. Fort Benton (1865) *A civilian post had existed since 1847
2. Fort C.F. Smith (1866)
3. Fort Shaw (1867)
4. Fort Ellis (1867)
5. Fort Keogh (1876)
6. Fort Missoula (1877)

Nebraska
1. Fort Kearny (1848)
2. Fort McPherson (1863)
3. Fort Mitchell (1864)
4. Fort Omaha (1868)
5. Fort Robinson (1874)
6. Fort Hartsuff (1874)
7. Fort Niobrara (1880)

Nevada
1. Fort Churchill (1860)
2. Fort Halleck (1867)

New Mexico
1. Fort Union (1851)
2. Fort Burgwin (1852)
3. Fort Craig (1854)
4. Fort Stanton (1855)
5. Fort Wingate (1862)
6. Fort Sumner (1862)
7. Fort Bascom (1863)
8. Fort Cummings (1863)
9. Fort Seldon (1865)
1-. Fort Bayard (1866)

North Dakota
1. Fort Rice (1864)
2. Fort Buford (1866)
3. Fort Abraham Lincoln (1872)
4. Fort Yates (1874)

Oklahoma
1. Fort Gibson (1824)
2. Camp Supply (1868)
3. Fort Sill (1869)

Oregon
1. Fort Klamath (1863)

South Dakota
1. Fort Pierre (1855) *A civilian post had existed since 1832
2. Fort Randall (1856)
3. Fort Sully (1863)
4. Fort Meade (1878)

Texas
1. Fort Sam Houston (1845)
2. Fort Brown (1846)
3. Fort Bliss (1849)
4. Fort Duncan (1849)
5. Fort McIntosh (1849)

6. Fort Ringgold (1849)
7. Fort Inge (1849)
8. Fort Worth (1849)
9. Fort Belknap (1851)
10. Fort Clark (1852)
11. Fort McKavett (1852)
12. Fort Chadbourne (1852)
13. Fort Phantom Hill (1852)
14. Fort Davis (1854)
15. Fort Quitman (1858)
16. Fort Stockton (1859)
17. Fort Richardson (1867)
18. Fort Griffin (1867)
19. Fort Concho (1867)

Utah
1. Fort Douglas (1862)

Washington
1. Fort Vancouver (1849)
2. Fort Steilacoom (1849)
3. Fort Cascades (1855) * The most significant of three small blockhouse "forts" built to protect passage on the Columbia River.
4. Fort Simcoe (1856)
5. Fort Walla Walla (1858)
6. Fort Colville (1859)

Wyoming
1. Fort Laramie (1849)
2. Fort Bridger (1858) * A civilian post had existed since 1834
3. Fort Reno (1865)
4. Fort Phil Kearny (1866)
5. Fort D.A. Russell (1867)
6. Fort Fetterman (1867)

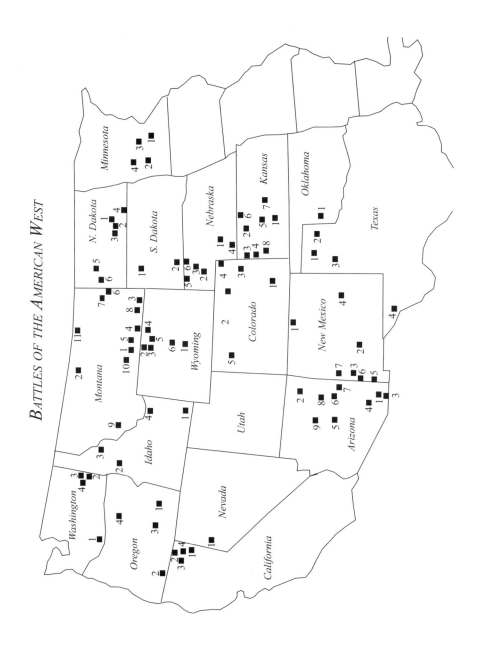

Arizona
1. Apache Pass, July 15-16, 1862
2. Canyon de Chelly, Jan. 12-14, 1864
3. Fort Buchanan, Feb. 17, 1865
4. Chiricahua Pass, October, 1869
5. Salt River Canyon, Dec. 28, 1872
6. Cibicue Creek, Aug. 30, 1881
7. Fort Apache, Sept. 1, 1881
8. Cedar Springs, Oct. 2, 1881
9. Big Dry Wash, July 17, 1882

California
1. Infernal Cavern, Sept. 28-29, 1867
2. Lava Beds, Dec. 3, 1872, Jan. 17, 1873, April 15-17, 1873
3. Sand Butte, April 26, 1873
4. Dry Lake, May 10, 1873

Colorado
1. Sand Creek, Nov. 29, 1864
2. Julesburg, Jan. 7, 1865, Feb. 2, 1865
3. Beecher Island, Sept. 17-19, 1868
4. Summit Springs, July 11, 1869
5. Milk Creek, Sept. 29-Oct. 5, 1879

Idaho
1. Bear River, Jan. 29, 1863
2. White Bird Canyon, June 17, 1877
3. Clearwater, July 11-12, 1877
4. Camas Meadows, Aug. 20, 1877

Kansas
1. Love's Defeat, June 7, 1847
2. Solomon Forks, July 1857
3. Kidder Battle, July 2, 1867
4. Fort Wallace, July 21, 1867, July 26, 1867
5. Saline River, August 1867
6. Prairie Dog Creek, Aug. 21, 1867
7. Plum Buttes Massacre, Sept. 9, 1867

8. Punished Woman's Fork, Sept. 27, 1878

Minnesota
1. New Ulm, Aug. 19, 1862, Aug. 23, 1862
2. Fort Ridgely, Aug. 20-22, 1862
3. Birch Coulee, Sept. 2, 1862
4. Wood Lake, Sept. 23, 1862

Montana
1. Hayfield Fight, Aug. 1, 1867
2. Marias River, Jan. 23, 1870
3. Powder River, March 17, 1876
4. Rosebud Creek, June 17, 1876
5. Little Bighorn, June 25, 1876
6. Cedar Creek, Oct. 21, 1876
7. Ash Creek, Dec. 18, 1876
8. Wolf Mtn., Jan. 8, 1877
9. Big Hole, Aug. 9, 1877
10. Canyon Creek, Sept. 13, 1877
11. Bear Paw Mtn., Sept. 30-Oct. 5, 1877

Nebraska
1. Plum Creek, Aug. 7, 1864
2. Mud Springs, Feb. 4-6, 1865
3. Rush Creek, Feb. 8-9, 1865
4. Forks of the Republican, June 24, 1867
5. Warbonnet Creek, July 17, 1876
6. Mackenzie's Raid, Oct. 23, 1876

Nevada
1. Pyramid Lake, June 2-4, 1860

New Mexico
1. Ojo Caliente, April 8, 1854
2. Cookes Canyon, Aug. 1861
3. Pinos Altos, Sept. 27, 1861
4. Pecos River, Jan. 4, 1864
5. Mount Gray, April 7, 1864
6. Doubtful Canyon, May 3, 1864
7. Fort Tularosa, May 14, 1880

North Dakota

1. Big Mound, July 24, 1863
2. Dead Buffalo Lake, July 26, 1863
3. Stony Lake, July 28, 1863
4. Whitestone Hill, Sept. 3-5, 1863
5. Killdeer Mtn., July 28, 1864
6. Badlands, Aug. 7-9, 1864

Oklahoma
1. Washita, Nov. 27, 1868

Oregon
1. Steens Mtn., Jan. 29, 1867
2. Lost River, Nov. 29, 1872
3. Silver Creek, June 23, 1878
4. Birch Creek, July 8, 1878

South Dakota
1. Slim Buttes, Sept. 9-10, 1876
2. Wounded Knee, Dec. 29, 1890

Texas
1. Adobe Walls, Nov. 29, 1864 June 27, 1874
2. North Fork of Red River, Sept. 28, 1872
3. Palo Duro Canyon, Sept. 28, 1874
4. Rattlesnake Canyon, Aug. 6, 1880

Washington
1. Battle of the Cascades, March 26-28, 1856
2. Tohotominne, May 17, 1856
3. Four Lakes, Sept. 1, 1858
4. Spokane Plains, Sept. 5, 1858

Wyoming
1. Platte Bridge, July 26, 1865
2. Tongue River, Aug. 28, 1865
3. Sawyer Fight, Aug. 31-Sept. 13, 1865
4. Fetterman Fight, Dec. 21, 1866
5. Wagon Box Fight, Aug. 2, 1867
6. Dull Knife Fight, Nov. 25, 1876

TALL IN THE SADDLE:

THE MOST NOTABLE (AND NOTORIOUS)

Among the officers who led forces across the American West there existed an exceptional few who by the nature of their actions – brilliant or catastrophic – or sometimes through luck, timing, or longevity, stood apart from the rest.

In some instances these leaders were not the most gifted or capable from among their contemporaries. Some held positions of enormous scope and responsibility. Others did not. Most, but not all, excelled as combat leaders. All of them, however, by the manner by which they discharged their duties – whether for good or for ill – shaped events that followed in significant and lasting ways.

JAMES H. CARLETON

In 1862, as the Civil War raged in the East, the Confederate States launched an invasion of the American West. Striking from Texas, rebel forces sought to secure the region's abundant gold and silver resources and perhaps in a grander scheme, capture seaports in Southern California. To repel the rebel advance, General James H. Carleton led Federal forces from California across Arizona and New Mexico. When the Confederates eventually abandoned their attempt, Carleton pushed his army into West Texas.

Although it was the Civil War that precipitated Carleton's presence in the area, when the rebel threat diminished he found himself primarily engaged in fighting Indians. For the remainder of the war, his army guarded the frontier against invasion while at the same time attempting to secure it against Indian raids notable for their scope and brutality.

It is in his role as Indian fighter that Carleton is best remembered. Employing Colonel "Kit" Carson as his primary field commander, Carleton was an implacable foe of the Native tribes, conducting campaigns known both for their harshness and success.

By the time Carleton arrived on the Texas border, he was already in his 23rd year of military service. Although he was regarded as a strict disciplinarian, by most accounts he was respected by his soldiers who apparently recognized and appreciated his experience and professionalism.

At the outset of the Civil War, Carleton was one of the longest-serving Union officers in the Far West. Carleton had been in the Regular Army since 1839. His first interactions with Native tribes had occurred as early as 1841 as a young officer posted in Indian Territory. Except for brief interludes, his entire career would be spent west of the Mississippi River.

Carleton was born at Bangor, Maine, in 1814. He served as an officer in a Maine militia unit during the 1838 border dispute with Canada – an undeclared, non-violent series of incidents called the Aroostook War. He

1

was commissioned as a lieutenant in the Regular Army the following year. As a young officer his first substantive duty was to take a company of 100 cavalrymen from Baltimore to New Orleans and then up the Mississippi and Arkansas Rivers to Fort Gibson, near the confluence of the Grand and Arkansas Rivers in Indian Territory (present-day Oklahoma).

At Fort Gibson, Carleton learned his trade leading border patrols, mapping remote areas, marking trails, and escorting wagon trains. He dealt with construction and supply issues and mastered the details of operating frontier outposts.

Two activities highlighted Carleton's assignment at Fort Gibson. His patrols disrupted the frontier slave trade (Kiowa and Comanche raiders regularly abducted slaves from Texas settlements and bartered them to slave-holding Creeks and Choctaws in return for blankets and guns). His most noted service, however, came in suppressing the production of raw whiskey which traders along the Red River in Texas distributed to the Native tribes in violation of Federal law.

The years 1842-1846 saw Carleton involved in several major expeditions as the nation's westward expansion began increasingly to brush against the central Plains region. From Fort Leavenworth, Kansas, Carleton led a unit of heavy cavalry to a location near present-day Council Bluffs, Iowa, where he established a post. Not long after, he was a member of a peaceful expedition that journeyed to Pawnee villages in Nebraska, exploring and mapping the Platte River region along the way. Late in 1844, he accompanied Colonel Stephen W. Kearny's dragoon force as it escorted an Oregon-bound party all the way to South Pass, Wyoming.

During the War with Mexico, Carleton commanded a dragoon company and was involved in heavy fighting at Buena Vista. Later, at the request of General John Wool, he performed a notable reconnaissance of the approaches to Saltillo prior to the battle there.

After brief postings at Carlisle Barracks in Pennsylvania and Fort Leavenworth, 1850 found Carleton in New Mexico in command of a cavalry unit assigned to escort duty along the Santa Fe Trail. In 1851, he assisted in building a post, Fort Union, near present-day Watrous in northeastern New Mexico, to protect travelers along the route. The following year he led a reconnaissance in force across eastern New Mexico in search of Mescalero Apaches.

In 1853, Carleton was assigned to command the cavalry outpost at Albuquerque. His duties there over the next two years involved exploring, examining the feasibility of a rail route through the region, and pursuing bands of Navajos and Apaches whose raids were devastating settlements throughout northern New Mexico. Carleton and his troopers, often accompanied by Kit Carson and New Mexico volunteers, were in the field much of the time

pursuing the raiders. Eventually, aided by
Pueblo Indian trackers, Carleton's squadrons
found a Jicarilla Apache encampment in
the Raton Mountains. Carleton and Carson
planned a surprise attack that caused the
Apaches to abandon their extensive campsite.
Eventually, pressure became too much for the
Native bands. Both the Navajos and Apaches
negotiated peace agreements which brought a
temporary calm to the volatile region.

Public Domain
James H. Carleton

In 1855, Carleton was directed by
Secretary of War Jefferson Davis to participate
in a study of European army tactics during the
Crimean War. For the next two years, working
out of Philadelphia, Carleton analyzed cavalry
components of the conflict, focusing most
closely on tactics used by Cossack horsemen. While his primary charter
was to explore cavalry-related aspects, his duties allowed him to examine
a broad spectrum of other matters as well: weapons, ammunition, clothing,
equipment, medical support, transportation, supply, construction, bridging
techniques, and much more.

When moving back to the West after finishing in Philadelphia, Carleton
commanded a group of recruit replacements headed for the 8th Infantry,
posted at the time in New Mexico. Ordered back east in 1858, he was tasked
with leading 700 soldiers bound for California via the Isthmus of Panama. For
Carleton, the journeys to New Mexico and California – military expeditions
of unusual length and duration – added to his already extensive experience in
moving large forces over long distances.

After arriving in California, Carleton was posted to Fort Tejon, near
Lebec, between present-day Bakersfield and Los Angeles, and assigned to
guard the nearby pass and escort mail stages. In April 1859 he was called
away from those duties to escort a military paymaster and investigate the
murky aftermath of a bloody incident that had occurred several months
before. On September 11, 1857, a party of more than 100 emigrants, members
of the Baker- Fancher train, had been massacred at a location in Utah known
as Mountain Meadows. Later published by Congress, Carleton's report on
the "Mountain Meadows Massacre" assigned the blame to members of the
Mormon community's Nauvoo Legion and their Paiute Indian allies.

Back at Fort Tejon for the next two years, Carleton led patrols across the
Mojave and built camps for travelers along the route to Salt Lake City. In
the spring of 1861, at the outset of the Civil War, he moved with a 50-man
company of dragoons to Los Angeles. In Southern California he organized

militia units and home guard companies in the area known to be active with Confederate sympathizers.

As increasing numbers of Regular Army troops were pulled from their western posts for shipment to the battlefields in the East, Carleton was directed to raise and organize volunteer infantry and cavalry units as replacements. Carleton quickly recruited a California volunteer army consisting of an infantry regiment and four companies of cavalry. Concurrently promoted to colonel of volunteers, he was given command of the "army" which was drawn heavily from the region around Sacramento and San Francisco. Wary of Confederate influence in Southern California, Carleton placed packets of troops around Los Angeles and San Bernadino. Eventually, Carleton would extend his security cordon all the way from San Diego to Fort Yuma, establishing checkpoints and recording detailed lists of travelers moving in and out of the region.

The spring of 1862 brought news of a Confederate invasion of New Mexico. Led by General Henry H. Sibley, rebel troops captured Albuquerque and Santa Fe and were poised to move farther west. A forward element had already advanced into Arizona and captured Tucson. Carleton's orders were to strike eastward, retake the posts that had been lost, and expel the Confederates from Arizona and New Mexico.

As Carleton readied the expedition, additional units joined his infantry and cavalry forces. Eventually, nearly 2,000 men from his original California Army, the Fifth California Infantry, Second California Cavalry, and a battery from the Third U.S. Artillery formed his legion, which he named the California Column.

Reflecting his experience, Carleton's army marched in a line of companies spread a day apart to allow wells and springs to replenish as the column moved forward. At the same time, they were close enough to be mutually supportive if placed under threat. In each group, infantry marched ahead to spare the troops from clouds of powdery alkali dust stirred up by the passing wagons. To avoid the suffocating heat, for the much of the journey Carleton moved his column at night, with only short marches broken by frequent rest periods during the daylight hours.

On May 20, 1862, an advance force of Carleton's men recaptured Tucson without a fight, the Confederates having evacuated the city a few days earlier. Carleton, newly appointed a brigadier general of volunteers, established a military government and as the bulk of his force flowed into the Tucson area continued a tortuous training program in the heat of southern Arizona. Carleton troopers were kept constantly busy drilling, moving supplies forward, guarding horses and mules, scouting, and repairing wagons.

After resting for a time around Tucson, Carleton put his main column in motion at the end of June. Moving along the Butterfield Overland Mail

4

Road, the army trekked across a landscape unusual in its variety. Mostly arid, the terrain alternated between rocky, hardpan soil, sand, and alkali dust that hung like a shroud over low points on the primitive roadbed. Vegetation was sparse, sometimes consisting only of mesquite thickets and occasional patches of Gila grass scattered along canyon floors.

Mid-July brought lead elements of the column to rising ground as the force neared the Chiricahua Mountains. There, at Apache Pass, about 20 miles east and south of Willcox in southeastern Arizona, the column's lead company was ambushed by a band of 500 well-armed Apaches. Sheltered behind barricades built of rocks and boulders, the Indians poured fire into the canyon floor about 300 – 400 feet below. Positioned above a stage station and spring located about two-thirds of the way through the four-mile long pass, the war party momentarily pinned down Carleton's troopers. As the struggle continued, the company commander, Captain Thomas L. Roberts, brought two 12-pounder howitzers into play, firing grapeshot that tore into the Apache attackers. As the momentum shifted, Roberts ordered a charge with fixed bayonets that cleared the Apaches from the hillside.

In August Carleton's entire force reached the Rio Grande. With the Confederates having withdrawn, Carleton requested permission to keep his forces in the area and extend the Union presence into West Texas. Later that month, Carleton succeeded General Edward R. S. Canby as commander of the Department of New Mexico, an immense region that encompassed all of the present-day states of New Mexico and Arizona. Concerned by the presence of Southern agents, Carleton continued the program of martial law instituted by Canby the previous year.

With the continuing threat of a renewed Confederate invasion, Carleton established a string of outposts across southern New Mexico and placed company-sized garrisons in the larger towns. He instituted an exhaustive regimen of patrols that searched for rebel infiltrators and confiscated Confederate property. As in California, he established a series of checkpoints that monitored travel in and out of the department, employing a widely disliked passport system of his own creation.

Carleton sent patrols across the international border at Juarez where they found large quantities of supplies cached there by the Confederates. A search of public and private buildings in El Paso found additional provisions and more than 100 rebel soldiers. Carleton paroled the prisoners and issued rations and clothing to them. All were sent to San Antonio, accompanied by two wagons to carry the wounded.

Carleton focused increasingly on improving security and increasing the military efficiency of his force. Training never ceased. He reorganized some of his units and equipped Kit Carson and his New Mexico volunteers with newer weapons. Worried that his original supply line – which extended from

5

the Pacific to the Rio Grande – might be severed, Carleton established a new route using the Santa Fe Trail to bring in supplies from Fort Leavenworth and other Kansas posts. Cavalry encampments were scattered along the route to shield the supply wagons from marauding tribesmen.

Inevitably, Carleton's attention was increasingly drawn to the threat posed by Apache and Navajo raiders who, mishandled and provoked by Confederate authorities during their occupation of the territory, had commenced all-out war in 1861. In the power vacuum that ensued when rebel forces vacated the region – an event that halted patrols and stopped the rations and gifts that had helped placate the tribes – the Mescalero Apaches and Navajos launched attacks throughout the region. In August, the month that Carleton arrived on the Rio Grande, Apaches killed nearly 50 settlers, took dozens of Anglo and Mexican children captive, and made off with hundreds of head of livestock.

In October, Carleton began a hard, unremitting campaign in which no quarter was to be given. He instructed his commanders to conduct no parlays with the Indians and to slay the men wherever they were found. (The policy was not universally applied by Kit Carson or other commanders.) Women and children were to be taken prisoner. Carleton intended to provide an object lesson, asserting that the Indians had robbed and murdered with impunity for too long.

Carleton was not the only commander or public official to advocate a policy of extreme harshness. Stunned by the atrocities committed by the tribes – roasting captives alive was not uncommon – even major newspapers sometimes advocated extermination of the Natives. Amid high emotions and growing public frustration with the number of attacks, Carleton sought to destroy the Indians or force them into submission.

Concentrating first on the Mescalero Apaches, through the winter of 1862-63, Carleton pushed his men relentlessly across the tribe's territory. Pressured constantly, the Apaches were kept on the move and their food, camps, and provisions destroyed. By the end of winter, the campaign was over. Exhausted and hungry, always under threat, the Apaches could take no more. Hundreds surrendered to Carleton's troops; others fled to Mexico.

Carleton moved the captives to Bosque Redondo, a forested area surrounded by plains along the Pecos River. There, in a 40-square mile tract, the Indians were interred and the area set aside as an intended reservation. Fort Sumner, a fairly large military post for its time, was established to guard the Indians.

Having quelled the Mescaleros, Carleton turned his attention to the Navajos. In a controversial decision, he determined to relocate the tribesmen in western New Mexico and eastern Arizona to Bosque Redondo. Carleton apparently concluded that the Navajos, among many other tribes, would pose a continuing menace and would join in future uprisings. Indeed, Navajo war

6

parties persisted in raiding settlements throughout the region, though on a smaller scale than the Apaches.

While the raids persisted, discoveries of silver and gold were at the same time attracting scores of immigrants to the area. Carleton thought it inevitable that the tribes would oppose the streams of travelers moving across their territory to reach the mineral fields. Perhaps coincidently, the enlistments of his California volunteers were about to expire. He may have felt their added strength was necessary to carry out his plan to move the thousands of tribesmen to a location hundreds of miles distant. Once concentrated at Bosque Redondo, fewer troops would be needed.

In the spring of 1863, Carleton set his troops in motion. When Navajos failed to attend a meeting called by Kit Carson to negotiate surrender terms, Carleton's units swept across Navajo territory. Led by Carson and his New Mexico volunteers and aided by Mexican guides, villages were found and destroyed as were crops and orchards. Flocks of sheep and herds of horses and cattle were killed or scattered. One by one, Navajo bands surrendered.

The "Long Walk" of the Navajo began in June 1864. Their journey from Arizona to eastern New Mexico took 18 days and covered about 450 miles. Altogether, a series of more than 50 marches lasting until the end of 1866 took the Navajo nation to Bosque Redondo. There, they were uneasily confined with the Mescalero Apaches, their bitter enemies. Eventually, nearly 10,000 Indians were placed at Bosque Redondo.

The consequences were disastrous. Mosquitos bred in the foul, standing water of the Pecos River producing pandemic outbreaks of malaria and dysentery. A prolonged drought seared the Indians' crops, destroying fields and garden plots. When the rains eventually came, the river flooded, ruining the tribes' irrigation systems. Suffocating heat added to the misery of malnutrition and disease. As early as 1865, some warriors began sneaking away to raid nearby settlements in search of food. By the time Bosque Redondo was abandoned in 1868 and the Navajos were allowed to walk back to their traditional tribal lands, more than a quarter had perished.

While the relocations of the Navajos to Bosque Redondo were ongoing, periodic clashes continued with other bands throughout the region. Carleton sought to punish Kiowas, Comanches, and Plains Apaches for their attacks on settlements and wagon trains. The largest of the resulting encounters took place 17 miles northeast of present-day Stinnett at a place called Adobe Walls in the Texas Panhandle.

On November 25, 1864, Carleton's field commander, Kit Carson, fought a difficult, eight-hour battle with perhaps as many as 1,200 – 1,400 warriors from several nearby villages. Carson, with a force of 260 cavalry, 75 infantry, and 72 Ute and Jicarilla Apache scouts, used the crumbling buildings of an abandoned trading post as cover in a defensive struggle. Aided by the clever use of two howitzers, Carson and his troops withstood repeated attacks before eventually withdrawing as ammunition began to run low. After burning a nearby Kiowa village, Carson took his force back to their main encampment.

Counting one Indian scout killed and four others wounded, Carson lost a total of six dead and twenty-five wounded. Estimates of Kiowa, Comanche, and Apache losses ranged from 60 to 160 killed or wounded. In the aftermath, both sides claimed success. It was one of the few times the Native tribes possessed a major battlefield at the end of the day.

The drawn battle at Adobe Walls would have little appreciable effect on Carleton's reputation. The same, however, could not be said of Bosque Redondo. As the "Long Walk" marches continued, public outcries grew in number and volume. Although the campaign provoked mixed reactions, as the months passed public sentiment toward Carleton turned increasingly negative.

When reports reached Washington, D.C., alarm was expressed by officials in the executive branch and by congressional leaders. A congressional committee traveled to New Mexico to hold hearings, eventually recommending an official inquiry. The resulting investigation by representatives from the Department of the Interior cleared Carleton of wrong-doing and commended his policies. Still, among New Mexico's citizenry, even the sizable segment that had witnessed Apache and Navajo depredations at close hand, public opinion tilted against Carleton.

Union forces had initially been hailed as liberators, as the Confederate threat receded, several of Carleton's policies caused increasing public indignation. Perhaps most despised was the passport program, accompanied as it was by an extensive series of checkpoints and military camps placed throughout the territory. Where Carleton insisted on passports as measure to enhance security, citizens and travelers tended to see them as an unnecessary irritant.

Protests grew and at some locations grand juries met to consider alleged abuses of martial law by soldiers under Carleton's command. Carleton also had collisions with an influential newspaper editor and key members of the New Mexico judiciary.

Newspaper articles reported growing public sentiment favoring the end of military rule and the restoration of civil government. The legal dispute involved questions regarding jurisdictional boundaries of military and civil courts. On at least two occasions, Carleton ordered the arrest of an associate justice of the territorial Supreme Court. For a time, the court could not meet for lack of a quorum.

Despite the allegations and the public furor, Carleton was brevetted major general in both the regular and volunteer army. Finally, on July 4, 1865, twelve weeks after Lee's surrender at Appomattox and seven weeks after the last battle of the Civil War, fought at Palmito Ranch in the southern-most tip of Texas, Carleton ended martial law and with it, the passport system.

When, in 1866, an election was held to select a territorial delegate to the U.S. Congress, voters chose one of Carleton's most bitter foes. Officials in the Andrew Johnson administration apparently interpreted the election result as a territory-wide repudiation of Carleton and his policies. On October 6, 1866, Carleton was reassigned. He was posted to the 4th Cavalry Regiment at San Antonio and reverted to his previous rank of lieutenant colonel. Embittered, he remained at that station and in that rank until his death from pneumonia on January 7, 1873. He was buried in Cambridge, Massachusetts.

Carleton was an early advocate of prohibition, forcibly suppressing liquor traffic and removing saloons from the proximity of military posts. At times he personally led soldiers in destroying brothels and evicting prostitutes. He viewed the Civil War as a crusade, taking it as his highest duty to crush the rebellion and preserve the Union – causes that perhaps in his mind justified measures others regarded as extreme.

There were other sides to Carleton, however. Harshness and irritability were counter-balanced by exceptional intelligence and creativity. A gifted writer, Charles Dickens and Henry Wadsworth Longfellow were among Carleton's correspondents. As a naturalist, he studied plants, animals, geology and weather. He collected specimens of rocks, mammals, insects, and meteorites that he shipped to Harvard University and the Smithsonian Institution.

Carleton married twice. A year after their marriage, his first wife, Henrietta Tracy Loring, died in 1841 at Fort Gibson, probably of typhoid fever. In 1849, while stationed in the Southwest, he married Sophia Garland Wolfe. Among their three surviving children (two others died in childbirth) was the journalist, playwright, and inventor, Henry Guy Carleton.

Carleton left a controversial legacy. The measures he took did indeed pacify an immense region at a critical moment in the nation's history. At the same time, the harshness of his actions and his prolonged suspension of civil liberties outraged friends and foes alike, ultimately causing his demise. Militarily, his defensive measures and logistical innovations thwarted Confederate ambitions in the Southwest. The system of forts he established helped provide the foundation for the future development of New Mexico and Arizona. Carleton's planning and execution of the movement of forces from California to the border of Texas – perhaps the longest overland expedition in American history – evidenced a sublime mastery of the military craft.

EUGENE A. CARR

F ew officers in American military history have led forces in harm's
way on so many occasions and for such an extended period of time
as Eugene Asa Carr. His career included an impressive record as a
combat leader during the Civil War as well as on the Great Plains and in the
Southwest. Most notably, he led the campaign that cleared the Cheyennes
from their fortress-like area along the Republican River in Nebraska and
defeated Chief Tall Bull's Dog Soldiers in a classic encounter at Summit
Springs, Colorado. Altogether, he participated in 40 major battles.

Carr was born in Erie County, New York, on March 20, 1830. At age 16
he entered West Point, graduating 19th of 44 in the class of 1850. Nicknamed
the "Black-bearded Cossack" for his most prominent physical feature, after
graduation Carr was posted to duties on the frontier. He was one of the few
commanders whose extensive career as an Indian fighter included service in
the West prior to the start of the Civil War. Carr served in Kansas, Nebraska,
and Texas, seeing his initial action as early as 1854 against Apaches near the
Sierra Diablo Mountains. On October 10 of that year, Carr, part of a 40-man
cavalry company tracking a band of 300 or so Lipan Apaches that had stolen
cattle from nearby ranches, was severely wounded. Typically, he stayed on
the field leading his men. Soon after, he was on the Great Plains participating
in Harney's Sioux Expedition in 1855 and shepherding Fort Riley, Kansas,
through a cholera outbreak later that year. In 1856-57, Carr helped maintain
order on the Kansas border and led a company in the so-called Mormon War.
In 1858, he accompanied Colonel Edwin V. Sumner on the Army's first major
reconnaissance of the Republican River Valley, an area whose name would
later be inextricably linked to his own. At the outbreak of the Civil War he
was in a command position at Fort Washita in Indian Territory.

Carr's Civil War service began early in the conflict and covered the
duration of the war in the western theater. He saw action at Wilson's Creek,
Pea Ridge, Port Gibson, Champion's Hill, Vicksburg, Camden, Little Rock,
Fort Blakely, and was part of the final drive towards Mobile. His actions at Pea
Ridge, where he was wounded several times while leading a division in the
fierce fighting around Elkhorn Tavern, were eventually recognized by award

of the Medal of Honor. Carr was commander of the cavalry division in the VII Corps, commander of the District of Little Rock, and finally commander of the 3rd Division of XVI Corps on the campaign against Mobile near the end of the conflict. By war's end, he was a brevet major general.

Public Domaine

Eugene A. Carr

For two years following the war, Carr was posted to Reconstruction duty in Arkansas and North Carolina. In 1868, he was again sent west to the frontier. There, along the Republican River, he led two expeditions that would forever tie his name to the military history of the central Plains.

Arcing north and south out of Kansas across most of southern Nebraska, the strategic value of the Republican River Valley was obvious long before a series of military campaigns brought notoriety to the region. From time immemorial, the Indians had used the valley as fortress, shelter, and hunting ground. It was a citadel: the Gibraltar of the Plains Indians.

The military importance of the area increased with each passing year as the frontier moved westward. Beginning in the 1850s, U.S. forces in considerable strength scouted the region in isolated forays that inevitably provoked clashes as the military units moved through the valley. After the Civil War, separate patrols escalated into a series of campaigns. Conducted each year, the expeditions were part of a larger whole, linked together by the military's overall strategic objective of subduing the tribes in the valley or driving them from it.

The first expedition in 1867, led by George Armstrong Custer with six companies of the 7th Cavalry, was inconclusive. The following year's expedition, led by Carr, while not yet decisive, would prove to be more significant.

Despite attempts by a congressional committee to reach agreement with warring tribes, in 1868 large bands of Indians resumed hostilities along and below the Republican River. To oppose them, Carr, a major in the Regular Army at the time, took the field with a contingent of the 5th U.S. Cavalry.

Carr was soldierly in appearance with a piercing gaze and full beard turned from black to gray in his later years. Less than average in height, his erect carriage made him appear taller. Carr was a scholar-warrior, widely read and intellectually curious, fearless on the battlefield. Unlike his contemporary, Ranald Mackenzie, Carr was known for his kind and considerate treatment of his officers and men. During the cholera outbreak at Fort Riley, he had

11

personally ministered to several of the stricken soldiers. A less than docile subordinate, he was a frequent thorn in the side of those above him in the chain of command.

In early October, Carr, posted in Washington, D.C., received orders to join the 5th U.S. Cavalry, "the Dandy Fifth," on the Kansas Plains. On October 18, 1868, with an escort of 100 troopers, Carr was hurrying to locate and join his command, already in the field, when his force was attacked by a large Sioux and Cheyenne war party near Beaver Creek, Kansas. Carr formed his supply wagons in an oval, placed his horses and mules inside, and for the next eight hours fought off repeated attacks by the 700 or more warriors who rode in constricting circles around his makeshift stockade. After a struggle through the heat of the day, the Indians withdrew in the face of increasing losses. Three of Carr's troopers were wounded.

Carr caught up with his command, seven cavalry companies and a contingent of scouts, on October 22 at Buffalo Tank, a railroad stop on the Kansas Pacific Railroad. Carr immediately set the force in motion towards Nebraska and the Republican River Valley. On October 27, near the Solomon River in northern Kansas, the cavalry's advance guard ran into a substantial force of Sioux and Cheyenne. The initial skirmish grew quickly into a full-fledged battle as 500 Indians joined the fray and Carr poured his entire command into the fight. A large, confused, running melee then resulted that continued for about six miles. At nightfall the Indians broke off the action after having lost about 30 warriors killed and wounded.

Unlike many battles on the Plains, which were intense spasm exchanges that were seldom of long duration, the first day's encounter was only the beginning of a prolonged period of violent, near-continuous action. For the next four days a furious running battle raged, tracing a long northward crescent across the Republican into Nebraska, west through the valley and then back again south to Beaver Creek.

The Sioux and Cheyenne losses were thought to be significant, and when the cavalry prepared to resume the attack at dawn on October 31, the Indians had vanished. Carr's efforts scattered the bands, pushing many of them south, driving them against Sheridan's forces waiting in Indian Territory.

From the government's perspective, the 1868 expedition had been more successful than the campaign of the previous year. Still, while the Indians had suffered substantial losses and had been temporarily dispersed, the danger along the Republican River valley had not been removed. Indeed, as events would show, the threat would soon reappear larger and more ominous than before.

In 1869, a short distance south of present-day Orleans, Nebraska, the Sioux massacred a party of United States surveyors near where Sappa Creek flows into the Republican River.

In the spring, Cheyenne Dog Soldiers, the tribe's elite warrior society, led by Chief Tall Bull and accompanied by large Sioux war parties, moved aggressively into the Republican Valley. Beginning on May 21, 1869, they launched a campaign of terror that cut a swath of destruction from the Saline River in Kansas to the Big Sandy in Nebraska. Moving swiftly, the Indians struck hunting parties, burned homesteads, derailed and nearly wiped out the crew of a Kansas Pacific train, and killed 13 persons in raids up and down the river. On May 30, war parties destroyed a Kansas settlement, killing an additional 13 settlers and kidnapping two women.

David Butler, governor of the two-year-old state of Nebraska, wrote to General C. C. Auger, commanding officer of the Military District of the Platte, imploring the Army to provide immediate assistance.

On June 9, a force under Carr's command left the post, moving first south and east along the Platte, then south to Medicine Creek, and then toward the lush valley of the Republican River. Their trek took them across rolling plains that rise gradually in elevation until they reach the foothills of the Rocky Mountains.

Carr's troopers reached the Republican on June 13 and camped at a point about four miles below the junction of the river and the mouth of Beaver Creek. These were the first in a series of moves that eventually formed an enormous horseshoe-shaped track that ranged over parts of Kansas, Nebraska, and Colorado. The campaign became known as the Republican River Expedition.

The frontier army was small, impoverished, and desperately undermanned at the time – the demobilization following the Civil War had been massive in scope and size – and throughout the five-week campaign Carr sent repeated requests for additional weapons, ambulances, and assorted provisions. Still, in the context of the times it was a sizable force that Carr took with him from Fort McPherson: eight companies of the 5th Cavalry (although none of the companies was at more than half authorized strength), two companies of Pawnee Scouts, and 54 over-loaded wagons as well as teamsters, wagon masters, and herders.

Carr was well-chosen to lead the expedition. The most famous personage on the campaign, however, was William F. Cody, Chief of Scouts of the 5th Cavalry. Carr and "Buffalo Bill" had previously served together and Carr, impressed with Cody's "skill, fighting, and marksmanship," requested that Cody lead the cavalry's contingent of scouts.

Carr, Cody, and the "Dandy Fifth" were unquestionably moving in harm's way. The Republican River Valley had long been a refuge for the Plains Indians. Now, in the spring of 1869, it was their last stronghold in the central Plains. They would not relinquish it easily.

Carr's force moved across terrain that was alternately rugged and sandy and, at the time, not well charted. The harsh landscape and the absence of roads and trails made it difficult for the wagons to keep up with the main body of troops. Breakdowns were frequent and the mules often played out from dragging wagons through the sand. To maintain the momentum of the pursuit, on two occasions Carr left a cavalry company and the wagon trains behind with orders to catch up later.

The journey to the south provided evidence of Cheyenne presence in the area. On the morning of June 12, a cavalry patrol was scouting along Deer Creek when it ran into a hunting party of about 20 Indians who fled before an attack could be organized.

Carr's men were narrowing the gap. He again stripped a group free of the main body and wagon train, sending three companies of cavalry and one company of Pawnee Scouts with three days of packs in pursuit of the Cheyennes. On July 4 the detached force came across a 12-person war party carrying a wounded brave on a litter. The Pawnee Scouts ran the Cheyennes down, scalped three of them and captured eight horses, two with Army brands.

Although skeptical of catching up with the main body of Cheyennes, who probably would have been warned by the surviving members of the Deer Creek hunting party, Carr put his entire force on the march. After backtracking momentarily to find a better route for his wagons, Carr then led his main body west through the difficult, sandy, inhospitable terrain of what is now eastern Colorado –a high, barren plain that farther west rises gradually into the foothills of the Rocky Mountains.

On July 10 troopers found a camp that the Indians had apparently abandoned earlier the same day and a heel mark left by a white woman's shoe. Carr halted at the encampment and readied his command for action.

Meanwhile, in recent days Tall Bull had first taken his band east toward Nebraska and the South Platte. Finding the Platte and other streams running too full for safe crossing, and worried that the route would take him in the direction of known military presence, he changed course. Lulled possibly by Carr's momentary backtracking in the past week into thinking that at least some of the force was being withdrawn, Tall Bull went into camp at White Butte Creek, near Summit Springs, Colorado. Carr was now 20 miles away.

Carr's provisions were running low and his men were tired. More critically, the cavalry's horses were by now ill-fed and exhausted. Carr formed his command, sorted by the physical condition of troopers and their animals. Only 244 out of 400 men from his seven cavalry companies and only 50 of 150 warriors in three companies of Pawnee Scouts would accompany him.

At Summit Springs, on July 11, Carr and his men surprised, out-fought, and overwhelmed their Indian adversaries. Guided by Bill Cody to the Cheyennes' camp in a small valley about 14 miles southwest of Sterling,

Colorado, Carr's outnumbered force slammed into Tall Bull's 500 Dog Soldiers from three sides, thoroughly routing them. The fight was brief and violent. Tall Bull and 51 other Cheyennes were killed. The remainder fled or were taken prisoner. Carr's after action report listed 274 horses, 144 mules, 9,300 pounds of dried meat, 84 complete lodges, 56 rifles, 22 revolvers, 40 bows and arrows, 50 pounds of gunpowder, 20 boxes of percussion caps, 17 sabers, 9 lances, and 20 tomahawks captured in the attack.

Troopers freed Maria Weichell, one of the women captured in Kansas. She was found wounded but alive near Tall Bull's lodge where, by some testimony, the chief had shot her during the attack. According to some participants, a second woman prisoner, Susanna Alderdice, was tomahawked by one of Tall Bull's wives and died soon after the battle. Carr's cavalrymen sustained only one casualty, a minor wound inflicted by an arrow.

Initiated by a classic cavalry charge, the battle was one of the few in the history of the frontier where reality would match the scenes depicted in western fiction.

For years a bastion of the Plains Indians, the Republican River Valley was finally cleared for settlement. The expedition broke the strength of the Cheyenne Dog Soldiers and eliminated the last Indian stronghold in the central Plains region.

In December 1868, between Republican River expeditions, Carr led a difficult reconnaissance from Fort Lyon, Colorado, to the Canadian River. Plagued throughout by severe weather, the campaign was notable mainly for having had for a time both "Buffalo Bill" Cody and "Wild Bill" Hickok assigned as scouts.

Carr was never very far from the action. Typical was an episode in south central Nebraska early in 1869. Spring of that year found the 5th Cavalry transferring from Fort Lyon, Colorado, to Fort McPherson, Nebraska, to take part in the Republican River Expedition. On May 14, soon after the unit had crossed into Nebraska, scouts came across an Indian trail near Medicine Creek. Carr detailed seven companies of cavalry to follow the trail.

Led by Buffalo Bill, the troopers pursued the difficult trail for two days, tracking the Indians several miles in an easterly direction. While the rest of the command watered its horses at a ford along Spring Creek, Carr sent a small group that included Cody on an advance scout to check on five Indians who had been seen in the far distance. Carr, anticipating trouble, sent a full cavalry company under the command of an experienced Civil War veteran, Lieutenant John Breckenridge Babcock, to support the reconnaissance.

Two miles from Spring Creek, as Babcock's troopers made contact with the scout party, both groups were ambushed and surrounded by an estimated 200 Indians who poured into the cavalrymen from hiding places in nearby gullies and ravines. Carr's arrival with the rest of the regiment ended a desperate struggle notable for Buffalo Bill being wounded in action and a Medal of Honor being awarded to Lieutenant Babcock.

By 1870, Carr was commander of Fort Mcpherson on the Nebraska frontier. In 1876, he was with Colonel Wesley Merritt and the 5th Cavalry at Warbonnet Creek, where he led the last great charge of the U.S. Cavalry, helping Merritt turn back the hundreds of Cheyennes attempting to join Crazy Horse and other "hostiles" on the warpath farther north. Carr accompanied the "Dandy Fifth" through the Sioux Campaign and led it at the Battle of Slim Buttes. He was in charge of the small garrison at Fort McPherson throughout the Cheyenne Outbreak from Indian Territory during the fall and winter of 1878. In 1879, he was named commander of the 6th Cavalry at Fort Lowell, Arizona. He served there for five years until being posted to Fort Wingate, New Mexico, in 1884.

Carr's service in the Southwest included the Victorio Campaign and, most notably, the battles of Cibecue (alternately, Cibicu) Creek and Fort Apache.

In late August 1881, Carr led a force comprised of five officers and 79 enlisted cavalrymen on a mission to apprehend a powerful Apache medicine man suspected of planning an uprising. Nock-ay-det-klinne (or, variously, Nook-ay-det-klinne, or Nochaydelklinne), mentor to Cochise and Geronimo, was a White Mountain Apache whose village was near Cibecue Creek in the interior of the Fort Apache Indian Reservation in eastern Arizona.

When the force arrived at the village, Nock-ay-det-klinne agreed to accompany Carr back to the fort. As the column moved along the trail away from the village, it became stretched out and broken as the medicine man, under guard by a sergeant and eight troopers near the rear of the file, found reasons to delay his departure. The procession was was shadowed by increasing numbers of armed Apaches.

As the front of the file moved toward Carr's planned campsite about two miles south of the village, a sharp bend in the trail momentarily blocked it from sight by the remainder of the column. It was apparently at this time that fighting erupted, with the Apaches initially focusing their attack on the rear of the column where Nock-ay-det-klinne rode with the contingent of nine soldiers. The Apache scouts mutinied, either instigating the assault or immediately joining in it. While much of the full encounter was fought at some distance with long range rifles, the initial clash involving the scouts – riding nearby or intermingled with the cavalrymen – was a violent, close-in encounter.

Despite the initial surprise, Carr rallied his troops and although some historians have criticized his handling of the episode, brought the separated parts of the column together and succeeded in driving off the attackers. Seven soldiers were killed at the scene and another later died of his wounds. Two more were wounded but safely evacuated. Eighteen Apaches, including Nock-ay-det-klinne, were killed.

Carr, concerned about the threat to Fort Apache, only lightly held by 60 soldiers, and wary of a potential ambush on the way back to the fort if he lingered at the scene of the fight, decided on a surprise night march to separate himself from the attackers whose strength he estimated at 60 during the initial attack, later joined by 200 or more during the course of the battle. After burying the dead, Carr destroyed the provisions that could not be carried. At 11 p.m., he began his move back to the fort, reaching it without incident in the afternoon of the following day.

Carr's premonition about a threat to the fort proved correct. Two days later the Apaches attacked in considerable force, making several assaults mostly at long range. The raiders were eventually driven off by heavy counter-fire after a struggle that lasted through the day and into the early evening. Three soldiers were wounded. Apache losses were unknown.

Cibecue Creek and Fort Apache would be the last of Carr's 40 major encounters. He retired from the military as a brigadier general in 1893.

Carr died in Washington, D.C. on December 2, 1910. He is buried at West Point.

JOHN M. CHIVINGTON

Many historians assign Colonel John M. Chivington the dubious distinction of being the most reviled of all the commanders who led government forces in the American West. Chivington's attack on a peaceable Southern Cheyenne village at Sand Creek, Colorado, on November 29, 1864, transformed an on-going Sioux uprising into a major war with Plains tribes. More than 150 Cheyennes were killed at Sand Creek. The majority were women and children. Atrocities inflicted on the remains further inflamed the Native bands, inducing many to join in the fighting. Public outrage provoked a Congressional inquiry that excoriated Chivington's conduct, effectively ending his military career and, later, his political ambitions.

Only the barest hints in John Chivington's earlier life might have foretold his actions at Sand Creek. He had been, after all, a Methodist minister with strong abolitionist views who at times held responsible positions in the church hierarchy.

Controversy, though, seemed to follow him. His near-belligerent abolitionist position prompted one pastoral move under the threat of violence. Other difficulties – including his aggressive commitment to military affairs – first disrupted his formal ministry and then eventually ended it. In his later life, accusations of professional and ethical misconduct further sullied his reputation.

Born in Lebanon, Ohio, on June 27, 1821, Chivington was drawn to a religious vocation in his early twenties after first working on the family farm and cutting and selling timber. He was ordained as a Methodist minister in 1844 at age 23. For nearly a decade, Chivington rode an extensive circuit, sometimes establishing congregations and supervising the construction of churches.

In 1853, church business took him to Kansas Territory. There, in the charged atmosphere of "Bleeding Kansas" his outspoken abolitionist views, forcefully expressed during sermons, placed him and others of like views in danger. On one occasion, Chivington placed two revolvers on the pulpit, essentially daring anyone to confront him. At the urging of officials and friends, he was transferred to a parish in Omaha, Nebraska Territory. Although the details remain unclear, Chivington had difficulties in his church dealings and remained in the post for only a year. After a brief time as presiding elder of the Nebraska City District, in May 1860, Chivington moved his family to Denver where he settled in as presiding elder of the church's Rocky Mountain District. Again, the appointment would be of relatively brief duration. He was not reappointed at the end of his two-year term. A friend later asserted that Chivington was removed from church duties because of his strong interest and involvement

Public Domain

John M. Chivington

in military activities. Although no longer presiding elder, Chivington maintained his affiliation with the church, serving on at least one executive board.

At the outset of the Civil War, Chivington was offered a commission as a military chaplain. He refused it, indicating that he preferred to serve in the combat arms. Soon after, he received a commission as a major in the First Colorado Volunteers.

Chivington would rather quickly play a part in the most substantive Civil War battle fought in the American West. In early 1862, Confederate General Henry Hopkins Sibley invaded New Mexico, seeking to secure the area's mineral resources for the Confederacy. Sibley's force eventually reached Glorietta Pass on the southern tip of the Sangre de Cristo Mountains, southeast of Santa Fe. There, on March 28, with forces under the direct command of William Scurry, his troops defeated a Union contingent led by Colonel John P. Slough.

Chivington, with 418 men, had been detached from Slough's main force a few days earlier. On March 26, Chivington's men surprised a Confederate force of 300 Texans near Apache Canyon. In the decisive victory that followed, Chivington's men killed four, wounded 20, and took 75 prisoners while losing five killed and 14 wounded.

Slough's intention for the forthcoming battle at Glorietta Pass was to have Chivington positioned to attack the Confederate flank while the main body of Union troops held Scurry at the mouth of the pass. Chivington took his position as directed but the flow of the battle brought neither Scurry's nor Slough's force to him. While Chivington was waiting, he learned that Sibley's supply train had been found nearby.

At a location known as Johnson's Ranch, Chivington's scouts under the command of Lieutenant Colonel Manuel Chaves of the Second New Mexico Infantry, discovered the wagons parked near the ranch buildings. Abandoning his position near the pass, Chivington moved his troops toward the ranch.

Reaching the scene, Chivington's men moved stealthily down a steep incline that sheltered the train, eventually finding cover close to the supply wagons. After waiting in concealment for about an hour, Chivington's troops sprang from their positions. Their assault took the rebels by surprise, scattering or capturing the small guard detail. Afterward, Chivington burned the supply wagons and shot or ran off the horses and mules.

Meanwhile, Slough's and Scurry's battle, fought not far away at Pigeon's Ranch, had ended in a rebel victory. When Chivington, having finished at Johnson's Ranch, moved to locate Slough, he came upon the Union force retreating from their encounter with Scurry.

As events unfolded, the Confederate triumph at Glorietta Pass counted for very little. Finding Slough now reinforced with Chivington's 400 soldiers and, more importantly, having lost the supplies necessary to sustain his troops in the field, Sibley was forced to end his campaign. The Confederates withdrew back to Texas and made no further attempt to invade New Mexico.

Although the discovery of the Confederate supply train was accidental, Chivington's response to the circumstance earned mostly favorable plaudits. He was appointed colonel a month after the battle. Others, then and later, were less impressed. By one account, the suggested route of attack came from a local official. According to some observers, Chivington's officers had argued at considerable length before he was convinced to go after the train. An editorial in the Albuquerque newspaper stated that one of Chivington's officers (Captain William H. Lewis) had in fact led the attack. Still other critics believed that had Chivington moved at the sound of gunfire to reinforce Slough at Pigeon's Ranch, his 400 men might have tilted that battle toward the Union force. Finally, in a foreshadowing of later events, some Confederate prisoners taken at Apache Canyon complained of Chivington's severe treatment of them.

Whatever the ground truth, Chivington emerged from the Glorietta Pass encounter with an enhanced reputation. Hailed as a hero, his star appeared in the ascendancy, complementing his early support for Colorado statehood as well as his own political ambitions.

His standing in the community solidified, Chivington remained in the military for the rest of the war, residing mainly in Denver. As the climactic event of his life approached, Chivington was 43 years old, a stocky man with a broad face, high forehead, mutton-chop sideburns and mustache. Chivington was robust in appearance, showing no residual effects from the small pox that had afflicted him two decades earlier.

Sand Creek, to which his name would forever be linked, occurred

November 29, 1864. In August, beginning at Plum Creek, Nebraska Territory, an Indian uprising mainly involving bands of Sioux at the outset had erupted across the central Plains. Reacting to the expulsion of their tribesmen from Minnesota after a conflagration there in 1862, and further alarmed by the increasing number of settlers and emigrants crossing their hunting grounds heading for California or the newly discovered gold fields in Colorado, the Sioux launched widespread, destructive raids that were exceptional in their violence. Near the Little Blue River in Nebraska, more than 100 settlers were killed. Nearly every stage station and road ranche on the overland trail came under attack. For a time, the entire trail was shut down from Fort Kearny, Nebraska Territory, to Denver and beyond.

Initially, the influx of settlers and travelers had prompted varying reactions among the tribes. In the early days of the mass migration, some regarded the travelers as a large tribe simply passing through. Over time, it became clear that the passages across Native territory were not isolated or temporary events. Indeed, the numbers increased from year to year.

In 1851, the Treaty of Fort Laramie had recognized Native domain over an immense territory that included parts of Wyoming, Nebraska, Colorado and Kansas. The pact covered hundreds of miles of the Great Plains all the way to the Rocky Mountains.

When, in late 1858, gold was discovered in the Colorado Rockies, the surge of migrants across Indian lands reached epic proportions. In February 1861, government representatives attempted to address the situation by negotiating a new agreement – the Treaty of Fort Wise – that, in return for providing annuities, reduced the Indian's reserve to less than a tenth of its former size. Six chiefs of the Southern Cheyenne, foremost among them Black Kettle, and four Arapaho chiefs, including Niwot, signed the treaty.

The signatory chiefs, however, represented only a portion of the Cheyenne and Arapaho nations. Others in the tribal group disavowed the treaty and refused to abide by it. Most notable among the dissenters were the Dog Soldiers, an elite band of Cheyenne warriors. The Dog Soldiers and their allies argued that the chiefs who signed the treaty did not represent the majority within the tribes and that the document had been agreed to without their consent. There were additional allegations of bribery and assertions that the chiefs did not understand what they were agreeing to. Further, those who opposed the treaty believed that the territory assigned to the Indians was not sufficient to sustain the tribes.

Government representatives, perhaps not fully understanding the complexities of Native culture, or the loose, decentralized structure within the tribes, regarded the treaty as binding among all tribesmen. Those who refused to adhere to it were regarded as hostile.

From the start, there was confusion about which groups were belligerent and which were not. For government officials, persistent questions – never fully resolved – remained regarding how to handle, recognize, and separate the non-hostile bands.

Into this powder keg environment stepped John Chivington. Chivington's views towards Indians seem somewhat implausible given his strong abolitionist sympathies. Nonetheless, they were notable for their extreme nature.

"I have come to kill Indians and believe it is right and honorable to use any means under God's heaven to kill Indians," he was quoted as saying. To an assembly of church deacons he said: "It is simply not possible for Indians to obey or even understand any treaty. I am fully satisfied, gentlemen, that to kill them is the only way we will every have peace and quiet in Colorado."

Such was the climate of the times that Chivington was not alone in holding these views. At about the same time, a front page editorial in a Denver newspaper advocated "extermination of the red devils."

Black Kettle, the Cheyenne chief who had signed the Treaty of Fort Wise, would become a major player in the unfolding tragedy. Long known for his peaceable views, in late September he had met with officials including Governor John Evans and Chivington, requesting guidance on measures to take to keep his 800 followers out of harm's way.

He was apparently given some rather vague advice to return to the reservation established by the Fort Wise treaty and to fly an American flag over his village. The flag, he is believed to have been informed, would show that the camp was non-hostile and would prevent it from being attacked. Though confused by the inconclusive outcome of the meeting and the ambiguous guidance that came from it, the chief moved as directed to the Fort Lyon area. (Fort Lyon was the former Fort Wise; the name was changed early in the Civil War.)

At Fort Lyon, the military post shadowing the reservation, Black Kettle was advised by the post commander to take his Cheyennes along with a smaller band of Arapahos led by Chief Niwot to a place about 40 miles away near Sand Creek. The officer, Major Edward W. Wynkoop, apparently believed that moving the Cheyennes and Arapahos to that location would reduce the potential for clashes with soldiers and keep them out of the path of migrant travelers. Meanwhile, Wynkoop promised, and provided, rations to the village.

When Wynkoop was temporarily succeeded as post commander by Major Scott J. Anthony, the rations were stopped. In the meantime, Black Kettle's camp remained at the site near Sand Creek.

In late November, as raids by belligerent groups continued along the trail, Chivington took the field with 700 troops from the 1st and 3rd Colorado Cavalry regiments and a company of New Mexico volunteers. Many of his men, particularly in the 3rd Colorado, were 100-day volunteers whose short terms of enlistment were about to expire. Among other possible motives for Chivington's attack, there is conjecture that he may have felt induced to use these forces prior to their release from duty.

After a difficult march over frozen ground covered much of the way by deep snow, Chivington took his force from its assembly area near Bijou Basin, about 80 miles southeast of Denver, to Fort Lyon, 260 miles distant. Chivington arrived at the fort on the afternoon of November 28. After confirming the location of the Indians' camp, he moved out at about 9 o'clock, trekking north on a night march that by sunrise brought his force to Black Kettle's village.

As with several aspects of the forthcoming fight, there is some uncertainty regarding the size of Black Kettle's camp. Many contemporary accounts place it at about 100 – 105 combined Cheyenne and Arapaho lodges, which likely sheltered about 500 total inhabitants. Black Kettle, believing he was assured of sanctuary, had released many of his warriors to go hunting. At the time of the attack, there may have been only 60 or so male Indians of all ages in the village.

In the early hours of November 29, Chivington, amidst loud cheering and general clamor, launched an all-out attack supported by artillery. Black Kettle ran up a white flag, hoisting it under or alongside the American flag that was already flying at the village. It was ignored. As the lines moved forward, two officers, Captain Silas Soule and Lieutenant Joseph Cannon, ordered their men not to fire, believing the village to be non-hostile.

The majority of Chivington's force attacked as ordered, however, commencing an action that persisted through late morning. The initial assault caused most of the inhabitants of the village to flee, racing away along both sides of the creek. The engagement quickly transformed into a series of running fights over an extended area as Chivington's men sought to chase down small groups of Indians desperate to escape.

Amidst the chaos, some Cheyennes managed to reach the camp's pony herd and escape on horseback. Many sought safety at another Cheyenne village not far away. Others moved upstream taking refuge in existing rifle pits or digging new ones along the banks of the creek. Though attacked and heavily fired upon, many in these groups survived. On the south bank, though, artillery fire took a toll of Indians attempting to break away from their attackers.

At one point, a large group of Cheyennes, perhaps 100 or more men, women, and children, clustered together, surrounded, seeking shelter along the creek bank. Eventually, as increasing numbers of troops reached the scene, about 200 soldiers were involved in what became the battle's largest single fight. In the struggle that followed, four or five soldiers were killed before resistance was subdued. An eyewitness later estimated Indian losses in that pocket at about 70 dead of which 30 or so were warriors and the remainder women and children. Artillery fire accounted for many of the casualties.

By mid-day most of Chivington's soldiers were back at the village site. At Chivington's order, lodges and other provisions were put to the torch. Of the 1,000 or so horses in the camp's pony herd, about 600 were captured. A small portion was later turned over to the Army quartermaster but few were fit for service.

Wounded Indians and others found alive inside the camp were killed by soldiers who roamed through the camp before and during its destruction. Almost all accounts of Sand Creek speak of horrific atrocities afflicted on Indian remains. Bodies were scalped and sexually mutilated. Body parts including fetuses and male and female genitalia were taken. Some were affixed to rifles and saddles. Others were publically displayed as trophies in Denver establishments.

Chivington's losses are thought to have numbered 24 killed and 52 wounded out of the 700 troopers committed to the fight. In some accounts, a substantial portion of those losses were said to have come from friendly fire – a contention disputed by some historians.

Estimates of Indian losses vary widely – from 150 to 400. In recent years, a figure of around 163 – 53 men and 110 women and children – has gained credence. Whatever the estimate, all accounts indicate that the majority of Indians killed, perhaps two thirds for more, were women and children. In his later testimony before Congress, Chivington portrayed a hostile camp of 1,100 – 1,200 inhabitants and estimated Indian losses of 500 – 600, all of them warriors.

In the days following the battle, Chivington arrested Captain Soule and five others who refused his orders to attack. When details of the massacre emerged, the Army dropped all charges. Less than a week after his release, before his testimony could be taken by a Congressional committee investigating Sand Creek, Soule was shot and killed by a supporter of Chivington while walking with his fiancé on a Denver street.

News of Chivington's attack and the atrocities perpetrated on the Indian remains circulated rapidly through the Plains tribes. Led by militants who believed Sand Creek justified going to war, the reaction was massive and violent. Even bands not primarily warlike felt threatened inside their designated safe areas.

Retaliation from Cheyennes and Arapahos came immediately. Soon after, they were joined by Brule and Oglala Sioux in launching raids on white settlements. Five weeks after Sand Creek, Julesburg, Colorado, was attacked. A second attack less than a month later by as many as 2,000 warriors sacked and burned the town. Fights at Mud Springs and Rush Creek, Nebraska, each involving hundreds of warriors, soon followed as the combined bands made their way to the Powder River county of Wyoming and Montana. There, they were joined by additional thousands of Northern Cheyennes, Arapahos, and Sioux. Chivington's actions at Sand Creek had transformed a Sioux uprising into a major war with the Plains tribes.

There can be little doubt of the extent of the Indians' outrage or of their hatred for Chivington. When fighting later erupted in the Powder River region, an Indian captive stated that in order for the Cheyennes to make peace, one condition had to be met: Chivington must be hanged.

Chivington was not hanged. Although the outrage expressed by the public and Congress was notable in its intensity, no civil or military charges were levied against him. Action by the Army was foreclosed when Chivington quickly left the military, apparently shielded by a general post-Civil War amnesty.

Though Chivington was never arraigned, the near-unanimous condemnation of his actions effectively foreclosed his return to the military as well as his later hopes for elected office.

A Joint Committee on the Conduct of the War stated in part that it "(could) hardly find fitting terms to describe (Chivington's) conduct," having concluded that he "deliberately planned and executed a foul massacre." The panel believed that Chivington had "full knowledge of (the Indians') friendly character having himself been instrumental to some extent in placing them (at Sand Creek)." In a particularly damning assessment, the committee report stated "the truth is that (Chivington) surprised and murdered, in cold blood, the unsuspecting men, women, and children who had every reason to believe they were under the protection of United States authorities." An Army judge publically labeled Sand Creek "a cowardly and cold-blooded slaughter." In October 1865, less than a year later, the Treaty of the Little Arkansas provided reparations for the outrages perpetrated at Sand Creek.

The question of "why?" will perhaps always perplex those who examine Chivington's actions. Many have speculated that Chivington's political ambitions were a factor. Chivington was already a noted figure in the territory from his success at Glorietta Pass and through his advocacy for statehood. Immediately after Sand Creek, Chivington returned to Denver and offered a highly exaggerated account of the fighting and the extent of the Indians' losses.

Over the years, those who have attempted to justify or mitigate Chivington's actions have noted that his attack occurred at a time when killing raids by Indians on whites – involving atrocities equaling the horror if not the number associated with Sand Creek – were common occurrences over hundreds of miles along the overland trail.

However, it was commonly understood that many of the Cheyenne bands were not hostile. Scouting of Black Kettle's village prior to the attack confirmed that no Dog Soldiers – the fierce military elite committed to war with the whites – were in his camp or part of his entourage. Indeed, as the Congressional report noted, Chivington himself was knowledgeable of Black Kettle's intent and the designation of the Sand Creek region as a sanctuary for his group.

Chivington spent the night before the battle at Fort Lyon and would have known from post officials that the Sand Creek village was not belligerent. While some have suggested that the recent transfer of post commander duties from Major Wynkoop to Major Anthony might have confused the circumstance, there is little evidence to support that contention. Anthony was clearly less sympathetic toward the Natives than was Wynkoop, but other than halting the flow of rations to Black Kettle, there is no indication that he took any force-related actions against them or that he considered them to be a threat.

Allegations of drunkenness on the part of Chivington's troops on the night before the battle have persisted through the years, as have assertions regarding their absence of discipline before and after the battle. Both charges are undoubtedly true, at least in part. There is, however, no testimony from any witness that Chivington tried at any time to prevent the atrocities inflicted by his troops.

For his part, Chivington remained unapologetic. For the remainder of his life, he concluded his public appearances saying "I stand by Sand Creek." Chivington justified his actions by citing orders from his superior, General Samuel Curtis directing him to attack hostile Indians wherever he found them. In his conditions for peace, Curtis had stipulated that Natives guilty of depredations had to be surrendered, stolen stock replaced, and Indian hostages taken to ensure compliance. In Chivington's narrative, Black Kettle had not formally or completely acquiesced to all provisions of the peace agreement – such as relinquishing weapons – which made him and his followers belligerents.

Even in an age when extreme views against Natives were rather commonplace, Chivington's went beyond those typical of the time, advocating the killing of Indians and extermination of the tribes. Underlying all else in the decision calculus that led Chivington to Sand Creek was an abject hatred of Indians.

For Black Kettle and the surviving members of his band, Sand Creek was but the first act of a final conclusive tragedy. Still refusing to take up arms, Black Kettle agreed to move his followers to Indian Territory (present-day Oklahoma). There, four years later in another battle surrounded by controversy, he and his wife were killed when their village along the Washita River was attacked by George Armstrong Custer and the 7th Cavalry.

26

Two months after Sand Creek, Chivington left the military service, mustering out on February 3, 1865. Forced from politics by public outrage, his first post-military venture was in a Nebraska freighting operation, an enterprise that failed because of his own machinations and contract violations. He moved for a time to Nebraska City, Nebraska, to administer his deceased son's estate. There, he seduced and married his daughter-in-law, an action publically repudiated by the bride's family. In 1871, his wife divorced him for non-support.

In 1868, Chivington dispensed with his hauling business and commenced a series of moves involving various enterprises that took him to Washington, D.C., Omaha, back to Washington, Troy, New York, to Washington again, and once more for a time to Nebraska City.

In 1871, by then in Cincinnati, Chivington married for a third time. He and his wife lived on a farm near the city from where he occasionally preached in local churches. Eventually, he campaigned for a seat in the state senate but withdrew when his involvement in Sand Creek became public knowledge.

In the early 1880s, he returned for a final time to Denver, moving through several jobs including marketing, under sheriff, and city sanitation inspector. Eventually, he was made city coroner. After a long and debilitating illness, he died on October 4, 1894. He is buried in Denver.

Allegations of wrongdoing and shady dealings (including taking money from the pockets of the deceased while he was coroner) dogged Chivington until the final days of his life. Others have suggested his involvement in a plethora of nefarious activities including forgery, arson, and insurance fraud. Over the course of three decades, his once promising reputation as the hero of Glorietta Pass vanished in a downward spiral of public revulsion and vilification.

At the time of Sand Creek, and for several years thereafter, Chivington served as a lay minister. In 1996, the United Methodist Church issued a public apology for Chivington's actions at Sand Creek.

In 1998, archeologists working with the National Park Service and representatives from several Plains tribes identified the site of the massacre. In Kiowa County, Colorado, artifacts including fragments of cannon balls were found along a section of Big Sandy Creek known as Dawson's Bend. In 2007, the Sand Creek Massacre National Historic Site was dedicated as part of the National Park system.

George R. Crook

As a leader in wars against the Native tribes in the American West, George Crook was a study in contrasts. In the field he was a relentless, implacable foe of those fighting against him. When the shooting stopped, he was a tireless defender of Indian rights, acting forcefully and speaking eloquently in opposing abuses inflicted on the tribes.

Only a handful of Army leaders fought Indians so long or in so many places. Crook's career as an Indian fighter stretched from the 1850s to the 1880s. He waged war against Native bands in the Pacific Northwest, the Great Plains, and in the Southwest.

Likewise, few leaders knew the Indians or understood their cultures as well as Crook – and perhaps none were as well respected by them.

Though not an intellectual, Crook was an innovative military leader, pioneering the use of mule pack trains and the employment of Native scouts. Neither his innovations nor his attitude towards Indians found wide acceptance among his colleagues.

To his soldiers, George Crook was "as plain as an old stick." He shunned ceremony and elaborate uniforms. On campaigns, his attire generally consisted of moccasins, a flannel shirt, and old canvas hunting garb topped by a slouch hat or pith helmet that shielded notable blue-grey eyes. Most expeditions found him at the head of the column riding his favorite mule, with a rifle slung across the saddle.

Broad shouldered, lean and athletic, Crook stood slightly over 6 feet tall. His fair hair was almost always closely cropped. His beard, though, was sizable and especially in his later years formed his most prominent feature. Crook wore his whiskers parted at the point of his chin, forming separate, several-inches-long extensions. In the field, he sometimes wore them braided or tied at either side of his face. In combination, the beard, an aquiline nose, firm mouth, and piercing eyes, formed an imposing presence.

Crook was not a formidable personality, however. While genial by nature, he maintained a quiet reserve that held most others at a respectful distance. Soft-spoken and deliberate in manner, Crook's professional approach was to offer general guidance to subordinates rather than issuing explicit

orders. Crook's early campaigns in the Pacific
Northwest led him to the same conclusions that
Ranald Mackenzie reached in the Southwest:
relentless pursuit was an effective tactic and
winter campaigns, when the tribe's mobility
was reduced, held special promise.

Crook is best remembered for two
major innovations. The first was the use of
pack mules on campaign. Frustrated by the
difficulties associated with supply wagons
and teams and their limited ability – on many
occasions *inability* – to move across rugged
terrain, Crook rather quickly discovered the
utility of mules.

Mathew Brady, Library of Congress
George R. Crook

Crook first used mules in a major way
in 1867, employing three pack trains on
expeditions that year. His chief packer, a
civilian employee named Thomas Moore, would remain with Crook for the
next 20 years. Over those two decades, beginning with the selection process
– mules were specially chosen and specifically trained for pack train duty –
Crook and Moore continued to refine their operations.

Crook's concepts turned the employment of mules into a military art.
Every part of the process – organization, equipment, utilization – was studied,
tested, and improved. Mules had been used to some degree previously, but
Crook incorporated mule pack trains into an integrated system for campaigns
against the Native tribes.

On expeditions carried out over hundreds of miles across some of the
continent's most difficult and varied landscape, the superiority of pack mules
over supply wagons was clearly demonstrated. Mules could climb mountains,
negotiate arroyos, and move single file through narrow defiles, traversing the
most extreme terrain while carrying remarkable loads. Average-sized packs
weighed 250 pounds to which an additional 100 pounds could be added if
necessary.

Mules proved especially well suited to the environment of the American
West: they were hardy, seemingly tireless, and could subsist on native grasses
for fodder. And, importantly, on the march they could keep up with cavalry
horses. The animals' durability and stamina enabled Crook to maintain
consistent pressure and carry the fight to nomadic opponents noted for their
proficiency in mobile warfare.

Crook was also a pioneer in the employment of Native scouts. While
other commanders used them, none employed them in such large numbers or
in such an encompassing manner as did George Crook. Crook paid his scouts

regular soldiers' compensation and placed special value on their tracking skills, knowledge of the terrain and understanding of their kinsmen's habits and intentions. When possible he recruited from the hostile tribe, believing that the presence of his scouts fostered dissension among the band being pursued and perhaps ultimately helped to defeat them psychologically as well as militarily. Then too, any tribesman employed as a scout was one less rifle that could be used against him. On reservations and in prisoner holding camps under his jurisdiction, Crook employed Native policemen and used Native councils to adjudicate offenses and disputes.

Crook was born September 8, 1828, near Taylorsville, Ohio, the ninth of 10 children of a farm family. He had little interest in books and not much formal education. When he was 19, a chance encounter with a congressman resulted in an appointment to West Point. There, his conduct was exceptional – he received few demerits – but his academic performance was less than stellar. Crook graduated in 1852 ranked 38th in a class of 43. Though pleasant, Crook was taciturn by nature and did not have a wide circle of acquaintances. One of his closest companions was his fellow cadet Philip H. Sheridan. Though substantially disrupted by a disagreement during the Civil War – Crook believed Sheridan had unjustly claimed credit for a successful action he (Crook) had taken – their relationship remained shakily in place for more than 30 years until irreparably severed over a dispute concerning Crook's handling of the Apache chief Geronimo.

After graduating from West Point, Crook's first posting was to the Pacific Northwest. Assigned to the 4th Infantry operating mainly along the Oregon-California border, Crook began his career as an Indian fighter. It was a vocation that would consume three and a half decades of his life and most of his military career.

Crook arrived in the Pacific Northwest at a time when the Native bands were still reeling from their initial experiences with the surge of emigrants drawn into the region by the California gold rush. Clashes were frequent with several tribes and for much of the next seven years, Crook led or participated in a number of expeditions against Native bands along the Rogue and Pitt Rivers. On a scout in 1857, he was badly wounded when struck in the right hip by an arrow. This would be one of two wounds suffered by Crook during 30 years of Indian fighting and four years of sometimes heavy combat during the Civil War. (In 1862, he was wounded during a small battle at Lewisburg, Virginia, in the early days of the war.)

During his time in the Pacific Northwest, Crook learned his trade as a soldier, scouting, leading forces on the march, fighting, and building outposts. It was during these years as well that his views regarding the tribes began to form. He was appalled by their treatment, noting that the government had rejected several treaties negotiated with them in good faith and often failed to observe provisions of existing agreements.

In the lawless environment that prevailed in the region, abuses against Indians were indiscriminate and too often went unpunished. When the Indians met savagery with savagery, soldiers were sent to put down the uprisings, prompting a vicious, near-continuous cycle of violence.

Crook's reaction to these circumstances differed notably from most of his colleagues. Far more so than most, he was receptive to the tribes' positions. When possible, he chose diplomacy over firepower. In 1858, rather than attack a Rogue River village that harbored Indians accused of killing white men, he negotiated with the chief and secured their surrender without bloodshed.

Nonetheless, Crook remained a soldier at heart. Although he appreciated the tribes' dilemmas, before being called east at the outset of the Civil War, he led successful campaigns against the Nez Perce, Shoshone, and other groups in scattered actions across northern California, Oregon, and Washington.

Crook's Civil War service began in the early days of the conflict. He quickly rose from captain to colonel and then brigadier general of volunteers, commanding initially a unit of the 14th Infantry and then the 36th Ohio Volunteer Infantry regiment. Much of 1861 and early 1862 found his unit operating in the mountains of present-day West Virginia. There, one of his initial early successes came at Lewisburg, where he defeated a sizable Confederate force. Crook was well-suited to his service in West Virginia, drawing on his experience in the Pacific Northwest to track down irregular groups ("bushwhackers") who rampaged through the lawless territory robbing and killing. By the time of Antietam, in September 1862, he was a brigade commander in the IX Corps leading his troops in actions around South Mountain and nearby Sharpsburg.

In 1863, Crook was appointed commander of the 2nd Cavalry Division operating at the time in Tennessee. In September, he led that unit through the horrific fighting at Chickamauga. In clashes that followed, his division saw action at McMinnville and Farmington, Tennessee. In early 1864, Crook and his cavalry tore up tracks and disrupted rail traffic between eastern Tennessee and Lynchburg, Virginia. In August, he was named commander of the Department of West Virginia, and led an army during Sheridan's Shenandoah campaign.

In October 1864, Crook was promoted to major general of volunteers after several successful engagements, including major actions at Winchester, Fisher's Hill, and Cedar Creek.

On February 21, 1865, while riding with a few members of his staff, Crook was surprised and captured by rebel cavalry. Held at Libby Prison in Richmond, he was paroled after a month as part of a prisoner exchange.

Crook's release came as the war was drawing to a close. On his return to duty, he was immediately given command of the cavalry of the Army of the Potomac and led its several thousand horsemen at Dinwiddie Court House on March 31. Subsequently, Crook and his cavalry saw action in almost all of the war's final engagements closing with Appomattox on April 9.

In the war's aftermath, Crook soon found himself in familiar territory. After reverting to his Regular Army grade of captain, in mid-1866 Crook was promoted to lieutenant colonel in the 23rd Infantry, a newly formed unit designated for duty in the Northwest. By December, Crook was on-scene as commander of the District of Boise, Idaho Territory. He was quickly in the field, putting down scattered Indian uprisings across parts of northern California, eastern Oregon, Idaho, and Nevada. Crook led his cavalry companies in difficult operations against the Paiutes, Klamaths, and associated bands. Reprising the lessons he had learned in his first tour of duty in the Pacific Northwest, Crook employed large numbers of Indian scouts from various bands against the warring Paiutes.

It was on these expeditions that Crook first made extensive use of mule pack trains. The innovation allowed him generally unencumbered movement away from his home base and enabled him to stay in the field for extended periods of time. Crook continued his campaigns through the dead of winter, skirmishing, capturing women and children, and putting villages and provisions to the torch.

Crook's force of about 200 cavalrymen and Indian scouts spent much of their time on the move. Clashes were frequent. In March 1868, Crook launched a winter offensive from a camp in Oregon. Evidencing his usual inventiveness and his experience with military operations in winter, Crook had his troops smear their faces with burnt cork to prevent sun blindness. Within a few days, Crook found the hostile Paiutes and in a sharp encounter fought on March 17, defeated them soundly, inflicting heavy casualties. Three months after the campaign began, the renegade bands sued for peace.

In the talks that followed Crook displayed the tough, hard line negotiating skills that would form part of his later reputation. It was an approach that would serve him well over the coming years.

Crook's achievements against the Paiutes and his later defeat of a mixed war party of Paiutes, Pitt River, and Modoc bands at Infernal Cavern in California were well noted by higher authorities. Crook was appointed commander of the entire Department of the Columbia, bypassing several officers who were superior in grade. Crook's tenure in the department would last for about two years, further crowned by his success in putting down disaffected bands of Umatilla and Nez Perce.

Crook's unblemished series of triumphs added to his reputation within the Army establishment and placed his services in demand when Indian troubles flared up elsewhere. After twice turning down offers to place him in command of the Department of Arizona – where Apaches were raiding, killing settlers, and stealing livestock – in 1871, at the request of President Grant, Crook reported for the first of his two extended tours of duty in the Southwest. He would serve as department commander for the next two years.

The timing of Crook's arrival coincided with peace efforts authored by an official of the Grant Administration, a noted humanitarian named Vincent Colyer. Colyer would be followed by another peace embassy led by General O. O. Howard. Colyer attempted to convince the Native bands to surrender and move to reservations that would be established in the region. In meetings, Colyer believed he had received the grudging consent of at least some of the tribal leaders to remain peaceful.

Crook provided Colyer – and later, Howard – with all available assistance, but was politely candid in offering his professional opinion that the tribes would not seriously consider making peace until they had been defeated on the battlefield.

Crook similarly demurred to Howard, who was convinced that good faith dealings based on trust and peaceful intent would dissolve the warring bands. Crook observed that incessant warfare was an integral component of Apache culture. Therefore, in his view it was naïve to believe that anything other than military defeat could dissuade them from raiding and killing.

When hostilities resumed after Colyer and Howard departed the area, Crook launched what would turn out to be a successful, year and a half campaign against the Apaches. After carefully selecting officers knowledgeable of Indian affairs and capable of acting independently, in November 1872, Crook sent elements of the 1st and 5th U.S. Cavalries along with Native guides to pursue warring bands across much of south central Arizona.

As he had in the Northwest, Crook used mule pack trains to help maintain pressure on the nomadic tribesmen. To further improve speed and mobility, he stripped down campaign gear, requiring soldiers to carry only minimal bedding, clothing, and camping equipment. Through the course of the coming winter, Apache camps were attacked at night and burned to the ground. As tribesmen began surrendering in ever larger numbers, Crook recruited many of them for his scout companies, adding heft to his strike force while further demoralizing the bands that remained hostile. Crook ordered that women and children not be harmed and that prisoners be well treated.

In August 1873, Crook saturated the region with fast-moving, self-sustaining columns. Found by Crook's Apache scouts wherever they went, the renegades could not escape the ferocious pressure. Hounded by day, unable to cook because their campfires were seen by the scouts, unable to sleep because Crook's soldiers attacked at night, the chiefs conceded. After 18 months of being unremittingly chased and attacked, Apache leaders met to discuss peace with Crook at Camp Verde, about 40 miles south of Flagstaff in central Arizona.

As was his usual approach, Crook took a hard line. While offering to protect those Apaches who stopped their raids, he threatened to destroy all who refused to surrender. Crook sent spokesmen to talk with leaders of the groups that had not met with him at Camp Verde. Crook's campaign – called by some the Tonto Basin Expedition – succeeded in bringing several years of relative peace to the region.

When the Apaches surrendered, Crook initiated programs intended to change the tribe's warlike lifestyle and induce them to be more receptive to reservation life. He employed tribesmen to serve as police and instituted governing councils and a court system administered by Indian peers. To foster personal accountability, he developed a tag identification system that allowed the quick detection of individuals absent without authorization. Urged to facilitate Apache farming and livestock breeding, Crook provided instructions, tools, and animals while guaranteeing an assured market for the tribe's produce. He maintained close personal oversight of reservation affairs. Indian leaders regarded him as firm but fair. Crook's efforts achieved greater success than most other attempts at Native pacification and assimilation.

In March 1875, Crook was sent to Omaha, Nebraska, to command the Department of the Platte where he would soon be introduced to warfare as fought by the powerful tribes on the Great Plains.

Spring of 1875 was an unsettled time in the region. The recent discovery of gold in the Black Hills had generated an influx of thousands of gold seekers into an area assigned to the Sioux nation by an 1868 treaty. Attempts to buy the area from the Sioux failed as did initial, occasionally half-hearted attempts to prevent prospectors from flooding it – a task for which the small frontier army was woefully inadequate.

As the number of Sioux attacks on emigrants increased so too did their raids on peaceful tribes quartered along the Missouri River. Pressure for action became more insistent. Eventually, the Indian Bureau issued an ultimatum demanding that the Sioux return to agencies established in Nebraska and Dakota Territory, essentially declaring that any Indian found off the reservations would be regarded as hostile.

Action was soon forthcoming. In bitter weather, Crook launched an expedition from Fort Fetterman, near present-day Douglas, Wyoming, on March 1, 1876. Hoping to catch the Sioux unprepared in winter quarters and perhaps deliver a demoralizing blow that would quickly put an end to hostilities, Crook split his force and sent six cavalry companies, about 400 men, under the command of Colonel Joseph J. Reynolds to assault a supposed Sioux camp located along the Powder River in southeastern Montana.

Almost everything about the subsequent battle was mishandled. The camp that Reynolds attacked sheltered not Sioux but Northern Cheyennes. Reynolds' assault had the effect of bringing the Cheyennes into the war as active participants allied with the Sioux.

Reynolds and his cavalrymen struck the cold, snow-covered encampment on March 17. The attack first met with success, forcing the Cheyennes from the village and capturing most of their pony herd. However, while the soldiers were burning the lodges, the Indians counterattacked, reclaiming most of the horses and compelling Reynolds' men to retreat. The remains of a least some of the men killed in the battle were left behind on the battlefield.

Crook was outraged. In addition to his displeasure with the way the battle was fought, by some accounts he had planned to use the village's buffalo robes and meat supplies – all burned by Reynolds' troops – to help provision later stages of his winter campaign. Crook subsequently brought charges against Reynolds, effectively ending his military career.

In the freezing weather of the Wyoming winter, Crook called off the campaign and pulled the troops back to Fort Fetterman. Meanwhile, the Cheyennes' victory emboldened fellow tribesmen at the Red Cloud and Spotted Tail Agencies in the Panhandle of Nebraska, inducing hundreds to join the hostile bands in the field.

For the next two months, Crook re-provisioned. In late May as part of a large, three-pronged operation envisioned by Lieutenant General Philip H. Sheridan, Crook moved into southeastern Montana. As conceived by Sheridan, while Crook advanced from the south, a column led by Colonel John Gibbon would move from the west and another force under the overall command of General Alfred Terry would push from the north. Together, all would converge in the vicinity of the Little Bighorn where large numbers of hostiles were presumed to be gathering. There, they would destroy the Sioux and their allies, or hammer them into submission and force them to return to their reservations. General Terry's column assembled at Fort Abraham Lincoln, near present-day Bismarck, North Dakota. His force included the 7th Cavalry, led by Lieutenant Colonel George Armstrong Custer.

Crook left Fort Fetterman on May 29. Having assumed personal command of the expedition the day before, he took with him a force comprised of 15 companies from the 2nd and 3rd Cavalry and six companies from the 4th and 9th Infantry – altogether, about 1,200 men. At the time, it was the largest force sent against Indians in the American West. It was also one of the best provisioned. Crook moved north with a large wagon train and, as always, a sizable mule pack train. Indeed, Crook was known throughout the Army for his skill in preparing expeditions for duty in the field regardless of climate or terrain.

Receiving reports of Indian encampments in the vicinity of Rosebud Creek, Crook moved in that direction past the ruins of Fort Phil Kearny, burned by the Indians in the aftermath of Red Cloud's War. A story persists that Crook had received a warning from Crazy Horse not to move past the Tongue River. Whether true or not, in the morning hours of June 9, as Crook reached the river and made camp along it, warriors sheltered on bluffs along the opposite bank opened fire on Crook's men. Little damage was done – most of the Indians' fire struck tents that were empty at the time. Crook responded quickly, ordering three infantry companies to form a skirmish line along the bank to pin down the attackers while a battalion of cavalry raced across the river and moved up the bluffs in an all-out charge directed at the strength of the Indians' position. Under steady, accurate fire from the infantry and heavy attack from on-rushing cavalry, the Indians broke and ran.

Crook spent a few days after the encounter preparing for a march into terrain that was understood to be even more rugged but whose specific features were little known. He sent his wagons back to his camp at Goose Creek under the protection of 100 infantrymen. Two hundred additional infantry were placed on mules freed from their supply pack duties.

Accompanied by 250 newly hired Crow and Shoshone auxiliaries, at 5 o'clock in the morning on June 16, Crook crossed the Tongue River and moved toward Rosebud Creek. As usual, he traveled light. Troops carried four days of rations – hardtack, coffee and bacon in their saddlebags and 100 rounds of ammunition in cartridge belts and boxes. No tents were taken and only one blanket per man was allowed.

Early the next morning, Crook and his 1,200 troops collided with a major force of Sioux and Cheyennes. Led by a cadre of famed war chiefs that included Crazy Horse, the Indians struck first in a bitterly fought battle that covered acres of ground and lasted throughout the day.

The day had begun with reveille at 3 a.m. Crook's army was on the move by 6 o'clock. Two hours later, after sending the Crows and Shoshones ahead to scout, the column stopped momentarily to rest and feed the horses and mules. They halted in a large, bowl-like defile cut through by the Rosebud Creek which at that location ran generally west to east. The area was known as Dead Canyon.

About a half hour later the first shots were heard as Crook's Crow and Shoshone scouts raced back, warning of large numbers of Sioux and Cheyennes rapidly approaching the bivouac area. As the struggle developed, groups of cavalrymen were sometimes surrounded, pressed inside landscape notable for its sharp ridges and jagged outcroppings. Several well-led cavalry charges drove the attackers from vantage points that overlooked the battle area. Eventually, the struggle evolved into pockets of actions whose locations and participants shifted repeatedly inside and along the edge of an extended, three-mile long battle area.

At the outset, Sioux and Cheyennes in numbers seldom seen in Plains warfare occupied the ridges that enveloped the area where Crook's troops were resting. Crook responded by sending officers to rally his Crow and Shoshone scouts, shattered by the initial rush. Crook hoped that eventually their services might be restored to the point where he could send them against the flank of the attackers.

Meanwhile, he dispatched a full battalion of the 3rd Cavalry straight north to clear the bluffs of a large contingent of attackers. Other troops were directed south to occupy high ground in that area and prevent an attack from the rear. Infantry and dismounted cavalry were formed into skirmish lines facing Indians who confronted them from several quadrants around the contested ground. As action continued, a charge by a reinforced battalion struck Indians on the bluffs to Crook's left.

Led by Captain Anson Mills, Crook's initial assault against the northern bluffs was well-delivered. Racing nearly a half mile across spongy and uncertain soil and then continuing up a steep slope, in twenty minutes the ridge was cleared of hostiles. The Indians fled to still higher ground 600 yards away. Mills formed his command into a skirmish line, advanced against the second ridge and captured it also. After Mills took possession of the bluff, they were assaulted several times by groups of Sioux on horseback whose periodic rushes initially did little damage.

Other charges around the perimeter of the bowl by Crook's men were equally as successful. As Indians were driven from bluffs nearest the battle area, several groups coalesced to add pressure against Mills' position at the north end of the field. Another well-conducted charge provided momentary relief, buying time until reinforcements arrived.

As action continued to shift, many of the Indians who had been attacked by Mills moved to join fighting that broke out at other locations. At that point, Crook took Mills and his battalion out of the fight in the bowl area, ordering him to attack a village or villages thought to be located somewhere down Dead Canyon. Crook promised to support Mills with a follow-on combined force of infantry and cavalry. Mills' place in the line was filled by mule train packers and other civilian employees.

Meanwhile, Indians in large numbers, including some who had vacated the fight with Mills, attacked Crook's positions along the east and west edges of the field. For perhaps the next two hours charges by both sides were met with equal numbers of countercharges as fighting raged at several points around the perimeter.

As action flowed back and forth, a battalion on the left flank became separated from the main body of Crook's force. Caught ahead of the front line, the unit was quickly surrounded and in danger of being overrun. Their destruction was only narrowly averted when relief forces sent by two other units broke through to them. Eventually, perhaps taking note of Mills' movement toward their village, the Sioux broke off their attack and hurried over the bluffs near Dead Canyon.

Some have conjectured that Crazy Horse may have intended an ambush using a ploy similar to that employed in the Fetterman Fight a few years earlier: an attack followed by a feigned retreat to lure pursuers into a trap. If the supposition is valid, Dead Canyon was likely the prospective killing ground. Enclosed nearly its entire length by high walls accessible only at each end, it held more promise than even the Little Bighorn.

Mills and his men moved down the narrow defile of Dead Canyon in a column of twos. They had cleared the mouth and the canyon where yet another well-handled charge aided by Crow and Shoshone scouts drove away a cluster of Sioux who fled farther down the canyon. As they rode cautiously between towering walls, it became readily apparent that they were in danger of being cut off and sealed inside the canyon. It seems certain that Crook was not aware of the terrain or the threat that it posed, and it is unlikely at this point that he or his officers recognized the enormous number of hostiles facing them.

As Crook was preparing to reinforce Mills and flow additional troops into the canyon, an action that likely would have doomed even larger numbers, fate intervened. Crook realized he had far more wounded than he had anticipated. His doctors protested against being left behind relatively unprotected with the casualties while Crook moved the bulk of his forces through Dead Canyon.

Seeing other fights still on-going around the perimeter, Crook heeded his medical staff's concern, deciding that he could not leave the field. He concluded that with pressure off them elsewhere, the number of warriors facing Mills might be too many for him to handle.

Crook quickly sent a small cadre racing across the battlefield and through the canyon to order Mills back to Rosebud Creek. After a hard, desperate ride the couriers caught up with Mills seven miles down the canyon.

Fate again intervened.

Mills had stopped his unit for a brief rest at an area – almost the only one in its entire length – where Dead Canyon was cut by a small cross canyon. The small defile had an opening to the west. Although boulder-strewn and steep, its slope allowed Mills and his men to climb out of the canyon. They returned to Crook with great reluctance.

After a day-long fight, the Indians broke off contact. Although Crook claimed victory because he possessed the ground at the end of the day, in reality the battle was a stalemate. As the Indians moved north, Crook, after camping for the night on the battlefield, returned to his main base at Goose Creek, Wyoming. Having expended 25,000 rounds of ammunition, he re-provisioned, saw to the care of his wounded, and clamored for reinforcements.

Losses were heavy on both sides. Most sources place Crook's casualties at 10 killed and 21 wounded. Indians losses are most often cited at 11-13 killed and additional wounded, although by some accounts Crazy Horse is alleged to have later acknowledged as many as 36 killed.

Rosebud Creek was not Crook's finest hour. He was criticized from within his own ranks for having issued contradictory orders during the course of the fluid battle. Others said he had not done enough to support his Indian auxiliaries.

Crook's defenders disagree, arguing that these and other actions such as pulling out Mills' contingent from Dead Canyon reflect not inconsistency but the reality of a chaotic battlefield and the exercise of judicious caution. Still, critics insist, at Rosebud Creek Crook underestimated his enemy.

Some scholars have asserted that Crook may have been shaken by the fight. This was his first battle experience with Plains tribes. His previous encounters with Indians in the Pacific Northwest and in Arizona had generally consisted of short duration clashes involving smaller bands of warriors who often fled when assailed by Army forces in sizable numbers. At Rosebud Creek, the Indians initiated the battle and sustained it at length. Crook may have been surprised by their aggressiveness and certainly by their numbers. Thousands of Natives were in the area of Rosebud Creek on June 17, and as many as a thousand to fifteen hundred were thought to have been on the battlefield at any one time.

The relative discipline of the warriors was another aspect of Plains warfare that Crook probably had not anticipated. Although nothing like a formal chain of command existed among the warrior bands, the multiple attacks and counter-attacks at Rosebud Creek evidenced a greater degree of cohesion and organization that he had previously encountered.

More importantly in view of events that followed, Crook's return to Goose Creek took him away from the titanic clash that occurred along the Little Bighorn only eight days later.

At Goose Creek, Crook dispatched couriers to General Sheridan to advise him that hostiles were in the area in unprecedented numbers. When that information reached General Terry's headquarters at Fort Abraham Lincoln, Terry (and Custer) had already departed. The report did not reach Terry until after the Little Bighorn.

The fight at Rosebud Creek had nearly exhausted his supply of ammunition and his wounded clearly required treatment. Nonetheless, Crook's extended sojourn at Goose Creek has prompted considerable discussion. Crook did not take the field again until early August. In the meantime, his repeated requests for reinforcements had been addressed. Sheridan had sent Colonel Wesley Merritt and the 5th Cavalry to join Crook. While moving from Fort Robinson, Nebraska, to link up with Crook's force, Merritt reversed course to take on large numbers of Sioux and Cheyenne who had left the Red Cloud and Spotted Tail agencies to join the hostile bands. In a superbly handled battle fought at Warbonnet Creek on July 17, Merritt thoroughly defeated Little Wolf's Cheyennes and forced them back to their reservations.

For a time after Merritt and the 5th Cavalry joined him, Crook remained immobile with a force of 1,400 men under arms. Much to his chagrin, when Crook eventually took the field on August 5, five days later his column was combined for a time with Terry's command. The huge assemblage moved in concert for a time, marching first east toward the Powder River and then back north toward the Yellowstone. With nearly 4,000 men, the force was too large and unwieldy to be effective against fast-moving nomadic bands. Finally, on August 18, the groups were split. Terry went back to Fort Abraham Lincoln with the remainder of the 7th Cavalry. Other units went north in an attempt to prevent the hostiles from crossing into Canada. Gibbon's command returned to Montana.

Crook, with the largest contingent – 450 infantry, 1500 cavalry, and 280 Indian scouts – was momentarily left as the only force in active pursuit. As usual, he was relentless. His forthcoming campaign was become legendary in the annals of frontier warfare.

The trek inspired – or provoked – several nicknames. Crook's expedition was alternately dubbed the "Mud March," the "Horsemeat March," or the "Starvation March." Indeed, each of those titles speaks to a reality of conditions along the way.

After traveling a few days with Terry's column in the vicinity of the Powder and Yellowstone Rivers, Crook turned east into present-day South Dakota. For the next three weeks, pelted by cold, persistent rains, Crook and his men pursued a large band of Sioux believed to be somewhere in the area. Crook, seeking as always to travel fast and light, took only minimum supplies and rations. Eventually, two and a half days of full rations were stretched into more than two weeks of subsistence on the trail. When those provisions ran out, the troopers were relegated to eating wild onions and horse and mule meat from animals that had played out or were lame or injured. Little else was available to supplement their meager diet, the Indians having cleared most of the game from the area before the soldiers approached. Water holes were sparse in number and when found were sometimes alkaline. Wood was also lacking; sometimes not enough was available to brew morning coffee.

Despite the conditions, Crook pushed forward, sometimes covering as many as 30 miles in a day. The column carried nine litters. All were eventually in use, transporting sick or exhausted men. Others were carried on pack animals whose loads had been used up.

Compelled to address the dire conditions confronting him, Crook detailed Captain Mills and 150 men on the best available horses to ride to Deadwood, purchase supplies, and hurry them back to the column. On the evening of September 8, Mills happened upon a Sioux village consisting of about 37 lodges near a geological feature called Slim Buttes, nor far from present-day Reva, South Dakota.

Mills' troops surrounded the village and attacked it at dawn the following morning. Except for a small pocket of Sioux who held out for a time in a nearby cave, the village was overrun and the inhabitants killed, captured, or scattered. Mills quickly sent word of the attack to Crook, informing him that his troops had found ample provisions of dried buffalo meat and other food stuffs. Crook quickly brought the rest of his hungry troopers – about a thousand in number, including infantry, cavalry, and artillery – to the site.

In the meantime, Indian survivors of Mills' attack had gone to Crazy Horse's nearby encampment. Crazy Horse, with something between 600 and 800 warriors, set out to retake the village.

Crazy Horse's initial attack, launched from vantage points along the bluffs, caused Crook to form a defensive perimeter to protect his horse and mule herd. After anchoring that position, Crook's men formed a strong skirmish line led by four infantry companies followed by dismounted troops from three cavalry regiments. A difficult firefight lasting nearly an hour drove the Indians from the buttes. During a search of the village after the battle, Crook's troopers discovered several items captured by the Indians at the Little Bighorn, including the guidon of Company I, 7th Cavalry and the bloody gloves of Captain Miles Keogh, one of Custer's officers.

Crook lost three killed and thirteen wounded in the fight. In the combined struggle at the village and during Crazy Horse's attack, Sioux losses were thought to be about 10 killed with a further unknown number wounded. Crook's men took 23 prisoners and captured more than 100 Indian ponies. The dried buffalo meat and other provisions discovered at the village sustained the troopers until a supply column finally reached them on September 15. Crook then left for other duties, turning over command to Wesley Merritt who took the column first to Deadwood and then to Fort Robinson where the expedition ended.

Crook's victory at Slim Buttes was the Army's first triumph over warriors who had fought at the Little Bighorn or were already at war at the time of the battle.

For Crook and his men, the victory and the recovery of Little Bighorn artifacts likely provided some small sense of solace to what otherwise had been a tortuous campaign that had left them destitute and hungry. While Crook's dogged pursuit and the victory at Slim Buttes had not destroyed the hostile bands, it had forced them to break up and scatter. Crook later presided over a winter expedition that sent Colonel Ranald Mackenzie to attack a Northern Cheyenne camp on the Red Fork of the Powder River. Called the

Dull Knife Fight, Mackenzie's victory effectively took the Cheyennes out of the war. Soon after, Nelson Miles' triumph at Wolf Mountain, Montana, essentially did the same with the rest of the warring Sioux bands. By the spring of 1877, the Great Sioux War was over.

In October 1876, Crook sent Mackenzie to quash an incipient uprising led by two powerful chiefs. Sioux leaders Red Cloud and Red Leaf, embittered by the outcome of negotiations that had caused the tribe to relinquish the Black Hills, had left the Red Cloud Agency near Fort Robinson in the Nebraska Panhandle. Taking a sizable band of followers with them, they moved to a location about 30 miles away along Chadron Creek. There, they established camps and demanded that their government rations be delivered to them at that location.

Crook concluded that the situation had to be immediately addressed, otherwise the government's reservation system would be placed at risk. Even worse, the groups might decide to join hostile bands still on the warpath. On October 22, Mackenzie, leading eight companies of cavalry and a contingent of Pawnee Scouts, surrounded the two camps and ended the "revolt" without a shot being fired. The Indians surrendered immediately and were escorted back to the agency.

In the fall of the following year, Crook was part of the confused and unfortunate drama that concluded with the death of Crazy Horse. The Sioux war leader, along with 885 Oglala followers, had surrendered at Fort Robinson on May 6, 1877. For a time, they resided peacefully at the Red Cloud Agency. In late summer, a series of rumors almost certainly fabricated by Crazy Horse's rivals and others jealous of his influence, began circulating through the agency. In various iterations the stories alleged that Crazy Horse was preparing a breakout, intending to take hundreds with him in a renewed campaign; or, alternately, that he intended to kill an officer at Fort Robinson and take over the agency. Misunderstandings and egregious mis-translations added to the confusion.

On September 3, 1877, as rumors continued to build, Crook arranged to meet with Crazy Horse to settle the dispute. On his way to the meeting an Indian raced to him to warn of an assassination plot allegedly perpetrated by Crazy Horse (a claim that was later found to be fabricated).

Crook could afford to take no chances. A resumption of warfare by 2,000 of the world's best light cavalry was too ominous a consequence to risk. Within an hour, Crook ordered Crazy Horse's arrest, apparently intending that he be incarcerated at Fort Marion, Florida. In the meantime, Crazy Horse had gone to a nearby camp to visit a friend, a giant Oglala named Touch the Clouds. On September 5, escorted by friends and a company of cavalry, he was on his way back to Fort Robinson, where he arrived in late afternoon or early evening.

Not understanding that he was to be confined, he drew his knife and struggled when he was taken to the guardhouse and saw the cells and barred windows. The confused melee that followed spilled out into the grounds near the building where he was bayoneted – whether accidently or purposefully continues to be debated. The wound was mortal, lacerating both kidneys. He died a few hours later.

Crook then returned to Omaha to resume his duties as departmental commander. Notwithstanding his less than stellar performance at Rosebud Creek, the Great Sioux War had been brought to a conclusion under his general auspices. Ironically, though he was by now widely recognized as one of the Army's premier Indian fighters, his personal views towards the Natives grew ever more moderate. In 1878 and 1879, when the government again experienced problems with Bannocks and Northern Cheyennes, Crook's well-written official reports favored the Indians' positions.

The action for which Crook is most noted – and the one which most clearly expresses his opinions regarding Indian rights – occurred in April 1879. The Poncas, a small tribe whose historic homeland was in northeastern Nebraska, had initially been given a reservation near their tribal grounds. In 1877, after a confused process rife with misunderstandings, the tribe was forcibly moved to Indian Territory where they were settled on land insufficient to sustain them. By the spring of 1879, more than a third had died of malnutrition, malaria, and other diseases. One of those who died was the son of a Ponca chief, Standing Bear.

Standing Bear had promised his son that he would bury him in the Ponca homeland in Nebraska's Niobrara River Valley. Accompanied by 65 followers, Standing Bear carried his son's body north from Indian Territory. When they arrived at the Omaha Reservation in Nebraska, word of their presence reached government authorities. Secretary of Interior Carl Schurz directed Crook to arrest the Poncas and return them to Indian Territory.

Crook dutifully followed orders and arrested Standing Bear and his contingent. However, he delayed sending them back, keeping them at Fort Omaha so they could rest and recover. In the meantime, Crook secured aid for them from influential sources. Crook told the Ponca's saga to Thomas Tribles, editor of the Omaha newspaper. The story was soon reported nationwide. John L. Webster, a prominent attorney, agreed to assist Crook in a lawsuit and was soon joined by Andrew J. Poppelton, chief attorney of the Union Pacific Railroad, headquartered in Omaha.

In April 1879, the attorneys sued for a writ of *habeas corpus* in U.S. District Court in Omaha. When the case came to trial, Susette La Flesche, a well-educated bilingual Omaha Indian of mixed-race heritage, interpreted for Standing Bear, a man of surpassing eloquence. General Crook was named formal defendant because the Poncas were being held under his custody.

On May 12, Judge Elmer S. Dundy ruled that "an Indian is a person" within the meaning of the law, and thus entitled to its full rights and protections. The landmark decision freed Standing Bear and his followers. Swayed by public opinion, the administration of President Rutherford B. Hayes authorized the permanent return of the Poncas to the Niobrara River Valley. Crook was appointed to a commission that recommended that the Poncas be compensated for their losses and that schooling and farming supplies by furnished to them.

In 1882, with Chiricahuas again raiding and discontent spreading across the Apache reservations, Crook voluntarily accepted an assignment to return to Arizona as department commander. An initial inspection trip, the reinstatement of his earlier policies and his presence on the scene – Crook was warmly welcomed by the Apaches – did much to quell the unrest.

The Chiricahuas, though, posed a persisting problem. Led by war chiefs like Chato and Geronimo, hostile bands robbed and killed in the United States before taking sanctuary in the rugged Sierra Madre Mountains across the border in Mexico. In the spring of 1883, Crook mounted a major expedition consisting of a troop of cavalry, 200 Apache scouts, and 350 pack mules. On May 1, Crook crossed into Mexico – an existing convention between the nations allowed troops from each side to cross the border while in pursuit of hostiles – and moved into the Sierra Madres. On May 15, his scouts surprised and destroyed an Apache ranchero, killing nine renegades and capturing supplies and equipment in large quantities. Relentless as always, Crook continued his pursuit, pressing deeper into the mountains.

Hounded without respite, tired and hungry, Chiricahua leaders met with Crook and begged for peace, bringing a quick, conclusive end to the campaign. Crook returned to the United States with 52 Apache warriors, 273 women and children, and a promise from the chiefs that their remaining tribesmen would turn themselves in at the San Carlos Agency.

As on his earlier tour of duty in Arizona, Crook allowed Apache leaders to select the sites for their settlements and made them accountable for their bands' behavior. Native police patrolled the villages and Apache scouts preserved order across the reservations.

Crook's policies were met with wide disfavor by Indian agents and much of the officer corps. Among the most hostile critics was General Philip H. Sheridan, Commanding General of the United States Army, who had an abiding distaste for the use of Indian auxiliaries.

While disagreements between Crook and his superior continued to fester, on May 17, 1885, Geronimo and a large number of malcontents broke out of the agency, moving to hideouts in Mexico and then returning periodically to raid and kill in the United States. Crook's forces chased the Chiricahuas for 11 months before Geronimo agreed to negotiate.

At a meeting south of the border, Crook relayed the government's demand for unconditional surrender and advised Geronimo that the intention was to send all Chiricahuas to prison locations in the eastern United States. Crook bitterly opposed the portion of the plan that called for incarcerating his own Chiricahua scout allies along with the hostiles. In any event, Geronimo would agree only to two years' confinement after which he and his tribesmen would be allowed to return to reservations in Arizona. Crook, though outraged by the failure of the pact to differentiate between renegades and non-renegades – and determined to attempt to modify that portion of it – apparently thought the overall agreement involving Geronimo's surrender was likely as good a deal as was possible. However, when the telegraphed news of Geronimo's capitulation reached higher headquarters, General Sheridan rejected the terms, demanding instead that either the Chiricahuas surrender unconditionally or that Crook destroy them. Crook was now faced with repudiating the agreement he had negotiated.

He refused to do so.

The resulting impasse lasted only briefly. To Crook's dismay, Geronimo and several warriors again fled from custody following a drunken revel.

Crook regarded Sheridan's sharp reply to the news of Geronimo's escape to be an affront and an implicit censure of his policies. He requested to be immediately relieved of his command. The following day, Sheridan appointed General Nelson A. Miles to take his place. The relationship between Sheridan and Crook, already strained, was now irretrievably broken. It would remain so during the rest of the lives of both men.

In September 1886, Miles, the new commander of the Department of Arizona – essentially employing Crook's methods although with larger numbers of soldiers and fewer Native scouts – compelled the remaining hostiles to surrender. Following their capitulation, the Apaches were moved to Florida. Miles, an officer never known for his modesty, claimed responsibility for Geronimo's defeat.

A rift soon developed between Crook and Miles over which was due the most credit: Crook for devising the tactics and prescribing the campaign the led to the surrender of the majority of the renegades, or Miles for guiding it to its conclusion and achieving the final surrender. Crook was also distraught that Miles seemed to acquiesce to, or did little to oppose, the shipment of loyal Apache scouts to Florida prisons.

After being relieved of his command in the Southwest, Crook initially returned to his prior post in Omaha. In April 1888, he was promoted to major general and appointed commander of the Division of the Missouri – actions that he regarded as providing a degree of vindication for his accomplishments in Arizona.

In his later years, Crook became increasingly active in Indian rights movement and persisted in specific efforts to assist Chiricahuas incarcerated in Florida. To his consternation, provisions of the surrender agreement providing for renegades to be reunited with their families were not being adhered to by government authorities. Then too, the prison sites at Fort Pickens and Fort Marion were particularly ill-suited to Apaches accustomed to a dry, arid climate.

Long allied with the Indian Rights Association, Crook secured the help of the group in reuniting families and moving the Florida prisoners to Mount Vernon Barracks in Mobile, Alabama. Crook was welcomed warmly and with great respect by Apache leaders – allies and former foes alike – when he visited the facility shortly after the move. Seeing that the place offered at best only a marginal improvement over the sites in Florida, in 1889 Crook began a campaign to further move the Apaches to Fort Sill, Oklahoma. Crook's efforts, made with the government's permission, would eventually come to fruition in 1894.

Recognizing Crook's prestige among the Natives, early in 1889, he was appointed to a commission to gain the Sioux tribe's consent for adjustments to the treaty affecting the Great Sioux Reservation.

Crook's appointment as commander of the Division of the Missouri enabled him to take up residence at the Grand Pacific Hotel in Chicago. His headquarters was renowned for its informality: the atmosphere was casual and the entire staff wore civilian clothes.

Crook's sojourn in Chicago was one of the rare times during his long career when his wife accompanied him for an extended period. Crook had married Mary Tapscott Dailey, a young woman from Maryland on August 22, 1865, having met her during his Civil War service. Mary was not an active military wife, remaining mostly on the Dailey estate near Oakland, Maryland, only occasionally visiting Crook at his duty stations in the West.

On March 21, 1890, Crook died of a heart attack in his Chicago hotel suite. The heart condition was likely influenced by long years of exposure in harsh environments. Other factors may have contributed as well. Strains from his conflict with Nelson Miles and anxiety over the treatment of the Apaches posed heavy and disquieting burdens. Influenza contracted on a recent visit to Fort Sill – a trip made to further his proposal to move the Apaches to that location – likely further sapped his strength.

Crook was initially buried at Oakland, Maryland. He was later reinterred at Arlington National Cemetery. Perhaps his most fitting epitaph came from the Sioux chief Red Cloud who said Crook "never lied to us. His words give the people hope."

George Armstrong Custer

Over the full course of the nation's history, few officers who have worn an American military uniform have remained as controversial as George Armstrong Custer. Even today his legacy is not fully settled. Hailed initially as a martyred hero killed waging a gallant struggle against impossible odds, current scholarship typically casts him in a less favorable light. In recent years he has been more often characterized as a reckless glory-seeker who foolishly squandered the lives of 207 soldiers under his immediate command and another 57 slain elsewhere on blood-soaked grounds along a small river in southeastern Montana.

Those who attempt to justify some or all of Custer's actions on that fateful day assert that given the usual expectations of the time, his plan – dividing his 650-man force into three strike columns (a fourth contingent was left to guard his supply train) – was not inherently flawed. Indeed, Custer had used something quite similar at Washita in Indian Territory eight years before.

This time, however, he was confronted by perhaps the largest gathering of hostile Indians ever assembled on the North American continent. His apologists would say that he had no way of knowing that. No one in is coterie, even veteran frontiersmen, had experienced anything like it. Thus, they would argue that he may have understandably regarded scouting reports as alarmist and exaggerated.

Nonetheless, *all* of his scouts advised him of the immense size of the Indian encampment. His most veteran and trusted scouts cautioned him against advancing into the valley. Some prophesized their own deaths if they did so. Even Captain Frederick Benteen, a subordinate who hated Custer with an abiding passion, urged him not to split his force. Custer ignored him.

It is uncertain why he did so. Conjectures, though (which are all that we have) have not been lacking.

Foremost among them is that Custer thought his force had been detected and therefore felt compelled to attack quickly, before the element of surprise was completely lost. Directions from his commander, General Alfred Terry, were sufficiently flexible to permit an attack. Although the clearly preferred intention was for Custer to wait until Terry and Colonel John Gibbon arrived to join in the action, Custer was given latitude to attack if, in his judgment, conditions warranted. Given Custer's aggressiveness, it was almost certain that he would either ignore the orders he had been given or interpret them in a way that would take his force into a fight.

Many have noted that Custer was under a cloud at the time. He had recently testified before a House committee investigating charges of corruption in the War Department. By inference, he had implicated the Secretary of War, William W. Belknap, and President Grant's brother, Orvil. Grant was not a forgiving man. Only with great reluctance and the direct interventions of Generals Sherman, Sheridan, and Terry, had Custer even been allowed to accompany the expedition – and then only under the stipulation that he would go as Terry's subordinate. Thus, according to some, he may have seen the Little Bighorn as an opportunity to redeem his reputation.

Library of Congress
George Armstrong Custer

Finally, there is the reality of Custer's ego. As many have suggested, he may have simply thought that he and the 7th Cavalry could handle *any* Indian war party of *any* size.

Whatever the motives for the attack or the apparent failures of leadership, there can be no doubting of Custer's personal courage. Daring to the point of recklessness, he was a commander who led from the front. Through four years of horrific combat during the Civil War and in encounters across the Plains, he was invariably at the front of his troopers, leading the charge straight into the thick of battle. It was that place – in the noise, fury, danger, and excitement of close combat – that he seemed to seek out. Certainly, it was there that he excelled.

More so than most of his contemporaries, Custer was a complex personality whose actions were driven by an intriguing blend of daring, recklessness, ambition and, at times, blind foolishness bordering on irrationality.

More than a century and a quarter later, the fascination remains.

Called "Autie" by much of his family, George Armstrong Custer was a lithe, slender 6-footer. He weighed about 170 pounds and had broad shoulders and blue eyes. Except in campaigns, he wore his light, gold-tinged hair in long, curled ringlets, a style that provoked derision among some of his men and earned him a nickname – "Long Hair" – from his Native adversaries.

In garrison, Custer was a "dandy," adorning his ornate uniforms with colorful affectations almost inevitably topped by a broad-brimmed hat and a red kerchief. On expeditions, such as at the Little Bighorn, he cut his hair short and wore a buckskin jacket and trousers. The big hat and the red bandana remained fixtures on the campaign trail.

Among those who served under him Custer provoked mixed emotions. Almost all of his subordinates acknowledged his bravery under fire (during the Civil War, he had eleven horses, including two at Gettysburg, shot out from under him), and appreciated that when the 7th Cavalry charged, he was at its front. His extraordinary stamina was both admired and cursed by those who campaigned with him. His men nicknamed his "Iron Ass" because of his endurance in the saddle. On campaign, he was known to ride for 11 or 12 hours and then in his tent at night write newspaper articles and 40-page letters to his wife. He was, though, also regarded as a harsh disciplinarian with an aloof personality. Although he expressed pride in their achievements, Custer maintained little direct contact with his soldiers and was mostly indifferent to their hardships.

His wife, Elizabeth ('Libby") Bacon Custer, was a formidable personality in her own right. Libby Custer lived for 57 years after her husband fell at the Little Bighorn. Until her death in 1933, she devoted her life to defending Custer's reputation against increasing public sentiment that he was an unprincipled glory seeker.

Though a favorite of Generals Sherman and Sheridan, who appreciated his aggressiveness and fighting spirit, Custer was generally disliked by officer contemporaries. At the Battle of Washita Custer abandoned several wounded and dying men, making no apparent attempt, or at best an indifferent one, at rescue or recovery. Perhaps as many as 19 soldiers were left on the battlefield, subjected to mutilations that would be inevitably forthcoming from vengeful tribesmen. Throughout much of the Army, Custer was never forgiven.

Custer was born December 5, 1839, in New Rumley, Ohio. He spent a portion of his childhood in Monroe, Michigan, living with an older half-sister. In 1856, he taught grammar school for a brief time after completing his own studies. Restless as always, he rather quickly applied for, and received, an appointment to West Point.

Custer entered the academy in 1857. His tenure at West Point was not noted for its excellence. Nearly expelled on several occasions, he accumulated large numbers of demerits, often for instigating pranks. When his class graduated in June 1861, Custer was ranked last of 34 students.

In the military profession, opportunity and career advancement are often influenced by the timing of surrounding events. For Custer, who stepped almost directly from the parade ground at West Point onto the battlefields of the Civil War, the timing was impeccable. He fought in the war's first major engagement at Bull Run and its last at Appomattox. Indeed, his service record reads as a litany of the battles waged by the Army of the Potomac:

Bull Run, the Peninsula Campaign, Antietam, Chancellorsville, Gettysburg, the Overland Campaign, the Wilderness, Yellow Tavern, Trevilian Station, the Shenandoah Valley Campaign, Culpepper Court House, Winchester, Fisher's Hill, Cedar Creek, Waynesboro, Dinwiddie Court House, the Siege of Petersburg, Five Forks, Appomattox.

At the outset of the war, Custer's obvious dash and willingness to take on all tasks caused Generals Philip Kearny, George McClellan, and Alfred Pleasonton – successively – to name him as their aide-de-camp.

Custer's first of many brevet promotions came soon after, following exceptional performances at Aldie, Brandy Station, and during the Rappahannock Campaign. Effective June 29, 1863, he was appointed brevet brigadier general of volunteers. He was 23 years old.

A few days later, on July 3, on the third day of the Battle of Gettysburg, General Robert E. Lee sent J. E. B. Stuart's cavalry on a sweep around the Union left flank, seeking to strike the Federals from the rear while the massed forces of Generals George Pickett, James Pettigrew, and Isaac Trimble (the assault commonly known as Pickett's Charge) hammered at the front. If the center of the line could be severed the battle and perhaps with it the war, could be won. Custer, commander of the Michigan Brigade, was initially detailed to move his unit to a different location in the field. He prevailed upon his commander, General David Gregg, to allow the brigade to remain in place. It was well that Gregg agreed to let him stay, for Custer's actions that day contributed mightily to the Union victory. In what quickly developed into one of the largest cavalry clashes of the war, Custer took his unit into the thick of an hours-long melee, leading charge after charge into the maelstrom. By the time Stuart finally withdrew, Custer's brigade has lost more than 250 men, the most of any in the field that day.

Following the battle, Custer received a brevet promotion to major in the Regular Army. Soon after, in quick succession he received Regular Army brevets to lieutenant colonel and colonel for actions at Yellow Tavern and Winchester/Fisher's Hill. In October – still two months shy of his 25th birthday – he was appointed brevet major general of volunteers.

From September 30, 1864, until the close of the war, Custer commanded the 3rd Division of cavalry, leading the unit through battles at Cedar Creek , Waynesboro, Dinwiddie Court House, and Five Forks. For his service in the latter two battles, he was brevetted brigadier general in the Regular Army.

Custer was on the field at Appomattox when Lee surrendered. General Sheridan thought so highly of Custer's services that he purchased the table from the parlor at Wilmer McLean's house on which the surrender document had been signed and gave it to Libby Custer. (The table is now at the Smithsonian.)

Soon after the war ended, Custer reverted to his previous rank of captain.

He toyed for a time with accepting a mercenary command in Mexico, fighting for Benito Juarez's guerillas against Emperor Maxmilian and his French troops struggling for control of the country. Refused the necessary leave of absence and unwilling to resign his commission, Custer was unable to accept the senior position proffered by Juarez. Civilian employment and political prospects were also considered, but not for long and how seriously is uncertain. In the end, Custer chose to remain in the Army, accepting, at Sheridan's behest, a posting that eventually led him to Texas on Reconstruction duty.

In June 1865, at Alexandria, Louisiana, Custer began assembling the force that would handle occupation duties in Texas. In August, he led them on a difficult 18-day march to Hempstead, Texas. In October, he moved the unit to Austin where he became chief of cavalry for the Department of Texas.

Until they were mustered out of service beginning in November and replaced with Army regulars, Custer's initial cadre consisted of volunteer units. With the war over, the men were eager to go home and get on with their lives. They chafed, at times to the point of near mutiny, at Custer's harsh discipline.

In September 1866, Custer accompanied President Andrew Johnson on a national tour aimed at building support for Johnson's policies toward the defeated South. In his public comments, Custer joined Johnson in speaking in favor of moderation.

Soon after, Custer was appointed lieutenant colonel (and, at the request of Sheridan, brevet major general) in a new unit being formed at Fort Riley, Kansas. In October, shortly before his 27th birthday, Custer joined the 7th Cavalry. He would remain affiliated with the unit until his death a decade later.

In March 1867, Custer and the 7th took the field for the first time as part of an expedition led by General Winfield Scott Hancock. Intended to awe the southern Plains tribes into docility, the campaign accomplished very little. Hancock's 1,400-man force trekked several hundred miles but saw few Indians and succeeded only in burning an abandoned village.

Early summer of that year found Custer leading a large contingent of the 7th Cavalry from Fort Hays, Kansas, to Fort McPherson, near present-day North Platte, Nebraska. At Fort McPherson, Custer met with General Sherman, who shelved a grander plan and instead directed Custer to proceed southwest to the Republican River where Cheyenne and Sioux in large numbers were thought to be assembling.

Four days later, after moving through rugged, broken country, Custer's troops reached the forks of the Republican just south of present-day Benkelman, Nebraska. There, with six companies of the 7th Cavalry, the major portion of his force, he camped from June 22 until June 30.

After dispatching an 11-person courier detachment to Fort Sedgwick, Colorado, and a guarded wagon train to Fort Wallace, Kansas, to replenish his supplies on the morning of the 23rd, Custer and his men settled into their camp.

The stillness of the pre-dawn hours of the following morning was broken by a shot from a sentry followed by heavy shooting from around the camp's perimeter. During the night, a large Sioux war party led by chief Pawnee Killer and thought to number in the hundreds surrounded the 7th Cavalry's bivouac. Custer's account indicates that a group of about 50 warriors on horseback, their approach concealed by a deep ravine, made a dash toward the encampment. The picket's timely shot disrupted their attempt to race through the camp and stampede the cavalry's horses, which would then be caught by the warriors encircling the campsite. That outcome, Custer noted, might have allowed the Sioux "to finish us at their leisure."

The "particularly sharp conflict" was not of long duration. The Sioux, under brisk fire and seeing their plans foiled, withdrew to a safe location about a mile away. Custer's only casualty was the sentry, who was badly wounded and ridden over by the fleeing Indians. The war party's attempt to scalp him was thwarted by heavy fire from troopers who rushed out of the camp to retrieve him.

Later that day, Indians were again sighted near the cavalry's camp. Custer sent Captain Louis Hamilton, a grandson of Alexander Hamilton, and 40 troopers in pursuit. The small group of Indians – a decoy – moved gradually away, drawing the cavalrymen ever further from their base. Eventually the Indians split up and Hamilton divided his force into two detachments. Hamilton, with 25 troopers, followed the largest group. At a location about seven miles northwest of the campsite, with the two cavalry detachments now far apart, the Sioux sprang an ambush. A party of about 40-50 warriors hidden in a ravine surrounded the soldiers, circling them and firing over the necks of their ponies.

Hamilton defended quickly and well, dismounting his cavalry and forming them to repel several attacks. In the meantime, the party's doctor, who had somehow become separated from both detachments, heard the sound of fighting. Chased by a party of Indians, he made a narrow escape, racing back to the main camp to report Hamilton's plight. Assistance was immediately sent, led by Custer himself. When the relief party reached the scene, Custer found that Hamilton's detachment had beaten back the attacks, killing two Indians and wounding others. Hamilton's only casualty was a wounded cavalry horse.

In the following days, the small courier party sent to Fort Sedgwick returned safely from their mission through hazardous territory. The 16-wagon train sent to Fort Wallace was heavily attacked by 600-700 warriors near Butte

Creek, Kansas, on their return journey. The three-hour attack was eventually broken off when a relief force sent earlier as a precaution by Custer appeared on the horizon.

Replenished with supplies brought by the wagon train to the Republican River bivouac, Custer, acting on new instructions from General Sherman, struck west up the north fork of the Republican – a route that took the cavalry from their campsite, past present-day Parks and Haigler, Nebraska, and into Colorado. Several miles inside eastern Colorado, the force turned north and made a grueling march that eventually brought them to the Platte River 50 miles west of Fort Sedgwick.

At this point Custer received disturbing news that a courier detachment composed of an officer, 10 enlisted men and a scout, had left Fort Sedgwick with dispatches for him several days before. The young officer in charge, Lieutenant Lyman Kidder, was directed to proceed to the forks of the Republican where Custer was still presumed to be camped. In reality, Custer and his command were by then 100 or more miles to the northwest.

Finding the camp on the forks of the Republican vacated, the courier party apparently misread Custer's trail, believing him to be headed south toward Fort Wallace. The path took the small unit deep into the same territory where several hundred warriors had so recently attacked Custer's wagon train. Custer realized the danger to the courier party and turned his force back, first to the forks of the Republican and then, correctly surmising what must have happened, immediately moved toward Fort Wallace, 80 desperate miles to the south.

On the morning of the July 12, several miles down the road near a small rivulet called Beaver Creek, the fate of the courier party was determined. In Custer's words "Lying in irregular order, and within a very limited circle, were the mangled bodies of the poor (party) so brutally hacked and disfigured as to be beyond recognition as human beings. Every individual in the party had been scalped and his skull broken .... Even the clothes of all the party had been carried away; some of the bodies were lying in beds of ashes, with partly burned fragments of wood near them, showing that the savages had put some of the to death by the terrible tortures of fire. The sinews of the arms and legs had been cut away, the nose of every man hacked off, and the features otherwise so defaced that it would have been scarcely possible for even a relative to recognize a single one of the unfortunate victims .... Each body was pierced by from 20 to 50 arrows ...."

In many ways, it was the same fate that would befall the soldiers of the 7th Cavalry eight years and eleven months later.

For Custer any favorable after effects from having led his first expedition on the Great Plains were quickly washed away. On July 21, he was placed under arrest. What precipitated a main charge against him was an event that characterized Custer's impetuous irresponsibility. In essence, he missed his wife and without permission left his post to see her. Libby was at the time at Fort Riley, 275 miles east of Custer's duty station at Fort Wallace. Custer took with him four officers and 72 men in an effort to justify his dash across Kansas on military grounds. He had, though, left without authorization and was charged with being absent without leave and conduct prejudicial to good order and discipline.

The eight total charges – he would be convicted on all of them – also included some related to a recent incident when Custer had ordered 13 troopers who had deserted to be ridden down and shot. Three were wounded, one fatally, as Custer made a public display of denying medical assistance when the soldiers were returned to the fort. During his earlier sojourn in Texas, in an attempt to quell desertions among disgruntled volunteers waiting to be released from service, he had executed one soldier and feigned shooting another. His scheme in Kansas was essentially a reprise of his mock execution strategy. It succeeded mainly in appalling most of his contemporaries.

The court-martial board that tried Custer convened at Fort Leavenworth. On October 11, he was found guilty on all specifications and suspended from rank and pay for one year.

As was often the case with Custer, help would be forthcoming from a familiar source. General Philip H. Sheridan, Custer's patron, replaced Winfield Scott Hancock as commander of the Department of the Missouri. Sheridan had a warm friendship – indeed, almost a father-son relationship – with Custer, dating back to their close association during the Civil War. Sheridan himself was a relentless fighter and likely saw a similar quality in Custer; he respected his young colleague's energy, aggressiveness, and near-recklessness under fire. Sheridan allowed Custer and Libby to stay for an extended period in his (Sheridan's) quarters at Fort Leavenworth. In October 1868, he restored Custer to field command of the 7th Cavalry and sent the unit on a winter campaign against hostile bands thought to be sheltering in Indian Territory somewhere near the headwaters of the Red River.

As conceived by Sheridan, the campaign would consist of three columns. Two outer ones led by Colonel Eugene A. Carr and Colonel Andrew W. Evans would operate on each side of Custer. The two wings would press the hostiles toward their camps and toward Custer, whose command would strike the decisive blow directly at the villages.

Carr, with seven companies of the 5th Cavalry, left from Fort Lyon, Colorado. Evans, with six companies of cavalry, two of infantry, and four howitzers, moved from Fort Bascom, New Mexico. Both would converge toward Custer, who on November 22, 1868, departed Fort Supply, Indian Territory, just east of the Oklahoma Panhandle in present-day Woodward County. Custer moved west with 11 companies of the 7th Cavalry totaling about 800 men. As events would unfold, horrific weather hindered the columns of Carr and Evans and lessened their impact on the campaign.

On November 26, a reconnaissance party found a substantial trail, probably made by war parties returning from killing raids on settlements in Kansas. Scouts tracked their route and later in the day a patrol personally led by Custer confirmed the location of a sizable village on the Washita River near the present-day city of Cheyenne in western Oklahoma. Custer brought his officers to a vantage point from where they could visualize the battlefield and their places in the forthcoming fight.

Custer attacked at sunrise on November 27. As he would at the Little Bighorn, Custer divided his command, this time, having surrounded the village, he would strike from all four sides. The details of his attack are not universally agreed on. Though Custer later wrote of attacking from all sides, some scholars describe a charge from three directions. Others believe a single, powerful blow was struck by Custer and the purpose of the units around the periphery was mainly to chase down Indians attempting to flee.

In the bitter cold dawn, Custer's horsemen charged through drifted snow and ice, taking the sleeping village by surprise. Custer led the attack from the north, racing into battle accompanied by the rousing strains of the melody *Garry Owen*, a favorite his, played by the 7th Cavalry band in the center of the line. Although policing up continued into the afternoon, the heaviest fighting lasted only a matter of minutes and even scattered shooting was probably over by mid-morning.

Custer's men burned all of the 51 lodges, destroying 1,000 buffalo robes and hundreds of pounds of lead, powder, blankets, and other provender. After allowing 53 women and children captives to choose their own horses, in a tactic that would be widely emulated he shot the remainder of the village's 700-900 ponies, eliminating the feared mobility of some of the world's most skilled horsemen.

Although Custer was unaware of it at the time, the village he attacked was only the western-most of several Native camps strung along the valley for perhaps as many as 10 miles. Altogether, possibly 2,000 warriors – Kiowa, Arapaho, Cheyenne, Commanche, and Apache – were sheltering in nearby camps.

As the struggle commenced, Major Joel Elliott, commanding the eastern-most side of Custer's divided forces, saw Indians attempting to escape from Custer's assault on the village. Probably unknown to Custer, Elliott took a squad of about 17 men (accounts range from 14-18) and set out after them, moving eastward down the south side of the Washita River. After a chase of two miles they caught and killed two Indians near what is now known as Sergeant Major Creek. Elliott and his small company then continued east only a short distance before they were engulfed by warriors in large numbers racing from villages scattered along the valley floor.

Elliott dismounted his men, placing them in a defensive circle where they lay prone in a hollow of tall grass. Fighting for their lives from behind any semblance of shelter they could find, their struggle did not last long. Elliott and his men were quickly overrun. All of them – those killed outright as well some captured alive – were horrifically mutilated.

Custer made no serious attempt to reach Elliott's party although by some accounts their plight may have been observed by at least some participants on his own battlefield. Custer's portion of the fight was by then finished or nearly so. Those sympathetic to him argue that he saw hundreds of warriors riding up the valley from nearby camps and appropriately retreated from the area in late afternoon having achieved his main mission, the destruction of the village. Another view has him believing that Elliott was still actively scouting and would rejoin him later.

Casualties of both sides remain somewhat uncertain. Recent scholarship places Custer's losses at 21 officers and men killed and 13 wounded. Estimates of Indian losses vary widely. Custer's official report, widely disputed, claimed 103 killed. A later Army study put the figure at about 50 killed and a like number wounded. Native sources asserted 11-18 warriors and at least 17 – although some figures are much higher – women and children killed.

The Battle of Washita remains controversial. Adding to the poignancy is that the village belonged to Black Kettle, a Cheyenne chief noted for his peaceful intentions. It has been Black Kettle's camp at Sand Creek that was destroyed by John Chivington's militia in November 1864 while flying both a white flag and an American flag to signal the group's non-hostile disposition. Dozens had been killed and Black Kettle's wife had been wounded several times. Subsequently, Black Kettle agreed to move his band to Indian Territory in hopes of separating them from hostilities on-going elsewhere across the Plains.

Only a few days before Custer's attack, Black Kettle and other chiefs had visited General William B. Hazen, commander of the Southern Indian District, to reaffirm their desire for peace and seek protection from attacks. Black Kettle told Hazen that he wanted no part in any war, but acknowledged that there were young warriors in the villages that he and other chiefs could not control. Born to a lifestyle where raiding was an integral component of their warrior culture, the young males wanted to continue fighting. Conversely, Black Kettle, who had been to Washington, D.C., and had witnessed the numbers and looming power of the white society, recognized the futility of further struggle. He became one of the strongest advocates and most visionary advocates for peace among the Native leaders.

The senior leaders on the Army side, General William T. Sherman, commanding general of the U.S. Army, and Philip Sheridan, commander of the Division of the Missouri, were not known for benign dispositions. Both agreed that the Indians could be defeated only by striking the Native camps during the winter months.

Sherman, though, while sending Sheridan to fight the hostiles, had directed General Hazen to establish a haven for the bands that wished to avoid war. The Kiowa-Comanche Reservation, headquartered at Fort Cobb in Indian Territory, was designated as an asylum area.

When Black Kettle asked Hazen for sanctuary, he was forthright in acknowledging that some of his young men had been involved in raids and that he could not control them. Hazen, too, was forthright – and like many of the personalities associated with Washita, he faced a dilemma. Since the raiding parties could not be prevented from moving in and out of the friendly villages, Hazen said he could not assure refuge to those that Sheridan had orders to destroy. Because some of the young men in Black Kettle's village were known to be raiders, Hazen told the chief that he would first have to make peace with General Sheridan and his field commanders.

Hazen advised the Native leaders to return to their camps and negotiate with General Sheridan's commanders; he (Hazen) was subordinate to Sheridan and it was Sheridan's policies that would have to be followed. Disappointed with Hazen's advice, it is believed that several of his group, including perhaps his wife, urged him to move his camp closer to others and seek greater safety in numbers. He chose not to do so, apparently believing that there was no immediate danger.

It is certain that there were warriors in the camps who had perpetrated attacks on white populations in western Kansas, southwest Colorado, and northwest Texas. Evidence of their raids was found by Custer's troops. It seems equally as certain that they were a minority of the village inhabitants. Thus the dilemma – although it appears that neither Custer nor Sheridan would have regarded it as such – of how to differentiate the hostiles from all the rest. If there were such a way to accomplish that, it was neither tried nor considered. Custer did not know whose camp it was, but it would not have mattered. His orders from Sheridan were to "destroy the village and ponies, to kill the warriors, and bring back the women and children."

It seems incongruous that with Custer's reputation the Army would later choose him as a peace envoy. But, indeed, after Washita, that is precisely what happened. With the government of a mind to pursue, at least temporarily, a peace policy, Custer was sent to find the Cheyennes and talk with them about ending hostilities and moving to reservations.

Taking only a small party with him, Custer journeyed to the *Llano Estacado,* the Staked Plains, of West Texas. There, at considerable personal risk, he met with Cheyenne leaders. During the negotiations that followed, as the peace pipe was smoked and passed, Rock Forehead, one of the Cheyenne chiefs, is thought to have told Custer that if he ever went against the pipe – that is, made war on the tribes – he and all of his men would be killed.

One of those who accompanied Custer when he travelled to meet the chiefs was an attractive Cheyenne girl. The young woman, whose name is most often written as Mon-na-she-tah, was one of the 53 captives taking during the attack on Black Kettle's village. Mon-na-she-tah and others were first taken to Fort Riley. There, when Custer's peace mission was formed, Custer or others may have thought the benign intentions of the small group traveling deep into hostile territory might be more clearly signaled if women were included in the party.

Mon-na-she-tah remains a controversial part of Custer's story. Some speculate that Custer may have fathered her child, a son named Yellow Swallow, born at Fort Riley in 1869. Dissenters assert that if she did have a child, the father was more likely Custer's brother Tom.

Some scholars dismiss the story completely. When Rock Forehead's band moved to a reservation, Mon-na-she-tah went with him, after which she is lost to history as is her son, Yellow Swallow.

Following Washita, Custer and the 7th Cavalry remained on the Plains until 1871. In March of that year, the regiment was sent south on Reconstruction duty. Serving primarily in Kentucky and South Carolina, for the next two years, the 7th carried out court orders, broke up illegal distilleries, and opposed the emerging growth of the Ku Klux Klan. Custer chafed at the nature of the "political" duty and the absence of combat.

Custer's frustration was greatly eased for a time when in January 1872, his friend Sheridan invited him to partake in what was to become perhaps the world's most famous buffalo hunt. Organized by Sheridan, who served as host, the event was held on behalf of Grand Duke Alexis, third son of Czar Alexander II of Russia, as part of his royal visit. The entourage was joined by William F. "Buffalo Bill" Cody and accompanied by two companies of cavalry who set up the camp and with a considerable train of wagons and extra horses, provided service and protection. Aided by Chief Spotted Tail and a party of Sioux, the Indians helped find the bison herd and assisted in the successful hunt. Ranging over parts of southwestern Nebraska along Red Willow Creek, the occasion was conducted in safari-like conditions. Large tents, at least some with carpeted floors, champagne, cigars, and mountains of rich food greatly eased the hardships of the trail. A band provided additional entertainment.

During their time together Custer and the Grand Duke became close friends. When Alexis returned from the visits farther west, Custer accompanied him on his journey to St. Louis, New Orleans, and Florida. They corresponded until Custer's death four years later.

In February 1873, the 7th Cavalry was reassigned to the Department of the Missouri. The unit took steamboats up the Mississippi to Cairo, Illinois, and boarded trains to Yankton, Dakota Territory (end of track). From Yankton, the unit marched the last 300 miles to Fort Rice, about 30 miles south of present-day Mandan, North Dakota.

They were at Fort Rice only a short time. On June 10, Custer led 11 companies of infantry, artillery, and a wagon train on a westward trek to join what became known as the Yellowstone Expedition. With the Northern Pacific Railroad about to lay tracks, the purpose of the campaign under the overall command of Colonel David S. Stanley of the 22nd Infantry, was to protect the railroad's survey crews and to signal to area tribes that force would be used if necessary to ensure the railroad's completion.

Custer at first clashed with Stanley who objected to Custer's insolence in attempting to handle the 7th as essentially an independent command. Though the differences were eventually, mostly, smoothed over, Custer proved to be a less than eager subordinate. In a comment that echoed many others made about him over the years, one of Stanley's officers wrote that Custer was "selfishly indifferent to others and determined to make himself conspicuous at all hazards."

Before the 7th's part in the expedition ended on September 21, Custer was involved in two difficult fights. On August 4, 1873, Custer, with an advance cadre of about 80 men, was camped forward at a considerable distance from the main body of Stanley's troops. A small band of Sioux approached the camp, stampeded the horses, and decoyed Custer and a pursuing party into a trap. Custer and those with him barely escaped with their lives when reinforcements arrived.

The August 4 battle was fought on the Yellowstone River, not far from where it joins the Tongue River. A week later, on August 11, the 7th Cavalry fought the Sioux again, this time about three miles from the mouth of the Little Bighorn.

The end of the expedition took Custer and most of the 7th back to a new post, Fort Abraham Lincoln, newly constructed on the Missouri River near present-day Bismarck, North Dakota. Other companies were assigned to Fort Rice and Fort Totten, 13 miles south of Devils Lake, North Dakota. Fort Abraham Lincoln would be Custer's and Libby's home until his death.

Much to Custer's delight, during the following summer of 1874, he and 7th Cavalry were chosen to survey the Black Hills. Although an 1868 treaty had promised the hills to the Sioux in perpetuity and closed the territory to white transit and occupation, raids on settlers by Lakota warriors thought to be striking out of the Black Hills sanctuary brought calls for intervention.

The country's economic condition at the time – a severe depression – added to the pressure on government authorities. Rumors of gold deposits provided inducement to establish an Army post in the hills. A fort, it was thought, might deter raids and in the best case – if gold was indeed discovered – prevent an influx of miners while protecting the Lakota lands.

Along with an extensive wagon train, a photographer and three newspaper reporters, Custer took two miners with him to help determine the validity of reports that gold was present in large quantities inside the treaty area. When the presence of gold was confirmed, Custer orchestrated the announcement to the American public, resurrecting his status as a household name.

As was often the case with this complex man, the Black Hills Expedition revealed a paradox. Custer was more than a passable writer, the author of frequent articles published by major newspapers and journals. In a letter to the *New York Journal* penned just prior to leaving Fort Abraham Lincoln, he wrote: "We are goading the Indians to madness by invading their hallowed grounds and throwing them open to avenues of terrible revenge ...." And yet, this was the officer who not only led the expedition that eventually did exactly that, but quite obviously relished the opportunity to do so.

Attempting to defuse the situation, in September 1875, government authorities began negotiations to buy the Black Hills from the Sioux. The Sioux refused to sell, considering the region sacred ground. Up to that point, the Army had managed to keep the hills relatively free of miners. But, when negotiations failed, the small, undermanned garrisons could no longer prevent swarms of prospectors from surging into the territory. The resulting Black Hills gold rush lasted through the fall and winter of 1875-76.

Late in the year, a decision by the Secretary of the Interior added to the underlying tension. Zachariah Chandler prohibited the Sioux from hunting in unceded territory. An attempt was made, not universally successful, to notify all Sioux bands to be on reservations by January 31, 1876. Any Native found away from a reservation after that date was to be presumed as hostile.

When the January 31 deadline passed, the Army set in motion a grand scheme to destroy the hostile bands or force them onto reservations. Orchestrated by General Sheridan, the plan called for a three-pronged advance that would eventually converge in southeastern Montana where the tribes were thought to be gathering. When the southern strike force commanded by General George Crook turned back at Rosebud Creek, the remaining wings under Colonel John Gibbon and General Alfred Terry were left to carry the battle to the non-treaty bands in the valley of the Little Bighorn.

Considering what happened next and the conspicuous place the Little Bighorn inhabits in the nation's history, it is ironic to recall that Custer almost missed the battle. His testimony -- by some accounts shallow and based on hearsay – to a Congressional committee investigating the selling of exclusive trading rights at military installations along the Upper Missouri River implicated the Secretary of War, William Belknap, and by association

President Grant's brother Orvil in the scandal. Grant initially forbade Custer's participation in the campaign. It was only through the interventions of Sherman, Sheridan, and Terry, who pleaded Custer's case to Grant, that Custer was allowed to proceed. Grant's approval was reluctantly given and came with the stipulation that Custer was not to be placed in a command position.

While Custer was eager to see action again, he was less than pleased with his assigned role. He was seldom a good follower under any circumstance and being made subordinate to General Terry was particularly galling. Compared to himself, Custer saw Terry as a novice when it came to fighting Indians. On his journey back from the East to rejoin the 7th, Custer allegedly told a compatriot that he would "cut loose" of Terry when conditions allowed. Unfortunately, perhaps, for Custer and the men under him, Terry's orders would be flexible enough to allow him to do that.

Custer's rendezvous with destiny began on May 17, 1876. As the regimental band played *The Girl I Left Behind Me,* Custer left Fort Abraham Lincoln accompanying Terry with all 12 companies of the 7th Cavalry, three infantry companies, and a battery of Gatling guns. Libby rode with him to the first campsite, about 13 miles away along the Heart River.

Already disconcerted by a strange weather phenomena that had occurred as the column left the fort – a temperature inversion combined with fog and mist reflected in the morning light made it appear that part of the 7th Cavalry was marching in the clouds – she bade him a tearful farewell the next morning and returned to the fort. Libby was 34 years old at the time. Custer would have been 37 the following December. She would not see him again.

The long trek across present-day North Dakota into southern Montana continued into June, aided on at least one occasion by Custer's adept routing of the column through the Badlands. Meanwhile, the steamer *Far West* journeyed up the Missouri River on to the Little Missouri and eventually down the Yellowstone to the mouth of the Little Bighorn, carrying 200 tons of supplies for the expedition. Earlier, three companies of the 6th Infantry moved from Fort Buford to set up a supply depot. That force would later intersect with Terry on May 29 near the mouth of the Powder River.

Colonel John Gibbon, with five companies of the 7th Infantry and four companies of the 2nd Cavalry, began his march on March 30 from Fort Ellis in western Montana. On his way to meet Terry and Custer, he had passed close to a large Indian encampment on the Rosebud. On June 9, Gibbon met with Terry on the *Far West.* Terry's initial plan was revised a bit at the time based on Gibbon's May 26 sighting of the village on the way to the rendezvous. Terry decided that a reconnaissance was called for and turned to an unexpected source.

Major Marcus Reno was a less experienced Indian fighter than Custer.

Terry's appointment of him to lead a sizable scout force may have been intended as a pointed reminder to Custer of his subordinate status. Reno left with six cavalry companies, a Gatling gun, and about 70 pack animals in mid-afternoon on June 10. Reno twice deviated from Terry's instructions. On the second occasion, a week into the reconnaissance, after turning west toward Rosebud Creek, he found evidence of increasing Indian presence as well as a wide trail. Reno's scouts loosely established the site of a village about a day away from Reno's location at the time. Uncertain of his rations if the trek persisted, with his soldiers tired and horses weakened by arduous terrain, Reno heeded the advice of his scouts and declined further pursuit. After 10 days and a march of 250 miles, Reno rejoined the main column on June 20. Terry was irritated that he had moved toward the Rosebud against instructions, but recognized that Reno had brought back useful information. Custer chastised him for not bringing the Indians to battle or at least following the trail far enough to determine if it turned.

After Reno returned, Terry met with Gibbon and Custer on the afternoon of the June 21ˢᵗ in the wardroom of the *Far West*. Their meeting focused on preventing the Indians from escaping. Warriors were known to be leaving reservations to link up with hostile bands already in the field. It was thought that the size of the warrior contingent might have at best doubled from the 1,000 originally estimated as Sioux tribesmen were joined by Cheyenne and Arapaho allies. Still, it was assumed that once attacked the Indians would flee, most likely to the south.

As devised by Terry, the strategy that flowed from that assumption as well as from Reno's scout and other scattered reports, called for one column to march up the Rosebud before turning west to the source of the Little Bighorn. The force would then move down the valley of that river where it was anticipated – correctly – that the hostiles would be found.

Meanwhile, the second column would march west up the Yellowstone River to the Bighorn, and then trek down that stream before following its tributary, the Little Bighorn. That approach, it was felt, would foreclose any attempted escape to the north. Trapped between the two converging columns, the Indians would either choose to fight and be beaten into submission, or surrender outright.

Terry realized speed was imperative. The great fear was that, as had happened in the past, the Indians would scatter when threatened with a sizable force. A great opportunity could be lost. Accordingly, Terry sent Custer up the Rosebud with the 7th Cavalry. Meanwhile, Gibbon's mixed column of cavalry and infantry with Terry accompanying it would proceed up the Yellowstone. As the forces came together with the Indians trapped between them, Gibbon's force would form the anvil to Custer's hammer.

Custer moved out at noon on June 22, heading up the Rosebud with 12 companies of the 7th Cavalry – 600 officers and men accompanied by 50 Crow and Arikara scouts and civilian employees. Terry's general orders to him were to check the Indian trail that Reno had seen earlier and that Terry assumed would cut over to the Little Bighorn. Terry, though, was concerned by the possibility that the Indians might escape to the south. Thus, he told Custer the even if the trail turned west as anticipated, he was to proceed up the Rosebud to the headwaters of the Tongue River before moving west to the Little Bighorn. That would, he believed, assure that the Indians had not escaped while allowing Gibbon's column sufficient time to move into position from the north.

Having turned down Terry's offer of four additional companies and two Gatling guns, Custer set a grueling pace, covering 80 or more miles across rugged terrain over the next two and a half days.

Hard marches first brought his column to the area where Reno had tracked the westward movement of a large band a few days before. On June 24, scouts identified an immense trail – easily a half-mile wide – that swung west toward the Little Bighorn. Custer ignored Terry's orders to bypass the track and turned instead to follow it.

Terry's orders to Custer had an escape clause – or at least Custer must have interpreted them as such. Terry had instructed him to use his own judgment if exceptional circumstances warranted. Custer was never known to pass up the opportunity for a fight. At about this time or soon after, he began to get reports – at least some were erroneous – that his column had been detected. In one instance, two Indians were seen leading a horse that had possibly strayed. In another, seven Sioux were seen on a ridgeline. Still later, three warriors were observed opening boxes of hardtack that had fallen off pack mules along the line of march. Finally, two Indians were seen close to the column and Custer's own scouts said they had seen the 7th's cooking fires from a distance and presumed the hostiles had, too.

Custer, concerned that the element of surprise might be lost and that the village would break up before he could get to it, abandoned his plan to attack on the morning of the 26th when it was anticipated that Gibbon's force would reach the north end of the valley.

Custer pushed him men hard, following the enormous trail for 28 miles, continuing through the night before finally going into camp at 2:30 in the morning of June 25. While his soldiers slept, his scouts reported finding an Indian village of enormous size 15 miles away. By 8 o'clock Custer had the 7th Cavalry in the saddle again, moving west. By noon the column reached the divide between the Rosebud and the Little Bighorn.

On the way to the valley of the Little Bighorn and later as he prepared his attack, Custer's scouts advised him of the immense number of signs they were picking up. Most said they had never seen evidence of so many Indians in one place. One scout told Custer that the 7th Cavalry did not have enough bullets to shoot all the Indians they would find in the valley.

Approaching the Little Bighorn, Custer brought his force to a high tabletop bluff. From there he could see only a portion of the valley, much of which was obscured by bluffs as upstream the river swung for a time back to the west. When eventually revealed in its entirety, the village was about a half mile to a mile wide and five to six miles long. Two smaller creeks flowed into the river from the south. At the southern end, the Little Bighorn twisted back and forth past a stand of cottonwood trees along with occasional ash and willows. Bluffs two- to three-hundred feet high lined the east bank and swept abruptly down to the river.

The immense encampment spread over the valley floor along the west bank of the river. Tepees in village circles containing Hunkpapas, San-Arcs, Minneconjous, Oglalas, Brules, and Cheyennes stretched south to north along the river's edge. Altogether, 8,000 – 10,000 Indians may have been camped there, of which possibly 2,500 were warriors. An enormous pony herd with as many as 20,000 horses grazed on flat land west and north of the village. Neither the full panorama of the valley nor the size of the Indian encampment would be visible to Custer until later in the fight.

Custer split his force into three segments. These were led by Major Marcus Reno with A, G, and M companies, comprising about 140 men; Captain Frederick Benteen with 125 men of D, H, and K companies, and Custer himself who took five companies with 225 troopers. Custer then further divided his immediate command into two wings led by Captain George Yates with E and F companies and by Captain Miles Keogh who took C, I, and L companies. A fourth portion of the force, Company B, led by Captain Thomas McDougall, was assigned to escort the slower moving pack train carrying supplies and extra ammunition.

Custer ordered Benteen to move south and west toward the far ridge line to keep Indians from escaping in that direction. The long left hook would also shield Custer's anticipated attack as he moved against the main village.

Reno's three companies would initiate the battle with an attack on the south end of the encampment. Soon after Reno struck the village, Custer would sweep down upon it from the east and north. Custer's assault would particularly threaten the women and children. If experience held true, capturing women and children and holding them as hostages would cause the Indians to surrender or break off the fight.

For two hours or more after dispatching Benteen, Custer rode with Reno, their column coming at about two o'clock to a large, recently abandoned campsite. From a nearby rise, in the distance scouts saw a party of about 50 warriors moving away towards the valley. Custer directed Reno to pursue the Indians and attack the village – a task Custer would have viewed with increasing urgency after having received an erroneous report that the Indians were scattering. In the meantime, Custer marched north with his five companies, climbing and moving across the rugged bluffs and ravines on the east bank of the river.

Reno moved out with about 140 troopers and 35 Arikara scouts, pushing ahead about three miles before reaching the valley floor and sighting the Little Bighorn in mid-afternoon. The distance to the south end of the village – about two miles – was further than it had appeared from the heights. He was informed that far from racing away from him, the Indians were in fact moving towards him in large numbers. Reno reformed his men and ordered a charge. Given the distance and the tired horses, their advance was probably more of a fast trot, or slow gallop.

The 7th's Arikara scouts struck first, making off with some horses and killing perhaps 10 women and children gathering wild turnips south of the first circle of tepees. Reno formed his three companies line abreast across the valley floor. As they continued forward, increasing numbers of warriors began leaving the village and moving towards them. Still at some distance from the encampment, and seeing a shallow ditch ahead that would disrupt the attack, Reno dismounted his troops and formed a firing line stretching 250 yards generally east to west along the valley floor. It was now about 3:30 in the afternoon and Reno's force was a half mile from the south end of the village. Some distance behind the skirmishers, every fourth trooper held the reins of cavalry mounts belonging to troopers manning the firing line.

The first wave of Indians struck them soon afterwards. A brisk exchange of fire continued for several minutes with initial casualties dropping on both sides. Several minutes after the shooting began Arikara scouts on the extreme left end of Reno's line gave way. As more warriors joined the fight, the Indians extended their assault to the west, lapping around the cavalrymen's left flank, exposing Reno's entire front. Reno's troops pivoted, swinging like a closing gate into a timbered area lining the east bank of the river.

Some later suggested that Reno might have been better served by staying in the timber and making his stand there, rather than breaking out and retreating to high grounds along the bluffs. He indeed took heavy casualties along the way and on the bluff itself, but as with much about the Little Bighorn, uncertainties abound. His supply situation likely defined his decision to fall back – though few applaud the manner in which the retreat was conducted. He apparently believed, as did at least some of his officers, that his three companies would be inevitably overrun by the masses of warriors pouring at them from the nearby village.

As the firing grew in intensity, Reno asked another officer, Captain Myles Moylan, for his opinion. Moylan recommended they get out of the timber. Soon after, Arikara scout Bloody Knife, standing next to Reno, was shot in the head. Brain matter and blood splattered over Reno, perhaps further shaking him.

Amid confusion, contradictory orders, and decisions made and reversed, Reno led a panicked retreat out of the woods. There was no bugler with his three companies, so many of his orders could not be heard. Several of his men were left behind. Some were caught and killed; others hid in the timber. Altogether, 15 went missing. Most made their way to Reno the following day.

Without establishing a rear guard, Reno, his troops struggling to follow him, bolted out of the trees. As fast as their tired mounts would allow, they raced to the river, crossed it, and labored to reach the bluffs south and slightly east of the timbered area.

There was nothing gallant about Reno's dash to the hillside. Many of the troopers were killed crossing the stream as the Indians chased them, sometimes riding alongside and moving among them, shooting and clubbing troopers at close range. A sharp embankment that led down to the river and a narrow slit up the opposite bank that provided the nearest exit from it formed a killing ground.

Slowed by the constricted passages at those locations, the troopers clustered together and were slain in large numbers. Altogether, three officers and 29 enlisted men and scouts were killed and left behind. Seven more were severely wounded. Counting the 15 men missing from the fight in the trees, Reno had lost 40 percent of his force.

Chased all the way, Reno ran the gauntlet, leading his struggling column in a desperate scramble to the top of a bluff now known as Reno Hill, about a mile and a half distant from their position in the woods. There, the troopers formed a hurried defense and began fighting off attacks that followed immediately.

Not long after, Benteen with his three companies reached Reno's embattled troopers. Benteen had found little activity on his scout to the south and west. He had received a note from Custer ordering him to "come quick," but no one knew where Custer was. With Reno under attack and imploring him to stay, Benteen added his force to Reno's and remained on the hill.

Sometime after 3 o'clock, many of the Indians broke away from their attacks on Reno and hurried off to the north. Soon after, a terrific burst of firing was heard from that direction. With their view blocked by higher bluffs, the Reno's troopers could not see the activity that prompted periodic spasms of heavy fire.

Reno and Benteen did not initially respond to the noise in the distance. Eventually, Captain Thomas Weir, commanding Troop D, despairing of the prospects of his colleagues, who though unseen were undoubtedly under attack, moved without orders toward the sound of the guns. Benteen initially and then Reno later, followed. Weir moved his company to higher ground

(Weir Point) a mile and a half north of Reno Hill. About four miles farther north he could see an immense throng of Indians. Amidst dust and smoke, the warriors appeared to be circling, firing at objects on the ground.

Within minutes the mass of Indians broke away from that activity and began racing towards Weir. Clearly outgunned, Weir fought a rear guard action and the troopers retreated back to their original position on Reno Hill. Heavy fighting continued through the afternoon and lasted until darkness fell at 9 o'clock at night. The cavalrymen used lulls in the action to improve their improvised barricades, using saddles, boxes from pack trains and rifle pits hastily dug with hands, knives, spoons, and tin cups. The growing number of wounded were placed in a large depression in the middle of the hill top, treated by the expedition's only surviving doctor. Pack animals and mounts were given shelter, though minimal, nearby.

Fighting resumed at 2:30 in the morning (June 26), with the shooting at first coming from long range. The troopers made several charges to drive the warriors back from the shaky perimeter. Sniping from long distance then resumed and continued until about 3 o'clock in the afternoon.

That evening the cavalrymen on Reno Hill observed an immense dust cloud as the entire village picked up and moved away from the valley. Reno's and Benteen's companies remained in position through the night. By morning, although it was not fully certain at the time, the Indians were gone.

While Reno's fight is less remembered that Custer's "last stand" battle, there can be no denying the intensity with which it was fought. Eighteen troopers were killed and another 52 wounded in the bitter combat along and atop the hillside. For two days, Reno and Benteen with fewer than 400 soldiers, scouts, and civilian packers, had held off possibly 2,000 Sioux and Cheyenne warriors.

Like many aspects of the Little Bighorn odyssey, Reno's and Benteen's conduct has been the subject of controversy. Reno was observed drinking from a flask on occasion during the battle. Whether he was inebriated at any point remains an open question. Libby Custer and other detractors asserted that had Reno continued his charge at the outset of the fight and swept into the village, the outcome of the battle would have been a victory for the cavalry. Reno eventually asked that a formal court of inquiry examine his conduct during the battle. The court exonerated him, concluding that his force would have been annihilated if he had pushed further.

Benteen was later hailed as the "great hero of the battle." By most accounts, he handled much of the defense on Reno Hill. At first, through fatigue and stubbornness, he failed to order the troopers under his immediate command to fortify their positions. While others were building barricades, he allowed his soldiers to rest. When attackers later struck his sector, his men suffered as a result and had to build hasty shelters under fire, sometimes taking material from other fortifications along the defensive circle. He was lauded, however, even by Reno, for rallying the troops and personally leading a charge that repelled a heavy attack against a two-company sector during a crisis point in the battle. Repeatedly exposing himself to fire, he encouraged the men along the firing line of the tenuously held perimeter.

After splitting his force, Custer with five companies angled to the right, moving up the bluffs along the east bank of the river. He halted just below the crest of a high butte. There for the first time he could see the full panorama of the Indian camp spread for miles along the valley floor. From there also, he could see Reno fully engaged. How long he remained at that location is uncertain. Now finally aware of the massive force opposing him, he sent a courier with a note to Benteen asking him to "come quick" and bring the pack animals.

It appears from battlefield archeology that at this point Custer again split his command with some going toward the river. Those soldiers were stopped cold and the survivors attempted to rejoin Custer.

Custer and the bulk of the command continued north. But the advance was stopped by a huge force of warriors led by Oglala Chief Crazy Horse that had crossed the river downstream. The whole of Custer's command – the surviving members of five companies – were now essentially spread across what today is called Battle Ridge. By this time, they were under attack from all directions, their numbers whittled down as the fight continued to grow in intensity. Years later, one Indian participant said that the shooting sounded like the tearing of a cloth; that is, so heavy that there were no distinguishable intervals between shots.

The duration of the battle is uncertain. It did not last long: perhaps as little as 30 minutes, at most an hour. When it was over, Custer and 207 of those under his immediate command lay dead, scattered across the landscape from near the river in the south, up the ravine to Battle Ridge, and then north to Last Stand Hill. Several bodies, including Custer's, were found in a cluster a few yards below the crest. They were apparently killed in a final stand, ringed by cavalry horses shot to form a final redoubt.

Custer's body was found half reclining, lying at an angle across two fallen cavalrymen. He had been shot twice. The first, killing, shot was a massive wound high on his left chest. The second was a gunshot to his left temple. The irregular circle of bodies near Custer included his brother Tom. Custer's brother Boston and his nephew Autie Reed were slain about 100 yards away down the hillside to the west. Custer's brother-in-law "Jimmi" Calhoun was found with his company some distance to the south along the ridge. Although Custer's corpse was stripped, almost alone among the 200 dead, his body was not mutilated. With few exceptions, all others were found naked and butchered.

Terry arrived in the area with Gibbon's column on June 27, eventually linking up with Reno and Benteen at their position on Reno Hill. Custer's fate, and that of his men, was initially unknown to them. As Terry's column moved to meet Reno, Gibbon's chief scout, Lieutenant James Bradley, discovered bodies first seen as white objects scattered across a distant hillside.

The final death toll at the Little Bighorn surpassed all other battles waged across the American West. All of the men serving immediately under him – 13 officers, 191 enlisted men, and 4 civilian scouts – were killed. Reno lost another 57 – three officers, 48 enlisted men, and 6 scouts. Another 62 wounded were transported back to Fort Abraham Lincoln on the *Far West*.

On June 28, the bodies were initially interred in shallow, sketchily dug graves. Only three shovels could be found – both columns were traveling light. Knives and spoons were used to complete the task. Custer and his brother Tom were buried side-by-side after being covered by pieces of tent canvas and blankets. In October of the following year, remains thought to be Custer's were reburied with full military honors at West Point.

Nonetheless, as has often been noted, the Little Bighorn – the Natives' greatest triumph – was the beginning of the end for the warring tribes. Three weeks after the battle, at Warbonnet Creek, Nebraska, Wesley Merritt and the 5th Cavalry turned back hundreds of Cheyennes attempting to join the hostile bands in the field. By fall nearly a third of all U.S. military strength had been concentrated in the theater. Gifted commanders such as Crook, Ranald Mackenzie, and Nelson Miles won a series of victories. By the following summer, the war was over.

The "Last Stand" rivets us still. In the long stream of history, the identities of few commanders are so directly linked with a specific battle as is Custer's with the Little Bighorn. The names seem almost inseparable. It was defeat, not victory, that made Custer immortal.

OFFICERS OF THE 7TH CAVALRY

Almost alone among the nation's historic battles, the names of subordinate officers who fought at the Little Bighorn are surprisingly familiar to sizable segments of the American populace – testimony, yet again, to the pervasive hold the "Last Stand" has on the country's consciousness.

On that fateful day, Custer divided his command into three battalions. Brief sketches of the principal officers in each unit follow.

Custer's Battalion

Captain Thomas Custer, aide-de-camp
Thomas Ward Custer, younger brother of George Armstrong Custer, was the only soldier to be awarded two Medals of Honor for service during the

Civil War. At the Little Bighorn he fought with an unmatched fury and is thought to have been one of the last to die on Last Stand Hill. His body was found within a few feet of his brother's.

Tom Custer was nominally the commander of Company C but served as George's aide-de-camp during the Little Bighorn expedition. Recently promoted to captain, he had been in the 7th Cavalry since 1866. Unlike his teetotalling brother, he was known as somewhat of a drinker and gambler. About the same height as George and with the same sturdy build, his cheek was scarred by a wound suffered during the Civil War when a bullet had skimmed along his right jaw.

Tom had enlisted as a private in that conflict at age 16 after an attempt to do so at age 15 had been rebuffed. He initially saw service in the western theater, achieving the rank of corporal. In 1864, at age 19, George arranged for him to receive a commission and serve as his aide-de-camp. The two of them saw heavy action at Waynesboro, Dinwiddie Court House, Five Forks, Namozine Church, Saylor's Creek, and the closing actions at Appomattox.

His Medals of Honor came within three days of each other. In almost other-worldly acts of heroism, he captured Confederate battle flags on April 3 and April 6, 1865, at Namozine Church and Saylor's Creek, Virginia.

At Namozine Church, Custer leaped a barricade while under heavy fire. As rebel troops fell back in surprise and confusion, he seized the enemy colors (2nd North Carolina Cavalry) and ordered the Confederate soldiers to surrender. He personally took three officers and 11 enlisted men prisoners, then commandeered another horse – his own having been shot during the charge – and returned to battle.

At Saylor's Creek 72 hours later, he charged rebel breastworks, leaping over the barricade under intense fire. Landing in the midst of enemy troops who surrounded him, he fired his pistol at the three closest to him, scattering them. Seeing the Confederates attempting to rally towards their colors, he raced forward. Though wounded in the face, he shot the rebel color bearer, wrested the flag from him as he was falling and returned with the colors to Union lines.

Twenty years old when he joined the 7th Cavalry at its formation, he was wounded again at Washita in 1868 and accompanied the unit on the Yellowstone and Black Hills Expeditions of 1873 and 1874.

Perhaps because of his bravery during the battle or earlier incidents with Indian leaders, his body was found horrifically mutilated and smashed, with his skull crushed and flattened, eyes and tongue ripped out, and throat slit. His remains were identified only by a "TWC" tattoo (Thomas Ward Custer) on his arm.

Thomas's remains were eventually buried at Fort Leavenworth National Cemetery in Kansas.

Captain Myles Keogh

Described by some as the handsomest man in the regiment, Myles Keogh brought a fascinating background and considerable experience to his duties with the 7th Cavalry.

Born near the Irish village of Leighlinbridge in 1840, in his late teens Keogh joined the Papal Army of Pope Pius IX and fought with other Catholic volunteers during a conflict with Piedmont-Sardinia. His obvious abilities resulted in a promotion to lieutenant and following the war led to an appointment with the Vatican Guard.

In 1862, Keogh came to the United States where he was commissioned as a captain and appointed as aide-de-camp to Union general James Shields. After action in the Shenandoah Valley, he transferred to the staff of Colonel John Buford and served with him through the battles of Antietam and Gettysburg. Later, as aide-de-camp to General George Stoneman, he was with Sherman's army during the Atlanta Campaign and on the March to the Sea. Extolled on several occasions for his courteous manner, soldierly appearance, and dash in combat, Keogh ended the war as a brevet lieutenant colonel.

While his military background in Europe and during the Civil War was notable, prior to the Little Bighorn, Keogh's battlefield experience with the 7th Cavalry was limited. Though he had joined the unit when it was organized in July 1866, he was on detached duty or away on extended leave of absence during the Battle of Washita and the Yellowstone and Black Hills Expeditions. He did, however, lead his company on escort on mail protection duties.

When Custer divided the portion of the force under his personal command at the Little Bighorn, Keogh was placed in charge of the right wing, composed of Companies C, I, and L. As the battle commenced, his force held high ground along the southern end of Battle Ridge, perhaps to secure that position in anticipation of Benteen's arrival. Eventually overrun by swarms of attackers moving up from the east and south, Keogh and a small group made a stand along the east side of the ridge.

Keogh's body was found in a cluster with the first sergeant of the three companies, a bugler, and a guidon bearer. They may have attempted a rearguard covering action while others struggled to flee towards Custer, fighting farther north along Last Stand Hill. Or, a few of his colleagues may simply have closed around him when he initially fell, shot through the left knee. Keogh's body was stripped, but for reasons not certain, was one of the few other than Custer's that was not mutilated. Eleven weeks later at the Battle of Slim Buttes, Keogh's bloody glove and the Company I guidon were recovered by troops under the command of General George Crook.

Keogh's name is further linked with the battle in an unusual way. Though wounded seven times, his horse Comanche was the lone survivor of the Custer battle. The horse became the revered mascot of the 7th Cavalry. Placed in the care of Private Gustive Korn, Comanche lived until 1890. His death, at age 29, was marked by full military honors.

Captain George Yates

Of the 7th Cavalry officers who commanded more than a company-sized contingent at the Little Bighorn, George Yates is the least known. When Custer further apportioned his force after separating from Reno and Benteen, Yates was given command of the left wing, Companies E and F, of the cadre that moved north with Custer along the bluffs east of the river.

Yates was a long-time friend of Custer whom he first met in 1862 in their joint hometown of Monroe, Michigan, while convalescing from a wound suffered at Fredericksburg. A veteran of some of the Civil War's bloodiest battles, Yates saw action at First Bull Run, Antietam, Fredericksburg, and Gettysburg. Through Custer's help, Yates was appointed to a position that placed him close to Custer for much of the war. A highly capable officer, Yates finished the conflict as a brevet lieutenant colonel.

Yates remained in the Army after the war and following brief service at Fort McPherson, Nebraska, joined the 7th Cavalry in June, 1867. At age 33, with thinning blond hair and a carefully clipped moustache, Yates was renowned for his immaculate appearance. For many years the commander of F Company, Yates' unit eventually came to mirror their leader's impeccable bearing and attire. Throughout the 7th Cavalry, F Company became known as the "Bandbox Troops" for their sparkling, squared-away appearance.

At the Little Bighorn, Yates fought early in the battle at Medicine Tail Coulee and later moved with Custer to Last Stand Hill, where his body was found a short distance to the left of Custer's.

Buried initially where he fell, a year later his body was exhumed and reinterred at Fort Leavenworth National Cemetery where his remains were placed next to Tom Custer's.

Yates' wife Annie shared a lifelong friendship with Libby Custer.

Reno's Battalion

Major Marcus Reno

Other than Custer himself, Marcus Reno may be the most controversial figure associated with the Battle of the Little Bighorn. Critics question his handling of the attack at the south end of the village; his later decision to leave the shelter of the trees east of the river; his precipitous flight to Reno Hill; his conduct of the fight there; and his reluctance to march to the sound of guns and move in the direction of Custer's fight on Last Stand Hill. To be sure, except for the manner of his disorganized, every man for himself, race to the bluffs, he has defenders for each of those and other actions as well.

Born in Carrollton, Illinois, in 1834, Reno was an 1857 graduate (20th in a class of 38) of West Point. After an initial posting in the Pacific Northwest, his Civil War service began as a cavalry officer. He soon saw action at Antietam, was later injured at Kelly's Ford, and subsequently fought at Gettysburg, Cold Harbor, Trevilian Station, and Cedar Creek. Brevetted numerous times, he ended the war as a brevet brigadier general.

At the conclusion of the conflict, Reno reverted to his permanent grade of captain and was posted to Fort Vancouver in Washington Territory. In 1868, he was promoted to major, the rank he held at the Little Bighorn. In December, 1868, he joined the 7th Cavalry. He led a three-company Northern Boundary Expedition in 1874 and served as commander at Fort Abraham Lincoln during Custer's absences.

During the battle, Reno's (and Benteen's) hesitancy to respond to the sound of gunfire in the north remains the subject of particular debate. Only when Captain Thomas Weir unilaterally advanced his company in that direction did Reno and Benteen eventually follow. When the contingent reached the high ground at what is now called Weir Point, they saw only dust and circling Indians in the distance and soon retreated to Reno Hill when hundreds of warriors began moving towards them. Frederick Benteen later alleged that Reno was ready to abandon his wounded on the battlefield and lead a breakout party.

In the immediate aftermath of the Little Bighorn battle, Reno was assigned to command Fort Abercrombie in Dakota Territory, 220 miles northeast of Bismarck on the Dakota-Minnesota border. Six months later he was charged with making unwanted advances toward the wife of James Bell, another 7th Cavalry officer. Complaints of public indecency associated with drunkenness followed. A court of inquiry convened at St. Paul, Minnesota, recommended dismissal from service but President Rutherford B. Hayes commuted the sentence to suspension of rank and pay for two years.

Reno had returned to active duty only a short time when he was again court-martialed. As before, drinking was a factor although this time the accusation was that he had peeked through a window at the daughter of Samuel Sturgis, the 7th Cavalry's commanding officer. He was convicted and dismissed from service. Subsequently, Reno worked for the Bureau of Pensions in Washington, D.C.

A portrait artist would have cast Reno in somber shades: swarthy complexion, dark hair, dark eyes – all converging from a morose, dour personality. Reno was long known as being a heavy imbiber. Reno's isolation and drinking apparently became more pronounced following the death of his vivacious first wife in 1874 while he was in the field. A second marriage in 1887 lasted only a short time.

In March 1889, Reno, then 54 years old, was operated on for cancer of the tongue. He died of pneumonia a few days after surgery. In 1967, at the request of a family member, a military board reexamined documents associated with the 1880 court-martial. The board reversed the decision, concluding that Reno's dismissal from service had been improper.

Originally buried in an unmarked grave in Washington, D.C., Reno's remains were later reburied in the Custer National Cemetery on the battlefield of the Little Bighorn.

Benteen's Battalion

Frederick Benteen

At the time of the Little Bighorn, Frederick Benteen looked like an aging cherub. Large, striking blue eyes peered from an oval face topped with snow white hair. Some photos show him in repose smoking a curved pipe. The appearance was misleading. Though soft-spoken, Benteen was in fact an irascible, cantankerous individual who seemed almost genetically predisposed to quarrels with his commanding officers. No matter who they were, Benteen argued with them in face-to-face exchanges, condemned them in gatherings of officers, and complained about them in articles written for newspapers. Custer, Sturgis, Howard and others tolerated, barely, Benteen's public bitterness and carping. Eventually, George Crook did not. Benteen was court-martialed and left the Army not long after.

There was, however, little question of Benteen's abilities or personal courage. In combat, he was a brave and inspiring leader. It may well be that on June 25 and 26, 1876, his leadership saved the 7th Cavalry from total destruction.

Benteen was born August 24, 1834, in Petersburg, Virginia. His early schooling in that city included some training in drill, possibly his only formal military education. In 1849, the family moved to St. Louis, Missouri. When the Civil War began, Benteen's decision to join the Union Army provoked a crisis within his secessionist-leaning family. In September 1861, he was appointed a first lieutenant in a Missouri cavalry regiment.

Benteen's Civil War service was almost entirely in the western theater. He fought in several major battles – Wilson's Creek, Pea Ridge, Vicksburg -- and in an almost limitless number of smaller battles and skirmishes including Florence, Cane Creek, Iuka, Jackson, Bolivar, and Pleasant Hill. As a brigade commander he led forces on the Big Blue, at the Little Osage Crossing, Charlot, Montevallo, Selma, and Columbus. He was brevetted to major and lieutenant colonel for his service at Osage and during the raid on Columbus. For a short time after the war, he commanded a "Buffalo Soldier" unit until it was disbanded.

In early 1867, Benteen, a captain, was assigned to the 7th Cavalry. For the next 16 years, until 1882, he was H Company commander. In August 1868, Benteen led a contingent of about 30 troopers to the first major victory achieved by the soldiers of the new regiment. Near Fort Zarah, Kansas, about five miles from the present-day city of Great Bend, he charged what was initially thought to be a raiding party of about 50 warriors. In fact, more than 200 Cheyennes were swarming around an embattled ranch. Despite being outnumbered, Benteen's troopers tore into the war party, drove it away, and then chased the hostiles relentlessly through the entire day.

Benteen accompanied Custer on the controversial campaign that culminated in the attack on Black Kettle's camp on the Washita on November 27, 1868. During the fight Major Joel Elliott, a close friend of Benteen, and 19 men were killed while chasing warriors attempting to escape. Benteen believed Custer had abandoned Elliott during the fight (the remains were left on the battlefield) and never forgave him. From their first meeting Benteen had disliked Custer, believing him to be a self-serving braggart. Benteen later wrote a letter to a St. Louis newspaper chastising Custer's actions during the battle. It was the first of others that would follow over the years.

At the Little Bighorn, Benteen was given command of companies H, D, and K, and sent on a wide swing left, west of the river, to scout and foreclose an escape in that direction from Indians fleeing the anticipated battle. The reconnaissance proved fruitless. As he turned back toward the main column, he was met by a courier from Custer urging him to hurry and bring packs (supplies, including reserves of ammunition, carried by pack mules). Interestingly, the pack train was not with Benteen. It was, in fact, farther south and east trailing the main column. By this time Custer, high on the eastern bluff, had seen the full scope of the immense Indian camp and realized he would need Benteen's manpower and more ammunition that he had with him.

The note from Custer prompted one of the many controversies regarding the battle. As Benteen moved toward Custer, having decided that the "come on … be quick" emphasis in Custer's note overrode the immediate request for packs (which would have required him to wait for the arrival of the pack train), he came upon Marcus Reno's troops fighting for survival on a bluff east of the river. Reno's battalion had been shot apart in a fight near the south end of the village. What was left of the unit had fled in disorder to the location now known as Reno Hill. There, mostly surrounded and under fire, they were running low on ammunition. Reno, superior in rank, pleaded with Benteen to stay, fearing otherwise the position would be overrun. Benteen agreed. Arguments continue on whether he should have ignored Reno's circumstance and fought his way to Custer.

As Benteen's and Reno's soldiers positioned themselves on the hill, heavy fire was heard to the north. Neither officer initially responded to it. Captain

Thomas Weir, realizing that it had to be Custer engaged, moved his company toward the shooting. Benteen first and then Reno eventually followed. The combined force had gotten as far as Weir Point, still three to four miles south of Custer, when, threatened by the looming presence of hundreds of warriors, they were forced to return to their positions on Reno Hill. There, through the rest of that day and the next, they fought off attacks that threatened to overwhelm and destroy them.

Benteen was at his worst and best during those actions. Marcus Reno was clearly shaken, his effectiveness questionable. As acknowledged by almost every trooper on the hill, Benteen became the de facto commander. At one point, he may have dissuaded Reno from leaving the position and abandoning the wounded. Benteen was not without fault, however. On the night of June 25, while the other companies entrenched and fortified their positions along the perimeter, Benteen told his soldiers to go to sleep. Either out of fatigue – he hadn't slept for essentially three days – or stubbornness, or disrespect for Reno's leadership, Benteen's unfortunate decision cost the lives of some of his soldiers when fighting resumed early the next morning and nearly resulted in his position being overrun.

Through the remainder of the day, however, he likely saved the position on Reno Hill. As the fight persisted, he convinced Reno to shift troops to an embattled sector, and when the Indians threatened to break through the defenses, he personally led two charges that drove them away. His calm demeanor, encouraging and rallying his men, walking along the line exposed to fire, was often recalled by survivors.

The Little Bighorn did not end Benteen's days as an Indian fighter. The following year, still a member of the 7th Cavalry, he performed well during the Nez Perce War. His contributions at the Battle of Canyon Creek on September 13, 1877, and his earlier service at the Little Bighorn earned him a brevet promotion to brigadier general.

In 1879, he testified at Marcus Reno's court of inquiry. He did not impugn Reno.

In 1882, Benteen was finally promoted to major and transferred to the 9th Cavalry. Four years later, a combination of circumstances led to his departure from the Army. A dispute over delays and lack of promised supplies for construction of a new post that Benteen had been ordered to build on the Ute Reservation in Utah brought him into a conflict with General George Crook. A letter in the *Kansas City Times* described in detail the problems at the new installation. Benteen denied writing it, but the letter clearly expressed his views regarding shoddy workmanship and the charging of excessive fees. Meanwhile, Benteen was alleged to have begun drinking heavily and on at least one occasion to have conducted himself in an unseemly manner in the presence of female guests.

The letter to the Kansas City newspaper did not reflect well on General Crook. Unlike Custer and other of Benteen's past commanding officers, Crook was not willing to leave the issue with Benteen unaddressed. In a court-martial trial that lasted 17 days in late February and early March 1887, Benteen was found guilty on three counts of drunkenness and of conduct unbecoming an officer. He was sentenced to dismissal from service. President Grover Cleveland mitigated the dismissal from service sentence to suspension of rank and duty for one year at half pay. After a short, final assignment at Fort Niobrara, Nebraska, Benteen requested and received a medical discharge. He left the Army on July 7, 1888.

Benteen was a man of legendary personal courage. At the Little Bighorn, though wounded in his thumb and having had the heel of a boot blown off by rifle fire, he continued to move along the line, steadying the troops, and then led the charges that dispelled the immediate danger.

He was described by contemporaries as tall and broad-shouldered, with muscular arms and huge hands. The latter aided him in his great passion in life: baseball. From members of H Company, he formed the Benteen Nine, which with great success for years took on all comers from other Army units and nearby communities. If not the best disciplined or sharpest appearing of the 7th Cavalry's 12 companies, because of baseball H Company became one of the most cohesive. In later life, Benteen blamed baseball for pain in his hands, no doubt exacerbated by the mostly bare-handed nature of the sport during that era.

Benteen died on June 23, 1898 in Atlanta, Georgia. Originally buried in that city, in November 1902, his remains were reburied at Arlington National Cemetery.

William S. Harney

Brigadier General William S. Harney led Army forces on the federal government's first military campaign against the Plains Indians. On September 3, 1855, near present-day Lewellen, Nebraska, Harney's force defeated bands of Brule and Oglala Sioux led predominately by Chief Little Thunder.

Harney's expedition was one of the most effective ever undertaken against the Plains tribes. The scope of Harney's victory so shocked the Sioux nation, the largest and most belligerent of the Native bands, that its 10,000 warriors remained relatively peaceful, and travel on the overland trail was mostly unmolested for almost a decade.

Like certain of his contemporaries – Custer, Mackenzie, and Miles foremost among them – Harney's legacy is difficult to place in balance. Of his courage, daring, organizational skill, and innovative leadership there can be no question. Yet apparent also were less positive traits – an impulsive, vindictive personality prone to eruptions of brutality. Harney's lack of tact was legendary; the Army court-martialed him four times. He was tried in a civil court in St. Louis for allegedly bludgeoning to death a black female servant who had lost his keys. Forced to hurriedly leave town, he was later found not guilty of the charge.

Harney's record in combat was long and distinguished even before fate brought him to the frontier as the earliest of the major military leaders in the American West. From the time he was commissioned as a second lieutenant in 1818, he fought in all of the nation's conflicts, beginning with a struggle against Jean Lafitte's pirates, and extending through the Black Hawk War, the Seminole wars, and the war with Mexico. As with General George S. Patton a century later, the Army was apparently willing to overlook the contentious, at times violent, personality in return for his obvious skills as a combat leader.

When the Civil War began, Harney was one of only four generals in the Regular Army, outranked only by Winfield Scott and John C. Wool.

Like his contemporary Ranald Mackenzie, Harney exhibited a complex and at times seemingly contradictory personality. Like Mackenzie, Harney was an implacable foe of the Indians, believing that peace on the frontier was impossible unless the tribes were utterly crushed. However, when the Indians succumbed and moved to reservations, there was no stronger advocate for their care and well-being than William S. Harney. As a key member of several government commissions that negotiated treaties with the Plains Indians, Harney earned the Indian name "Man-who-always-kept-his-word."

Public Domain
William S. Harney

Renowned for his dash and ferocity on the battlefield, Harney's principal hobby as a young officer was raising flowers and vegetables. He was not an easy man to categorize.

Harney was born April 22, 1800, near Nashville, Tennessee. His first of many experiences under fire took place in Louisiana, where as an 18-year old newly commissioned second lieutenant, he helped force Jean Lafitte to move his operations out of the United States. The encounter with Lafitte provided affirmation to Harney that his career was well-chosen. He was tall – 6 feet, 4 inches – ramrod-straight, with an impressive soldierly bearing. In later life, a well-trimmed white beard accentuated blue eyes that were sometimes described as fierce in appearance. He rather quickly earned a reputation – carried with him throughout his career – as a blunt, rough individual proud of his accomplishments and his reputation for exceptional leadership on the battlefield. His harsh, discourteous manner alienated many of his colleagues and subordinate officers. He was, however, solicitous of the well-being of his enlisted soldiers and was generally respected by them. Harney disliked military details and trivialities, but became known as one of the nation's most bold and effective soldiers.

Blue Water, the western battle that Harney would become most known for, was not his first experience on the frontier. Remarkably, thirty years before, in 1825, he accompanied General Henry Atkinson on an expedition up the Missouri that successfully concluded treaties with several tribes.

During the Seminole War, Harney was an advocate of what might in later years have been called civic action, seeking to win the Indians over rather than confronting them militarily. Among other gestures, he was known for challenging Indian warriors to foot races near the fort.

Still, when combat was required, he proved to be an innovative, aggressive leader. During the second war with the Seminoles, Harney led forces on quick canoe-borne raids that contributed substantially to the success of General William Worth's counter-insurgency campaign.

Eight years later when war erupted with Mexico, Harney was given command of the 2nd U.S. Dragoons, serving first in the north with John E. Wool's forces under the overall command of Zachary Taylor. Harney's excellent performance was well-noted. After the Battle of Buena Vista, Winfield Scott ordered him south to serve as the Army's senior cavalry officer during the campaign that captured Mexico City and ended the war. Harney fought with particular distinction at Cerro Gordo and soon after received a brevet promotion to brigadier general.

For a time immediately following the war, Harney served as commander of Military District Number Five, which comprised most of the settled portion of the new state of Texas.

In 1854, Harney was on leave in France when he was summoned back to take the field against the Lakota Sioux. It would be the government's first campaign against the Plains Indians and it would result in the battle for which Harney's service on the Great Plains is most remembered.

The battle, one of the most savage of all encounters between the Army and the Plains tribes, took place on September 3, 1855 near Lewellen, Nebraska, in the valley of a stream now called Blue Creek. By the usual standards of Plains warfare, the numbers involved were huge and the casualties were high in a fight that eventually covered acres of ground both at the scene of the main combat and during the pursuit that followed.

Although the significance of the battle has long been apparent, confusion remains regarding several of its features. For example, the encounter is increasingly referred to as the Battle of Ash Hollow. In reality, the battle occurred about six miles northwest of the famous Oregon Trail site, across the North Platte River in a broad valley formed by a creek referred to in the 1850s as the Blue Water. The popular perception of the clash has also changed over the years. The initial public reaction – widespread acclaim – was later followed by labels such as "Harney's Massacre." For a time, soldiers who fought in the battle were sometimes branded "butchers" and "squaw killers." In recent years, those harsh judgments have mostly reversed.

The direct cause of the 1855 battle was an episode that came to be known as the Grattan Massacre. In 1854, a band of Oglala and Brule Sioux led by Chief Conquering Bear was camped near Fort Laramie, about two miles from present-day Lingle, Wyoming, awaiting allotments of food promised by an 1851 treaty. The provisions were late in reaching them, by one account perhaps by as much as two months. While the Indians were waiting, a contingent of Mormons on the way to Utah – the Hans Peter Olson Company – traveled through the region. When the party neared the Indian camp one of its livestock, "a sickly, half-starved cow," either wandered away or frightened, wound up in the Indian camp. The Mormons made no large effort to have the cow returned to their herd. The Sioux regarded the animal as abandoned and killed and ate it. When the Mormons reported the incident at Fort Laramie, the Indians – in accordance with the treaty provisions and in order to receive their annuities – at first promised to turn over the Indians who had killed the cow.

While not regarding the latest episode as being particularly serious, the commander of Fort Laramie eventually decided to send Second Lieutenant John Grattan to bring in the Indian perpetrators.

Grattan, a recent graduate of West Point, is described in some accounts as being inexperienced, quick tempered, and anxious for action. Grattan took 27 soldiers, another officer, an interpreter and two cannon with him. Some sources assert that Grattan was handicapped in that his interpreter, a man named Lucien Auguste, was thoroughly disliked by the Indians and quite possibly drunk when he accompanied Grattan. By one account, a local trader warned the lieutenant that Auguste could cause trouble at the Indian camp. In later years, General Harney, who led the forces that fought in the battle precipitated by Grattan's actions, came to suspect that Grattan himself may have been drinking.

When Grattan's force reached the encampment, Chief Conquering Bear, despite several attempts, was unable to get the Indian who had committed the offense to give himself up. Grattan then moved his men to the center of the camp and placed his cannon in position facing the lodge of the Indian who had killed the cow. One last, unsuccessful, attempt was made to secure his surrender. At that point, a gun went off. It is uncertain who fired it, Indian or soldier. The shot sparked a spasm of heavy firing by both sides. Volleys were unleashed from both cannons and Chief Conquering Bear fell almost immediately.

When the melee eventually ended, Grattan and all but one of his men were killed. That one had his tongue cut out and died later at the Fort Laramie hospital. Chief Little Thunder, who would later confront General Harney on the Blue Water, was in the Indian's camp during the clash. Ironically, Little Thunder was apparently one of the pacifiers who, after Grattan and his party had been killed, talked some of the more violent and excited Indians out of attacking Fort Laramie and attempting to burn the post.

In the immediate aftermath of the Grattan incident, an attempt was made to round up all friendly and peaceable Indians and shelter them near Fort Laramie. Eventually, in hopes of diffusing the situation, the Indian agent directed the Brule to move to the south side of the North Platte River. Little Thunder's band did not comply with the orders. His group was thought to harbor participants involved in the recent robbery of a mail train and the murders of mail contractors. Many of those involved in the Grattan episode were with Little Thunder as well. Whatever considerations motivated them, the decision not to go to Fort Laramie violated the government's directive.

In the meantime, a number of incidents quickly followed the Grattan affair. From August 1854 through August 1855, hostile Sioux bands (not the majority) launched a series of raids that involved murders, the theft of mules and mail, and the burning of hay, corrals, and stations.

The public outcry from the Grattan incident and the depredations that followed compelled Congress to act. Secretary of War Jefferson Davis advised President Franklin Pierce to take military action. Davis's report, along with Commanding General of the Army Winfield Scott's recommendation for a punitive expedition, set in motion events that would bring General Harney and his troopers to west central Nebraska the following year.

On October 26, 1854, the War Department named General Harney to lead the campaign. Harney, on vacation in Paris, hurried back to the United States. After first meeting with President Pierce and General Scott, he moved on to Jefferson Barracks in St. Louis. There, he began assembling troops and supplies. Lieutenant Colonel Philip St. George Cooke, a veteran of the Mexican War and an experienced Indian fighter, was assigned to command the cavalry component of Harney's force.

In early August, 1855, having first moved to Fort Leavenworth, Kansas, Harney was ready to begin. With 600 cavalry, infantry, and artillerymen consisting of the 2nd Dragoons, five companies of the 6th Infantry, one company from the 10th Infantry, and a battery of the 4th Artillery, Harney moved north and west into Nebraska. When he left Fort Leavenworth, he took with him the largest force that had ever entered Indian territory.

Harney's plan was ambitious: one wing of a giant pincer would travel north up the Missouri and establish a base at Fort Pierre; the other, led by Harney himself, would move along the "Great Platte River Road" toward Fort Laramie. Eventually, the wings of the enormous double envelopment would converge to squeeze the Sioux into submission. Harney's aim was to find the Indians and either force them to fight or keep them on the move, disrupting their activities and perhaps causing the warriors to separate themselves from the rest of the group. If the latter occurred, the onset of winter might cause the Indians to surrender or face starvation.

As events unfolded, low water on the Missouri River delayed the shipment of troops and supplies to Fort Pierre and the northern arm of the force assembled too late to contribute to the campaign.

At Fort Leavenworth Harney was delayed for a time by torrential storms before eventually moving his troopers to a camp near Fort Kearny, Nebraska. Along the route, Harney was unexpectedly joined by Lieutenant G. K. Warren, a topographical engineer, and a party of seven men. The addition of Warren to the expedition was a fortunate occurrence, both for Harney and for historians. Warren was a superb officer who participated directly in the key events associated with the campaign and recorded his observations in a daily journal.

On August 24, Harney left the Fort Kearny bivouac and continued his trek along the Platte River. Nine days later, on September 2nd, his force crossed to the North Platte and reached the vicinity of the Blue Water Creek. By the time camp was made that night in a flat meadow area west and a bit north of Ash Hollow, Harney's horses and men were approaching exhaustion.

Until that day, few Indians had been sighted. That circumstance changed as Harney's force descended the gorge of Ash Hollow to reach their campsite. From the bluffs in the Ash Hollow area several Indian lodges were visible in the distance via telescope. An eastbound wagon train reported the presence of numerous lodges and identified Little Thunder as the chief. Later still, the expedition's guide, Joseph Tesson, located the Indian's main camp on Blue Water Creek, a few miles distant to the north from both Ash Hollow and the North Platte River. Undetected at the time was a second, smaller camp still farther north on the west bank of the creek.

Harney's bivouac was on the south side of the North Platte River a short distance from where Blue Water Creek converges with it. They made a "cold" camp that evening; no fires were permitted so as not to disclose the location or size of the force. The men settled in for a short night after replenishing their canteens and eating wild grapes and plums that grew in abundance near the river.

Harney met with his officers that evening and laid out an aggressive plan of attack that would strike the Indians from two directions. Colonel Cooke would set out early with his cavalry and some mounted infantry, moving east and north in a half circle until his force was on the other side of the Indian camp. There they would wait, hidden, until they heard firing, then attack the village from the rear. In the meantime, Harney's infantry would delay its start in order to approach the Indian camp at daybreak when Harney intended to launch a frontal attack. If the Indians retreated, they would be driven into Cooke's on-rushing cavalry. If they fought in place, they would eventually be surrounded as Cooke's force moved from the north to pin them against Harney's infantry and artillery.

Despite having been warned of Harney's approach by an Indian agent, Little Thunder's band had chosen to ignore orders to move south or return to Fort Laramie. Encamped near Blue Water Creek, they were drying out buffalo meat taken during a recent hunt. Their decision not to move was likely influenced by the desire to stay in place until the meat was cured. Whatever the total combination of factors that went into their choice – which the chiefs had debated during a recent council – the Indians apparently misunderstood Harney's intentions and the strength of his contingent, either believing that

Haney would not attack or, as some have reported, thinking that they could defeat any white force sent against them.

On the morning of September 3, the Indians were clustered in two villages along the west side of Blue Water Creek. Forty-one Brule lodges were located four miles north of the North Platte River. An additional 11 Oglala lodges formed a smaller camp three miles farther north.

By most contemporary accounts, in combination the 52 lodges housed about 250 Indians. That would place about five Indians in each lodge. Some scholars have noted that the usual estimate is seven to eight individuals per lodge. If the latter figure portrays the true picture at Blue Water, there may have been as many as 400 Indians encamped at the two locations.

Moving toward them in the early dawn hours were 500 troopers: infantry, cavalry, and artillery. (Harney's total force consisted of 600 soldiers. The figure of 500 for the attack subtracts out the number in the wagon train escort and those who dropped out during the march or were too lame to participate in the attack.)

When the troops crossed the North Platte River, the terrain they moved through was shaped by the meanderings of the Blue Water Creek. At the time of the battle, the creek was "about 20 feet wide and 2 to 10 feet deep flowing over a rocky or sandy bottom." The banks were "abrupt and 3 to 4 feet high."

The valley itself is about a half mile wide, bounded on the east by low sand hills. The hills on the east are modest in height and have the appearance of gentle, rolling mounds.

The bluffs that form the west wall are steep, rugged, cut by narrow ravines, and characterized by sharp outcroppings of rocks whose twisted crags form small caves or niches between the coarse formations. Small mesas periodically appear along the west face; the tops of the bluffs are relatively flat as they continue north through the valley.

Cooke's force moved out at 3 a.m. in order to be in place behind the Indian village prior to Harney's attack. Cooke took with him two companies of the 2nd Dragoons, one light company of the 4th Artillery, and one company of the 10th Infantry, about 150 men in all. The latter (artillery and infantry) were mounted on this occasion to enable them to reach their distant positions in time. Led by the scout Joseph Tesson, after crossing the river they trekked east behind the sand hills, skirting the far side to avoid detection.

Harney delayed by a half hour his originally intended jump off time, deciding an extra 30 minutes would bring the village into clear view at the time his force arrived in front of it. At 4:30 a.m., along with his staff and five companies of the 6th Infantry, Harney crossed the North Platte River. Keeping to the east side of the small valley, his troops moved north toward the Indian village.

At the north end of the valley, events required a quick modification to

Harney's plan. As Cooke's forces turned west to position themselves in back of the Brule encampment, they discovered the smaller Oglala village. Saved by Tesson's scouting, they did not stumble into the camp. After already having traveled about five miles, Cooke moved still farther north in order to place himself on the reverse side of what was now known to be a combined camp, larger and more extensive than expected. Still, soon after sunrise, he located a promising position on a ridge and the bank of a dry creek bed about a half mile north of the Oglala village. Keeping his cavalry in readiness and out of sight, he placed his now dismounted artillerymen and infantry in prone positions to block the Indians' anticipated escape route. There he remained for the next two hours waiting to move into action at the sound of firing from Harney's attack.

To the south, Harney's movement also met with unforeseen circumstances. About a mile into his march toward the Brule village his approach was detected and, soon after, lodges were struck and the Indians began to withdraw quickly up the valley to the north. After moving some distance in that direction, they halted and a parley ensued between Harney and the village chiefs.

As often occurs in the "fog of war," opinions differ regarding the meeting or meetings that followed. One version, said to come from Indian informants, was that Little Thunder asked for a conference to gain time to dismantle and move the camp. When Little Thunder, along with chiefs Spotted Tail and Iron Shell, rode from the village carrying a white flag, Harney – having fought Indians since the Seminole Wars in Florida – was not taken in by the ruse. While expressing his willingness to talk, he kept his infantry on the move. Alarmed, the chiefs broke off the talks and raced toward their camp at full speed. According to this account, soldiers fired at the chiefs as they galloped away.

The journals of two officers, Captain J. B. L. Todd and Lieutenant G. K. Warren, and a separate newspaper article provide a somewhat different version. All agree that the Indians first asked for a parley that Harney ignored. Warren relates that at the time Harney's force reached Blue Water Creek, the Indians, on the opposite side of the stream, had moved a considerable distance up the valley. Concerned that he might lose contact with the Brules and not be able to bring them to battle, Harney sent his interpreter to talk with Little Thunder "in order to gain time and learn something of the disposition of the Indians." Harney may have had another motive as well. By this time, he had received information that some of the ground traversed by Cooke's troops earlier that morning – especially an area of spongy soil – was not conducive to cavalry. Therefore, he may have agreed to a meeting to assure that Cooke's men had sufficient time to reach their positions and be in place to spring the trap. Whatever Harney's intent, Little Thunder agreed to meet with him but only if the troops were stopped.

Messages, carried by the interpreter, flowed back and forth until eventually both sides, infantry and Indians, halted with the creek separating them, Indians to the west, Harney's infantry on the east side. Harney and Little Thunder met near a rock outcropping projecting from a low bluff on the east bank of the creek. The location was about a half mile downstream (south) of the large camp. While the talks were on-going, some of the Indians, possibly wary of a trap, began moving up the ravines and small canyons, seeking refuge in the caves and brush in the hills to the west.

When the talks began, Harney dismounted in front of his skirmish line and waited for Little Thunder, who raced at full speed to meet him and stopped suddenly 30-40 feet away. The talks lasted for perhaps as much as an hour. Harney castigated the chief for the Grattan incident, the murders of the mail party, and the frequent attacks on wagon trains. Little Thunder replied that he could not contain the young people in his village, but that he himself was friendly and did not wish to fight. As the talks continued, Little Thunder became visibly more uneasy. By Warren's account, Harney told the chief that no attack would be launched until he returned to his camp and that if his young men wanted a battle, there would be one. Warren says Harney told Little Thunder that if he (Little Thunder) wanted sanctuary, he should leave the area immediately.

Much remains uncertain about this series of meetings. Sioux lore asserts that the soldiers began firing while the chief was meeting with Harney under a white flag. The journals of the officers involved in the parley are consistent in stating that the firing did not begin until Little Thunder returned to his camp.

Meanwhile, Cooke's forces, waiting at the north end of the valley, had also been discovered. An Indian woman and two children walking along the west side of the stream had seen the soldiers hidden in the grass. The woman hurried back to warn the encampment. Two young warriors immediately rode out and challenged the soldiers to fight. Cooke declined to do so, staying at the ready in accordance with Harney's plan, holding off his attack until he heard firing from the south.

Sounds from Harney's battle were not long in coming. According to many accounts, after Little Thunder declined Harney's offer of safety and returned to his camp, the infantry advance resumed and the order to fire was almost immediately given.

The din that reached Cooke's men came mostly from a heavy assault by two companies of Harney's infantry. Attacking diagonally west and north, they moved across Blue Water Creek and up the valley. Their spirited attack drove the Indians to the bluffs on the west side of the valley where they sought refuge and firing positions among the ragged outcroppings and limestone caves. As the Indians took shelter along the valley wall, the infantry companies sustained their attack, working up the steep slopes and through sharp ravines despite heavy fire. While the two companies were charging the heights, a third was sent north along the creek in what turned out to be a mostly futile attempt to catch in the flank any Indians retreating toward the east from this first phase of the engagement.

Cooke's force, positioned north of the upper camp, moved out at the sound of the first volleys from Harney's battle, galloping in a column of fours across the valley racing for the bluffs in the enemy's rear. Cooke peeled off three companies and sent them on a sweep to the reverse side of the bluffs to close the west wall of the valley as an escape route. An additional company of mounted infantry was sent straight down the valley in an attempt to seal off a gap in the hills which was correctly anticipated as a possible avenue for retreat.

As the cavalry raced south to meet the oncoming infantry, the Indians were pinned between the sides of Harney's rapidly closing vise. In a matter of minutes, as the trap swung shut, the valley of Blue Water Creek and its adjoining western bluff became the scene of carnage.

Exposed to withering fire in the open and about to be overrun from the north and south, abandoning their possessions, most of the Indians fled initially to the caves and rocky outcroppings on the heights along the west side of the valley. There they were soon assaulted by the two companies of infantry moving up the valley floor and by the three companies of Cooke's cavalry coming over the tops of the bluffs behind them. Heavy fighting quickly spread across the hillsides as the Indians fired from rock formations and niches in the jagged limestone in a desperate attempt to repel attackers now enveloping them from both front and rear.

The first phase of the battle was notable for its fury. The infantry, employing new, recently issued long-range rifles (U.S. Rifle-Musket Model 1855, a .58 caliber muzzle loading percussion rifle; Harney's cavalrymen were armed with the Sharps Carbine, Model 1852, a .52 caliber breech-loading percussion rifle), exacted a fearful toll as targets presented themselves along the hillside and in the crags, crannies, and underbrush on the faces and tops of the bluffs. It is possible that the Indians were surprised by the range of the new weapons and underestimated the extent of their lethal fire. Heavy broadsides into the caves and twisted rocks caused horrific casualties from ricochets as well as from direct fire.

Harney placed his artillery at the south end of the battle area on a small mesa at the base of the hills where the Indians had fled. That vantage point enabled the batteries to maintain a steady fire into the caves and rake the hillsides where a rain of arrows and bullets was coming from the Indian defenders.

The fight along the bluffs was short but vicious as the Indians resisted fiercely, returning the concentrated fire being poured into their lodgments up and down the bluffs. Eventually, the fire from the cavalry shooting down from the top of the hills and the increasingly heavy assault by the infantry as more and more soldiers reached the bluffs became too severe to withstand; the intensity of the attacks coming from both the front and the rear forced the Indians to abandon their positions. They fled – desperate, headlong, and mostly unorganized – away from the hillside, racing towards and then across the creek, seeking escape through the gap area between the sand hills on the east rim of the valley.

The report of one of the infantry company commanders describes the Indians being driven initially up the hillside where "the cavalry made its appearance directly in front of them. They turned and attempted to escape by the only avenue now left open to them, a ravine in front and to my right. As they passed, from a high commanding point we poured a plunging fire on them with our long range rifles … The party was compact, and as one of their people fell, others jumped from their horses and picked them up, replaced or carried them off. A few moments after, the cavalry came down and our work ceased."

Sent by Cooke to "the nearest practicable descent," a company of cavalry worked its way down the hillside and charged after the fleeing Brules and Oglalas in an all-out pursuit that carried through the gap and extended several miles beyond. The company of mounted infantry that Cooke had earlier dispatched down the valley as a blocking force was hampered by terrain, spongy soil, cumbersome infantry rifles, and the lack of experienced horsemen. Those factors as well as a poor choice of position reduced their effectiveness and prevented them from completely stopping the flow of retreating Indians who were already under continuous fire from the cavalry coming down the bluffs after them and from the infantry companies shooting from vantage points on the hillsides.

The infantry company sent north along the creek by Harney at the outset of the battle in an attempt to catch the Indians in the flank along their anticipated line of retreat had little success. The distance was too great for the infantry to arrive in time to seal off the escape and too far also to reach with effective rifle fire. The major combat on the western hillsides and along the valley floor was over by mid-morning.

The cavalry company sent by Cooke formed the vanguard of the pursuit outside the valley. Those troopers were soon joined by mounted infantry and other units dispatched by General Harney from his headquarters on a high mesa called Rattlesnake Hill midway along the west wall of the valley. The Indians fled down the slopes, through the gap and scattered into small parties, racing in every direction through the rolling table land. Those with fresher ponies often managed to escape, although "(t)here was much slaughter in the pursuit, which extended from five to eight miles."

Viewing the pursuit from Rattlesnake Hill, Harney ordered a recall, fearing that the Indians' better knowledge of the terrain might place in jeopardy small groups of cavalry involved in a chase. However, many of his horsemen were too distant to hear the bugle and it was almost midday before all returned and were accounted for. The headcount revealed that one trooper – who had probably raced too far ahead of the rest of the pursuit – was missing.

Harney's after action report cited 86 Indians killed, six wounded and more than 50 women and children captured. Sioux tradition numbers the captives at 100 or more. A few days later, the bodies of several Indians were found near the banks of the Platte River along the route of the bloody retreat from the Blue Water. That consideration may account for another source's placing the Indian casualties at 136 killed.

According the Harney, "(t)he casualties of my command amounted to four killed, four severely wounded, three slightly wounded, and one missing, supposed to be killed or captured by the enemy." It is possible that one of the wounded soldiers later died. A journal entry written the following year by an emigrant on a wagon train traveling through Ash Hollow states: "We passed the graves of five soldiers who were killed in September, 1855, in an action between the Sioux and U.S. soldiers." Cooke's mounted force sustained the majority of Harney's casualties, a reflection of the extent of their involvement and the intensity of the combat they engaged in.

Cooke's men claimed 74 Indians killed, five wounded, and 42 women and children captured. The infantry declared 12 male Indians killed and 10 or12 women and children captured. Apparent from the statistics is that most male Indians who did not break out were killed. Little Thunder, though wounded, was one of those who managed to escape as did several other chiefs including Spotted Tail and Iron Shell.

Hailed as heroes in the immediate aftermath of the conflict, Harney's troops later came under criticism particularly for alleged atrocities perpetrated against Indian women and children during the course of the battle. Over time, these actions sometimes drew comparison with the infamous "Sand Creek Massacre." In that incident, on November 29, 1864, near Sand Creek, Colorado, Colonel John Chivington led a group of Colorado volunteer militia in an attack on a peaceful village of Cheyenne and Arapaho that claimed more than a hundred lives.

The comparison between Blue Water and Sand Creek, Harney and Chivington, has been found to be unfortunate. The actions of Harney's Regular Army troops on that September day in 1855 bore little resemblance to the outrages inflicted by Chivington's militia nine years later. While at

Blue Water adult male Indians and often boys "fought with great ferocity (and) were given no quarter," most recent researchers have concluded that, unlike Chivington's militia, the soldiers in Harney's expedition did not deliberately attack the innocent. There were casualties among the women and children in the crags and rock formations where they had sought haven along with braves who fired from the same positions in a futile attempt to fight off attackers and protect those sheltered with them. Others occurred on the hillside during efforts to flee "when distance or strangeness of dress or the camouflage of terrain sometimes prevented recognition of sex or age differences." Accounts indicate that General Harney was prompt in detailing soldiers to recover the wounded on both sides.

Contemporary reports indicate that most of Harney's men were appalled by the carnage, especially that inflicted on refugees in the rock crevasses where many women and children were killed by the soldiers as they sheltered there. The expedition's medical officer was officially commended for being "indefatigable in his attention to the suffering wounded, both of our troops and the enemy."

Few sites are as mournful as a battlefield in the aftermath of the fury. The scene at Blue Water was especially poignant. In the rush to the bluffs early in the battle and during the headlong flight at its conclusion, the Indians had abandoned their possessions: buffalo skins, parfleches, cradleboards, cooked meat, robes, tepees, lodge poles, pots – all the belongings that helped bring life to what scant hours before had been a large, busy, and productive village. Dead and wounded of both sides lay fallen across the rocks, scattered over the hillsides and along the escape route east across the valley to the space between the sand hills and beyond.

After the battle, Harney established a new camp close to the battlefield. Search parties found articles that established the presence of hostiles in Little Thunder's camp and confirmed their connection with the Grattan Massacre, the mail train murders and other atrocities. The scalps of two white women were discovered on the body of a dead warrior.

After leaving a small force at a newly constructed sod fortification named Fort Grattan, on September 9 Harney, with the main body of his troops, left the Ash Hollow area and moved northwest toward Fort Laramie. There, marauding Sioux had recently ran off with 80 head of the fort's livestock. Other bands of Sioux, however, traveled to the fort to negotiate a peaceful settlement.

Harney met with the non-belligerents, smoked the peace pipe, and directed that the Sioux return stolen property, turn over the Indians guilty of murder, and make no more attacks on the overland trail. The chiefs present at the meeting were not able to answer on behalf of the greater Sioux nation.

Determined to send a message and prosecute the guilty, Harney took 450 men and 25 mountain men scouts and set out in pursuit.

The weather was already marginal – 28 degrees above zero – when Harney left Fort Laramie on September 29. Nonetheless, Harney's troops moved quickly. The mountain men scoured enormous areas in a series of scouts, soon confirming that the Indians had dispersed into small bands. Harney sent a portion of his force back to winter at Fort Laramie, then continued with the remainder of his troops tracking east across the Dakota Badlands towards Fort Pierre. Snow fell as early as October 4, but Harney persisted, reaching the outpost on October 20. No soldiers were lost on the journey. Harney had demonstrated that military operations could be conducted on the northern Plains even under bitter conditions. It was a lesson that Mackenzie, Miles, Sheridan and others would apply in full measure in the years that followed.

Fort Pierre was a disheveled former American Fur Company trading post where the government had directed Harney to establish a military installation. Though inadequate, through a bitter winter the post would house six companies of the 2nd Infantry and four of the 2nd Dragoons. As soon as possible, Harney shifted the units a considerable distance south and east to a more suitable location that became Fort Randall.

During Harney's stay in Fort Pierre, he visited isolated outposts in the dead of winter. At an encampment near the Niobrara River, in temperatures near zero and with three feet of snow on the ground, he arrested the post commander for not taking sufficient care of his soldiers and horses. Harney stayed at the location for two months, building a sheltered enclosure for the soldiers.

In February, 1856, he returned to Fort Pierre and arranged for a spring council with Sioux leaders. Nearly all the Sioux bands attended. Their leaders arrived at Fort Pierre with a better understanding of Harney's temperament and intentions. They complied with Harney's demands, surrendering three warriors implicated in the stage coach attacks and returning several of the animals stolen from Fort Laramie the previous fall.

Earlier, during Harney's trek to Fort Pierre, other Sioux – Minneconjou this time – had arrived at the fort under a white flag, stating to Harney's representatives that they wanted nothing more to do with "Mad Bear" (Harney). On November 2 the group returned additional horses stolen at Fort Laramie.

Six days later another Sioux band arrived intending to sue for peace. Harney, who by then had arrived at the post, told the assembled Sioux leaders that he would meet with representatives from the entire Sioux nation in 100 days, asking that 10 leaders from each band meet with him in council at that time. Harney sent word to the major chiefs that he would consider their failure to attend the meeting as an indication that they were still at war.

The Indians honored Harney's request, meeting with him at Fort Pierre on March 1. As was usual with Harney, he spoke in blunt terms, telling the chiefs that he believed the buffalo would disappear and that eventually the Sioux would have to adapt to a different lifestyle. Harney laid out several conditions to the assembled leaders – their thefts of horses must stop; attacks on the Pawnees, their historic rivals, must end; the goods they had stolen must be returned; the warrior who had stolen the Mormon's cow (and precipitated the "Grattan Massacre") must be surrendered, and that there must be no more attacks on travelers along the overland trail.

In return, Harney promised that the government would protect them from white intrusions, resume their annuities, and return all Indian prisoners of war not involved in the stage coach attacks. Harney selected Sioux leaders and assigned each of them 100 warriors to help carry out the terms of the agreement. As a further gesture of goodwill, Harney began using Indians as couriers to deliver military messages and distributed excess clothing items to the tribesmen.

At least one Indian agent thought Harney's pact was the best peace agreement ever bartered between the two parties. Even the Oglala, one of the most belligerent bands, came to the fort asking to be part of Harney's peace program.

Harney turned the official ratification, held on May 20, 1856, into a memorable occasion. Nearly 5,000 Sioux camped near the post to observe it. The Sioux turned over to Harney the warrior that had killed the Mormon's cow. In a major show, Harney arrested the man, locked him in the guardhouse – and released him the following day.

Following his extended discussions and successful treaty negotiations with the Sioux, Harney suggested that the government treat the Sioux bands as one nation and that it be kept in check by a separate Army unit specifically assigned to that task. In later years, Ranald Mackenzie, Philip H. Sheridan and others would come to share his view that the Indians would struggle until every avenue of resistance was closed to them. They would surrender without fanfare, he believed, only when they had no other alternatives remaining.

Harney's victory at the Battle of the Blue Water and the agreement he negotiated in its aftermath kept the peace on the frontier for most of the following decade until August 1864 saw the first in a series of massive uprisings.

In the late 1850s, Harney led troops charged with upholding federal authority in "Bleeding Kansas." He briefly commanded an expedition in the "Mormon War," but was recalled to Kansas when conditions deteriorated there.

In 1859, while commanding the Department of Oregon, he was involved in the international incident that became known as the Pig War. San Juan

Island, off the coast of Washington near Vancouver, was at the time subject to competing claims by the British and the Americans. When a pig owned by a British national caused damage to an American's property, Harney sent troops led by George Pickett, later the Confederate general known for the famous charge at Gettysburg, to demand reparations. The British refused, nearly precipitating a shooting war. Tension continued until General Winfield Scott negotiated an agreement that allowed dual occupancy of the island until an international tribunal could adjudicate the competing claims. (An international court later ruled in favor of the United States.) Harney's impulsiveness and lack of tact did not contribute to the peaceful outcome and he was eventually recalled.

The run-up to the Civil War found Harney commanding the Department of the West with Headquarters at Jefferson Barracks in St. Louis, Missouri. The sympathies of the political leadership of the state, like those of the populace, were split between pro- and anti-secessionists. When President Lincoln called for troops to suppress the rebellion, Claiborne Jackson, the pro-slavery governor, refused to comply, conspiring instead to bring Missouri into the Confederacy through military means if necessary.

Events soon spiraled out of control. On May 10, 1861, acting without Harney's approval, Captain Nathaniel Lyon led an unofficial contingent of "Home Guard" unionists to capture a force of Missouri state militia who were poised to seize the federal arsenal. In the aftermath of the clash, a riot erupted in St. Louis. The state legislature followed by recognizing the militia and designating it the Missouri State Guard, further authorizing it to resist any incursion by federal troops.

Harney was appalled and, perhaps rare for him, worked to ease the tensions. He reached an agreement with Missouri State Guard commander Sterling Price that allowed Price and the State Guard to control much of Missouri, while troops loyal to the Union held sway in and around St. Louis.

It is possible that Harney, no diplomat, was naïve in his dealings or, alternately, that he sought to postpone bloodshed in the vain hope that a resolution to the national crisis might still be found. Nonetheless, Harney's actions were unacceptable to Republican state party leaders already suspicious of Harney's Southern birth. On May 30, they succeeded in persuading the Lincoln administration to replace Harney with Lyon.

Harney was recalled to Washington, D.C., for consultation, but was captured by Confederates while en route as the train passed through Harper's Ferry, Virginia. Harney was later taken to General Robert E. Lee, who offered him a command position in the Confederate Army. When Harney refused, Lee allowed him to resume his journey to Washington. There, to his surprise, he was relieved of his command in Missouri.

Harney spent the next two years in Washington in administrative duties before retiring from the Army on August 1, 1863. Two years later he was made a brevet major general in recognition of his long service.

Winfield Scott, Commanding General of the United States Army – no friend of the acerbic Harney – expressed his displeasure that Harney had been removed from command. Later, President Lincoln was alleged to have said that cashiering Harney had been one his administration's greatest mistakes.

Harney's service to the United States was not yet complete, however. He was recalled on various occasions to serve on Indian commissions and as an emissary to the northern tribes. In those duties he was consistent in his appeals for the government to honor its commitments and treat the Native tribes fairly. Considering his legendary lack of tact, Harney exhibited remarkable forbearance in his negotiations with Indian leaders, sitting patiently for hours listening to the ritual, rambling prologues that eventually led to substantive talks. In 1868, he was involved in the treaty discussions at both Fort Laramie and Fort Rice and for a time was put in charge of disbursements to the tribes and administrative matters in the treaty area. By the time of his death the Indians regarded him as one of the most trusted and widely respected of the government representatives: The-man-who-always-kept-his-word.

Harney died at Orlando, Florida on May 9, 1889. He is buried at Arlington National Cemetery.

Oliver O. Howard

L ike several other of his contemporaries, General O. O. Howard is best remembered in American history for his extensive, though sometimes checkered, service during the Civil War. After a brief interregnum following that conflict, Howard spent the greater part of a decade in the Pacific Northwest. Beginning in 1874 and for several years thereafter, as commander of the District of the Columbia, Howard led forces through major Native uprisings in the region, confronting warring bands of Nez Perce, Bannock, Paiute, and Sheepeater tribesmen. His time on the frontier is most notable for his role in the Nez Perce War and, in particular, for his epic pursuit of Chief Joseph and the Nez Perce tribe.

Howard was born in Leeds, Maine, on November 8, 1830. In 1850, at age 19, he graduated from Bowdoin College and entered the United States Military Academy that same year. He graduated from West Point in 1854, ranked fourth in a class of 46.

Commissioned as an ordnance officer, Howard first moved through short tours of duty at the Watervliet Arsenal near Troy, New York, and the Kennebec Arsenal in Augusta, Maine. In 1857, he was transferred to Florida and saw action against the Seminoles.

Always a deeply religious man, in Florida Howard experienced a conversion to evangelical Christianity that influenced the remainder of his life as a soldier and citizen. For a time, Howard pondered resigning from the military to enter the ministry. Eventually, the Civil War suspended further consideration; he would remain in the Army for another 37 years. His religious proclivities would, however, earn him the nickname the "Christian General." The title was not always expressed charitably by the troops who served under him. Howard was known for his strict military and moral discipline and for requiring his troops to attend prayer and temperance meetings.

After a year in Florida, Howard returned to West Point where he taught mathematics until Fort Sumter drew the nation into conflict. Howard's wartime service began almost immediately. Appointed colonel in the Third Maine Infantry regiment, he was in temporary command of a brigade at the First Battle of Bull Run. His performance there was undistinguished; the

unit was driven from the field. Unlike many
other commanders on both sides, though, he
managed to keep his force reasonably intact
while retiring in good order from Chinn Ridge.
He was later promoted to brigadier general and
given permanent command of the unit. In the
midst of heavy action at the battle of Fair Oaks
on June 1, 1862, Howard was struck twice in
the right arm. The wounds were severe and
subsequently required amputation. Thirty-one
years later, Howard received a belated Medal
of Honor for his service during the battle.

Howard recovered from surgery in time
to participate in the fight at Antietam, taking
command of a division after General John
Sedgwick was wounded. On December 13,

Mathew Brady, Public Domain
Oliver O. Howard

1862, his division, along with several others, was unsuccessful in the attack
on Marye's Height during the bloody engagement at Fredericksburg. Having
been promoted to major general in November 1862, Howard subsequently
took command of XI Corps, replacing General Franz Sigel. His tenure with
the corps was not crowned with laurels. The unit was comprised mainly of
German immigrants, many of whom spoke little or no English. The troops
were openly resentful of Howard and vocal in their demands to have Sigel
reinstated.

On May 2, 1863, at Chancellorsville, disaster – much of it of his own
making – struck Howard and XI Corps. Posted at the extreme right of the
Army of the Potomac's line, Howard left his flank "in the air," neither
anchored to a natural obstacle nor safely entrenched. Warnings of Confederate
troop movements were disregarded and the unit was shattered when attacked
by General "Stonewall" Jackson's entire corps. Though Howard's personal
bravery in trying to rally his force was notable, the rout that ensued threatened
to engulf much of the Union Army. A campaign that had begun with high
hopes and much promise ended in catastrophe.

Two months later, XI Corps faced near calamity again. At Gettysburg on
July 1, the unit was routed for a second time, forced into a panicked retreat
through the streets of the town leaving prisoners behind. On this occasion
much of the fault was due to the actions of one of his division commanders,
Francis Barlow, who mismanaged a portion of the XI Corps defensive
front. Though Howard abandoned positions west of town, his foresight in
posting troops on Cemetery Hill before the battle provided a strong fallback
position. Howard helped organize defenses on the hill preventing another
Chancellorsville-like debacle. For a time, the consecutive setbacks at

Chancellorsville and Gettysburg earned the general, whose standard signature was "O. O. Howard," the occasional nickname "Uh-oh" Howard.

XI Corps spent the remainder of the three-day battle on defense around Cemetery Hill, repulsing attacks and assisting on periphery in rebuffing Pickett's Charge on July 3. Howard's role in the fight was not without controversy. When General John Reynolds was killed early in the fighting, Howard became the ranking Union general on the field. General Meade, travelling toward Gettysburg with the remainder of the Army of the Potomac, sent General Winfield S. Hancock with written orders for Hancock to assume command until Meade's arrival. When Hancock reached the battlefield, Howard, who was senior to Hancock in date of rank, refused to relinquish command. The issue between the men was settled by compromise until Meade arrived on the field. In councils of war held at Meade's headquarters to decide whether to stay or retreat, Howard was a strong advocate for continuing the fight at Gettysburg.

Howard was 32 years old at the time. Photographs taken soon after the battle reveal a strong face framed by a full head of dark hair and beard. He stood 5 feet 9 inches tall with a slender build and pale complexion. Articulate and polished in manner, he was lauded in at least one newspaper account for his exceptional coolness under fire after taking command from the fallen Reynolds.

Later that year, Howard and his corps were sent west to Tennessee to join the Army of the Cumberland. At Chattanooga they were part of the assault that cleared Missionary Ridge. Later, he took command of the newly formed IV Corps and led that unit through much of General William T. Sherman's Atlanta Campaign. He was wounded again at Pickett's Mill. In July 1864, when General James B. McPherson was killed near Atlanta, Howard became commander of the Army of the Tennessee and led that force to victories against Confederate General John Bell Hood at Ezra Church and Jonesboro. Subsequently, the Army of the Tennessee, with Howard in command, served as Sherman's right wing on the March to the Sea. As the war progressed, Howard developed into an effective corps commander and became a favorite of General Sherman.

Always a strong abolitionist, after the war Howard was named commissioner of the Freedman's Bureau (initially called the Army's Bureau of Refugees, Freedmen, and Abandoned Lands), charged with integrating freed slaves into society. He remained in the position from May 1865 until July 1874, organizing and administering reconstruction programs, setting labor policy, distributing food rations, establishing schools and courts, and providing medical care.

In 1872, President Ulysses S. Grant detailed Howard on a special mission to negotiate with Chiricahua Apache leader Cochise in an attempt to end years of raids on American settlers. Accompanied by Tom Jeffords, a white frontiersman friend of Cochise, Howard traveled almost alone deep into the Apache heartland. After spending 11 days with Cochise and other Apache tribal leaders, the negotiators reached an agreement. Criticized by some government officials as being overly generous, the settlement granted the Apaches a large portion of southern Arizona as a reservation. With notable exceptions, the pact held generally firm until a year or so after Cochise's death four years later.

Although some Apaches, possibly the majority, remained on the reservation and refrained from attacks, raids by others continued well into the next decade. With some justification, Howard's humanitarian contemporaries hailed the "glass half full" success of his mission. With perhaps equal justification, General Crook and others who supported a harder line criticized the result, believing a warrior culture hundreds of years old would not cease fighting unless defeated on the battlefield.

After nine difficult, often contentious years with the Freedman's Bureau, in 1874 Howard was appointed commander of the Department of the Columbia with headquarters at Fort Vancouver, Washington Territory. Howard's name is most notably linked with the American West through his service in that position during the Nez Perce War.

In the summer of 1877, the Wallowa band of the Nez Perce tribe refused to cede the remaining portion of the tribe's traditional homeland in northeast Oregon. The Nez Perce had originally signed a treaty with the government in 1855 that give the tribe extensive land in Idaho, Oregon, and Washington Territory. When gold was later discovered in 1860 on the tribe's remaining land, the government could not forestall the flow of gold seekers and other immigrants into the territory. In 1863, a second treaty greatly reduced the size of the Nez Perce reservation. Several bands of Nez Perce refused to sign the pact, asserting that its provisions separated them from their ancestral homelands in the Wallowa Valley. The disagreement caused a schism with the tribe, sizable numbers of whom did not move to the new reservation.

After a period of uncertainty and changes of mind at the presidential level, the Grant Administration eventually decided to transfer the entire tribe to a reservation in Idaho. Preliminary meetings with the non-treaty chiefs failed to produce an agreement to move to the new agency. Eventually, General Howard wearied of the inconclusive talks and gave the tribe a 30-day ultimatum to relocate. By many accounts, the time was insufficient to accommodate the task although considerable portions of the tribe made preparations to comply.

Others did not.

As the deadline neared, a group of outraged young warriors sought retribution for past white transgressions against the tribe. Perhaps as many as 18 settlers living along the Salmon River were killed. Some were alleged to have committed violent acts against members of the tribe; almost all were thought to be trespassing on Nez Perce land. With the initial bloodletting, many Nez Perce – including among them those who had attempted to comply with government orders – apparently believed the die had been cast and that a peaceful outcome was no longer possible.

When word of the settlers' deaths reached Howard, he dispatched a 130-man force from Fort Lapwai in northern Idaho Territory. Howard's response was the first in a series of actions that culminated in one of the most remarkable episodes in American military history. For the next three months 800 Nez Perce held U.S. forces at bay during an epic 1,200-mile journey across parts of Oregon, Idaho, and Montana. The tribe's odyssey took them over the Bitterroot Mountains, south through a portion of Yellowstone Park, and back north to within 40 miles of the Canadian border. Rebuffed by Crow allies in their quest for assistance, the tribe determined to seek safety in Canada, intending to shelter there with Sitting Bull's band of Sioux that had crossed the border during the Army's relentless campaign after the Little Bighorn.

From mid-June 1877 until early October a series of battles, some led personally by General Howard others by officers under his command, were fought across the high frontier of the American Northwest. During four decades of sporadic warfare against Native tribes across the West, the Army would find the Nez Perce to be among their most formidable adversaries. Nez Perce warriors, who probably numbered 150-200, were renowned for their marksmanship. Excellent horsemen, their hardy, superbly trained Appaloosa ponies would prove more than a match for the cavalry's horses. The band was led by adroit, military proficient war chiefs whose sophisticated tactics included advance scouts, rear guard actions, flanking moves, skirmish lines and field fortifications. Even General Sherman, Commanding General of the United States Army, was moved to comment that the Nez Perce retreat was one of the most extraordinary events of the Indian wars.

The Battle of White Bird, or White Bird Canyon, was the first clash of the Nez Perce War. The force Howard dispatched in response to the deaths of the settlers along the Salmon River consisted of 106 cavalrymen, 11 civilian volunteers and 13 trusty Nez Perce serving as scouts. Two company commanders, both captains – David Perry (Company F) and Joel Trimble (Company H) – led the assigned units. Perhaps believing that the small force could handle any difficulties and that conflict was unlikely, Howard misjudged the gravity of the situation and did not accompany the expedition.

On June 17, southwest of Grangeville in Idaho County, the forces came together. As the troopers approached, five or six Nez Perce moved out under a white flag, seeking to negotiate. For reasons never explained, perhaps startled or by accident, one of the cavalry's civilian scouts fired at the Indians. The cavalry commanders were quickly disadvantaged when one trumpeter was killed at long range as he was attempting to sound assembly and a second was discovered to have lost his bugle during the march. Both commanders at first dismounted their men and formed an extended skirmish line with the civilian volunteers holding the extreme eastern edge. Within minutes the volunteers were struck by Nez Perce hidden along the valley floor. That portion of the front quickly came apart. Most of the civilians fled.

In rapid succession, two events then placed the entire cavalry force in jeopardy. An attempted cavalry charge by Captain Perry never materialized because of the lack of a trumpeter to sound assembly. Soon after, elsewhere along the trail Captain Trimble attempted to deploy and maintain a line of mounted cavalry – a disastrous tactic given the inexperienced troops and poorly trained horses. Rather quickly, both flanks gave way.

Seeking to establish a rally point, Trimble sent seven men to high ground on the field. Orders for the remaining troopers to move to that area were misinterpreted as calling for a general withdrawal, which was soon joined in an all-out flight by Perry's company as well. Pursuit by the Nez Perce was immediate and deadly. One group of soldiers – reports vary from eight to 18 – were trapped in a closed ravine. All were killed when they ran out of ammunition.

The bulk of the cavalry forces fled southwest up steep canyon walls where they regrouped along flatter ridge lines at the top. A fighting retreat of several miles followed before the remnants of the column were saved by the arrival of fresh volunteers.

The battle was over by mid-morning. It was a disaster for the U.S. Army. Thirty-four cavalrymen were killed and two more, as well as two civilians, wounded. Nez Perce losses were believed to have numbered only three wounded. Additionally, warriors retrieved an extensive amount of weapons and ammunition taken from slain cavalrymen or otherwise left behind on the battlefield.

Realizing that further hostilities were inevitable and wary that other tribes might join the Nez Perce uprising, Howard called for additional troops – eventually, about 2,000 from posts around the country would be sent to the area – and made plans for an extended pursuit.

Howard arrived in the White Bird area several days later with a force of 400 men. By that time, however, the Nez Perce had crossed the Salmon River. During the months' long chase that followed, river crossings would prove to be another skill the Nez Perce possessed in abundance. While Howard and his command crossed the Salmon with considerable difficulty, the Nez Perce moved several hundred men, women, and children, along with tepees, camp equipment, two thousand horses and other livestock back and forth with relative ease.

After the debacle at White Bird Canyon, Howard took personal command of the expedition. Not quite a month later, after crossing the Salmon and the South Fork of the Clearwater River, with a force of 440 cavalry and another 160 civilian volunteers and scouts, he caught up with the Nez Perce at the base of the Idaho Panhandle.

In the meantime, in early July the war chief Looking Glass and his band joined the Nez Perce, adding numbers and strength to the group opposing Howard. Ranches and farms, perhaps as many as 30, were burned as the tribe moved east across the traditional tribal lands.

On July 8, civilian scouts reported the location of the Nez Perce camp to Howard. Contrary to the tribe's expectations, Howard approached their village from the south after following a fork of the Clearwater River through exceptionally rugged country. When Howard reached the site on July 11, he occupied a high ridge overlooking the valley and the encampment below. After placing howitzers and Gatling guns on the elevated ground, Howard opened the attack with an artillery barrage. The Nez Perce responded quickly, sending warriors to contest the hilltop and slow Howard's advance. Working under fire, the Nez Perce hastily assembled a stone fortification. Shooting from behind the barricade, their steady fire halted Howard's cavalry and gave other tribesmen time to set up defensive positions along a tableland above the side of the river.

The fight continued through the day, ending with both sides settled into fortified lines. On July 12, the fighting opened with Howard's force facing Nez Perce sheltered in a defensive perimeter about one and a half by two miles long stretched along the river.

As Howard was preparing a battalion-sized attack along the right side of the line, an unanticipated event changed the complexion of the battle. As the assault was about to be launched, a 120-mule pack train carrying supplies to Howard reached the battlefield. Visible to all, its appearance surprised both the cavalrymen and the Nez Perce.

Captain Marcus Miller, his force in readiness to lead the planned attack, moved immediately to secure the pack train. Finding his men well forward toward the Nez Perce line and receiving little opposing fire – the Nez Perce were perhaps still puzzled by the pack train's appearance – Miller suddenly ordered a charge. Startled, the Nez Perce retreated in haste, crossing the river and abandoning the village. Howard's men advanced all along the line and took possession of the camp.

The results of the Clearwater struggle were mixed for both sides. Howard had taken the village, captured some Nez Perce supplies, and kept the tribe on the run. But, the battle was a costly one. Cavalry losses amounted to 15 killed and 25 wounded with another two civilians killed and one wounded. Nez Perce losses were thought to number about four killed and six wounded. The Nez Perce had seen their village destroyed along with much of their camp equipment. The bulk of the tribe had escaped, though, and importantly, they had gotten away with their pony herd intact. Although about 30 Nez Perce surrendered to Howard a few days later the tribe's overall strength, enhanced by the addition of Looking Glass and his band, remained larger than at the outset of the fighting.

Encamped near Kamiah, Howard learned that the Nez Perce were leaving the Weippe Prairie, a grassy, relatively level area across the river. The modest-sized force of cavalry and scouts that Howard sent to check on the tribe's movement was ambushed by the Nez Perce. Two of the reconnaissance party were killed and one wounded, but not before confirming that the tribe was headed east through the Lolo Pass. Before exiting the region completely, Nez Perce raiders doubled back to the Kamiah area and made off with several hundred horses. On July 25, they crossed into Montana.

Having earlier received approval from General Sherman to ignore departmental boundaries and continue the pursuit wherever it took him, Howard, with a force numbering about 700, cautiously followed along the Lolo Trail. He did not resume the chase until July 30.

Far behind, Howard telegraphed ahead and arranged for Colonel John Gibbon to move against the Nez Perce from his post at Fort Shaw, Montana. Gibbon managed to catch the tribe and surprise their sleeping camp. The resulting battle of the Big Hole was costly to both sides. The Nez Perce lost as many as 70-90 killed, of whom perhaps 30 were warriors – the most casualties the tribe would suffer in any battle during the war.

The following day, accurate long-range fire kept Gibbon's soldiers immobile while the Nez Perce slipped away. The fight cost Gibbon 31 soldiers killed. Short of food and water and with 40 wounded men to attend to, he remained in place and awaited Howard's arrival. After a tortuous 71-mile ride over the previous 24 hours, Howard and a small advance party reached Gibbon on August 11. Gibbon's troops were in no shape to continue the chase, having lost almost a third of their force in the bitter fight on August 9. Soon after, Howard's entire column arrived on scene and Howard resumed his pursuit, turning his force south toward Yellowstone Park.

Meanwhile, the Nez Perce had first moved southeast into Montana, then back into Idaho through the Bannock Pass and finally once again into southern Montana through the valley of the Lemhi River. Howard took a more direct route aiming to intercept the tribe somewhere near the national park.

Bloodshed erupted in spasms during the Nez Perce's march. Perhaps as retribution for the losses suffered at Big Hole, young warriors killed ranchers and attacked a wagon train while the tribe moved through Idaho into Montana. Howard took his column on a parallel track north of the Nez Perce. As the tribe turned northeast, he altered his route, cutting sharply east and south to interpose his force on the Nez Perce path.

Howard had begun this leg of the campaign with 310 soldiers and several dozen civilian volunteers and Indian scouts. He was joined on the trail by an additional group of 39 volunteers and a 50-man company of cavalry. By August 19, he was in southeastern Idaho at a place called Camas Meadows, a fertile prairie split by Camas and Spring Creeks. He had pushed hard and was now only a short distance behind the Nez Perce who had vacated their campsite the preceding day.

Howard bivouacked in the meadows that night, naming the place Camp Calloway after the leader of the Virginia City volunteers. Howard took special pains to fortify the position, placing extra sentries on all sides of the encampment. Nonetheless, at 4 o'clock the next morning, Nez Perce raiders struck the camp. Having noted the heavy guard details, the Indians discarded their notion to directly attack Howard's camp. Instead, they took aim at his more vulnerable horse herd.

When the raiders reached the edge of the camp, one was seen by a sentry who sounded the alarm. At about the same time, a shot was fired, by whom remains uncertain. Heavy firing commenced immediately, although in the darkness few on either side were hit. The early alarm prevented the Nez Perce from releasing large numbers of cavalry horses from their picket lines. Many of Howard's pack mules were free roaming, however, and the raiders concentrated on stampeding those animals. Altogether about 200 mules and 20 horses belonging to the Virginia City volunteers were captured or set loose in the noise and confusion.

At sunup, Howard sent a strong force of 150 cavalry to chase the Indians and recover loose stock. About eight miles from the camp, the cavalrymen were ambushed by a rear guard left in place by the raiders. While the main party drove the captured stock toward the Nez Perce village, the attackers took advantage of outcroppings black lava, copses of aspen trees, and broken terrain sprinkled with sagebrush to bring Howard's men under fire and delay their pursuit.

Soon after the attack began, a handful of Nez Perce formed a thin skirmish line across a narrow meadow. The cavalry commander deployed his troops along a small ridge that bordered the field and though ineffective at long distance, began taking the Indians under fire. Soon at least one cavalryman was hit by return fire and it was discovered that the skirmish line was a distraction that allowed other Nez Perce hidden in the rocks to creep up on both sides of the dismounted cavalry.

The cavalry commander sounded a retreat to escape the enfilading fire, but one of the three company commanders chose not to obey the order. The captain and 50 of his men shifted to a strong position but were followed and surrounded by Nez Perce warriors. Trapped inside an improvised redoubt, for perhaps as long as three hours the troopers struggled to fight off their attackers. Howard eventually received word that the cavalry companies were in trouble and left quickly with reinforcements. At mid-afternoon he reached the besieged company, still holding out in rifle pits strung along a series of small ridges that sheltered their horses in the shallow ground in between.

The cavalry company had lost two killed and about a half dozen wounded during what became known as the Camas Meadows battle. Nez Perce losses are not certain but may have numbered two warriors wounded. The Nez Perce had not managed to capture the cavalry's horse herd, but the 200 mules taken on the raid inhibited Howard's mobility.

Howard chose not to pursue aggressively. When he did resume the chase he moved slowly and with caution. The night after the battle he was reinforced with 280 infantrymen and two days after that with about 50 additional Bannock scouts. Some of the latter quit a short time later, disenchanted by the slow pace of Howard's pursuit.

When the Nez Perce vacated the Camas Meadows area, they crossed again into Montana, moving toward the wilderness region in and near Yellowstone Park. Howard halted the chase for a few days, resting his weary troops near a sizable body of water called Henry's Lake. General Philip H. Sheridan began moving veteran cavalry and infantry units along with experienced scouts into Montana.

When the Nez Perce left the Yellowstone Park area they first sought, but were refused, assistance from their Crow allies. Denied help, they headed generally north toward sanctuary in Canada. The chase was picked up by Colonel Samuel Sturgis and six companies of the 7th Cavalry. Sturgis began the pursuit on August 12. After an exhausting trek, he caught the Nez Perce on September 13, about 10 miles north of Laurel, Montana. In the running fight that followed, Sturgis was not able to stop the Nez Perce but managed to capture 400 or so of the tribe's pony herd. Both sides sustained casualties in the clash although the cavalry companies suffered more heavily.

His horses completely spent by the fight and the hard riding over the previous month, Sturgis was unable to continue. Two days after the battle, he was joined by Howard who resumed command and again pushed his troopers after the Nez Perce. Howard moved at a steady pace but was by this time probably two or more days behind in the chase. Unbeknownst to the tribe, however, a second column had joined the pursuit and was moving rapidly towards them.

Leaving from Fort Keogh, Montana, Colonel Nelson A. Miles led several companies of the 2nd and 7th Cavalry, elements of the 5th infantry and a contingent of superb Cheyenne and Lakota scouts – probably 520 men, altogether – on a 160-mile forced march. Moving from the southeast, Miles intercepted the Nez Perce on September 30 near Snake Creek in present-day Blaine County, Montana. By then the tribe was within 40 miles of the Canadian border.

Believing they had won the race with Howard, and unaware that Miles had entered the chase, the Nez Perce made a leisurely camp prior to the final push to the border. Miles' force was detected only at the last moment; still, the Indians put up a hurried, ferocious defense. Both sides suffered heavy casualties during the bloody day of battle that followed. Miles then settled into a siege operation. The camp was surrounded and Miles' Native scouts made off with most of the Nez Perce's pony herd.

On October 4, Howard and his force reached the scene, further sealing the fate of the trapped encampment. Without horses, running low on food and short of blankets in the bitter cold, Chief Joseph surrendered the majority of the Nez Perce the following day. A much smaller group led by White Bird managed to slip away into Canada.

By the standards of warfare across the American West, the battle was relatively costly, with most of the casualties occurring in the extraordinary violence of the first day. The Army's losses numbered 21 killed and 26 wounded (one source places Miles' losses at 31 killed and 47 wounded). Nez Perce losses were thought to be about 25 killed and another 50 to 60 wounded.

The Battle of Bear Paw, as the fight became known, ended the Nez Perce War. Both Howard and Miles promised Chief Joseph that the tribe could return to their traditional homeland in Wallowa Valley. Over the strong objections of both men, higher authorities instead ordered the tribe to Fort Leavenworth, Kansas. Later, the Nez Perce were sent to Indian Territory before eventually being allowed to return to Oregon in 1885.

Estimates of casualties for the entire conflict vary considerably. Army losses are generally placed at about 123 soldiers and 55 civilians killed with another 152 wounded. Nez Perce casualties are thought to be in the range of 150-200 killed (not all were warriors) and another 100 or more wounded. About 400-450 surrendered with Chief Joseph.

The Nez Perces' capitulation sparked a lifelong quarrel between Miles and Howard, each claiming credit for the victory and for the capture of Chief Joseph.

As fate would have it, Howard's Indian-fighting days were not to end with Chief Joseph's surrender. The late 1870s were a volatile time in the history of the Pacific Northwest. Over the next 24 months Howard would find himself engaged in two more conflicts with Native tribes. Though smaller in scope and less well remembered than the Nez Perce War, the Bannock War in 1878 and the Sheepeater War of 1879 took additional lives, consumed additional resources, and required the commitment of sizable forces. As department commander, Howard was in overall charge of both campaigns, at times personally leading troops in the field and on others directing the operations of subordinate commanders.

Several conditions, many of long duration, precipitated the Bannock War. In 1866, the Bannocks, whose traditional homeland was along the Snake River Plains of southern Idaho, were urged to move to a camp near Boise City in an attempt to peacefully separate them from the influx of immigrant farmers flowing into the territory. In 1869, the somewhat informal attempt was replaced by relocation to an officially established reservation at Fort Hall.

The transfer severed the Bannocks from their historic grounds and strained the tribe's cultural/religious beliefs which were tied to that specific region. Eventually, the pressure became too much and in May 1878, a large band including 200 warriors left Fort Hall for the Big Camas Prairie area. Bannock history was closely tied to the prairie locale, which for decades the tribe had frequented to harvest camas roots. Friction soon developed with a few white settlers who had livestock in the region. Two settlers were wounded and a third was killed in the following days.

The territorial governor contacted Howard on May 30, advising of the outbreak of violence. A cavalry force under Captain Reuben F. Bernard was dispatched for the Boise area and hurried to the scene. Bernard's force reached the Bannock camp on June 2 and after a near-bloodless confrontation forced the Indians into retreat. The Bannocks moved generally west, eventually raiding along the Snake River where several settlers were killed. By shifting westward, the tribe hoped to connect with Paiute allies. Meanwhile, Bernard's column was bulked up by additional cavalry companies sent by Howard and by the arrival of local militia volunteers.

The war's first real fighting took place on June 8 near South Mountain, a tiny hamlet in southwestern Idaho, about five miles from the Oregon border. In the struggle that erupted in and around the small mining camp, two militia volunteers and several Bannocks, including their principal chief, Buffalo Horn, were killed. Bested in the clash, the Bannocks fled farther west, aiming towards Oregon and Paiute friends while raiding mining camps along the way. The spreading violence prompted state and territorial governments in California, Nevada, and Utah to send militia units to supplement Howard's forces.

Bernard maintained a hot pursuit through the Jordan Valley, across Steens Mountain in southeastern Oregon and points farther west. Bernard's force – four companies designated as the expedition's Left Column by Howard – caught the Bannocks on June 23, forcing a battle at Silver Creek in southern

Idaho. The encounter cost Bernard two or three troopers killed. A sizable but undetermined number of Bannocks were casualties as well. The Bannocks stole away during the night, but lost their camp and most of its contents as the cavalry swept through the village. On June 25, Howard met with Bernard to plan the closing moves of the campaign.

On June 29, Bannocks were caught again in a skirmish near Canyon City. The arrival of Bernard's cavalry shortly after the clash prompted the Bannocks to push toward Fox Valley.

On July 8, a force personally led by Howard intercepted the tribe at the junction of a small creek and the Columbia River. In a surprise attack led by Bernard, Howard advanced his force against Bannocks entrenched amid rugged bluffs and along the crest of a steep hill. Bannock warriors fell back, driven from three successive positions before making a stand in a grove of heavy timber. As the fighting developed, Howard's troops flanked the Indian's defense and forced them to flee. Five soldiers were wounded, one of whom later died of his wounds, in the sharp encounter. The Bannocks also suffered casualties and were forced by Howard's attack to retreat to the southeast, altering their course away from prospective help that awaited them farther north.

On July 12, in a related incident, a cavalry unit inadvertently collided with a large band of Umatilla warriors, potential allies of the Bannocks. Worried by the influx of militia forces, the band had left the nearby Umatilla Reservation, apparently with the intention of joining the Bannocks. Confronted by the cavalry, the Umatillas surrendered immediately and – perhaps induced by a large bounty on the head of Chief Egan, the Bannock's leader – agreed to join the troopers in the fight. A short time later the Umatillas went to the nearby Bannock camp and either by subterfuge or attack, killed Chief Egan and several others.

On July 20, a cavalry force met and defeated a Bannock band in the canyon of the North Fork of the John Day River. The clash further split the Bannocks, who fled in confusion down the battlefield.

By the end of July, Howard shifted the focus of the campaign to tracking and running down a number of smaller, shattered groups. Multiple pursuits, difficult but relentless, followed. Small skirmishes over a widely scattered area took place through the next two months with a final sharp encounter occurring in mid-September. Eventually, exhausted and under continuous threat, nearly all the Bannocks returned to the Fort Hall Reservation. Those few that did not remained in tiny groups and hunted peacefully. Over time, most later ventured back to the reservation as well.

The Sheepeater War of 1879 was the last Indian war fought in the Pacific Northwest. Numbering about 300-500, the Sheepeaters were a nomadic band of Western Shoshone whose name derived from a standard fixture of their diet, Rocky Mountain sheep. Although the tribe ranged widely through the region, the campaign that would come to bear their name took place primarily in central Idaho.

As was so often the case in clashes between Natives and white immigrants the specific causes of the conflict are disputed. The core story, though, has familiar overtones. The influx of settlers and miners following the discovery of gold in the area impinged on the Indians' life style. The Sheepeaters, in turn, were accused of killing prospectors and ranchers. Multiple killings in early 1879 prompted Howard to send forces against the tribe. He led a three-column campaign, sending forces north from Boise, southeast from Camp Howard at Grangeville, and east from the Umatilla agency. All would converge in the vicinity of Payette Lake, near present-day McCall, Idaho.

Ten days into the march, after pushing through deep snow and fording flooded streams, the force from Boise arrived at the hamlet of Orogrande. Led by Captain Bernard, the cavalry companies reached the town on June 8. They found it mostly destroyed. After waiting for his supply train to catch up with him, Bernard resumed his pursuit across difficult, poorly charted terrain, moving along barely navigable portions of the Salmon River. Well into their months' long trek, Bernard's force marched up the Middle Fork of the Salmon, spending several weeks slogging through inhospitable landscape and inclement weather.

While Bernard moved up the Middle Fork, the column from Camp Howard reached Big Creek Canyon near the South Fork. On July 28, scouts detected Indians signs. Shortly after, the unit, led by a young lieutenant, was attacked from all sides while moving through a canyon. Two troopers were wounded and the column was forced to withdraw. Two miles away, the unit reorganized but the following day the troopers were attacked again, this time from two sides.

As the fight intensified, the Indians set fire to the area near the soldiers' position, seeking to burn them out. The cavalry's first sergeant set a backfire near the cavalrymen's lines that prevented flames from reaching the entrenched troopers. The Sheepeaters left the battle site that night. The soldiers left the following day. Forced by severe terrain to abandon portions of their gear and supplies, the unit returned to Camp Howard to re-equip.

In the meantime, after a temporary diversion, Bernard requested that reinforcements and provisions meet him at the South Fork of the Salmon River. The column from the Umatilla agency – two companies of cavalry and Native scouts – eventually linked up with him near the hot springs along the North Payette River.

A march of several days took the combined columns through recently abandoned campsites and belongings discarded by the band as the Indians struggled to stay ahead of their pursuers. Reaching the area where the Camp

Howard column had fought its battle, scouts found the main Sheepeater village a few miles distant. Bernard hurried his troops to the scene, but found an empty camp which he quickly burned.

In the days ahead, the Sheepeaters split into smaller groups. All except the tiniest clusters were chased and kept on the move. Periodic raids by small groups of warriors occurred as the Indians tried to stave off the relentless pursuit. Casualties, though not large in number, were inflicted by both sides. As the chase drew on, Howard rotated some units temporarily back to Camp Howard where they were rested, resupplied and then quickly returned to the field.

In mid-September, as Howard's push continued, the cavalrymen came upon a mostly abandoned camp recently left in great haste by the Sheepeaters. A handful of captives were taken. One, possibly a war chief, promised to bring in the remainder of the band who were still on the loose. Two weeks later, cavalry officers accompanied by Umatilla scouts negotiated the surrender of the Sheepeater band. By October 1, the campaign was over. The Sheepeaters were taken first to Vancouver Barracks and were subsequently resettled on the Fort Hill Reservation.

The Sheepeater War was a conflict devoid of major battles. Waged mostly by company-sized units, the struggle developed as a series of running clashes waged over an enormous territory. Though not often in the field during the course of the war, Howard's campaign design – continuous pursuit from several directions – eventually exhausted the Sheepeaters. It was not elegant and it was not fast, but in the end it was effective. Stripped of their provisions, hungry and ground down from the relentless chase, the band eventually surrendered.

Howard's service in the Pacific Northwest continued until 1881, when he left for a two-year tour as Superintendent of the United States Military Academy. His final assignments included command positions with the Department of the Platte, the Department of the Pacific, and the Department of the East. Howard was in the latter office, with headquarters on Governors Island in New York harbor, when he retired from the Army in 1894.

General Howard's profound humanitarian convictions were evidenced by the major role he played in establishing Howard University in Washington, D.C., as a college for African-American students. He served as the school's president from 1869-1874. In 1895, he founded Lincoln Memorial University in Harrogate, Tennessee, to provide education opportunities to "mountain whites."

Howard died at Burlington, Vermont, on October 26, 1909, and was buried in Lake View Cemetery in that city.

Ranald S. Mackenzie

anald Mackenzie was one of the first of the U.S. Army's senior field
commanders to wage war against the Indians with consistent success.
Having taught himself to "think like an Indian," he turned many of
the Native tribes' war-fighting methods against them and was undefeated in
encounters that spanned much of the American West. Despite darker sides to
Mackenzie's service, there can be no questioning of his accomplishments,
his brilliance as a commander, or his personal bravery. On battlefields
throughout Texas, the central Plains, and the Southwest, Mackenzie was often
the government's "firefighter," given the most difficult tasks in the direst of
circumstances. During the course of his entire career fighting Indians across
a substantial part of the continent, he lost fewer men than did Custer in one
horrific afternoon of combat.

Ranald Mackenzie was born July 27, 1840, in New York City, the first
child of an often-absent naval officer known for his demanding and autocratic
leadership style. When Mackenzie was eight years old, his father died of
a heart attack leaving the family with only modest resources. Growing up,
Mackenzie was ambivalent about a career choice. He briefly studied law, and
then attended Williams College for a time before receiving an appointment
to West Point. There, he eventually settled in and his considerable talents
became evident. He graduated first of 28 in the Academy's class of 1862.

Mackenzie's subsequent Civil War service was truly extraordinary.
Referred to by Ulysses S. Grant as "the most promising young officer" in the
Union Army, Mackenzie was brevetted *seven* times during the war. Within
two years he had fought in eight major engagements including Second Bull
Run, Antietam, and Gettysburg. Later, he led cavalry forces in the Shenandoah
Valley Campaign, at the Battle of Five Forks, and in the war's concluding
encounters at Petersburg and around Appomattox. Wounded six times (his
nickname "Bad Hand" resulted from losing parts of two fingers during the
siege of Petersburg), his battlefield "presence" and personally courage were
universally acknowledged. When Lee surrendered the Confederate Army,
Mackenzie took custody of the captured property. When the war ended, he
was a brevet major general.

Mackenzie's extraordinary talent as a combat leader came as a surprise to many who had known him before he entered the military. Shy and reserved, with delicate features, as a youth Mackenzie was afflicted with a speech impediment (a slight lisp) and had a rather high, shrill voice that never completely changed. Although he grew tall and rugged in appearance, issues with his speech and voice persisted and he never became comfortable speaking in public. At Williams College he had a wide circle of friends who described him as quiet and modest and remembered his smile and earnest gray eyes.

Public Domain
Ranald S. Mackenzie

West Point and, perhaps especially, his Civil War experience seem to have changed him. In later years military colleagues would characterize him using phrases such as "alone and aloof" and "cold and efficient." By temperament, he became "high strung" – nervous, impatient, and irritable.

From his earliest days in the military, Mackenzie gained a reputation for his meticulous approach to duty and for his willingness to assume responsibility and take the initiative with or without orders. The men who served under Mackenzie often disliked him – sometimes intensely – for his harsh discipline. Almost all, however, recognized his exceptional abilities as a trainer and leader and greatly respected his bravery under fire. In balance, many of his soldiers may have seen the latter qualities as being more compelling – when Mackenzie served as commander of the 41st Infantry, the regiment had the lowest desertion rate in the Army.

Still, there were aspects to his service that make his career more difficult than most to place in balance. At times his discipline was so harsh that he was known to his soldiers as the "Perpetual Punisher" he took his forces on extra legal, cross-border excursions; and he was sometimes criticized for his treatment of the Native tribes that he was sent to subdue. (Although here, as in many areas, there is contradiction: one of Mackenzie's proudest achievements was preventing a shooting war with the Ute tribe.) His legacy is further blurred by the mental instability that afflicted him in later years and forced his retirement from the Army.

Mackenzie's career is perhaps best recalled for his leadership on battlefields and in campaigns against opponents adept in guerrilla warfare. There, he was without peer.

Mackenzie's service following the Civil War was almost entirely in the West. From 1867-1875, first as commander of the 41st Infantry, a Buffalo

Soldier unit, and later as commander of the 4th U.S. Cavalry, Mackenzie was posted at various times at Fort Brown, Fort Clark, Fort McKavett, Fort Concho and Fort Richardson in Texas and at Fort Sill in Indian Territory (present-day Oklahoma). In October 1871, Mackenzie was wounded for a seventh time during a skirmish with Comanches at Blanco Canyon. Mackenzie's service during this period was highlighted by triumphs at the Battle of the North Fork of the Red River (1872) and at the Battle of Palo Duro Canyon (1874).

Two aspects of the Battle of the North Fork brought Mackenzie notoriety as an Indian fighter. The first was that the campaign and its climactic struggle were waged in the *Llano Estacado*, the "Staked Plains" of West Texas, an immense region of rugged, inhospitable terrain that had long been the nearly impenetrable stronghold of warring bands. The second was that it was likely during this expedition that Mackenzie developed a strategy for defeating the Plains Indians.

Striking out of the *Llano Estacado*, for years the Comanches had raided ranches, stolen cattle, and indulged in illicit *Comanchero* trade. From the time of the U.S. Army's arrival in the region, the Staked Plains had been a forbidden zone – a sanctuary from which the Comanches operated with near-impunity from refuges in hidden canyons, seemingly swallowed up in the vast, flat emptiness. On July 21, 1872, aided by information on trails, routes, and water provided by a captured *Comenchero* cattle thief, Mackenzie with 284 officers and men of the 4th Cavalry and 24th Infantry, plus Indian scouts, began a reconnaissance that stretched all the way west to Fort Sumner, New Mexico, then north, and finally back east to the Texas Panhandle. After resupplying and resting his command, on September 21, Mackenzie moved north toward the headwaters of the Red River, along the way leaving a supply cache and a security detail near present-day Clarendon, Texas.

On September 29, leading a force of seven officers, 215 enlisted men, and nine scouts, Mackenzie came upon a substantial Indian village located near present-day Lefors, Texas. The 262 lodges, probably housing well over a thousand Indians, were situated on the North Fork of the Red River about seven miles from the mouth of McClellan Creek. After first resting men and horses, Mackenzie formed his troopers into columns of four and prepared for a charge.

Mackenzie attacked at 4 p.m., taking the village completely by surprise. One company made straight for the Indians' horses, stampeding or capturing the herd. Meanwhile, Mackenzie's remaining columns tore through the village before fanning out in pursuit of the masses of Indians that were put to flight. Except for a group of 80 or so warriors who were killed or scattered after a brisk fight near a creek bank, major resistance was quickly overcome. It is likely that the most intense combat lasted for no more than half an hour. Lodges, stores of meat, robes, clothing, camp supplies and utensils were burned. Hundreds of horses and mules were captured, although some were recovered by Comanche raids the following night on Mackenzie's camp. Mackenzie's after action report cited 23 Comanches confirmed killed, although other bodies may have been hidden to prevent desecration by Mackenzie's Indian scouts. Some estimates place the Comanche dead at 50 or more. The 130 Comanches taken prisoner were later exchanged for the band's promise to go back to the Indian agency and to return white captives held by the tribe. Mackenzie's losses were two troopers killed and two seriously wounded. (Some sources say three killed and three wounded.)

The win at the North Fork was of special significance. For the first time, the Army had struck at the heart of the Comanches' fortress. Mackenzie had mastered terrain that the Indians had considered inviolable. Capturing the horse herd took away the Indians' mobility and with it their capability to hunt and conduct raids. With their horses gone, their supplies and their village destroyed, the Indians could not survive except on reservations. It was a lesson that Mackenzie and other army leaders would apply often in the future.

The Battle of the North Fork was a precursor both to the Red River War and to the way that conflict would be fought by the Army. Conditions in the region had steadily worsened following the 1867 agreement (the Medicine Lodge Treaty) that established two reservations in Indian Territory. Some Comanche, Kiowa, Southern Cheyenne, and Arapaho bands moved to the reservations. Other sub-tribes, though, refused to sign and remained "hostile." Indian raids from inside and outside the reservations soon followed. For the reservation Indians, strife was sometimes a response to the tardiness in receipt – or absence – of the food and provisions promised by the government. For both treaty and non-treaty Indians, war was a reaction to encroaching settlement and to the hundreds of commercial buffalo hunters who swarmed through the area, ignoring provisions of the treaty. Between 1874 and 1878 hunters all but exterminated the great southern herd of American bison. As conditions deteriorated, large numbers of Indians from several tribes resolved to make a final attempt to drive the intruders from the Plains. Conversely, for the Army the year 1874 brought a concerted attempt to pacify the Texas frontier.

An attack in late June by 300 or more Indians on a buffalo hunter encampment at Adobe Walls provided the catalyst for government action against the southern Plains tribes. Eventually, five columns of troops moving from different points of the compass converged on the Texas Panhandle and tributaries of the Red River. Mackenzie's column, sweeping north from Fort Concho (near San Angelo), was part of a plan aimed at maintaining a continuous offensive, pressuring the Indians from all directions until they were forced into submission.

The Army on this occasion was well-provisioned for an extended campaign. The soldiers' unremitting pursuit and the tightening ring thrown across the Panhandle made it the scene of frequent clashes. More than 20 battles were fought before the Red River War officially ended in June 1875. The decisive fight came at Palo Duro Canyon, where the majority of Indians had taken refuge from the threatening columns. The U.S. forces that fought and won the battle were led by Ranald Mackenzie.

In late September, Mackenzie moved north toward the canyon with his column, comprised mainly of the 4th U.S. Cavalry accompanied by infantry and associated scouts. Long regarded as a safe haven by the Native tribes, Mackenzie believed, correctly, that large numbers of Indians would be assembled there. During the night of 25 September, Comanches attacked Mackenzie's camp near Tula Canyon. Anticipating a possible assault, Mackenzie had posted a greatly reinforced picket line that succeeded in driving off the raiders. The respite was brief, however; the Comanches resumed their attack the following morning. Repulsed again after a three mile running fight, the Indians broke off the encounter. For a time, Mackenzie's scouts lost the trail. The Comanches had vanished, as if they had been swallowed up by the earth.

In fact, they had.

Eventually, Mackenzie's troops picked up several small trails that fed into a single larger one. They had found the path to Palo Duro Canyon.

Two days after the running fight, they reached the rim of the canyon. There, below, were bands of Kiowa, Comanche, and Southern Cheyenne spread over as many as five villages in a winter encampment. Bisected by a small stream, the succession of campsites stretched for miles along the canyon floor. At the point where Mackenzie's troops reached it, the canyon was about a half mile wide, with walls almost vertical in places that fell 500 feet to the floor below. Soon after, a search revealed a path of sorts down the south rim.

Mackenzie wasted no time, attacking in the early hours of September 28. Aimed at taking the sleeping villages unaware, Mackenzie's attempt at surprise met with only partial success. By one account, the soldiers' presence was detected by an Indian chief. Although killed in the early moments of the fight, Comanche leader Red Warbonnet got off a warning shot. Another version has Mackenzie's column being spotted by an Indian sentry who yelled, fired his weapon, and disappeared. Whoever fired the warning shot, few Indians except perhaps some in the first village, seemed to pay much attention to it. Sweeping down the rim, Mackenzie's troops charged along the floor of the canyon, racing through and destroying the Comanche village. The shock and chaos of the assault on the first cluster of Comanche lodges spread instant panic through the other villages. Lodges were abandoned and flight began almost immediately as large numbers attempted to escape Mackenzie's trap and reach the open Plains. Few succeeded. Though Mackenzie's troops were subjected to sniping fire from the canyon walls, resistance was scattered and ineffectual. By nightfall Mackenzie's soldiers had taken the five villages and destroyed their contents. More than 2,000 Indian ponies were captured. About 1,450 were eventually shot to prevent them from falling back into Indian hands. In the aftermath, the scene was one of complete devastation. In addition to horses, camp paraphernalia and the Indians' entire winter food supply were destroyed.

The casualties at Palo Duro Canyon were remarkably light. Mackenzie lost only one soldier. Overwhelmed almost immediately, only three Indians were killed. Still, the defeat was total. The loss at Palo Duro Canyon along with unrelenting military pressure from several directions decided the campaign. Dismounted and hungry, pursued incessantly, within a month large numbers of Indian bands began returning to their reservations. When Quannah Parker's band surrendered the following summer, the Red River War was officially over.

Mackenzie returned to Fort Sill in Indian Territory after the clash at Palo Duro Canyon. Ironically, many of the Indians from the Palo Duro encampments were initially interred there. Frustrated with the reservation system and the deplorable conditions he found, Mackenzie ordered his soldiers to build houses for the Indians and, despite objections from the Indian Bureau, issued rations from military stores to the internees.

By most accounts, the Fort Sill Indians respected Mackenzie and understood and appreciated his attempts to feed, clothe, and house them. At the same time, as some historians have noted, they knew this was the officer who had pursued them relentlessly. Thus, while they may have welcomed his compassion, it is likely that their feelings of appreciation were also tinged with fear.

While at Fort Sill, Mackenzie suffered a near-fatal accident, striking his head after a fall from a wagon. Mackenzie remained in a near-coma for two or three days. The severity of the accident has led many to conjecture that the fall contributed to the mental problems that afflicted Mackenzie a few years later.

In 1873, in the interregnum between the battles at the North Fork and Palo Duro Canyon, Mackenzie was posted to Fort Clark, near Brackettville, with orders to stop the theft of livestock from Texas ranches by Indians raiding across the border from Mexico. On May 18, in an extralegal excursion (several sources make it fairly certain that this and later raids had the tacit – or more – approval of President Grant and Mackenzie's superior officer, Lieutenant General Philip Sheridan), Mackenzie struck across the border into Coahuila, Mexico.

In January 1873, Grant had realigned U.S. forces along the border and warned that the Mexican government would be held responsible for the persistent and at times devastating Indians raids coming across the Rio Grande. In addition to killings and kidnappings, the attacks had inflicted an estimated 50 million dollars in property damage to Texans, mostly from attacks on ranches and wagon trains and thefts of horses and cattle.

Finding the raider's village near Remolino, Mackenzie burned it and returned with 40 captives and 65 horses that had been stolen in Texas. Additionally, evidence was found that appeared to show that stolen horses and cattle had been delivered to prominent Mexicans, probably with the collusion of elements in the Mexican government. More importantly, Mackenzie's victory at Remolino showed the raiding Kickapoo and Lipan Apaches that Mexico was no longer a safe haven. The presence of the hostages combined with Mackenzie's aggressive border patrols put an end to the raids.

Mackenzie believed that Mexico's failure to control the Indians along the border was due mainly to internal problems within the Mexican government. He proposed an agreement that would allow troops from both countries to cross the border when in hot pursuit of marauders. Mexico agreed to help stop border incursions, although the full scope of Mackenzie's proposal was not initially enacted. Later, during his duties in Arizona and New Mexico, a more complete arrangement would be reached with Mexican authorities.

Following Custer's defeat at the Little Bighorn in June 1876, Mackenzie was sent north to Camp Robinson in the northwest panhandle of Nebraska. (Camp Robinson would be officially designated a fort in January 1878.) The Great Sioux War was raging and although Wesley Merritt's victory at Warbonnet Creek in July had stopped the flow of Indians leaving reservations to join the warring bands, conditions remained unsettled. Hundreds of hostiles led by Crazy Horse, Sitting Bull, Dull Knife, and other war chiefs were still in the field and posed continuing threats.

After a failed attempt the previous year, in 1876 government commissioners met with representatives for a second time to negotiate a treaty that would relinquish Sioux claims to the Black Hills. In late September, after several days of confusion and disputes, commissioners secured sufficient signatures from the reluctant and sometimes bewildered chiefs to claim dubious title to the Black Hills region.

The negotiation process was hostile from the start; after one particularly angry session an embittered Sioux chief walked out, taking his followers with him. More importantly, after the treaty was signed two influential Indian leaders, Red Cloud and Red Leaf, infuriated by the results, took their followers away from the Red Cloud Agency. Thirty miles from the post, at Chadron Creek, they established new camps and demanded that government rations be delivered to them at those locations rather than at the agency. General

George Crook, department commander, arrived at Camp Robinson in mid-October. Perhaps fearing the precedent and a breakdown in the government's reservation system if the situation was left unaddressed, Crook concluded that the Indians must return to the agency, even if force was required to make them do so. Concerned also that the bands might break away to join the still-hostile groups farther north, Crook determined on immediate action.

On October 22, Mackenzie led a sizable force on a fast-moving night march that took them to the Chadron Creek area. There, close against the hostile camps, eight companies from the 4th and 5th U.S. Cavalry accompanied by 40 Pawnee Scouts waited for daybreak. At sunrise, in a daring and well-conceived strike, the scouts captured the pony herds while four companies of cavalry surrounded each camp.

Both villages surrendered immediately. The firearms of 150 warriors were confiscated along with more than 700 horses. The Indians were taken back to the agency the same day. Women and children and the aged and infirm were permitted to ride. Warriors, marvelous horsemen who practically lived on horseback, were required to walk the entire 30 miles.

As best as can be determined, not a shot was fired; but, for the Indians the defeat was crushing, total, as surely as if bodies had been left strewn on the battlefield.

The effects were felt almost immediately.

Red Cloud from that point resumed his role as an advocate for cooperation and the door was slammed on the possibility that the bands might unite with Crazy Horse or other groups still at war.

A month after his successful raid on the camps along Chadron Creek, Mackenzie moved from Camp Robinson against a large group of hostiles believed to be congregating near present-day Kaycee, Wyoming. Led by Dull Knife and Little Wolf, the band of Northern Cheyenne was thought to number about 400 warriors. With a force of 800 or more consisting of elements of the 2nd, 3rd, 4th, and 5th Cavalry regiments, accompanied by Indian scouts, Mackenzie tracked west into Wyoming Territory. In late November, Pawnee scouts found the Cheyennes along a fork of the Powder River in the southern Bighorn Mountains.

Located in a gorge bounded by towering walls and bisected by a swift, ice-choked river, the Cheyennes set their camp in a relatively open area where the canyon widened out. The site was difficult to approach: the main canyon was further cut by several smaller lateral chasms, each with fast-moving streams that fed the larger river. The Cheyennes considered the place impregnable.

Mackenzie's troopers reached the area of the canyon on the night of the 24th. Moving through the pre-dawn hours of the following morning, their path dimly illuminated by moonlight on the snow-covered ground, Mackenzie timed his approach to arrive at the campsite just before sunrise.

Mackenzie waited, his troopers standing in ranks, holding their horses in the biting cold, then attacked the encampment of 173 lodges at daybreak. Numbering 1,300 inhabitants, the village was home to almost the entire Northern Cheyenne tribe. In bitterly cold weather the initial assault drove some of the warriors, many of whom were ill-clad or naked, into the frozen countryside. Mackenzie's troopers captured the Cheyenne pony herd early in the battle. Soon after, Company A of the 4th Cavalry was sent to prevent the Indians' desperate, nearly successful, attempt to retrieve it. The Cheyennes resisted fiercely and at one point trapped the company in a steep ravine, firing down on it from both sides. As the fighting intensified, Mackenzie first sent one, then two companies into the fray. The relief force charged on foot and the fighting became hand to hand as the struggle continued to escalate. For a time the battle hung in balance as the entire cavalry force was committed to the struggle in the ravine and to other fights around the campsite. Eventually, with the assistance of several of his Indian scouts who provided heavy covering fire from nearby higher ground, Mackenzie's 5th Cavalry troopers rescued their embattled comrades and cleared the ravine, killing about 20 Cheyennes.

Meanwhile, a cavalry company raced through the encampment, eventually taking two hillocks that commanded the immediate battle area. After a difficult struggle Mackenzie's men secured the village, although they were harassed by Cheyenne warriors who fired from nearby rocks and high ground before retreating from the area.

The battle, which became known as the Dull Knife Fight, was prolonged and bitter. Mackenzie lost six killed including the Company A commander, and 26 wounded. Losses among the Northern Cheyenne were put at 25 killed – although it is likely that the actual number was substantially higher – with an additional unspecified number wounded. Mackenzie's troopers torched the lodges and their contents, destroying the Cheyennes' entire winter food supply, and took with them 600-700 captured horses. Among the items found in the village were a 7th Cavalry guidon and other gear taken by Indians who had fought Custer at the Little Bighorn.

The Dull Knife Fight essentially ended major Cheyenne participation in the Great Sioux War, leaving only Crazy Horse's band of Lakota Sioux as the major hostile band continuing to resist the government.

In 1877, Indians resumed cross-border raids from Mexico into south Texas. Major General Edward Ord had already made cross-border forays, but in March 1878, Mackenzie was sent to Fort Clark to help deal with the incursions. As before, he instituted a system of active, far-ranging patrols and in June led an expedition into Mexico. Mackenzie hired a former *Comanchero* who had contacts with the bandits. Carefully gathering intelligence, Mackenzie learned the location and identities of the responsible parties. His major incursion, aimed at causing the Mexican government to take action against the Indians, eventually led to increased cooperation between military units of both nations. By late fall of that year the raids had ceased.

Later, when additional Mexican forces were transferred to the border, coordinated efforts between U.S. and Mexican forces led to the eventual defeat of marauding Apache bands in the 1880s.

In October, again functioning as the Army's trouble-shooter, Mackenzie was sent with six companies of cavalry to the Los Pinos Agency in Colorado. Utes at the agency were refusing to follow the provisions of a recent treaty that required the tribe to move to Utah. Mackenzie averted the threatened uprising by advising the chiefs that the only alternative was war. Two days later, the tribe began its move. Mackenzie regarded the peaceful solution to the Ute controversy, where one wrong move could have led to war, as one of the great achievements of his life.

The final stages of Mackenzie's career as an Indian fighter continued to be crowned with success. In the fall of 1881, he moved with his cavalry to Arizona to command field operations aimed at subduing warring Apaches. In September of that year fighting had again erupted when Apaches killed U.S. cavalrymen at a bloody fight at Cibecue Creek. On September 25, Mackenzie arrived at Fort Apache, having moved his battalion nearly 1,000 miles, mostly by train, from Gunnison, Colorado. Overcoming a convoluted organizational structure, Mackenzie positioned troops at key locations, worked effectively with Mexican authorities, and using techniques perfected elsewhere, rather quickly quelled the modest uprising. In October, after conducting a short but effective campaign, he was reassigned to command the District of New Mexico.

Once again tasked with pacifying Apaches who were launching cross-border raids, as well as with putting down a threatened uprising by restless Navajos, Mackenzie quickly developed good working relationships with Mexican forces. On one occasion, one of his units chased a large band of Apaches into the path of Mexican troops who killed 78 of the Indians. Mackenzie's astute measures defused further incidents. Within a year the Army was firmly in control.

On October 13, 1883, Mackenzie was promoted and assigned to the Department of Texas in San Antonio. His days as an Indian fighter were over.

Within weeks of assuming his post as commander of the Department of Texas, Mackenzie's mental state rapidly deteriorated, perhaps as a consequence of the head injury suffered from the fall at Fort Sill. Others have postulated that his condition was the residual effect of sunstroke and prolonged illnesses suffered as a child. Syphilis has also been mentioned as a possibility. Some modern scholars believe his affliction was the result of the cumulative effects of wounds, years of stress, and fatigue – and that today his mental state would be diagnosed as post-traumatic stress disorder. Whatever the cause, his behavior became increasingly erratic. He was retired from the Army and was placed for a time in an asylum. His death on January 19, 1889, left to history's judgment a military career that was an intriguing blend of harshness and brilliance. Mackenzie's aggressive disposition to wage total war was abetted by his unquestioned personal courage. Counterbalancing his willingness to stretch legalities and invite criticism for his tactics was a record of sustained success on the battlefield.

He is buried at West Point.

Wesley Merritt

O n July 17, 1876 – three weeks after the Little Bighorn – a slender, soft-spoken cavalry officer defeated hundreds of Sioux and Northern Cheyenne attempting to join Crazy Horse, Sitting Bull, and other noted war chiefs. His triumph in a little known and vastly unappreciated battle at Warbonnet Creek, Nebraska, shut off the flow of Indians to the battlefields farther north. Wesley Merritt's victory was the beginning of the end for the Plains Indians. After Warbonnet Creek, they never again prevailed on a major battlefield. By the following summer, the war on the Plains was over.

Wesley Merritt was born in New York City in 1836 and graduated from West Point in 1860, ranked 22nd of 41 in class standing. After initial postings with cavalry units in Utah, he was recalled to Washington, D.C., at the outbreak of the Civil War. He remained there in duties associated with the defense of the city and in aide de camp and adjutant positions until April 1863, when he was named adjutant to the commander of the Army of the Potomac Cavalry Corps. In May, he participated in Stoneman's Raid in fighting around Chancellorsville. Soon after, Merritt was given command of the 2nd Cavalry. He led that unit at the Battle of Brandy Station, the largest cavalry battle of the war, and at the Battle of Upperville. He was cited for his "gallant and meritorious service" in both battles.

In the cavalry reorganization that followed, Merritt was jumped in grade from captain to brigadier general. Collectively, Merritt, along with Elon Farnsworth (later killed at Gettysburg) and George Armstrong Custer, were known to the American public as the "boy generals."

At Gettysburg, Merritt's unit guarded Union lines of communication during the opening phase of the battle and participated in an attack on the Confederate right flank on the final day of combat.

In December 1863, Merritt took command of the 1st Division of the Cavalry Corps and led it during Grant's Overland Campaign. Merritt and his unit saw major action at the Battle of Yellow Tavern, during which Confederate cavalry leader J. E. B. Stuart was killed.

In August 1864, Merritt's division was transferred to General Philip Sheridan's newly formed Army of the Shenandoah and served with Sheridan throughout the Valley Campaign. Sheridan quickly came to respect the young officer and the two of them formed a friendship that lasted throughout their lifetimes. Merritt received a brevet promotion to major general after routing Confederates at the Third Battle of Winchester on September 19, 1864.

As second in command to Sheridan during the Appomattox Campaign that closed the war, Merritt was again cited for bravery at the Battle of Five Forks. He was named as one of the commissioners to oversee the Confederate surrender at Appomattox Court House.

In mid-1865, Merritt was given command of the cavalry forces of the Military District of the Southwest, commanded by Sheridan. In

Public Domain
Wesley Merritt

July of that year he led his cavalry units on a month-long, 600-mile trek from Shreveport, Louisiana, to San Antonio, Texas, where they formed part of the Union's occupation forces in the region. Merritt remained in Texas until mid-1876, serving for a decade as commander of the newly-formed 9th Cavalry, a "Buffalo Soldier" unit charged with tracking down renegades and Indian raiders.

Merritt's connection with the central Plains began on July 1, 1876, when he took command of the 5th Cavalry, engaged in operations in the Panhandle of Nebraska. A few days later, less than a month after Custer's defeat at the Little Bighorn, Merritt and the 5th Cavalry fought and won one of the most significant but little remembered battles in the annals of Great Plains warfare.

Waged near a small stream in extreme northwestern Nebraska, the Battle of Warbonnet Creek came after a series of calamitous defeats inflicted on U.S. military forces sent to quell the massive uprising that had exploded across the Plains. Culminating with the catastrophe at the Little Bighorn, Indians repeatedly battered army units led by some of the nation's most famous commanders.

Custer's defeat at Little Bighorn on June 25, and the defeat of a column led by General George Crook a week earlier on the Rosebud, left the nation thunder-struck. By the standards of Plains warfare, the casualties were staggering. Amid shock and anger came calls for action.

More ominously, as word of Custer's defeat spread through the tribes, hundreds of warriors made preparations to leave their reservations and join the hostile bands on the warpath in the north.

Even before the debacles at Rosebud Creek and the Little Bighorn, Sheridan, concerned by reports of Indians leaving the Red Cloud and Spotted

Tail agencies in northwestern Nebraska, had ordered the 5th Cavalry to move to the region and cut the "feeder-trail" linking the reservations with the Powder River area where large numbers of hostiles were rapidly assembling.

Initial elements of the 5th Cavalry, sent from posts scattered across the central Plains, arrived in Wyoming in early June. Subsequently, at Fort Laramie, eight full companies came together. Soon after, the force moved out to take blocking positions along the Indian trail.

On July 1, as the unit maintained its vigil on the trail, Wesley Merritt took command of the regiment. Colonel Merritt replaced elderly Colonel William Emory, an 1831 graduate of West Point, who retired after having for several years exercised only administrative command of the unit. Operational command in the field was held by Lieutenant Colonel Eugene A. Carr. When Merritt assumed command, he chose to exercise operational as well as administrative control. Carr remained with the unit and fought with it at Warbonnet Creek. During the following campaign and the Battle of Slim Buttes, Merritt commanded the expedition's combined cavalry contingent while Carr led the 5th Cavalry component.

Quiet and unpretentious, noted for his coolness under fire, Merritt was highly regarded, having been brevetted to major general for his exceptional service during the Civil War. Dark-haired, of average height and build, Merritt was clean-shaven early in his military career before allowing himself a modest mustache as he grew more senior in rank. Merritt knew the territory well, having spent several months in the area serving as Cavalry Inspector for the Military Department of the Missouri, serving under department commander Lieutenant General Philip H. Sheridan – duties that enabled him to function as General Sheridan's personal investigator and troubleshooter.

At the 5th Cavalry's main camp northwest of the Red Cloud Agency in Nebraska, brief lulls were broken by intermittent skirmishes as groups of warriors pushed away from the agency. Merritt responded by moving the camp closer to the Indian trail and launching an aggressive series of scouts. The move to the new camp brought with it an added sign of peril: Merritt's soldiers found recently dug rifle pits and the bodies of Black Hills miners killed by the Indians.

Merritt kept his troops at the new campsite for the next several days while patrols scoured the area. Those activities ended on July 12, when Sheridan, apparently responding to General Crook's continued pleas for reinforcements, ordered Merritt to return to Fort Laramie to refit and then to join Crook in northern Wyoming.

The return to Fort Laramie was well under way and the unit was going into camp after a march of 16 miles when Merritt received word from the commander of Camp Robinson that hundreds of Cheyenne were planning to leave the Red Cloud Agency and join the warring bands farther north.

Merritt reacted quickly. Advising Crook and Sheridan of his decision, over the next two days he backtracked 51 miles to a point on the road between Fort Laramie and the Red Cloud Agency. There, he camped the night of July 14. Concluding that a further advance of his entire force toward the agency might provoke a fight before he was ready – and determined to verify the accuracy of the information he had received – Merritt sent a cavalry company to investigate the situation at the agency.

By midday on July 15 he had received word that 800 or more Cheyenne and Sioux led by Chief Little Wolf were planning to leave the agency that day or soon after. Merritt realized that it was crucial to shut off the flow of additional warriors to the hostiles who had already fought the cavalry to a standstill.

Within an hour of receiving the news, Merritt personally led seven cavalry companies deep into northwestern Nebraska. Merritt's goal was to get ahead of the Cheyenne and position himself across their line of march. If he could beat the Cheyenne to the trail, he intended to meet them head on and force them back to the agency.

Time was of the essence. Even if they left on Sunday the 16th, the Indians would need only a 28-mile ride to reach the junction in the trail. Merritt would have to travel three times that distance. To do it, he needed to retrace his path to the north and turn east across the Indians' most likely route. By 10 o'clock that night, Merritt had taken his men 35 miles. After a brief stop to rest and feed the horses, by 5 a.m. they were on the march again.

At midday they reached a palisaded camp along Sage Creek guarded by a company of infantry. There, they rested for an hour, ate a quick lunch, and further lightened their loads. Merritt's cavalrymen broke open ammunition boxes and stuffed their pockets and belts with cartridges.

Merritt decided to leave his heavy supply wagons at Sage Creek and take only light company wagons with three days' rations. Merritt's infantry company was loaded into the bigger wagons and directed to follow and catch up when they could. Their approach toward Warbonnet Creek the next morning would influence events in the battle that followed.

At 8 o'clock that night – July 16th – Merritt's cavalry reached Warbonnet Creek. They had marched 85 miles in 31 hours … and they had beaten the Indians to the vital crossing.

"Buffalo Bill" Cody, the 5th Cavalry's Chief Scout, and his men were posted well out on the eastward flank as Merritt drove his force toward the junction. Cody returned from a reconnaissance that night, assuring Merritt that the Indians were still positioned southeast – between Merritt's troops and the reservation. Large numbers of hostiles were moving towards them, however, and would probably reach the crossing early the next day. Indeed, Little Wolf's Cheyenne, having heard of the battle with Custer, were already on the move, hurrying to add their numbers to the hundreds already on the warpath in Wyoming and Montana. That night they were camped about seven miles southeast of Merritt's men on Warbonnet Creek.

The 5th Cavalry bivouacked in light timber on a small plateau near a line of bluffs. Shielded behind the western slope of the ridges, Merritt's encampment could not be seen by hostiles moving up the trail from the east and southeast. Only a few fires were allowed, and those were dug deep into holes so the flames could not be seen. One entire company was placed on guard duty, positioned in hollows and ravines where they could see objects silhouetted against the sky.

In the pre-dawn hours, details in the landscape began to emerge as the blackness receded. To the west, the lightening sky revealed the rolling hills of the higher ground crossed by the regiment the night before. Immediately to the east, Warbonnet Creek extended across the 5th Cavalry's front in a series of loops and curls that began in the southeast and traversed north before twisting back toward the left edge of Merritt's camp. A portion of the creek to the north was rimmed by a thin, snake-like tree line as the stream bent back and twisted its way to the South Fork of the Cheyenne River. Beyond the creek was a relatively flat area that extended 300 to 400 hundred yards before meeting a series of low ridges that pointed in the direction of the creek. The ridges varied slightly in height and the space between them was flat. In some places, the field of vision from these low spots and from the smaller ridges was obscured by the slightly higher ground on either side.

Merritt's sentinels were placed on two small, sharply pointed hills that formed distinct spikes in the skyline. The southernmost hill was about 90 feet high and 400 yards away from the tree line and ridge that hid the 5th Cavalry. The second hill, not quite as high, was about 100 yards closer to camp.

The knolls provided unobstructed views to the southeast, the direction from which the Indians would most likely come. The trail the Indians would use passed only a short distance to the right of the southernmost knoll. There, it crossed a shallow ravine. As the ravine and the trail wound their ways separately north, the ground between them rose sharply, concealing one from the other.

Merritt had been up since 3:30 a.m., joined within an hour by the entire regiment. In the pre-dawn quiet, the troopers huddled around shielded fires boiling coffee and frying salt pork. Soon, the "Dandy Fifth" was ready to mount up: 330 enlisted men, 16 officers, a doctor, and five scouts including and led by Cody.

At about 4:15, as sentries watched from the top of the tallest hill, several Cheyenne warriors in groups of two or three appeared at the head of a ravine about two miles to the southeast. Merritt came to the knoll with three of his staff, quickly followed by two scouts and about a half dozen cavalrymen.

They were soon joined by Cody, returning from an early morning scout during which he had located the Indians' main camp. The entire group had dismounted behind the hill and crawled to a vantage point at the top, peeking over at the spectacle unfolding before them. Merritt ordered the 5th to saddle up and mount, the order passed quietly from trooper to trooper. Six companies then moved forward, angling south, hidden by the sheltering bluffs as they waited in line only 200 yards from the trail and the ravine crossing.

The Indians, sent by Little Wolf to scout ahead, rode slowly in the direction of the outpost on the hillock and the 5th Cavalry's encampment. Moving in a pattern momentarily inexplicable, a number of warriors suddenly darted halfway up the wall of the ravine and began looking intently to the west. The initial band moving up the draw was soon joined by others. By 5 a.m. dozens of Indians were visible, lining the hillsides a mile and a half away, all fixated by some occurrence out on the western horizon.

The explanation soon became clear. Merritt's supply train – the heavy wagons he had left at Sage Creek – were coming into view as tiny dots far out on the higher ground of the western rim. In a superb logistical feat, after tending his mules and piling infantrymen on top of his supplies, Lieutenant William P. Hall had brought his train ahead on an all-night march. From a distance, with the infantry in the wagons concealed beneath wagon tarps, the Indians likely believed it to be a civilian train bound for the Black Hills, and ripe for picking.

As Merritt and the small group with him watched, several warriors broke away from the main body on a facing ridge. Charging headlong down the slope, the party raced directly towards them at full speed. Again, the observers on the hill were left with no immediate explanation. Again, when it came, the answer lay to the west. Behind them, popping up suddenly over a high point on the prairie, no more than a mile to the southwest, two couriers carrying dispatches to Merritt galloped into view, visible not only to the cavalrymen on the hillock but also to the Cheyenne who were moving swiftly to intercept them. The Indians were not seen by the couriers who, believing Merritt's camp was near, had hurried ahead of the protection of the oncoming supply train. To those on the knoll, it was apparent they would meet near the junction where the trail and the ravine came together.

Contemporary accounts credit Cody with proposing that he, along with two scouts and six troopers, cut the Indians off before they could surprise the couriers. Merritt ordered Lieutenant Charles King, in charge of the sentries on the hill, to signal when the time was right for Cody and his party to burst from cover and confront the fast-approaching Indians.

Staying out of sight, Cody and his men scrambled down the backside of the hill, mounted their horses and, still concealed, rode to a spot near the head of the ravine. There, they waited for the signal from King. When the Cheyennes were about 90 yards away, King signaled for Cody to attack. Cody's party sprang from their hiding place, tore headlong around the shoulder of the bluff and, firing as they rode, charged straight towards the onrushing warriors.

Startled, the Cheyennes momentarily halted and began answering the attack, firing volleys toward Cody and at the hillside outpost. Their leader, Yellow Hair, bent low over his pony's neck, fired a round that narrowly missed Merritt as he ran to join Lieutenant King at the top of the knoll.

Cody's charge carried his squad straight into the advancing Cheyennes. In the melee that followed – an episode still wrapped in controversy – Cody and Yellow Hair engaged one-on-one. Accounts vary as to the nature and duration of the individual combat that resulted in Yellow Hair's death.

The developing clash between Cody's small force and Yellow Hair's Cheyennes caused action to erupt both west and east from the scene of their encounter. Out on the prairie to the west, at the sound of the first volley and with Indians now visible to them, Lieutenant Hall broke out his infantry from under the wagon tarps and deployed them in skirmish position to protect the supply train. To the east, the mass of Indians on the ridge opposite Warbonnet Creek began a dash to the scene of the fight.

The Indians' bid to rescue their colleagues had carried them about halfway across the open ground toward the creek when Merritt ordered the 5th Cavalry to move against them. Sweeping both north and south around the tallest conical hill, three companies – B, K, and I – reached open ground, formed into line, and charged. Line abreast, guidons snapping in the breeze, in a classic cavalry charge – possibly the last in American history – the three veteran companies, about 147 troopers, lit into the oncoming Indians.

Stunned by the sight of the wave of blue about to slam into them, the Cheyenne turned their ponies and took flight. Merritt's cavalry chased the Indians closely for about three miles as the Cheyenne abandoned their possessions and raced in panic to the southeast toward the reservation. Sounds of the battle from Warbonnet Creek and the chase that followed carried to Little Wolf's camp seven miles away. Realizing that their path was now blocked and the goal of joining their allies was no longer attainable, they hurriedly dismantled their village and began the trek back to the Red Cloud Agency, leaving behind several lodges and hundreds of pounds of provisions.

Correctly sensing that the fight had gone out of the Indians, Merritt's directed the cavalry to follow the Cheyenne in a loose pursuit over the next 30 miles, intent mainly on keeping them on the move toward the agencies. Stringing out his forces over an extended front to prevent flanking attempts by groups of hostiles, Merritt's wide net rolled southeastward, folding the mass of Indians within it and keeping them always pointed toward the reservations. There, without further opposition, they arrived that night and the following day.

Losses on both sides were minimal. The 5th's only casualty occurred during the chase when a cavalryman's horse fell down an embankment, injuring the trooper. Several accounts cite the Indians' only loss as Yellow Hair. Others indicate that during the chase, at least six Cheyenne were killed and perhaps another five wounded. Soon after the battle, Eugene A. Carr, who led the 5th Cavalry's charge that morning and participated in the pursuit, wrote to his wife that three Indians were killed.

The next day, July18, Merritt telegraphed the results of the battle to Sheridan in Chicago and to Sherman and the administration in Washington. The same day, the 5th began the trip back to Fort Laramie, arriving there on the 21st. As was usual with Merritt, he did not tarry. The 5th took on supplies and re-shod their horses on the 22nd. At 6 a.m. on July 23, they marched north to join Crook.

Merritt's conduct immediately following the battle was noteworthy. During the Indians' panic-stricken flight, it would certainly have been possible to have killed or maimed them in large numbers. Merritt chose instead to follow and push them back to their agencies. Given that Warbonnet Creek occurred less than a month after the Little Bighorn and the public likely would have supported a more aggressive outcome, his restraint was commendable.

Merritt was initially criticized in some quarters for not immediately responding to Crook's pleas for reinforcement. Time has muted that criticism. Crook continually appealed for additional manpower although he remained static in garrison with more than a 1,000 men – already too many to chase quick moving and rapidly dissolving bands of hostiles. Merritt's victory at Warbonnet Creek prevented large numbers of Cheyenne and Sioux from combining with the hostiles that tormented Crook that summer, and provided far more effective service than joining him quickly in an already cumbersome camp.

Merritt's legacy – and that of the 5th Cavalry – was that for more than a month they blocked the vital trail used by the Indians to reach the hostiles in Wyoming and Montana. Then, when the first major war party headed northwest, the defeat that Merritt and the 5th Cavalry inflicted on them was decisive – both militarily and psychologically. After Warbonnet Creek, the Cheyenne and Sioux made no other significant attempts to leave their agencies and join their allies in combat.

For the military, and the country, Warbonnet Creek played an important role in helping restore morale and confidence. Merritt and his 5th Cavalry outgeneraled, outrode, and outfought a dangerous foe. Their actions turned large numbers of hostiles around, prevented others from joining, and took all of them permanently out of the war. The victory at Warbonnet Creek was, in the words of one scholar, "timely, professionally executed, and desperately needed."

After the fight at Warbonnet Creek, Merritt moved north with Crook and on August 3 joined General Alfred Terry. For a time the two columns merged and moved generally eastward with more than 4,000 men. After Terry split off, dispatching units in an attempt to prevent hostiles from reaching Canada, Crook's contingent continued a difficult trek toward the Little Missouri. Crook stripped his force of non-essentials, attempting to travel fast and light. Their grueling, controversial pursuit was maintained in the face of horrific weather. In its latter stages the expedition, with Merritt leading the combined cavalry division – 10 companies of the 5th Cavalry, five companies of the 2nd Cavalry, and 10 companies of the 3rd Cavalry – was reduced to half rations supplanted by mule and horse meat from cavalry mounts "played out" by starvation and exhaustion.

In early September, 150 troops dispatched on a supply replenishment mission ran into a Sioux village near present-day Reva, South Dakota. The troops surrounded the village, located near a geologic feature called "Slim Buttes," and attacked at dawn on September 9, inflicting several casualties.

Indian survivors made contact with Crazy Horse who, with 600-800 warriors, moved quickly toward the destroyed village. In the meantime, Crook's full contingent, the 5th Cavalry, along with various other cavalry, infantry, and artillery units – totaling slightly more than 1,000 combatants – arrived on scene.

During the fight at Slim Buttes, Merritt's troops pushed the Indians initially from the high ground and, ultimately, from the field. Later, he took command of the entire expedition, guiding it back to Fort Robinson, as Crook departed for other duties.

While Warbonnet Creek shut down the flow of Indian reinforcements, the victory at Slim Buttes was the first for government forces over hostile groups who were in the field at the time of the Little Bighorn. Merritt's leadership played a vital role in each triumph. In the turbulent history of warfare on the Great Plains both battles were significant. By the middle of the following year, Crazy Horse, leading one of the last major hostile groups, surrendered at Camp Robinson, Nebraska.

Aside from his achievements at Warbonnet Creek and Slim Buttes, Merritt's most notable service on the Plains took place three years later during the Ute War of 1879. In early October of that year, he led a relief force of 250 troopers of the 5th Cavalry on a 170-mile forced march to rescue 200 or more soldiers trapped and besieged after a six-day battle with Utes along the Milk River in northern Colorado. Merritt's march, from Fort D. A. Warren near Cheyenne, Wyoming, would in later years be studied for the speed and consummate professionalism with which it was conducted. Merritt's timely arrival on scene prompted the surrender of the Ute Chief and essentially ended the war.

Merritt served on the frontier until 1882 when he was named Superintendent of West Point. He held that post until 1887.

Merritt is sometimes credited with inaugurating the Army's first war game maneuvers. He was an advocate for continuing professional education for the officer corps.

In April 1887, Merritt was promoted to brigadier general and assigned as Commander of the Department of the Missouri. In 1889, he accompanied troops to present-day Oklahoma to help maintain order during the land rush that opened the territory to settlers.

With the outbreak of the Spanish-American War, Merritt was given command of the U.S. Army's VIII Corps. After Admiral George Dewey defeated the Spanish fleet at Manila Bay, Merritt's forces took the city in August 1898. Merritt served briefly as military governor of the Philippines and later advised the U.S. commissioners who negotiated the Treaty of Paris that ended the war.

Merritt retired from the Army in 1900. Like his contemporary, Eugene A. Carr, he died in 1910 and was buried at West Point.

Nelson A. Miles

F ew combat leaders during the nation's Indian wars fought on so many battlefields or over such varied landscapes as Nelson Miles. Fewer still did so with more consistent success. On fields of strife across Texas, the central and northern Plains, Arizona, and the Pacific Northwest, Miles led U.S. Army forces to an uninterrupted string of victories.

Miles was born in 1839 on a farm near Westminster, Massachusetts. For a time in his youth, he worked as a clerk in a crockery store. Unlike the majority of his army contemporaries, Miles did not attend a military academy. Rather, on his own initiative, he secured military instruction from a former officer in the French army. His service during the Civil War was noted for its extent and for his personal heroism. With the Army of the Potomac, he fought at Fair Oaks, Antietam, Fredericksburg, Chancellorsville, the Wilderness, Spotsylvania, Petersburg, and the closing campaign at Appomattox – all of the Army of the Potomac's major battles except Gettysburg (when he was recovering from wounds). Miles was wounded four times and eventually received the Medal of Honor for his actions at Chancellorsville.

For a short time immediately following the war, Miles commanded the District of Fort Monroe where he supervised the incarceration of Confederate President Jefferson Davis. Miles drew criticism for having for a time placed Davis in shackles.

Miles was known as a highly competent, innovative combat leader with unquestionable personal courage. Some biographers have commented that unlike many successful military commanders, Miles actually *looked* like a hero. Tall and muscular with broad shoulders, intense blue eyes and a jaunty mustache, he cut a dashing figure.

There were, however, episodes during the course of his long and remarkable service that temper his legacy. There were, for example, lifelong feuds with other senior officers about who should receive credit for victories to which each of them had contributed. There were later questions about credit withheld from a deserving subordinate and about the handling of a peace agreement. Later still, at Wounded Knee, there were disputed murmurs that his aggressiveness as overall director of operations may have contributed to the violent outcome.

To many, Miles seemed an abrasive personality. Although grade reductions and restorations of permanent ranks were pro forma during the Army's massive drawdown after the Civil War, he was vocally indignant about his reduced rank. (Miles was promoted to colonel in the Regular Army in 1866. He had been advanced to brevet major general during the war.) By some accounts, he was unabashed in his efforts to accelerate his own advancement. Married to the niece of General William T. Sherman and the governor of Ohio, he was not above appealing directly to them as well as to President Ulysses S. Grant for assistance with his career. Vain and ambitious, he spoke openly about his own aspirations for high political office. Because of his political networking, Miles was not well liked by many of his senior officer colleagues. He was, however, popular in the ranks and well-respected by his troops who recognized his obvious competence and valued his experience.

Brands Studio, Public Domain
Nelson A. Miles

Miles's service after the Civil War was almost entirely on the nation's frontier. He saw action on battlefields that extended from the plains of Texas westward across the continent.

In the Red River or Buffalo War of 1874-75, a conflict primarily aimed at forcing belligerent Kiowa, Comanche, and Cheyenne bands onto government agencies, Miles led a mixed unit of cavalry and infantry from Fort Leavenworth, Kansas, to the Texas Plains. Miles' force was one of five columns that pressured the warring bands and, aided by Ranald Mackenzie's victory against Comanches in the Battle of Palo Duro Canyon, forced their surrender.

On the northern Plains, the early months of 1876 brought a string of defeats to the U.S. Army that culminated in the disaster at the Little Bighorn. Along with other units sent from distant locations, Miles and the 5th Infantry were called from Kansas as the Army attempted to regain the initiative.

Major goals of the campaign were to bolster the garrisons at each Indian agency and establish a permanent presence on the Yellowstone River. Like the Republican River in the central Plains, the Yellowstone area was of special importance to the nomadic tribes. The region's grass, water, and plentiful buffalo provided shelter and sustenance to the warring groups. Now, aroused by several victories and led by legendary war chiefs, thousands of Lakota

Sioux and Northern Cheyenne warriors waited along the Yellowstone and its tributaries for the Army's arrival.

Miles, with six companies of the U.S. 5th Infantry, arrived in the area in early August aboard the steamer *E. H. Durfee*. Initially given command of a 10-company wing of a large expedition under the overall command of General Alfred Terry, Miles remained with the massive force for only a short time. On August 10, Terry's column met with that of General George Crook coming up from the south. The two units moved together for a time but the 4,000-man combined force was too large for tracking, chasing, and fighting small, fast-moving bands of hostiles.

Miles was soon released to return to the Rosebud Creek area. Transported from there downriver on the steamer *Far West* he, along with Colonel Elwell S. Otis, established posts along the Tongue River where that stream emerges from the Yellowstone. The cantonments – on the north bank of the Yellowstone, at the mouth of the Powder River, and at O'Fallon's Creek (later moved to the Glendive Creek area) – covered major fords and were intended to keep hostiles from using them as escape routes. Miles also kept a company aboard the *Far West* as a floating, mobile reserve.

Miles quartered the bulk of his troops at an extensive camp on the Tongue River. From there he headed up four major expeditions against the Sioux. Aimed at ultimately driving the hostile bands back to the agencies, Miles's sorties pursued the Indians relentlessly, destroying provisions and keeping the hostiles constantly on the move.

From the Tongue River, Miles struck one of the campaign's first successful blows. When a replenishment wagon train failed to reach his encampment as expected, he put the 5th Infantry on the march. Moving down the Yellowstone, his troops found the train besieged by Sitting Bull's warriors. Miles' soldiers rescued the train and then followed Sitting Bull's band as the Indians moved north.

At Cedar Creek on October 21, Miles destroyed Sitting Bull's village in a battle conducted in textbook fashion. Miles assigned five companies as skirmishers across a broad front, skillfully deployed three others as reserves, and made exceptional use of two artillery pieces. Two additional companies shielded the artillery and guarded the supply train. The Sioux were likely surprised by the accurate, sustained firepower of well-trained infantry equipped with long-range Springfield rifles. Though heavily outnumbered, Miles' troopers pressed the attack, forcing the Sioux back. Several strong counterattacks led by Gall and other war chiefs eventually failed after heavy fighting. Before scattering, the Sioux attempted to set fire to the prairie. When that failed they fled, abandoning their camp, which Miles quickly burned.

By this time the massive coalition of Indian forces that had fought on the Little Bighorn had dispersed into smaller, but still lethal, bands. The scattering of the hostile groups changed the nature of the Great Sioux War. Campaigns were now characterized by multiple operations against separated bands moving across a landscape so immense it was called the "Big Open" by the Native tribes.

In early November, Miles returned briefly to Tongue River to resupply before moving back north to the Missouri River. To more effectively scour the countryside, Miles separated the 5th Infantry into three independent commands. On December 18, one of those columns – three companies commanded by Lieutenant Frank Baldwin – caught Sitting Bull's Hunkpapa Sioux on Ash Creek near the Yellowstone divide. Sitting Bull's village of about 120 lodges was again destroyed as were many of the band's horses and mules. Bereft of food, shelter, and supplies, Sitting Bull's military strength was effectively destroyed. Not long after, wary of the Army's persistent aggressiveness even in the face of horrific weather conditions, he took his followers to Canada and removed himself from the war.

It had long been Miles' contention that if Sitting Bull and Crazy Horse – the charismatic leaders of the warrior bands – were defeated, the scope of the Native uprising would be materially diminished if not ended entirely. Now, having dispatched Sitting Bull, Miles set his sights on Crazy Horse.

Late in 1876, with Crook still in the field and Ranald Mackenzie having defeated Dull Knife and the Northern Cheyenne at the Battle of Red Fork of the Powder River, Miles learned of Crazy Horse's presence along the Wolf Mountains. On December 29, Miles took seven companies and artillery in pursuit, moving southwest through the Tongue River Valley. His men were superbly equipped for the arctic-like conditions. Blankets had been cut up for underwear; buffalo overcoats had been issued as had overshoes, leggings, woolen face masks, and fur caps and gloves. Miles forced a relentless pace, tracking hostiles who had been pillaging near the cantonment, believing that the raiders would lead him to Crazy Horse and the main encampment of Sioux and Northern Cheyenne.

However, by contemporary accounts, Crazy Horse had apparently envisioned the raiders as a decoy party intended to lure Miles away from his post and into an ambush – a reprise of the ploy used in the Fetterman Massacre along the Bozeman Trail a decade earlier.

As events unfolded, the ambush plan went awry when, on January 7, 1877, a handful of scouts sent ahead by Miles captured a small group of Indians along the suspected route to Crazy Horse's camp. In a subsequent attempt to rescue the captives, the decoy party launched a premature attack, striking the troopers before Crazy Horse and the main body of warriors were on hand to fully spring the trap.

Although the major components on neither side had reached the scene, the preliminary battle on January 7 was hotly contested. Jumped by 40-50 warriors hidden in brush, the scouts sought refuge in a thin line of timber a few hundred yards distant, having two horses shot from under them along the way. Making barricades of fallen trees and boulders, the outnumbered scouts fought off several attempts to rush and overwhelm their position. As the shooting grew more intense, additional numbers of Indians, likely 100 or more, joined in the attack, taking up positions in surrounding rocks and on nearby hillsides.

At the sound of firing, Miles, camped a short distance away, sent an infantry company and an artillery piece to relieve the besieged scouting party. Heavy small arms fire persisted for an hour or more before shells from Miles' artillery piece induced the Indians to break off their attack and begin a slow retreat. By nightfall, the valley was quiet and the scouts and the relief force sent by Miles had returned safely to camp.

After leaving the main cantonment in late December, traveling through periodic snow flurries and temperatures that sometimes reached 30 degrees below zero, Miles had brought his 436-man force to a horseshoe bend in the Tongue River. His troops were making an early camp there when the fighting began between the scouts and the decoy party.

Miles had chosen excellent defensive ground for his encampment. The horseshoe configuration of the river shielded the camp on three sides. To the southwest, a plateau topped by a small knoll – later to be known as Battle Butte – provided a mostly unobstructed view of the valley

After sending troops to assist the scouts, Miles had formed skirmish lines that wrapped the bivouac site in a protective ring. When the shooting ended at dusk, Miles – anticipating a possible assault on the camp the following day – put two full companies on guard duty along the projected line of attack.

Miles' premonition was correct: Crazy Horse did indeed attack the following day, although the assault did not come completely from the quadrant he anticipated.

Crazy Horse, unaware that the decoy party had already skirmished with elements of Miles' force, planned to follow the Tongue River to within a few miles of the army camp, where the force would split. Half of the 800 warriors, mostly Northern Cheyennes, would cross the river, use the hills to mask their approach, and move against the soldiers' encampment from the south. Crazy Horse with his 400 Lakotas would continue along the river and attack from the west.

Believing an assault would come entirely from that direction, Miles sent Company E, 5th Infantry to the high, unobstructed ground on Battle Butte. The 80-foot sheer face on the west side of the butte would channel any frontal assault to a quarter-mile wide opening between the butte and a line of bluffs north of the camp. To cover that gap, Miles placed Company K, 5th Infantry in a group of cottonwood trees along the river bank.

Apparently thinking they had achieved surprise, Crazy Horse and his Lakota warriors streamed along the northern bank of the river, making no attempt at concealment as they neared Miles' fortifications. Miles, though, had his force up at 4 a.m., and had immediately sent out scouts to scour the area, a task made more difficult by more the three feet of recently fallen snow.

Despite the cold and the masking snow cover, Miles' veteran contingent of scouts detected Crazy Horse's advance and raced back to warn the camp. Miles quickly rode to the Battle Butte plateau where, through field glasses, he watched Crazy Horse's large force move through the foothills west of the cantonment.

Miles later commented on an interesting aspect of the battle: many of the Indians dismounted and fought the battle on foot, forming firing lines a few hundred yards from Company K's position in the cottonwoods.

Miles quickly positioned his units to receive the attack. Pointing with a small stick that he carried with him through the battle, he sent Company A, 5th Infantry and some mounted infantrymen to join the company and artillerymen already stationed on Battle Butte, then shifted his two artillery pieces to the northwestern edge of the plateau. He next sent two additional companies to support Company K, now heavily dug in among the cottonwoods. On the opposite river bank, Company E, 22nd Infantry, moved to Company K's left. On the right, on the south bank near the supply wagons, Miles posted Company F, 22nd Infantry. Two companies, C and D of the 5th Infantry were kept in reserve inside the horseshoe formed by the bend in the river.

Miles' dispositions were timely and well-conceived. At around 7 a.m., the Indians' initial assault, mounted by Lakotas and Cheyennes in large numbers led by Crazy Horse, struck Company K's entrenched positions in the trees along the river. The heavy attack was thrown back by Company K's riflemen, supported by Companies E and F on the flanks and well-placed artillery rounds from the cannons atop Battle Butte.

Driven back by intense fire, the Indians retreated into the nearby hills, regrouped, and charged again. The second of several subsequent assaults struck the far eastern extremity of Company K's position in an attempt to collapse the line and force the unit to retreat across the river. Each attempt was blown apart by heavy rifle fire and shells from Miles' artillery.

Fighting near Company K's section lasted through the early morning. Eventually, Crazy Horse shifted his attack still farther east, occupying bluffs that overlooked portions of Miles' camp. Covering fire from the heights enabled groups of warriors to cross the river and move through the valley to high ground southeast of the campsite.

While the battle raged to the west, a group of 400 or more Indians, mostly Northern Cheyennes led by Medicine Bear, crossed from the north bank of the frozen river and moved toward the hills south of Battle Butte. Their approach was seen by the Company E commander atop the plateau who shifted his line, extending it from the center of the mesa and wrapping it amid rugged outcroppings along the southwestern edge. The rocks in the sector formed a natural barricade from which Miles' riflemen met Medicine Bear's approach with volley fire aided by artillery support.

As the Indians pressed forward, Company E shifted to the southern base of the knoll to meet the attack. Medicine Bear's assault now reached a key point: if the Indians overran the defending company, Miles' troops and his artillery positions elsewhere north on the plateau would be exposed to attack with little cover. Miles was now ringed in on three sides: Medicine Bear's warriors pressed forward from the south while others under Crazy Horse held the valley to the northwest and, after crossing the river east of the camp, now controlled a line of bluffs to the southeast.

With the nearest assistance several hundred miles away, Miles boldly took the offensive. First taking on the most ominous threat, he sent Company A against the large numbers of warriors now gathered on three ridges arrayed one behind the other about a quarter of a mile from his post on Battle Butte and pulled his two reserve companies to positions on the plateau.

Company A moved over mostly open ground to attack the ridge line 400 yards distant. Clad in heavy buffalo coats as protection against the bitter cold, the skirmish line trod across snow-covered ground, pressing their attack while taking fire from Indians shooting down from the heights.

The company's determined attack cleared the first of the three ridges, smaller by half than the two immediately in back of it. However, the company's follow-on attack on the two higher ridges eventually stalled, the victim of numbers, natural obstacles, and exhaustion. Miles saw the attack losing momentum and sent Company D, 5th Infantry to reinforce the assault.

After crossing the valley floor, Company D moved to the left of the embattled company already fighting on the ridge and continued up the face to the second, taller hill. Meeting fierce resistance, the troops slowly inched their way up the steep, icy ridge.

As D Company struggled their way up the hill, an unusual episode took place that influenced the future of the battle. In an attempt to rally the warriors fighting on the ridges, Big Crow, a prominent, much-venerated Northern Cheyenne medicine man, began to dance atop the third, highest ridge. Clad in vivid red, he believed himself immune from harm by the soldiers' rifles. For a considerable time, fully exposed to fire, Big Crow did indeed seem to be impervious to injury. Eventually, however, shells from two troopers firing from 200 yards away struck him and he fell mortally wounded in the snow. The loss of their medicine man seemed to dishearten many of the Northern Cheyenne warriors, some of whom began to drift away from the battlefield.

The fighting ebbed for only a moment, however. Crazy Horse, after circling around the fighting in the northern part of the valley and crossing the river east of the soldiers' camp, led a ferocious attack that threatened to overwhelm the soldiers on the ridge. Rallying about 300 Lakotas, he boldly struck at the two embattled companies. Moving over a terrain feature that connected the two ridges, Crazy Horse's assault carried to within 50 yards of D Company's forward line.

Again the battle hung in the balance. Although fighting continued to the north around K Company's entrenchments in the cottonwoods and in the south where Medicine Bear's men moved against Battle Butte, Miles saw that the two companies – A and D – struggling on the ridge were in jeopardy. Indeed, his entire force would be threatened unless Crazy Horse's Lakotas could be driven from the third ridge. Miles committed his last reserve unit, Company C, to the fight.

Instead of launching C Company to directly reinforce the troops already engaged on the ridges, Miles sent it straight at the third ridge. The C Company commander took his unit to the base of the ridge and then ordered his men to charge. Although the commander's horse was shot out from under him, the company moved inexorably up the hill under heavy fire.

As Company C fought its way up the ridge, troopers found a drainage runnel that provided access to the Lakotas fighting on the connecting ground between the second and third ridges. At this point, 500 combatants were mixed in a desperate struggle that lasted through the morning. The Indians fiercely held their ground before continued pressure from the advancing troopers caused them to fall back to positions along the crest of the third ridge. There, concealed among jagged outcroppings, fallen trees, and hidden ravines, they established a formidable redoubt and held the advancing troops at bay with plunging fire from their Winchester and Sharps rifles.

The warriors' strong fortification and heavy, sustained fire was visible from Miles' command post on Battle Butte. Miles ordered the position shelled by his two artillery pieces. Explosions in the rocks and timber eventually began to take a toll, causing the Indians to begin a slow retreat off the ridge and into the valley. Their withdrawal was orderly and well-conducted: the warriors periodically halted, reformed their firing lines, and continued the battle against the advancing troops.

The Army pressed the pursuit for about an hour. Around noon, heavy snow began to fall. With visibility increasingly poor, his troops exhausted, ammunition low, and the Indians moving away from the battlefield, the chase was called to a halt.

As the weather rapidly deteriorated into blizzard conditions, warriors fighting Miles' troops in the north along the cottonwoods by the river and in the south close to Battle Butte also withdrew from the area, using the blinding snowfall to shield their retreat. After five intense hours of combat, the battle was over.

Despite the large numbers of combatants and the enormous expenditure of ammunition by both sides, the casualties were fairly light. One soldier was killed on the scene, another later died of wounds, and seven others were wounded. The extent of Indian losses is uncertain

The next day Miles led a six-company reconnaissance in force through the valley along the Indians' line of retreat. Carcasses of dead horses were found as were numerous pools of blood congealed on the frozen ground. The pools marked locations where the Sioux and Cheyenne wounded had been dragged through the snow. Miles noted that the blood trails continued for five miles.

Crazy Horse's retreat took him and his followers toward the Bighorn Mountains 70 miles to the south. In the midst of a Montana winter, it was an inhospitable place with little game, marginal shelter, and implacable Crow enemies. Losses in supplies and ammunition precluded Crazy Horse and his Sioux and Cheyenne followers from resuming their attacks.

Wolf Mountain and similar clashes subsequently affirmed General Philip Sheridan's conviction – firmly shared by Miles – that the best way to defeat the wide-ranging Plains Indians was to wage war year-round, including, most particularly, campaigning through the deep winter months when the Indians were in semi-permanent camps, food was scare, and the pony herds were weak.

Later, the significance of the battle would become fully apparent: Wolf Mountain was Crazy Horse's final attempt to wage offensive warfare against the U.S. Army. Four months later, in May, he surrendered with 800 followers and 2,000 ponies at Camp Robinson, Nebraska.

By April 1877, Minneconjou Sioux Chief Lame Deer and his followers were regarded as the most threatening band of hostiles still at large. Lame Deer had sworn never to surrender.

Miles now made Lame Deer his personal focus. Difficult tracking through the Tongue River Valley to Rosebud Creek and subsequently down a small tributary today called Lame Deer Creek, brought Miles and his troopers to Lame Deer's village. Miles attacked the 60 lodges at dawn on May 7, killing Lame Deer and several others and destroying the Minneconjou's pony herd.

Except for the few scattered survivors of Lame Deer's camp, after Miles' victory warring bands almost entirely disappeared from the "Big Open." Through the summer and fall of 1877, Miles coordinated what in a later time would be called "search and destroy" missions, keeping independent columns on constant move through the region. On July 3, the last shots in the war were exchanged when one of Miles' detached units traded fire with a small band of Sioux.

By September, the remainder of Lame Deer's band turned themselves in at the Spotted Tail Agency in Nebraska. The Army, well equipped, adequately provisioned, highly mobile, striking regardless of terrain or weather conditions, had at long last adopted a strategy that led to victory. The Native bands, weary, hungry, and suffering, were now all in Canada or on reservations. Across the "Big Open" there remained only abandoned campsites. The Great Sioux War was over.

The end of the war brought little respite for Miles and the 5th Infantry. Violence had flared that summer in the Northwest, where portions of the Nez Perce tribe objected to General Oliver O. Howard's demand that they move to government agencies. Evading Howard's pursuit, the tribe had engaged on a legendary trek. Led by Chief Joseph and others, their journey had brought them all the way from their homeland near Wallowa Valley, Oregon, across Idaho and Montana Territories. By the end of September, after several battles and narrow escapes, they were only 40 miles from Canada and safety.

Lagging behind in the chase, on September 12 General Howard had sent a message to Miles at Fort Keogh, Montana, asking for his assistance. Miles received Howard's note on September 17 and left the following day with a force of 520 soldiers, civilian employees, and scouts.

Moving northwest, diagonally with the Nez Perce's anticipated line of march, Miles took his mixed cavalry/infantry force on a rapid 160-mile march toward the Canadian border. On September 29 in the midst of a heavy snow storm, scouts found the Indians' trail. The following day, north of the Bear Paw Mountains along Sand Creek, they located their encampment.

Fearing that the tribe would resume their flight, Miles moved out at 2:30 in the morning. As his column approached the village he ordered an attack, sending a battalion of the 2nd Cavalry – about 160 troopers – to assault the camp. A battalion of the 7th Cavalry, with 100 troopers, was assigned to follow the 2nd Cavalry's charge and support the attack. The remainder of Miles' force, about 145 mounted infantrymen from the 5th Infantry, followed in reserve bringing with them a cannon and the pack train. First at a trot, then at a gallop, and finally at an all-out charge, the first wave of cavalry raced toward the fortified camp.

Believing they had eluded Howard and not anticipating Miles' approach, the Nez Perce were resting prior to making a final, short push into Canada. Only minutes before the attack, Nez Perce scouts detected Miles's column advancing toward the village. The Nez Perce were among the most militarily proficient of all the Native tribes; despite the brief warning time, warriors responded quickly and well. From rifle pits, rugged ground, and a ravine near the ridge traversed by the cavalry, they rose up and fired on the onrushing horsemen. Renowned throughout the region as superb marksmen, their steady fire killed and wounded several soldiers, forcing the first-arriving company to withdraw about 250-300 yards. Two other companies then struck at the front and were similarly repulsed by Nez Perce firing from behind a near-vertical embankment.

Miles then sent two dismounted companies of the 7th Cavalry and his infantry units to occupy high ground and form a fighting front. By about 3 p.m. all was in place for an attack by the combined force. The attack, against well-conceived barricades manned by skilled fighters, was thrown back with heavy losses. By nightfall on September 30, Miles had lost 18 dead and 48 wounded. The Nez Perce were thought to have lost 22 warriors killed including three of the most prominent leaders. They had also lost much of their horse herd, captured by Miles's scouts and a small unit of cavalry around the time of the initial attack.

Both sides fortified their positions during the snow and bitter cold of the night that followed. Nez Perce dug shelters for the women and children and rifle pits that covered all approaches to the camp, which measured about 250 yards along each side in a nearly square configuration. The rifle pits were manned by about 100 warriors each armed with three or more weapons – largesse from successful encounters during their epic march.

By now, Miles had the camp surrounded. Rather than storming the village and subjecting his troops to further lethal fire from the well-positioned defenders, he shifted tactics and placed the encampment under siege. Miles' 12-pounder Napoleon cannon arrived that evening and the following morning Miles began shelling the village.

Fitful negotiations began fairly soon but agreement was not initially forthcoming. Shelling continued through October 3, but the Nez Perce were well dug in and the firing, though prolonged, did little physical damage. Psychologically, however, the pounding may have exacted a toll; apparently at about that time many of those inside the besieged camp began to despair of their circumstances.

Their prospects were further dimmed with the arrival of General Howard and an advance force in the evening of October 4. Howard, the senior officer on the field, allowed Miles to retain tactical control of the siege.

Miles agreed with Howard's suggestion that two friendly Nez Perce accompanying his column be sent to the village to plead for an end to the fighting. On October 5 at 8 o'clock in the morning, firing ceased as the envoys made their way into the camp. This time, with the Nez Perce cold, hungry, and having lost most of their horses, Chief Joseph agreed to surrender – an occasion immortalized by his words, "From where the sun now stands, I will fight no more forever."

Chief Joseph's agreement covered only that portion – a substantial majority – of the Nez Perce tribesmen that were directly affiliated with him. Altogether 431 Nez Perce – 79 men, 178 women, and 174 children –

surrendered or were captured by Miles' troops. Another smaller group, led by White Bird, did not surrender and managed to slip through Army lines and reach Canada. Miles' scouts reported that the soldiers had captured more than 1,500 horses during the course of the battle.

Miles provided food and blankets to the Nez Perce and promised Chief Joseph that the tribe would be allowed to return to reservations in their homeland. Over the forceful objections of Miles and Howard, General William T. Sherman, Commanding General of the United States Army, overruled that decision. Instead, the Nez Perce were first sent by train to Fort Leavenworth, Kansas, and later to Indian Territory (present-day Oklahoma). They were eventually allowed to return to the Pacific Northwest in 1885.

Although some sources place the figures higher, total losses from the five-day siege are thought to number 21 soldiers killed and a substantial number of additional wounded of whom three died later. Most of the casualties occurred during the cavalry charge on the first day of fighting. Nez Perce losses are not known with certainty, but probably numbered about 25 killed, including several of the tribe's most prominent leaders, with another 50 or 60 wounded.

Miles was effusive in his praise of the Nez Perce warriors, describing the fight at Bear Paw Mountain as the fiercest of any Indian battle he had ever been involved in. His view that the Nez Perce movement was unequalled in the history of Indian warfare was shared by several others. General Sherman stated that the Nez Perce "fought with almost scientific skill, using advance and rear guards, skirmish lines and field fortifications."

The war's aftermath was not without controversy. Although Colonels John Gibbon and Samuel Sturgis had also led forces pursuing the Nez Perce, Miles and Howard precipitated an argument that lasted the rest of their lives about which of them should receive credit for Chief Joseph's surrender.

Miles' Nez Perce expedition was noted for his pioneering work with heliograph communications. A decade later in the Southwest his adroit use of signal mirrors to communicate over long distances – a facility acquired from his experience against the Nez Perce – would play a role in the campaign against Geronimo's Apaches.

On April 28, 1886, Miles arrived in the Southwest to replace General George Crook as commander of U.S. forces in the region. Hostilities had resumed on May 17 of the previous year when Geronimo with about 35 warriors and 100 or so followers fled the San Carlos Reservation in Arizona. Over the next several months of fitful encounters, promises of surrender made and broken, and extended chases over rugged country along the border and into Mexico, Geronimo raided settlements, stole livestock, and killed 75 American citizens, 10 soldiers, 12 Apaches, and an unknown number of Mexicans.

Crook had relied primarily on Apache scouts in his efforts to track down Geronimo. Miles did not emphasize their use to the same degree. Instead, he posted infantry at key passes and water holes. As in Montana, he made effective use of heliograph equipment placed on mountain tops to communicate over the territory's vast distances. Miles formed a special unit to track Geronimo's band.

Chases, often anti-climactic, covered hundreds of miles and took Miles' special force well across the border. Much of April through August was spent in Mexican territory. After weeks of fruitless efforts, Miles' unit made contact with Geronimo and his followers, now worn down by constant pressure and movement.

In mid-July, Miles sent Lieutenant Charles Gatewood, an Apache speaker knowledgeable of the tribe's customs, to negotiate with Geronimo. On August 24, after an arduous journey, Gatewood found the Apache chief. Despite difficult negotiations and several changes of mind, they reached agreement the following day. Geronimo formally surrendered to Miles on September 4 at a site south of Rodeo, New Mexico, near Apache, Arizona.

Geronimo's surrender brought closure to an epic period in American history. His raids were the last significant guerrilla activity in the United States. Where once thousands of Native warriors roamed and raided the Plains east to west from the Missouri River to the Pacific Coast and north to south from the Canadian to the Mexican border, Geronimo's band at the time of his surrender consisted of 16 warriors, 12 women, and six children.

Miles' actions during and after Geronimo's surrender have sometimes been called into question. By several, but not all, accounts he withheld credit from Captain Gatewood for that officer's role in negotiating the surrender. When Geronimo and his followers were sent to Fort Marion, Florida, the exile group included Apaches who had helped Miles during the conflict. Some versions of the episode have Miles proposing that action or agreeing with it, even though sending them with the hostiles was contrary to an agreement made with them earlier. Crook bitterly opposed the incarceration of the scouts and the resulting enmity between the two men lasted until Crook's death four years later.

In 1890, Miles directed the Army's overall response to the "Ghost Dance" scare then sweeping across the Plains tribes. The Ghost Dance was part of a mystical set of beliefs preached by a Paiute Shaman named Wovoka. Wovoka, also known as Jack Wilson, prophesied that the entire Indian race, living and dead, would be reunited on a regenerated earth free from death, disease, or misery. When that cosmic event occurred, the buffalo would be restored and the white men would disappear. The dance was an important part of the prophecy; the more often it was performed, the sooner the prediction would come to pass. There were variations in the dance ritual. Unique to the Sioux was the belief that Ghost Shirts would protect them from soldiers' bullets.

The Ghost Dance originated in western Nevada among the Paiute tribe. By the spring of 1890 it had reached the Pine Ridge Reservation in South Dakota. The Ghost Dance provoked concern bordering on hysteria from settlers and Indian agents who interpreted the promised disappearance of the white man as a violent threat to their safety.

In response to appeals for protection, the government moved large numbers of additional troops into the region. On December 15, Sitting Bull, a Ghost Dance advocate, was killed during an altercation when tribal police attempted to arrest him.

Amidst confusion and rising tensions the tragedy at Wounded Knee occurred two weeks later. Miles was not at Wounded Knee and not in direct command of forces in the field. He criticized the on-scene commander, Colonel James Forsyth, and later filed charges against him. (Secretary of War Redfield Proctor eventually dropped the charges and exonerated Forsythe.) In later years Miles' harshest critics suggested that his aggressive actions to contain the Ghost Dance scare might have panicked the Lakota Sioux and set in motion the events that culminated in bloodshed. Others find the alleged connection less than distinct. The Wounded Knee aspersions did not prevent Miles' later selection as Commanding General of the United States Army.

Wounded Knee was the last major encounter between government forces and Indians in the United States. The Ghost Dance movement died out soon after. Its demise closed Miles' career as an Indian fighter.

In 1894, after his service in the Indian Wars, Miles directed the 12,000-man force sent by government to put down the Pullman Strike. On October 5, 1895, he was appointed Commanding General of the U.S. Army, a post he held until his retirement as a lieutenant general in 1903. In 1898, he led the U.S. forces that captured Puerto Rico during the Spanish-American War.

Miles' brusque manner made him few friends. Already made uncomfortable – or envious – by his political connections, many of his fellow officers were openly wary. Negative views of Miles' actions and accomplishments expressed by contemporaries, though perhaps animated by their personal discomfort with him, make aspects of Miles' career difficult to assess.

The one sure measure was his consistent success on the battlefield.

Miles died in 1925 in Washington, D.C., and is buried at Arlington National Cemetery.

Frank J. North

Frank North never achieved the highest ranks in the military; never had
overall command of a large force in combat; and there is no single
campaign or battle to which is name is inextricably attached. Yet is his
role on the frontier was often as vital as any senior officer's. North is included
in these pages because he may well have been America's greatest leader of
indigenous forces.

For a 14-year period between 1864 and 1877, North led the Pawnee Scouts,
a unit seldom exceeding 100 – 150 warriors. During the course of dozens of
encounters, North's band established a well-justified reputation as preeminent
scouts, trackers, and fearsome fighters. Fluent in the Pawnee language,
understanding and respectful of the tribe's customs and religion, North was
venerated by the warriors who fought for him.

While various military leaders had used small numbers of Natives as scouts,
none had been constituted as formed units or organized on a quasi-permanent
basis. Although other names have sometimes been mentioned, credit for the
Scouts' formation is most often given to General Samuel R. Curtis. Curtis
had become inadvertently acquainted with Frank North when they shared a
stagecoach journey sometime in the spring or summer of 1864. Impressed by
the young man's experience with the Pawnees and his understanding of military
tactics, Curtis asked him to help form of unit of scouts to assist the Army's
hard-pressed forces during the Great Sioux War of that year. With Curtis's
support, North quickly organized a company of 77 warriors. For the Pawnees,
the opportunity must have seemed like a godsend: the Scouts could roam free of
the reservation and wage war against their historic enemy.

Perhaps because of his youth, North was not initially given command of
the unit, serving instead as second in command to Joseph McFadden, an older
man who, like North, had an affiliation with the Pawnee Agency. The choice
of McFadden to lead the company proved to be unfortunate. McFadden was
little respected by the Pawnee warriors who were generally indifferent to his
instructions.

When results from the Scouts' initial employment in the field were modest
at best, North was given command. He remained in that position for the entire
course of the unit's existence. Initially commissioned as a captain, his obvious

competence and the Scouts' success resulted in his eventual promotion to major. For more than a decade, the Scouts were typically mustered in each year for the course of the fighting season. Then, in a recurring pattern, they would be released and again reassembled the following year.

Early difficulties with supplies and pay when the unit was led by McFadden were resolved under North's stewardship. During the short time under McFadden, the Pawnees had to furnish their own mounts and much of their equipment. Pay was a persistent issue. By contrast, North assured that his men were provisioned with horses, ammunition, saddles, blankets and uniforms (although some preferred to strip to breech-clothes before going into battle). Notably, the Scouts received the same pay as Army soldiers.

Nebraska State Historical Society
Frank J. North

North was born at Ludlowville, New York, on March 10, 1840. Later that same year, the family relocated to Plymouth, Ohio. The Norths remained there until Frank was 16 before moving farther west to Omaha, Nebraska Territory. North's father perished in a blizzard the following spring while leading a survey party. North and an elder brother assumed care of the family and in 1858 moved to Columbus, Nebraska, where North engaged in farming and freighting. After three years he took a job on the Pawnee Reservation near Genoa, Nebraska. North served as the agency's clerk and interpreter, having learned the Pawnee language during his freighting venture, often hauling logs from a nearby sawmill to the reservation. He may have had an initial acquaintance with the Pawnees' Caddo tongue while trapping and trading in the Omaha area while the family resided there.

Ramrod straight, tall and slender at 6 feet 2 inches tall, North earned an early reputation among whites and Natives for reliability and scrupulous honesty. He was widely respected throughout the Pawnee tribe whose leaders over the years made numerous references to the fact that he never told them a lie and never deceived them.

The Scouts' first campaign was generally unproductive. Responding to the massive uprising that shut down hundreds of miles of overland trail, General Curtis pushed a sizable force from Fort Kearny into Native territory. Curtis split his command, sending General Robert B. Mitchell west toward the head of the Solomon River, while he and Colonel Robert R. Livingston moved down the Solomon from the east. Although some experience was gained in conducting long distance, extended campaigns, little was directly accomplished and the Scouts' performance under McFadden was less than stellar.

The initial organization of the Scouts and the nature of the unit's affiliation with the Army structure were at the outset rather loose and quasi-official. On all future campaigns, the Scouts would be officially mustered in to government service and operate as an integral component of the military establishment.

With North now in command, the unit was officially mustered in as Company A, Pawnee Scouts on January 13, 1865. It would prove to be a busy year. Depredations along the overland trail brought North and his Pawnees to Fort Kearny in late February. Soon after, a small 25-man detachment was sent to scout along the Niobrara River.

Bigger plans were afoot, however, and the Scouts would play a major role in the events that followed. On July 30, General Patrick E. Connor, commander of the recently established District of the Plains, left Fort Laramie with 558 soldiers, 195 teamsters and wagon masters, and 197 Indians, 95 of whom were Pawnees led by Frank North.

Connor's expedition was intended as one of three columns that would strike into the Indians' heartland. Two others, led by Colonel Nelson Cole and Lieutenant Colonel Samuel Walker, would leave from Omaha and converge on the Powder River area. Plagued by inclement weather, late-arriving supplies, poor contractor support, atrocious scouting, and Cheyenne resistance, the columns led by Cole and Walker became a perfect storm of futility. Connor later had to divert forces to assist in their rescue.

On the trail, North's Scouts ranged far and wide, returning periodically to camp to report to North, sometimes bringing in scalps they had taken and horses they had captured, before disappearing again. On August 11, Connor's column reached the Powder River about 175 miles north of Fort Laramie. North's scouts discovered the remnants of a large village, probably 150 or more lodges sited along the river. In the residue of the camp, Connor's soldiers found scraps of telegrams taken by the Indians during their January raids on Julesburg, Colorado, and the scalp of at least one white man. Soon after, the Scouts intercepted a small raiding party and in an all-out charge, killed all five of them.

A day or two later, North and a small group were on a scout when they were attacked by a sizable Sioux war party. North became separated from his companions and as he sought safety, his horse was killed. Bob White, a Pawnee sergeant, came to his aid. Although ordered by North to break away and bring help, Bob White refused, instead staying to fight beside him. Together the two of them fought off Sioux attackers until other Scouts came to their rescue. North's near-miraculous survival further enhanced his exceptional reputation among the Pawnees. On August 16, an event occurred that contributed to the Scouts' growing legend. At 2 o'clock in the morning, a group of Cheyennes were sighted on a bluff not far from Fort Connor, a newly constructed post. Connor ordered

North and 40 Pawnees to go after them. North and his Scouts traveled 60 miles, crossing the Powder River seven times that night, never losing the trail. At sunup they overtook the Cheyennes, killed them all – possibly 24 in number – and returned to the camp later than afternoon. North turned over to Connor 16 horses and 12 mules with government brands along with considerable quantities of coffee, sugar, tobacco, and other supplies the Cheyennes had taken on raids along the trail.

Increasingly frequent sightings and contact made it event that hostile Sioux and Cheyenne were nearby in considerable numbers. On August 20, North sent a small company of Scouts after a war party spotted about six miles from the post. The Pawnees killed one of the raiders, thought to be a chief.

On the move again August 25-28, North sent a detachment to check on a rising column of smoke seen in the distance. Jim Bridger, accompanying the scouting party, discovered an Arapaho camp on the banks of the Tongue River. Connor brought his main force to the area during the night of August 28 and attacked the next morning.

The Arapaho village was situated on a large mesa, 500-600 yards across with the camp stretched along the left side. When Connor sounded the charge, North's Pawnees pitched into the village. Along with Connor and some troopers, a handful of Scouts – perhaps 15 in number – pushed entirely through the camp and engaged in an extended chase. Eventually, their horses tiring, Connor and his party of about 30 halted momentarily. The Arapaho band, far larger in number at this point, chose the moment to regroup and attack. Connor and the Scouts made a fighting retreat back to the village which Connor ordered destroyed. Altogether 250 lodges were burned along with tons of meat, robes, and supplies. Sixty-three Arapahos were killed during the fighting.

After the battle, Connor sent North and his Scouts ahead with a herd of 500-600 ponies captured from the Arapahos. Although under frequent attack from raiding parties, the Scouts safely conveyed the mounts to Fort Connor. When Connor returned to the fort, he published orders singling out North and 15 of his Scouts for conspicuous bravery during the campaign.

In the meantime, the whereabouts of the Cole-Walker expedition that was supposed to join Connor's column was unknown. Worried about their well-being, Connor sent North to investigate.

On September 15, North informed Connor that he had discovered about 250 dead cavalry horses belonging to Cole's expedition about 50 miles away. Always forging ahead and looking for targets, North had also located a large village. He then traveled 50 miles through the night to deliver his report.

With North's information, contact was made with Cole's party after Connor sent two of North's Pawnees ahead to locate them. Cole's force was in dire straits, nearly out of food and many of their horses dead or played out. Connor quickly sent supplies that sustained the party along with directions that guided them to Fort Connor. Accounts vary, but one version has Frank North being the first to reach Cole's column.

The government's forthcoming decision to launch peace talks halted Connor's Powder River Expedition. North and his Scouts had provided almost the only bright spots in what was otherwise a mostly expensive and unproductive campaign.

The Scouts' unit history provides a terse recap of the company's activities during the year:

"Organized at Columbus, Nebraska, January 13, 1865. Attached to District of Nebraska at Fort Kearny, February 1865. At Fort Rankin April 1865. Power River Expedition June 30 – October 7, 1865. Action at Tongue River August 28. Action at Powder River September 1-8. Operations on Plains against Indians; protected lines of communication and emigrants until April 1866."

In January and February 1866, North and his Scouts accompanied an expedition intended to track down hostiles in southwestern Nebraska and northwestern Kansas. Led by Lieutenant R. H. Brown of the 12th Missouri Cavalry, in addition to seven companies from that unit, the force consisted of five companies of the 1st Nebraska, six companies of the 7th Iowa, a company from the 6th Regiment of "Galvanized Yankees" (former Confederate soldiers released from Union prison camps in return for their promise of service on the Plains), and a combined detachment of the 2nd U.S. Cavalry and the 18th Infantry. The column left Fort Cottonwood (later Fort McPherson) on January 6 and moved initially to the south fork of the Republican River. After a minor skirmish on January 23 and few Indians sighted, the force returned to the fort. Brown and his men reached the post on February 19 after a 300-mile trek covering 44 days. The Pawnee Scouts were mustered out of service on April 1, 1866.

As would be the usual pattern, the Scouts' absence from military events on the Plains did not last long. Though there was a temporary lull in major campaigns in the Plains region, the next four years proved to be busy ones for the unit as North and his Pawnees scouted, escorted settlers, and guarded trails.

The year 1867 brought a new assignment for the Scouts. With the Northern Pacific Railroad laying tracks west of Grand Island, Nebraska, Sioux and Cheyenne resistance became increasingly fierce as the rails extended deeper into territory where the tribes had historically hunted and roamed at will. General Christopher C. Auger, regional commander, asked North to recruit four companies of Scouts to protect the railroad workers.

North and his men performed that mission effectively, shielding the workers as the rails pushed west through the Platte Valley. As the weeks went by, North and his Scouts were also called upon to respond to incidents that occurred along completed portions of the track. One episode, illustrative of others, occurred in August 1867, near present-day Lexington, Nebraska, where a large party of Cheyennes ambushed, plundered, and burned a train.

A trap was laid by a Cheyenne war party led by a chief named Turkey Leg. The ambush site was about four miles west of Plum Creek Station at a point where the tracks traced a gentle curve and passed over a small bridge or culvert spanning a narrow gully. At the trestle the Indians removed the rails and tilted them so that one end of each protruded two to three feet above the track bed. Ties were piled against the rails for support and the entire structure was lashed together by wire cut from the telegraph line that paralleled the tracks. The Indians apparently hoped that the barricade arrangement would rip out the underside of the train carriage as it passed over, or at the minimum rupture the cylinders on each side of the locomotive. When the barricade was in place, the Indians hid in the nearby ravines and tall grass and waited for traffic along the track.

The first activity came after midnight in the form of a hand-car sent ahead of a train. Accounts vary from three to six as to the number of men on the car and their immediate fate. Whatever the number, the crew was apparently distracted by the sight of Indians and did not see the barricade. The hand-car slammed into the barrier and all of the men were thrown from it. The Indians swarmed over them and by most versions all but one were killed almost instantly. The survivor was hurled some distance from the car and tried to hide in the prairie grass. Caught by one of the Cheyennes, he was knocked unconscious and scalped. Something then caught the attention of the Indians, perhaps the approach of the train, and the warrior dropped the scalp and rode off elsewhere. The crewman, William Thompson, awoke, found his own scalp, and after passing out again eventually revived in the cool night air. Finding a place to hide, he watched disaster unfold as the Indians destroyed the train and slaughtered its crew. Later, with the Indians drunk on liquor pilfered from the freight cars, he made his way to the nearest station where his wounds were treated.

Meanwhile, unaware of the peril that awaited a short distance down the tracks, the train was fast approaching. As the train sped towards the blockade, the crew eventually saw the barrier and the dislodged rails in the engine's headlights. The engineer tried to reverse the locomotive, but the train was moving too fast to stop. A series of catastrophic events soon took place, each adding to the horror that preceded it.

As the train, brakes screeching, slammed into the barricade, the fireman was flung against or into the locomotive's open firebox and was roasted alive. In the chaos of the derailment, the engineer was hurled through the locomotive's window and nearly disemboweled as he struck a metal object in the cab. He charred body was later found surrounded by burning cars and cargo.

Within moments, the area around the ravine was transformed into a nightmarish scene. Shattered cars and freight were strewn over the landscape. Fires began quickly, started partly by the flames ejected from the locomotive's mangled firebox. Two flat cars loaded with bricks were catapulted over the engine and landed several feet beyond it while the remainder of the train telescoped against the engine and ground itself apart. The conductor, riding at the back of the train, saw what happened to the engineer and fireman and ran into the night to escape capture and warn a second train known to be following along the track a short distance behind.

The crewman managed to escape marauding Cheyennes and flag down the second train, which reversed back to the nearest station, arriving there at about 2 o'clock in the morning. Attempts to form an immediate rescue party were not successful and it was mid-morning before a force from the local area made its way to the ambush site.

Not long after, Frank North, commanding a company of Pawnee Scouts and a few soldiers, brought his contingent to the scene of the attack. He followed the attackers' trail long enough to confirm they were Cheyennes. North chose not to pursue them, believing that if they were not followed the Cheyennes would return to raid again in the same area. Accordingly, he went into camp at Plum Creek and waited for them to reappear.

They did so, about 10 days later. Warned by one of his detached scouts that the Cheyennes were moving toward him from the south, Major North moved his force to the Plum Creek overland stage station. There, he intended to rest his men and horses overnight.

The Pawnee Scouts, however, wanted to identify the approaching party before darkness set in. North consented and allowed 48 Scouts led by two young cavalry officers and accompanied by two sergeants to move out and locate the incoming raiders. Leaving immediately, the company rode almost directly south, crossed the Platte and followed the river bank in an easterly direction until they were within about a mile and a half of Plum Creek.

There, they collided with the Cheyennes.

For generations, the Cheyennes along with their traditional allies, the Sioux, had been the bitter foes of the Pawnee. Theirs was a years-long struggle fought with little quarter given: each found inventive and horrific ways to torture prisoners, raid, and terrorize their opponents. Now, at the sight of their mortal enemies, both parties readied for a clash.

The Cheyennes – about 150 in all, by most estimates – quickly mounted and the mayhem occurred as opposing sides met on the banks of Plum Creek. Though the Scouts numbered only 52 total (counting the two officers and two NCOs), they charged at full fury. The speed of their attack and the cohesion of the smaller group carried them into and through the Cheyennes who fled in panic and confusion, overwhelmed by the ferocity of the assault. The Pawnees' wrath was not soon abated and they raced after the Cheyennes, pursuing them for miles as they rushed toward the Republican Valley. The killing and scalping ceased only when nightfall put an end to the chase.

When the bloodlust was over, 15 Cheyennes had been killed and scalped. The Pawnees also returned with 35 horses and mules. Two captives – one a 16-year old nephew of Turkey Leg – were also taken and later exchanged for settler hostages held by the Cheyennes.

The encounter had an important consequence; the victory of North's Pawnee Scouts markedly slowed Cheyenne attacks on the railroad.

Events of the year provided a singular honor for North and his Scouts: they were chosen to escort General William T. Sherman, Commanding General of the United States Army, from the end of track to Fort Laramie. The following year, 1868, saw North and the Scouts engaged in near-continuous duty along the Union Pacific Line.

Farther south, violence again erupted on a major scale in the Republican River Valley. In May and June 1869, Cheyenne Dog Soldiers – the tribe's warrior elite – launched almost daily attacks on prairie settlements. Led by Chief Tall Bull, the Cheyennes killed settlers, took women captives, and ran off with perhaps 500 head of horses and cattle.

The military sent Brigadier General Eugene A. Carr with five companies of the 5th Cavalry and 150 Pawnee Scouts led by Frank North in pursuit. North's Pawnees quickly picked up the trail and guided Carr's column west and then north in a giant, horseshoe-shaped arc that over the coming weeks would eventually cover hundreds of miles and become one of the epic campaigns on the western frontier. Ironically, Carr at first objected when North and the Scouts were assigned to the expedition. His attitude rather quickly changed, however, and on future campaigns he explicitly requested their presence.

For two days after entering the valley, Carr moved mostly west, crossing over Deer Creek before stopping early on June 15 to rest his troops at a campsite along the banks of Prairie Dog Creek. The troops bivouacked along the creek side with the Pawnee Scouts camped about a half mile from the cavalry. Carr's wagon train was positioned between the two camps. Apparently hidden in the tall grass throughout the day, in late afternoon the Indians attacked the wagon train area as Carr's men settled down for supper. During the chaos of the first few minutes, a teamster was wounded as Carr's troopers struggled to respond. The sudden attack was aimed at driving off the mule herd and thus immobilizing the wagon train carrying Carr's supplies.

Quick reaction by the Pawnee Scouts foiled the Cheyennes' plan. Before the cavalry could react, the Pawnees raced to their ponies and went after the attackers. Along with William F. "Buffalo Bill" Cody, chief scout of the 5th Cavalry – who had left his horse saddled – and Frank North, the Pawnees engaged the Cheyennes in a running battle that extended over several miles as the raiders hurried away to the south. As the chase continued, Cody and the Pawnees were joined by several companies of cavalry before night fell and the chase was broken off. The Pawnees killed two of the marauders before darkness obscured the trail. A few days later the column fought off a night attack again aimed at spooking the horse and mule herds.

As the trek continued, the Cheyennes did their usual masterful job of disguising their tracks. At one point the band split into two parties, leaving a plain, heavy trail to the right and a scattered, dim trail to the left. North correctly identified the clearer trail as a ruse intended to induce Carr's column to move in the wrong direction. Carr sent a decoy party (quickly returned) to feign following the heavier track and resumed the chase.

Believing the Cheyennes were close by, Carr quickened his pace. After moving 65 miles in a day through brutal heat, the Scouts found a recently abandoned campsite and the footprint of a white woman's shoe. At noon on July 11, one of North's Pawnees sighted Tall Bull's village near the Platte where the chief had camped waiting for high water to recede.

Led by Cody, North, and the Pawnees, Carr moved his column to the edge of a bluff. By most accounts, many of the Pawnees unsaddled their horses and stripped off their uniforms as they prepared for battle. Carr's force struck the village in an all-out charge, tearing through the camp as the Cheyennes fled in confusion. As the struggle continued, Tall Bull and about 13 others were cornered in a ravine where a fire fight erupted. After several minutes Tall Bull raised his head above the rim of the ravine and was shot and killed. Many accounts identify Frank North as the marksman who killed the chief.

The Battle of Summit Springs was one of the frontier army's most decisive victories. Tall Bull and 51 other Dog Soldiers were killed and 117 other Cheyennes were taken captive. Tepees, weapons, and tons of supplies were destroyed. Though wounded, one of the white women held captive by the Cheyennes was rescued. By several accounts, a second woman captive, perhaps along with her small child, was tomahawked and killed by the Cheyennes during the course of the battle.

Operations more routine in nature then persisted for a few years. In addition to his other duties, the years 1871-1876 found North employed as a post guide and interpreter at Fort Russell, near Cheyenne, Wyoming, and at Sidney Barracks in western Nebraska. Then, in 1876, North's services were again called upon in a major way. Outraged by the Black Hills Treaty which ceded grounds sacred to them, the Plains tribes again threatened violence across hundreds of miles of frontier. At General Sheridan's request, North went to Indian Territory where the Pawnee Reservation had been relocated. North had no trouble recruiting a full company of Scouts eager to get off the reservation, go after their ancient enemy, and serve under North's command.

Once formed, the Scouts eventually joined Ranald Mackenzie at what was then Camp Robinson in the Nebraska Panhandle. Energized by Custer's defeat at the Little Bighorn, hostiles in large numbers were in the field. At the Red Cloud Agency near Camp Robinson, two prominent Sioux chiefs, Red Cloud and Red

Leaf, left the agency in continuing protest against provisions of the Black Hills Treaty. Taking hundreds of followers with them, they established new camps 30 miles away from Chadron Creek, insisting that their rations be distributed to them at that location. Worried about a precedent that might destroy the reservation system as well as the possibility that hundreds of additional warriors might join the enormous numbers already waging war, department commander George Crook decided that the bands must be compelled to return to the agency.

Taking eight companies of cavalry and 40 Pawnee Scouts, Mackenzie moved out, reaching the hostile camp after marching through the night of October 22. At dawn the next morning, he sent the Pawnees to capture the twin villages' pony herds. Meanwhile, Mackenzie surrounded each camp with four companies of cavalry. The Indians surrendered immediately and their weapons and horses were confiscated. They were escorted back to the agency that day. With the Pawnees' assistance, Mackenzie's raid foreclosed additional threats from Sioux tribesmen at the agency.

A month later, North and the Scouts were again in action with Mackenzie, this time far to the west and north along the upper Powder River. Mackenzie pushed his 1,100-man force relentlessly through deep snow and frigid temperatures toward a hostile camp believed to be located on the Crazy Woman Fork of the Powder River.

Scouts guided Mackenzie through a gorge surrounded by high walls, cut by a fast-moving stream. Mackenzie stopped some distance away during the night. As dawn approached, he crept forward and positioned his force close to the village. At sunrise on November 25, a charge was sounded. Frank North and his brother Luther, along with the Pawnee Scouts, led the race to the village.

Most Cheyenne warriors – many of them almost naked in the cold – were driven from the village. The battle evolved into a prolonged and bitter contest as the Cheyennes rallied at the end of the gorge. Establishing a bastion on a low hill, their position commanded the field. Seeing that the redoubt was the key to the battle, Mackenzie sent forces to attack and capture the knoll which was taken after a hard fight.

For a time during the battle, a sizable number of Mackenzie's cavalrymen were trapped under fire in a ravine. North's sharp-shooting Pawnees knocked down several Cheyennes and helped hold attackers at bay until Mackenzie funneled additional troops to the area.

The Dull Knife Fight, as it came to be known, continued for an extended time as the Cheyennes fought a rear guard action aimed at allowing the tribes' women and children to escape. Later still, firing – though mostly ineffective – continued from ledges and canyon walls.

Casualties were taken on both sides, although it seems clear that the Cheyennes' losses were especially heavy. In the aftermath, all 183 of the village's lodges and its entire cache of supplies were burned. A considerable portion of the tribe's pony herd – 150 or more – was captured as well. The Dull Knife Fight essentially ended the Northern Cheyennes' resistance.

With the defeat of the Northern Cheyenne and victories over the Sioux by Miles, Mackenzie, and Crook, the war on the Plains was effectively over. Sitting Bull had fled to Canada during the winter of 1876 and Crazy Horse surrendered at Fort Robinson, Nebraska, in the spring of the following year. At long last, shooting had ceased in the "Big Open." With the coming of peace, the Pawnee Scouts were no longer needed. They were mustered out of service for a final time in April 1877.

After leaving the Army, North went into business with his close friend "Buffalo Bill" Cody, partnering with him in a cattle ranch at the head of the Dismal River in western Nebraska. In 1882, the two men sold the ranch and North was elected to the Nebraska legislature. After serving a two-year term he rejoined Cody, assisting with Cody's Wild West Exhibition. In 1884, while with the show in Hartford, Connecticut, North was severely injured in a riding accident. Near death for a time, he recovered sufficiently to rejoin Cody in New Orleans. In the spring of 1885, while traveling back to the Midwest on business connected with the show, he took ill and died a few days later, on March 14, at his home in Columbus, Nebraska. Three days later, after what his obituary described as the largest funeral ever held in the city, he was buried in Columbus.

Philip H. Sheridan

G eneral Philip H. Sheridan is a transcendent figure in American military history. Known for his service during the Civil War, Sheridan, along with Ulysses S. Grant and William T. Sherman, emerged from the conflict as one of a triumvirate of the most famous Union generals.

Overshadowed is Sheridan's long post-Civil War service directing operations against warring tribes in the American West. In actuality, Sheridan commanded a large frontier region for a longer time than any other officer. For the better part of two decades, he led the Division of the Missouri, a vast theater comprising almost half of the nation's territory. Sheridan's zone of responsibility extended north to south from the Canadian border to the tip of Texas and east to west from Chicago to the Rockies. Inside that enormous region were 175,000 Natives of various tribes.

To pacify and secure the region, Sheridan had remarkably few resources. By the 1870s, the entire Army of the United States numbered less than 25,000 enlisted men, down from the more than two million that had served during the Civil War. Sheridan's force was chronically undermanned. Most infantry companies had only 40 men assigned; cavalry companies only 50. Across three departments in the Division of the Missouri – the Platte, Dakota, and the Missouri – Sheridan's force averaged one trooper for 75 square miles of territory. In Texas, the fourth department, the ratio was even more extreme: one for every 120 square miles. His always underpaid and often undersupplied soldiers faced a warrior culture whose core elements were riding and fighting and whose leaders knew every terrain feature and the location of every water hole.

During Sheridan's tenure, the western frontier was the venue for almost constant military action. As division commander, Sheridan directed forces in the Red River War, the Ute War, and the Great Sioux War. Later still, as Commanding General of the United States Army, he oversaw operations against Geronimo's Apaches and other hostile tribes in the American Southwest.

The Red River War (1868-1869) first illustrated the concept of operations that would characterize Sheridan's generalship on the frontier. Using converging columns deployed from three locations, his forces struck the hostile tribes in winter quarters, destroying food, shelter, and provisions.

Though that strategy would be refined over time, Sheridan-directed

operations almost always featured multiple
columns and unremitting pressure regardless
of terrain and without respite during winter
months. Hostile bands were deprived of shelter,
sustenance, and mobility. Harassed incessantly,
the tribes were eventually drained of their will
to resist.

For the Natives the consequences were
devastating. For the government, soldiers, and
emigrants, the subjugation of the warring tribes
opened an immense portion of the continent to
unthreatened settlement and commerce.

Though Sheridan was known on occasion
to speak in sympathetic terms about the
Indians' plight, those remarks were reserved for
ruminations about why the tribes were induced

Mathew Brady, Public Domain
Philip H. Sheridan

to fight and conditions on the reservations (which he urged be improved). Once
the fighting began, he became an implacable foe, unapologetic for his actions
or those of his men. While he recognized that breaking up the Indians' lifestyle
was a major cause of the persistent warfare that plagued the Plains, Sheridan
placed no moral judgment on that series of events. Rather, he spoke in favor of
consistency in national policy, railing against programs that seemed to vacillate
between benign humanitarianism and stern oversight.

Sheridan agreed with placing the tribes on reservations and attempting
to convert them to modes of living more compatible with the greater U.S.
population. Like almost all military officers, he disagreed with the government's
approach. Sheridan advocated putting the reservations under military control.
That, in his judgment, would result in fairer treatment, better administration, and
eliminate the graft so prevalent in the Indian Bureau. Fairer treatment, though,
did not mean milder treatment. Sheridan was appalled by the lax standards on
many reservations. In his view, the tribes' warrior cultures predisposed them to
violence; thus, every infraction needed to be addressed until the cultures were
transformed.

Sheridan believed the clash between cultures was inevitable and that
prosecuting war with extreme measures would serve to shorten the conflict.
Perhaps drawing on his own experience as a junior officer in the Pacific
Northwest serving under George Wright – whose harsh tactics brought a quick
and permanent end to a war – and his own actions in the Civil War, he concluded,
like his friend and colleague William T. Sherman, that victory was not assured
until the enemy had been defeated psychologically and well as militarily. The
quickest, surest way to do that, in his view, was to punish the enemy with the

utmost severity, making every aspect of his continued existence difficult and uncertain.

The "only good Indian is a dead Indian" comment that is often attributed to Sheridan is perhaps apocryphal. He denied ever saying it. Nonetheless, Sheridan was a "total war" soldier. When forces under his command were engaged in a shooting war, he may well have applied similar sentiments to any foe who happened to be facing him at the time.

For nearly three decades, Sheridan played a prominent role in shaping and employing the Army that fought the Native tribes after the Civil War. The "winning of the West" (as seen from the settlers', soldiers', and government's perspective) may be credited to him as much as to any officer who saw service on the American frontier.

There is some dispute about Sheridan's date and place of birth. Most references cite March 6, 1831, at Albany, New York. Supposition persists, however, that he may have been born in Ireland (and that he, or perhaps his parents, fudged the location in the event he might later enter politics). Other suggested birthplaces have included Boston, Massachusetts, and Somerset, Ohio.

Sheridan was a diminutive 5 feet 4 inches tall. He had a swarthy complexion and a large head typically topped by a small, flat "pork pie" hat. President Lincoln described him as "A brown, chunky little chap with a long body, short legs, not enough neck to hang him and such long arms that if his ankles itch he can scratch them without stooping." To his men and the American public, he became "Little Phil."

Perhaps in a foreshadowing of his later aggressiveness on the battlefield, during his third year at West Point, Sheridan was suspended after a fight with a classmate. After sitting out for a year, he graduated with the class of 1853, ranked 34th of 52 cadets.

After graduation, Sheridan served for a short time at Fort Davis, Texas, a small post situated near the Rio Grande. His time there was brief; a few months later he was transferred to the 4th Infantry and posted to Camp Reading, California, at the northern end of the Sacramento Valley.

The Yakima War of 1855 brought Sheridan's first experience under fire. In March 1856, he led 40 dragoons to the rescue of a group of settlers under siege near Oregon Cascades. Though outnumbered, Sheridan's company tore into the attackers and drove them away from the embattled party. Sheridan was later reassigned to western Oregon, where he and his men guarded the Grande Ronde Indian Reservation. Sheridan served through the Yakima and Rogue River Wars under the overall command of General George Wright. Wright's use of superior firepower combined with harsh measures eradicated the threat – tactics no doubt recalled by the young officer in later years. Sheridan remained in the Pacific

Northwest for nearly six years, helping Wright and other commanders tame the Yakimas, Cascades, and other warring bands.

Sheridan was a 30-year old captain, still posted on the West Coast when the Civil War began. In September 1861, he was transferred east to join the 13th Infantry, but found himself shunted off to staff duties working on behalf of Generals Henry Halleck and Samuel Curtis. Though the duties were not to his liking, he performed them exceptionally well. Halleck, in particular, was reluctant to replace him. Eventually, Sheridan secured an appointment as commander of the 2nd Michigan Cavalry. From that point, his rise was meteoric. In some of the bloodiest fighting of the war, he earned a reputation for aggressiveness, tenacity, and personal courage. By September 1862, he was a brigadier general of volunteers.

After difficult struggles at Perryville and Stones River, where his counterattack turned an apparent defeat into an important, but costly, Union victory, he was promoted to major general of volunteers.

Sheridan and his unit fought well at the bloodbath at Chickamauga, but like Union forces other than those under George Thomas, were forced into a hurried retreat to Chattanooga. Sheridan apparently tried to rally his regiment to assist Thomas but was unsuccessful in stopping the panic-driven rush to safety.

If redemption was necessary, Chattanooga provided it. Surrounded for a time in the city, Union forces under the command of U. S. Grant – who had replaced William Rosecrans after Chickamauga – launched an attack. Sheridan led a bold, surprisingly successful charge up Missionary Ridge, capturing Grant's attention and earning his esteem. When Grant soon after moved east to assume command of all Union forces in the field, he took Sheridan with him, installing him as commander of the Army of the Potomac's cavalry.

Frustrated initially when the cavalry arm under General George G. Meade was confined to escort and reconnaissance roles, Grant eventually approved Sheridan's employment of the force as an offensive weapon. Sheridan quickly commenced a series of raids into Confederate territory. One, with as many as ten thousand horsemen, struck towards Richmond. Another killed Confederate cavalry leader J.E.B. Stuart at Yellow Tavern. Not all the raids were successful, but their cumulative impact and potential led Grant to give Sheridan an independent command.

Sheridan was subsequently sent to the Shenandoah Valley with orders to defeat rebel General Jubal Early, who maintained a formidable presence there, on occasion threatening Washington, D.C. Two initial victories drove Early south. Then, on October 19, 1864, at Cedar Creek, Early's forces attacked while Sheridan was 14 miles away traveling to a meeting at Winchester, Virginia. Early's attack carried through the Union lines, sending the Federals into an all-out retreat. Sheridan heard the distant firing, raced back to the battlefield, rallying and collecting his disorganized soldiers along the way. His personal example, galloping toward the enemy, waving his hat, calling to his men, turned the tide of battle. His reassembled troops slammed into the rebels, many of whom were busy looting the Union camp. Early's army was routed, forced from the valley for the final time. The poem, "Sheridan's Ride," made him and his horse Rienzi legends in the popular press. Sheridan's victory allowed him free rein to utterly destroy the food producing capacity of the valley, known as the "bread basket of the Confederacy." Grant had assigned him that task, advising him to demolish it to the point that "crows flying over it … will have to carry their own provender."

Sheridan was with Grant during the closing actions of the war. At Five Forks on April 1, 1865, his forces captured the vital crossroads, contributing greatly to Lee's decision to abandon the Petersburg-Richmond area and attempt to move his army to North Carolina and there link up with the remaining major Confederate force in the field. Grant sent Sheridan to intercept Lee as the Confederates made a desperate attempt to escape. Over the next several days as the armies moved west and slightly south across Virginia, Lee tried to slip past the Federals. In the end, Lee's genius was not enough. Sheridan's relentless pursuit was too much for Lee's starving, exhausted soldiers.

At Saylor's Creek on April 6, Sheridan caught an entire wing of the Confederate army and captured a quarter of the remaining rebel forces. A few days later, as Lee made a final attempt to reach a railroad, Sheridan blocked the way. Sheridan was with Grant in William McLean's parlor near Appomattox Court House when Lee surrendered.

After Appomattox, Sheridan was sent initially to the Texas border. With 50,000 troops, he provided moral and material support to the forces of Benito Juarez who were battling 40,000 French troops serving Emperor Maxmilian's bid to maintain control of Mexico.

His next stop was also a brief one. Assigned to Reconstruction duties in Louisiana and Texas, he was replaced on July 31, 1867, after charges that his administration was too harsh in its treatment of former Confederate officials.

His subsequent posting, as Commander of the Department of the Missouri, brought him directly into the Indian wars, an involvement that in some degree would continue through the remainder of his long career.

Although the Medicine Lodge Treaty, signed in October 1867, seemed to hold initial promise for pacifying the southern Plains, most of the tribes failed to settle on new territory provided to them by the government. In addition to the usual contentions for a considerable time Congress – tied up with impeachment proceedings for President Andrew Johnson – failed to appropriate funds for food, clothing, and other essentials promised by the treaty. Tribal leaders seldom had full control of their aggressive young warriors even under the best of circumstances. By the time the bill finally passed in July 1868, it was too late. A Cheyenne war party was the first to leave the reservation. In the coming weeks they were joined by Oglalas, Brules, and other Cheyenne bands, all combining in a series of raids on farms and settlements. Fifteen white men were killed, five women raped and others taken captive during the attacks. Farm buildings and other dwellings were burned over a widespread area.

Seeking to stop further violence, Sheridan sent two emissaries to discuss grievances with tribal leaders. The negotiators were attacked along the Solomon River. One was killed and the second wounded before fleeing the area.

Sheridan then ordered Cheyennes and Arapahos to return to their reservations as required by the treaty. They were also to turn over the leaders of the raids in Kansas – also a stipulation of the treaty. Both requests were refused. Believing at the time that he had too few soldiers to mount a summer campaign, Sheridan assigned his available forces to protect the Kansas Pacific Railroad and nearby settlements.

As he prepared for a campaign later in the year, in May 1868, Sheridan sent Colonel Benjamin Grierson from Fort Riley, Kansas, to reconnoiter and establish a post closer to the potential area of hostilities. On the junction of two waterways near a crossing point often used by Comanches on their raids into Texas, Grierson constructed the future Fort Sill.

In the meantime, hoping to distract the hostiles, Sheridan sent Lieutenant Colonel Alfred Sully with a sizable combined force of cavalry and infantry to strike Cheyenne and Arapaho camps south of the Arkansas River. A few skirmishes followed, but Sully did not move fast enough to close with the renegade bands. His expedition returned to Fort Dodge on September 18 without achieving significant results.

Conditions continued to deteriorate through the summer and fall. Subsequent to the earlier raids in Kansas, more than a hundred settlers had been killed and many women violated. Farmsteads and stage stations were burned and livestock numbering in the hundreds stolen. Throughout the Department of the Missouri, 18 soldiers were killed and other 43 wounded.

With public outrage building, Sheridan decided on a winter campaign. First, though, he wanted his main strike force to be commanded by an officer of his choice. George Armstrong Custer, a colleague from their Civil War days, had been court-martialed in October 1867. Custer had been suspended from active duty for a year. Intervening on his behalf, Sheridan succeeded in having Custer restored to duty before his suspension ended. On September 24, 1868, Sheridan telegraphed Custer as his home in Monroe, Michigan, advising him to report immediately.

Custer was assigned 11 companies of the 7th Cavalry, four companies of infantry, and the 19th Kansas Volunteer Cavalry. In a trek personally led for a time by Sheridan, on the 22nd of November, Custer's column reached Fort Supply in present-day Woodward County, Oklahoma, 100 miles south of Fort Dodge, Kansas.

Sheridan's idea for a winter campaign was not entirely new, but it did have numerous skeptics, including among them even some veteran frontiersmen. Sheridan, though, believed that well-clothed, well-fed soldiers could subsist in the bitter conditions long enough to find and strike the Native camps. His prospects for success were aided by the steady advance of rail lines across the Plains. Before the railroads, weather and distance considerations had favored the Indians, tucked away nearly out of reach on the vast expenses of the American West. Now, the progress of the rails allowed the buildup of supplies at distant depots, greatly increasing the Army's mobility and staying power.

As would be typical of Sheridan-conceived campaigns over the years, he envisioned several columns moving in concert. Major Andrew W. Evans with 500 men would move eastward from Fort Bascom, New Mexico, to the Canadian River region of the Texas Panhandle. Major (brevet brigadier general) Eugene A. Carr would push south from Fort Lyon, Colorado, with seven companies of the 5th Cavalry. Along the way Carr's column would be joined by five more companies already operating in the field. Together the combined force would the march farther south and east.

Carr's and Evan's columns were intended to push the Indians towards Sheridan's main column – led by Custer – coming towards them from the east. Once Custer's larger force made contact, Carr and Evans would block the Indians' escape to the west and north.

As events played out, supply snafus, organizational delays, and horrific weather prevented Evans and Carr from having much impact on the campaign. On November 27, Custer found Black Kettle's Southern Cheyenne camp, the western-most of a series of villages strung along the Washita River. In a costly, controversial encounter, Custer claimed 103 Cheyennes killed, including Black Kettle, and 53 captives taken. Custer lost 21 killed and 14 wounded.

On Christmas Day, Evans struck a combined Kiowa-Comanche village several miles south of the Washita battlefield along Soldier Spring. Evans' men destroyed food caches, lodges, and camp supplies. In the midst of a bitter winter, many of the hostiles returned to the reservation.

By the spring and summer of the following year, 1869, most of the renegade Sioux and Cheyennes had surrendered. The one major exception was perhaps the most fearsome band of all – Cheyenne Dog Soldiers led by Chief Tall Bull. After destructive raids along the Republican River Valley in Kansas and Nebraska, the Cheyennes moved north to join hostile bands of Sioux.

Sheridan sent Carr from his post at Fort Lyon to Fort McPherson in preparation for a major campaign to be launched from that location. After a legendary chase covering a hundreds of miles long horseshoe-shaped track the extended from central Nebraska into northern Kansas and eastern Colorado, Carr caught and defeated Tall Bull at Summit Springs, Colorado, on July 11, 1869. Tall Bull and 51 other warriors were killed, and all of the band's lodges, weapons, and supplies were destroyed. Carr's victory at Summit Springs broke the power of the Cheyennes. Nearly all of the few hostiles still in the field soon surrendered.

As conditions would show, Sheridan's campaign succeeded in achieving his three announced goals. The southern Plains tribes had been forced onto reservations. Hostiles had essentially been removed from the area between the Platte and Arkansas Rivers, assuring the security of railroads and settlements. Lastly, the Indians that had precipitated the raids had been severely punished.

While successful far beyond most past expeditions, the campaign had not yet been decisive. A few years later, the Red River War of 1874-1875 would complete the subjugation of the southern Plains tribes.

During his tenure as commander of the Division of the Missouri, Sheridan remarked often of his surprise at the rapid westward advance of the frontier. As early as 1872, he noted that much of Dakota, which only a year or two previously had been the domain of the warring tribes, was now transformed into farms and ranches. Previously barren country was providing sustenance to the rest of the country. Like most of his colleagues, he was impressed by the persistence of the pioneer families: the "Great American Desert" was indeed a myth.

Particularly in eastern Dakota Territory, conditions were fairly quiet. Sheridan suggested that in that region, while continuing to protect settlers from infrequent raids, the Army role could begin shifting towards exploring the remaining unsurveyed territory, protecting railroad crews as the track moved farther west, aiding civil authorities upholding the law in newly settled regions, and generally helping with the advance of civilization in the frontier regions.

Sheridan's observations regarding the spread of westward advancement were widely shared. Commissioner of Indian Affairs Francis A. Walker reported that by 1872, reservations west of the Missouri were already well-populated. Including older establishments, nearly 25,000 Indians dwelled on reservations. The Indians, it was reported, offered little trouble. Military protection was rarely necessary.

Still at large were about 11,000 "non-treaty" hostiles who had been pushed westward, deeper into Montana. For the next several years, these bands would engage in a life and death struggle with the frontier Army.

The westward march of the Northern Pacific Railroad provoked recurring clashes as tracks pushed further into the historic grounds of the Sioux nation. Sherman, Commanding General of the United States Army and Sheridan's immediate superior, believed that the railroads would advance settlement and ultimately help solve the "Indian problem." As white habitation increased, the tribes would be generally confined within the tracks of the Union and Northern Pacific railways, and the buffalo herds that sustained them would be split and diminished as well.

Like Sherman, Sheridan anticipated that the Sioux and their allies would eventually react with violence to the incursion. In a series of preemptive moves, Sheridan sent two powerful strike forces into the field in the spring of 1872. Colonel David S. Stanley, with 600 infantrymen, a battery of Gatling guns and 12-pounders, moved from Fort Rice to the mouth of the Powder River. Major E.M. Baker with 400 soldiers patrolled farther west of Stanley.

When Baker was forced to pull back after confronting hostiles in numbers seldom seen before, Army leaders took it as a signal that the task would be difficult and bloody. Shortly after, the tribes underlined their resolve with a direct attack on Fort Abraham Lincoln.

Sheridan responded by transferring Custer and the 7th Cavalry to man tht fort and others in the Upper Missouri. In doing so, Sheridan introduced a new dynamic into the conflict. Henceforth, the forts were changed from defensive bastions into bases of supply for cavalry forces that under aggressive commanders would range far and wide in pursuit of hostile tribesmen.

When violence flared again in the south, Sheridan's strategy was similar to that he had employed on the northern Plains in 1868-1869. Using climate as an ally, converging columns would keep the hostile bands constantly on the move causing them to expend their supplies. Eventually, Sheridan believed, the bands would be exhausted by the relentless pursuit and lose their will to resist. That, as well as his confidence that sooner or later one of the columns would find and defeat the war parties, would ultimately cause them to surrender.

To launch what would be known as the Red River War, Sheridan sent three columns from posts in Texas and Indian Territory toward the "Staked Plains" of West Texas, a historic and previously unconquered stronghold of the southern Plains tribes. Meanwhile, from forts in New Mexico and Kansas, two columns would press the Indians from the north and west. The five columns, totaling about 2,000 soldiers, would remain constantly on the move, harassing the tribes and battering them when they came in contact.

On August 31, 1874, Nelson Miles destroyed a village and all its associated property after a difficult, masterfully fought battle deep in West Texas. Miles used Gatling guns, howitzers, and repeated flanking movements to dislodge a combined force of 600 or so Kiowas and Cheyennes. After fixing some momentary supply problems, Miles chased the tribes through blizzards and the depths of a bitter cold winter.

On September 28, Ranald Mackenzie, after moving a force across the supposedly impregnable "Staked Plains," defeated a large, combined camp in the Palo Duro canyon. Of the 25 engagements fought during the war, Palo Duro was the largest and would have the most far-reaching consequences. Spurred by the efforts of Mackenzie and Miles, the five columns in the field eventually achieved the result Sheridan intended. During February and March 1875, hostile bands surrendered in droves at Fort Sill and the nearest Indian agencies. When the last war party surrendered in June, the war on the southern Plains was over.

Sheridan had defeated the tribes not by inflicting significant losses in battle, but through subjecting them to exposure and starvation, destroying their property and killing their livestock. In considerable measure, it was the sufferings of the family members that induced warriors to seek solace on reservations. Quick results, Sheridan believed, could only be achieved by making war on the entire tribe. It was total war – and it was brutally effective. In a sense, it was the Shenandoah Valley all over again.

As the war in the south was dying down, the focus of action was shifting farther north. Gold had been discovered in the Black Hills, a region granted to the Sioux by the Fort Laramie Treaty of 1868. As the cash-strapped government's behest, Sheridan sent George Armstrong Custer with six companies of the 7th Cavalry from Fort Abraham Lincoln to accompany mining experts and other interested parties. The expedition's reports of gold and glowing descriptions of remarkable landscape ratcheted up pressure from commercial interests to open the region.

Though economic considerations and commercial pressure may have weighed in Sheridan's assessment, his stated justification focused primarily on protection for the region's civilian population. The ostensible reason for the expedition was to explore suitable sites for the establishment of a fort. Sheridan had long favored a post in the area, believing it would control marauding Sioux who struck from the sanctuary to raid into Nebraska, Dakota, and Wyoming.

On November 3, 1875, Sheridan attended a meeting at the White House that established a policy toward the region that would shift considerably over the following months. Initially, the attempt was made to rigidly enforce the provisions of the Fort Laramie Treaty. Soldiers were ordered to prevent miners and other emigrants from entering the Black Hills. In the meantime, the government launched an ultimately unsuccessful attempt to buy the Black Hills, the *Paha Sapa* sacred ground, from the Sioux. Later, though white incursions remained officially prohibited, a decision was made to not restrict prospectors and others from entering the region – a task that the stretched, undermanned Army had difficulty carrying out under the best of circumstances.

A further decision, made late in the year, required all Indians to report to their agencies by January 31, 1876. Those who failed to comply would be regarded as hostile. In reality, given conditions of distance and weather, compliance was in most cases difficult and in many nearly impossible, even among bands that were disposed towards a peaceful outcome. Many, angered by the Black Hills imbroglio, were not.

Anticipating widespread non-compliance from the largest and most warlike tribes on the Plains, Sheridan initially planned on a winter campaign. The initial blow was to be struck by a force led by Colonel Joseph Reynolds under the overall command of General George Crook. However, Reynolds' defeat at Powder River on March 17, 1876, made a summer campaign inevitable.

Sheridan's plan for the summer involved a sizable portion of the U.S. Army forces in the west. General Alfred Terry with 1,200 men would move from Fort Abraham Lincoln. Terry's column included much of the 7th Cavalry under the command of George Armstrong Custer. Coming from the opposite direction, Colonel John Gibbon would bring 440 troopers from Fort Ellis, Montana. Finally, General George Crook with 1,100 men would press north from Fort Fetterman, Wyoming. The columns would converge in south central Montana in the vicinity of the Yellowstone and Powder Rivers.

The campaign was mishandled from the outset, beginning with Crook's withdrawal after a June 17 battle at Rosebud Creek. A litany of misadventures followed; Gibbon deferred a fight on his way east; communications between the columns was lacking; Terry's guidance to Custer was, perhaps intentionally, ambiguous; and Custer's decisions as he approached and entered the Little Bighorn battlefield have been questioned for more than a century and a quarter.

Sheridan was an indomitable, aggressive commander who was not daunted by adversity. Three weeks after Custer's defeat, Wesley Merritt and the 5th Cavalry – placed near Warbonnet Creek by Sheridan's foresight – turned back Sioux and Cheyennes attempting to join Crazy Horse and other hostiles in the north. He followed by sending Lieutenant Colonel Elwell S. Otis and Colonel Nelson Miles to reinforce the remnants of Terry's column and dispatched Wesley Merritt and the 5th Cavalry to join Crook.

In the months that followed, Crook, Miles, and Mackenzie chased down and defeated Crazy Horse, Sitting Bull, Lame Deer, and Dull Knife in a string of victories that ended the Great Sioux War. The campaign was model Sheridan: fast-moving, independent commands; multiple axes of attack; constant pursuit, even under bitter conditions; elimination of pony herds, thus immobilizing the nomadic tribesmen; destruction of shelters and food supplies. By the end of 1877, there was not a hostile Indian left in the "Big Open."

Far away from the Little Bighorn battlefield, conditions across the Great Plains remained unsettled. In the fall of 1876, the government made another attempt to acquire the Black Hills from the Sioux. In late September, after several days of confused and sometimes bitter disputes, commissioners secured sufficient signatures from the reluctant and sometimes bewildered chiefs to claim dubious title to the Black Hills region. Infuriated, two prominent Sioux chiefs, Red Cloud and Red Leaf, took their followers away from the Red Cloud Agency, located near Fort Robinson. Thirty miles north along Chadron Creek they established new camps and demanded that their government rations be delivered to them at those locations.

Sheridan sent Ranald Mackenzie to Fort Robinson to help quell the incidents that threatened the fragile peace in the region. Sheridan shared department commander George Crook's concern that acquiescing to the chiefs' demands might led to a breakdown in the government's reservation system. More immediate was the threat that the bands might break away and join the hostile groups still operating in the north.

Crook dispatched Mackenzie toward the camps with eight companies of cavalry and a contingent of Frank North's Pawnee Scouts. Mackenzie surrounded the camp, captured the pony herd, and ended the incipient uprising without a shot being fired.

The Little Bighorn campaign and the Great Sioux War caused Sheridan to further refine his strategy. Though converging columns would remain a central feature in his planning, the greater distances and the harsher climate on the northern Plains made that approach less effective than it had been farther south – a circumstance for which Sheridan is sometimes criticized for not having recognized more quickly. To complement that tactic, Sheridan placed troops on the tribes' favorite hunting grounds and established posts from which the Indians could be continuously watched and harassed until hunger drove them to the agencies. Reservations were then ringed with posts to prevent breakout raids.

In 1883, with William T. Sherman's retirement, Sheridan was appointed Commanding General of the United States Army. Conditions in the central and northern Plains were benign by that time. In the Southwest, however, small bands, mostly Apaches, continued to cause periodic disruptions. Led by Geronimo and others, the Apaches went through recurring cycles of subjugation, surrender, reservation domicile, break out, and resumption of warfare. General George Crook had succeeded by varying means, not all of them military, in whittling down the frequency of the raids and the size of the renegade parties.

In late March 1886, yet another breakout by Geronimo and about 40 followers caused Sheridan to fire off a caustic note to Crook, while at the same time rejecting Crook's negotiated settlement with a large band of Apaches who had recently surrendered. Contrary to Crook's terms, Sheridan demanded unconditional surrender.

The two officers already disliked one another. Among other things, Sheridan was not enamored of Crook's considerable use of Indian auxiliaries and thought Crook's treatment of the Apaches was too moderate. Greatly angered, on April 1, Crook asked to be reassigned. Sheridan immediately complied, transferring Crook to the Department of the Platte and naming Nelson Miles as his replacement. Miles, using many of Crook's tactics albeit with a harsher edge, eventually quelled the uprising and shipped Geronimo and others off to prison in Florida.

Although he lobbied for improved weapons and supported professional school for artillery, cavalry, infantry, and engineer training, Sheridan was rather conservative by nature. His tenure as commanding general was not known for radical reorganization or innovation.

Several lesser known facets of Sheridan's service highlight an exceptionally diverse career. In 1870, President Grant sent him to Europe to observe and report on the Franco-Prussian War. Sheridan was present at Napoleon III's surrender. In 1871, from his headquarters in the city, Sheridan coordinated relief efforts during the Great Chicago Fire. He was eventually placed in complete charge when the mayor placed the city under martial law.

To a considerable extent, it was through Sheridan's efforts that Yellowstone was conserved as a national park. Acting first in the mid-1870s, he advocated military control to prevent the loss of wildlife and natural features unique to the region. Later, when land developers and railroad interests threatened the park, Sheridan lobbied successfully to protect it. His efforts expanded the park's boundaries, constricted commercial ventures, and prohibited leases near the natural attractions. In 1886, after the park had suffered through a series of incompetent and nefarious superintendents, Sheridan sent in the 1st Cavalry. The military operated Yellowstone until 1916 when the newly formed National Park Service took over.

In the summer of 1888, about two months before his death, Sheridan finished writing his memoirs. Soon after, he was stricken with a massive heart attack in Washington, D.C., and was moved to his summer home in Norquitt, Massachusetts. On June 1, Congress, reacting to his fragile condition, promoted him to four star general. Sheridan died at his summer residence on August 5 at age 57. He was buried at Arlington National Cemetery near the Custis-Lee Mansion.

IN THE SHADOWS OF HISTORY

The contributions of the officers described in the following section ranged from exceptional to disastrous. Some carried out their duties capably but without special flair or fanfare for 20 to 30 years, often while posted at austere forts scattered across remote areas of the nation's frontier. Others saw action in an incredible number of engagements. Most, but not all, prevailed more often than not on the battlefield.

Though their names are typically not as well recalled as those of their more renowned contemporaries, all played roles in America's western saga. Their stories, and their legacies, deserve to be remembered.

Reuben F. Bernard

Counting Civil War encounters and clashes with Native tribes across the Southwest and Pacific Northwest, Reuben F. Bernard claimed to have fought in 103 battles and skirmishes during the course of his career.

Bernard was a rarity among his Army officer contemporaries: he came up through the ranks. Indeed, his first experiences as an Indian fighter occurred as an enlisted man prior to the Civil War. From 1855-1862, he fought against Chiricahua Apaches in New Mexico and Arizona. His abilities were noted and by the standards of the time he moved rapidly through the ranks from private to corporal to sergeant before being made first sergeant of a troop of 1st United States Dragoons.

Early in 1862, with the onset of the Civil War, Bernard was commissioned a second lieutenant in the 1st United States Cavalry. Though brevetted to lieutenant colonel and colonel at the close of the war, Bernard's permanent rank in the Regular Army was first lieutenant. In July 1866, he was promoted to captain and for all practical purposes held that rank through the duration of the Indian wars.

During his many skirmishes, Bernard most often led forces of company size or only slightly larger. That circumstance was not a reflection on his abilities; rather, it was indicative of the nature of many of the conflicts with the Native tribes. Most involved spasm encounters waged by nomadic tribesmen pursued by understrength cavalry units – evidence of the miniscule size of the Army at the time. As a captain, Bernard never served as a district or departmental commander. Although he commanded campaigns and expeditions, the forces involved were, with some exceptions, fairly modest in size.

Two of his most significant leadership roles occurred during the Bannock and Sheepeater wars in the Pacific Northwest. As General Oliver O. Howard's subordinate, Bernard led Howard's "Left Column," comprised of an augmented force of four cavalry companies that fought the Battle of Silver Creek against the Bannocks. During the middle and late stages of the Sheepeater conflict, Bernard had command of three companies and a large contingent of Native scouts – a sizable force given the modest number of troops committed to the conflict.

Bernard enlisted in the Army from his home state of Tennessee in 1855.

He was initially posted to Fort Craig, 35 miles south of Socorro, New Mexico, with the 1st Dragoons, his parent unit through the course of his enlisted service.

Bernard's talents were apparent and by 1861 he was first sergeant of Troop D. Later that year, already a veteran of several skirmishes with the Chiricahua Apaches, he was part of a relief column sent from Fort Breckinridge, located between present-day Mammoth and Winkelman, Arizona, to respond to a crisis precipitated by the arrest of Apache chief Cochise. The chief, erroneously accused of kidnapping the son of a nearby rancher, had escaped prior to Bernard's arrival. The chief proposed an exchange of prisoners – among those held by the cavalry were members of his family – in return for a cessation of hostilities.

Missouri History Museum
Reuben F. Bernard

Bernard counseled the lieutenant in charge, George N. Bascom, to accept the offer. Bascom refused, however, and more than a decade of violence ensued. The lieutenant later charged Bernard with insubordination. Bernard was tried by court-martial and acquitted.

When the Civil War began, Bernard and his unit, now designated the 1st United States Cavalry, were transferred to the eastern theater. The enormous expansion of the Union Army created a demand for qualified individuals to fill officer slots. Bernard's experience in the West made him well suited as an applicant. After serving a few months in an acting capacity, he was officially commissioned as a second lieutenant in the cavalry on July 17, 1862. Promotion to first lieutenant came the following June. Bernard would hold that rank in the Regular Army through the remainder of the war. He was brevetted four times for "gallant and meritorious service:" to captain on May 6, 1864 (Battle of Todd's Tavern, Virginia), to major August 28, 1864 (Battle of Smithfield, Virginia), and to lieutenant colonel and colonel, March 13, 1865 (for the totality of his service during the conflict).

Sent back to the West following the war, Bernard served as commander of Camp Lowell, located on the outskirts of present-day Tucson, through 1868 and the first few months of 1869. He then took command of Fort Bowie, near Willcox in southeast Arizona, and held that position through 1871.

His time at Fort Bowie was most notable for leading eight expeditions against the Chiricahua Apaches during several active months in 1869. The most successful of those campaigns occurred in October in response to a Chiricahua attack on a stage coach near Dragoon Springs (68 miles east of Tucson). The Indians' October 5 raid killed and mutilated a passenger and four soldier escorts.

Soon after, the raiders attacked six cowboys, killing one, and made off with more than a hundred head of cattle.

Reinforced by troops brought in from Camp Goodwin in present-day Graham County, Arizona, and Camp Crittenden, located three miles from Sonoita, Arizona, Bernard took the field to confront the Apaches. About 20 miles east of Willcox, he caught the band near the Chiricahua Pass. In three fights over a span of several days, Bernard's troops killed 30 of the warriors and retook livestock stolen by the Apaches on earlier raids. The most notable of the clashes occurred on October 20. Bernard and his 61-man patrol returned to the scene of a running fight that had taken place a few days earlier in which 12 Apaches had been killed. Picking up the trail left by the Indians after the first encounter, they pursued a band led by Cochise high into the Chiricahua Mountains.

The difficult track pointed toward a campsite recently abandoned near the foot of a mesa. As Bernard's troops reached the area, they were taken under fire by Apaches shooting from atop the butte. Jagged outcroppings and deep ravines cut each side of the mesa, hampering movement. Bernard dismounted his cavalrymen, formed a line and moved up the steep face of the bluff. Under intense fire, 32 soldiers struggled up the slope seeking shelter behind boulders and in stone cairns as they pushed forward.

Eventually, the line reached a rock ledge about 30 yards from the main body of Apaches. The landscape beyond the ledge was fully exposed to Apache fire which swept the field. For a time the soldiers were pinned at that location and lost two men killed and another wounded as the shooting grew in intensity. With his initial assault halted, Bernard launched a flank attack with the remainder of this company but found the Indians' position – on rugged, boulder-strewn ground at the top of the mesa – too strong to take with the relatively few soldiers he had available. Short of manpower and finding the patrol's horses also exposed to fire, Bernard ordered a withdrawal. Although it was Bernard who pulled his forces away from the battle, it was the Apaches who suffered most heavily, losing 18 warriors killed during the encounter.

After command duties in the Southwest, Bernard was posted to the Pacific Northwest where he would serve as key subordinate to General Oliver O. Howard during both the Bannock and Sheepeater Wars in the late 1870s.

First, though, there was a brief but bloody conflict – the Modoc War – to deal with. Fought in California against a small but lethal band of Modoc tribesmen, who made exceptional use of familiar, almost impossibly difficult terrain, the conflict was a severe test for Army forces. Bernard was involved in at least two encounters. On January 16, 1873, he led forces that clashed with the Modocs at Hospital Rock, two miles east of the tribe's lava bed fortress. The skirmish was a precursor to a costly battle fought in the Modoc's stronghold area the following day. Under the overall command of Colonel Frank Wheaton, with a force of two cavalry companies and a contingent of Klamath scouts, Bernard led the east wing of a pincer attack on the fortress. Bernard's role was to launch a spoiling attack and block the Modoc's escape route while the major assault struck from the west. The day-long battle, fought in fog and mist, was unsuccessful. The plan to unite the two wings was abandoned when both units were pinned down by heavy, mostly hidden, fire. At nightfall, Wheaton withdrew his troops from the battlefield. Bernard commanded forces through the remainder of the war which ended in June 1873 with the Modoc's surrender.

When war with the Bannocks erupted in May 1878, Bernard, commanding Company G of the 1st Cavalry, led the initial contingent of troops into the conflict area. On June 2, Bernard moved against the Bannock camp on the Big Camas Prairie. After a brief skirmish, his attack scattered the band which retreated to nearby lava beds. Not long after, as the violence spread and the scope of the uprising became apparent, General Howard assigned him as commander of a force of four companies – designated the "Left Column" – and sent him against the main body of hostiles.

In the early hours of June 23, Bernard's column struck the Bannock camp located along Silver Creek. The attack forced the Indians out of the village into a ravine that the Bannocks had previously prepared for defense. Action continued through the day and into the night as the soldiers pressed the Native's redoubt. When morning on June 24 found the tribe gone, Bernard destroyed the abandoned camp. The engagement cost the cavalry two killed and three wounded, one of whom died two days later. Bannock losses are uncertain but were believed to be substantial.

Bernard launched a vigorous pursuit of the fleeing Bannocks, eventually cutting loose entirely from his infantry contingent. Joined by an additional company on June 27, Bernard continued the chase, keeping his fresh horsemen constantly on the move. On June 29, Bernard, with a cavalry force numbering 350, arrived at Canyon City, shortly after the Bannocks had fought with a local militia unit. With the cavalry close at hand, the tribe continued its move toward Fox Valley, seeking assistance from potential allies.

On July 5, General Howard met the expedition in the field and assumed overall command. Further reinforced near Pilot Rock, Oregon, by the arrival of two additional companies, on July 7 the cavalrymen prepared for an attack on the main Bannock Camp. Discovered by scouts earlier in the day, the camp was located on harsh terrain near Birch Creek. Responding to orders by Howard, Bernard wasted no time in assaulting the camp. Striking at sunrise the following day, Bernard chose to attack with his cavalry dismounted, but moved horses along with the advancing troops to be ready for any sudden break from the scene by groups of warriors. Except for a contingent left to guard the pack animals, Bernard pressed the assault with his entire force. During the course of a day-long fight, the Bannocks were driven from three successive well-defended positions.

Finally, late in the day, a flanking move by Bernard caused the Indians to retreat a substantial distance – four or five miles – into the mountains. The latter portion of the Bannocks' struggle was fought as a delaying action to enable women, children, and part of the horse herd to escape. Bernard lost five men wounded, one of whom later died. The extent of the Bannocks' losses is unknown but several bodies were observed on the battlefield – an indication of substantial casualties, since the Indians seldom left dead or wounded warriors behind.

Worn out by the difficult pursuit over some of the region's harshest terrain, following the battle Bernard took most of his command to Fort Walla Walla, Washington, to rest and refit. The remainder of the war was essentially fought as a series of small-unit actions waged against dispersed bands of warriors. By the end of August, the fighting was over and the Bannocks were on the way back to their reservations. Bernard returned with Company G to the unit's duty station at Fort Boise.

Early in 1879, Bernard, still commanding Company G, was again a first responder, deploying with his unit at the outset of the Sheepeater War. Traveling through horrendous conditions and inhospitable terrain, Bernard and his men struck towards the hamlet of Orogrande, reaching it in early June. They found it totally destroyed with many buildings burned to the ground. For the next several weeks Bernard moved up the Middle Fork of the Salmon River. In what would become an epic pursuit, he and his men persevered though losses of animals, ammunition, and supplies. The column pressed on, often tormented by torrential downpours, cold nights, and high winds. Plentiful game sustained Bernard's 75 or so soldiers, scouts, and freight drivers.

Joined by two more companies and additional scouts near the hot springs at North Payette River, Bernard maintained his quick march, passing through areas recently burned by the Sheepeaters. The column again lost pack animals and supplies as the grueling trek continued. On August 11, a supply train reprovisioned Bernard's strike force.

Resupplied, the combined unit resumed the chase, closing the gap with the fleeing tribe. Bernard's troopers moved past recently abandoned campsites and Indian fish traps, as the trail became more obvious. At mid-month, scouts located a Sheepeater village a few miles in advance of the column. Bernard hurried his force to the site only to find it abandoned. Bernard's Umatilla scouts looted the village and Bernard burned what was left.

When the following morning brought reports that the tribe was still close by, Bernard split his column to search for the Indians. On August 20, one search party fought off an attack by a dozen or so raiders at a location known as Soldier Bar on Big Creek.

For a time Bernard maintained the hurried pursuit. The ground was broken and rocky and several horses broke down from exhaustion. One night, two dozen or more wandered off. Fortunately for the troopers, all were found the following day. Bernard returned briefly to Camp Howard, a nearby temporary post, to resupply.

On September 17, Bernard's soldiers again took up the chase. Rather quickly they came upon an Indian camp, but found the site mostly abandoned. The soldiers took a woman and some children captive before an unexpected event changed the course of the war. An Indian named Tanmanmo, possibly a war chief, surrendered to the soldiers. Believing that the Sheepeaters had enough of the fighting and the exhausting chase, he offered to bring in the rest of the warrior band in return for promised sanctuary for the tribe.

Two weeks later, two officers accompanied by about 20 Umatilla scouts negotiated the surrender of the Sheepeater band. After capitulating on October 1, the tribe was taken to Vancouver Barracks. A short time later they were resettled on the Fort Hall Reservation. Bernard's soldiers returned to Fort Boise after a campaign of more than 1,200 miles through mostly uncharted territory.

The Sheepeater conflict ended Bernard's Indian fighting days in the Pacific Northwest. More was to follow, however, although in a different part of the country.

With the Pacific Northwest pacified, Bernard's unit was among the forces transferred to the Southwest to confront the violent Apache uprisings that persisted there.

Numerous skirmishes followed, the most notable occurring in the confused aftermath of the Apache's ambush of General Eugene A. Carr's troops at Cibecue Creek on August 30, 1881, and the attempted attack on Fort Apache soon after. Fearing retribution, a sizable band of Ciricahuas fled toward Mexico raiding as they moved south. On October 2 they attacked a wagon train near Cedar Springs, Arizona, but were thwarted by the presence of nearby troops who immediately gave chase. Bernard, leading two companies of the 1st Cavalry, was joined by two additional companies from the 6th Cavalry in an extended running fight that lasted until 9 o'clock at night.

Late in the day the Indians were forced into nearby hills and made a stand there. Possibly to provide time for the women and children to escape with the band's livestock, at about 8 p.m. Apache warriors made an all-out rush at Bernard's troopers that carried to within a few feet of the Bernard's line.

The soldiers fought off the charge and held their ground until darkness eventually halted the fighting. The Apaches slipped away during the night carrying their casualties with them. Bernard and his composite cavalry units lost one killed and three wounded during the fight. Pursuit resumed the following day and extended all the way to the border before the Chiricahuas crossed into Mexico.

The skirmish was typical in many ways of the extraordinary number of small unit encounters fought by Bernard during the course of his long career. In 1890, Bernard received a brevet promotion to brigadier general for his service against the Apaches at Chiricahua Pass (October 1869), and later at Silver Creek, Oregon (June 23, 1878), and Birch Creek, Oregon (July 8, 1878) during the Bannock War.

After 41 years of service, Bernard retired from the Army in 1896 with the permanent rank of lieutenant colonel. After his retirement, he served as the first president of the Order of Indian Wars and as governor of the United States Soldiers Home in Washington, D.C. He held both of those positions until his death in Washington on November 17, 1903.

He was buried at Arlington National Cemetery.

Edward R. S. Canby

Two unusual aspects draw attention to the brief, bloody conflict known as the Modoc War. The first is location. Much of the fiercest fighting took place in California – not a place normally associated with Indian wars of the American West. Nonetheless, from November 29, 1872, until June 1, 1873, the bitter struggle raged across northern California and southern Oregon.

The second notable feature is that Modoc War was the only one of all the Indian wars in which a Regular Army general was killed. That officer was General Edward R. S. Canby. (Custer, although brevetted to major general during the Civil War, held the rank of lieutenant colonel in the Regular Army at the time of his death at the Little Bighorn.) A further irony is that Canby had little to do with the actual fighting. He was killed while serving as counselor to a peace commission.

Canby's death would be one of approximately 60 suffered by U.S. forces during the war. Another 50 or so soldiers were wounded. Given that only about 500-700 troops were committed to the fight, the percentage of casualties was unusually high. Modoc fighting skills certainly contributed to that outcome – a result made even more extraordinary by the fact that there were possibly only 50-55 Modoc warriors engaged in the war at any one time (the numbers most often quoted are 52-53; the highest cited by any source is 89). Terrain was also a predominate factor. The Modocs exploited their intimate knowledge of some of the most severe landscape in North America.

Major fighting on the lava beds near Tule Lake, California, took place on ground heavily concentrated with jagged outcroppings, caves, caverns, and razor-like ridges. Seams in the lava provided secluded trenches through which the Modocs moved undetected, shifting from location to location along interior lines.

Army units paid a heavy price for their assaults on what proved to be a formidable, if not impregnable, fortress. As the struggle shifted outside the lava beds, the landscape was only slightly less benign. Heavy timber and rugged mountains provided ample venues for defensive stands and ambushes.

Edward Richard Sprigg Canby was born November 9, 1817, at Piatt's Landing, Kentucky. He attended Wabash College for a time before receiving an appointment to West Point. Not an academician, he graduated in 1839 next to last in a class of 31. After commissioning, he was sent almost immediately to Florida where he served in the Second Seminole War. Duty in the war with Mexico followed a few years later. Notably, he was brevetted three times for his actions at Contreras, Churubusco, and Belen Gates. He also saw action at Veracruz and Cerro Gordo.

Theo. Lilienthal, Public Domain
Edward R. S. Canby

Canby became known through the small Army as an adept administrator. During the course of his 34-year career, he often found himself assigned to adjutant general and administrative duties.

Contemporary accounts indicate that he went about his job quietly, without flash or fanfare. His unobtrusive manner came across to some associates as stern or taciturn. It seems equally likely, however, that it reflected a natural modesty and reserve. After the Civil War, in difficult Reconstruction duties in the South, even his bitterest opponents came to regard him as firm, calm, and almost painfully honest. Canby carried himself like a soldier; his ramrod straight posture accentuated a tall, slender build. He remained clean-shaven, a rarity at the time.

Administrative duties, first in New York and later in California followed his service in Mexico. In California, a passable knowledge of Spanish helped him sort out disputed land titles. Postings in Wyoming, Utah, and New Mexico – where in 1860 he would wage a mostly unsuccessful campaign against Navajos – followed.

Canby was in command at Fort Defiance, New Mexico Territory, in present-day Apache County, Arizona, when the Civil War broke out. When Confederate forces invaded New Mexico early in 1862, Canby was beaten at the Battle of Valverde. In the aftermath, he placed a string of encampments along the Rio Grande, Pecos, and Canadian Rivers. His defensive strategy – the camps straddled the Confederates' supply routes and most likely avenues of attack – eventually forced the rebels to withdraw. The Union's strategic victory at Glorietta Pass caused the Confederates to abandon the invasion and retreat into Texas.

After Glorietta Pass, Canby was promoted to brigadier general and reassigned to the eastern theater. For a time after the New York City draft riots in 1863, he was posted to Washington, D.C., in duties he described as "Assistant Adjutant General" to the Secretary of War. His exceptional service in that capacity led to his promotion to major general.

In May 1864, Canby was sent west to replace the ineffectual Nathaniel P.

Banks after the failure of the Red River Expedition. Canby was later named commander of the Military District of Western Mississippi and was in those duties when he was wounded by a sniper while on a Union gunboat in Arkansas. As the war was drawing to a close in the spring of 1865, Canby organized the campaign against Mobile, Alabama, that led to the capture of the city on April 2.

Canby played an interesting role in Civil War history. Soon after the Mobile campaign he accepted the surrender of the last two Confederate armies in the west. On May 8, 1865, he took the surrender of rebel forces led by General Richard Taylor. Eighteen days later, on May 26, General Edmund Kirby Smith surrendered the last Confederate forces operating west of the Mississippi River. The capitulation of Smith's army, the last major rebel force in the field, effectively brought an end to the war.

After the war, Canby's administrative skills resulted in a number of postings in some of the more difficult billets in the postwar Army, commanding Union forces engaged in occupation duty in the South. In succession, he commanded in Louisiana; a district surrounding Washington, D.C., consisting of Delaware, Maryland, and portions of Virginia; North and South Carolina, and Texas. Those duties were interrupted only by an assignment to Washington, D.C., where Ulysses S. Grant, Commanding General of the United States Army, regarded him as indispensable.

In 1870, Canby was posted to the Pacific Northwest where he was eventually confronted by an incipient uprising by a small tribe whose homeland spanned portions of northern California and southern Oregon. Trouble had long been festering with the Modocs. Moved earlier to a reservation that also housed their historic enemies, the Klamath tribe, the Modocs had left the reservation for a time years before. When settler complaints again arose, the tribe was induced to return to the reservation in late 1869. They did not stay long. Immediately and repeatedly harassed by the Klamaths, the Modocs left the agency again in April 1870. Led by Chief Kientpoos – known to the white community as Captain Jack – 372 Modocs moved south to their home country along the Lost River.

On November 28, 1872, troops from Fort Klamath, Oregon, supplemented by local militia, under the overall command of Major John Green, were sent by the Bureau of Indian Affairs to induce the Modocs to return to the reservation. Discussions led by Captain James Jackson, the on-scene commander, initially appeared to offer promise of a peaceful outcome. Eventually, though, for reasons that are not certain, a skirmish developed. The Modocs resisted but ultimately fled as Green's troops burned their village. Casualties occurred on both sides. One soldier was killed and another wounded among Jackson's men and two were killed and three wounded among the Modocs.

The Modocs initially split into three groups. One, not under Captain Jack's command, killed 14 (or 18, the number is in dispute) male settlers in retaliation for Green's attack. Others led by Captain Jack moved across Tule Lake and entered the natural fortress formed by the lava beds. Eventually the three Modoc bands converged there under the loose overall command of Captain Jack.

Although Canby would play little direct part in the fighting, his plan for the campaign was to squeeze the Modocs by moving forces ever more tightly around the fortress and pressuring the Modocs to surrender. Skirmishes and ambushes followed rather quickly. On December 3, while moving along a dry creek bed, a local militia unit ventured close to Captain Jack's stronghold. The unit, perhaps numbering as many as 23 men, was surprised by Modoc attackers who killed everyone in the party. On December 21, Modoc raiders struck from their lava bed fortress, attacking an Army ammunition wagon at Land's Ranch.

Army reinforcements reached the area by mid-January 1873, bulking up the available force to about 400 troopers. The on-scene commander, Colonel Frank Wheaton, led U.S. Army soldiers as well as militia companies drawn from California and Oregon. Action was not long in coming. On January 16, 1873, troops led by Colonel Reuben F. Bernard skirmished with Modoc warriors near Hospital Rock.

The Army's major response was forthcoming on January 17. On a wet, foggy morning 300 or so troopers and local volunteers under the direct command of Frank Wheaton assaulted the stronghold. Taking advantage of the rugged landscape, the Modocs inflicted heavy casualties, defeating attacks from the east and west and forcing the troops – cold, exhausted, and confused by the intricate terrain – to abandon their assault leaving weapons and dead behind.

The battle was costly to the attackers. Thirty-five soldiers were killed or wounded. Modoc losses are uncertain but likely inconsequential as they deftly exploited the advantages offered by the terrain.

Parleys with Captain Jack conducted by Army leaders and government officials followed in the days ahead. The Modocs persisted in their request for a reservation on the Lost River. With the talks at an impasse, the Grant administration proposed a Peace Commission to meet with the Modocs. General Canby was appointed counselor to the commissioners. By some accounts, Captain Jack was disposed to negotiate a truce, if not a settlement, but was dissuaded by leaders of the band already indicted for the murders of the 14 (or 18) settlers. This version has Captain Jack brow-beaten into a plot to kill the peace commissioners sent by the government.

Although apparently warned of the plot beforehand by a friendly Modoc interpreter, Canby along with three other commissioners agreed to meet with the tribe's representatives on the morning of April 11. Different recollections of the meeting exist, but sometime during the session, soon after Captain Jack repeated – and was denied – his request for a Lost River reservation, he drew a hidden revolver and killed General Canby who, like the other commissioners, was unarmed. One other commissioner was killed by the Modoc chief, a third was wounded, and the fourth escaped unharmed. Canby's body was later recovered. He had been shot twice in the head and his throat had been slit.

Four days after the commissioners were killed, the Army retaliated. On April 15, forces led by Colonel Alvan C. Gillem launched a second assault on the fortress. (Colonel Wheaton had been sacked after the earlier, failed attack.) Gillem's plan to completely surround the stronghold did not come to fruition, but two days of hard fighting succeeded in cutting off the tribe from its Tule Lake water supply. The next morning, April 17, troops captured the fortress but found the Modocs had escaped through a hidden crevasse. Captain Jack took his followers south toward the Schonchin Lava Flow and replenished their water supply from nearby ice caves. The battle cost the Army seven killed and 13 wounded. Modoc casualties were believed to be light.

On April 26, as the Modocs journeyed south, they ambushed a 71-man cavalry patrol accompanied by scouts sent to look for them. They attacked as the soldiers were eating lunch near the base of Sand Butte (now called Hardin Butte). In a brief battle that probably lasted less than an hour, some troops fled in disorder. The Modoc attackers killed or wounded all 35 who stayed to fight. The catastrophic loss again caused the Army to change commanders. Colonel Gillem was replaced by Brigadier General Jefferson C. Davis.

Three weeks later, on May 11, the Modoc's fortunes began to turn when they were soundly defeated while attempting a surprise attack on soldiers camped near Dry Lake. In a headlong retreat, the tribe lost most of its horses and supplies. The death of a prominent war chief, killed during the battle, added to Modoc's devastation. Exhausted and under constant pursuit, quarrels broke out within the tribal group. One small band split off and moved west toward the present-day city of Dorris, California. Meanwhile, Captain Jack and a larger group trekked in the direction of Big Sand Butte, apparently intending to make a stand there.

In the days ahead, the smaller group was apprehended by the Army and quickly offered to help track down Captain Jack and turn him over to government authorities. They did so, and in early June 1873, Captain Jack surrendered at Willow Creek, California.

Although the numbers vary widely by source, statistics from the war paint a grim picture. The Army lost 55-67 killed and another 50 wounded. Somewhere between 16 and 20 civilians also died in the fighting. Modoc losses were thought to be considerably less: perhaps 17 warriors killed of whom four were executed after the fighting ended.

In the aftermath, leaders of the band that assisted the Army were granted amnesty. Ironically, it was this band that had killed the settlers and precipitated the war. The Modocs who had killed the peace commissioners were tried at Fort Klamath and convicted of murder. On October 3, 1873, four, including Captain

Jack, were hanged. Two others were imprisoned. Survivors of Captain Jack's band were exiled to an agency in Oklahoma.

Canby's remains were returned to Indianapolis, Indiana, where his family had a home. He was buried in that city at Crown Hill Cemetery on May 23, 1873. Among those who attended the ceremony were several prominent officers including Generals Sherman and Sheridan. Lew Wallace and Irwin McDowell served as pall bearers.

OTHER COMMANDERS DURING THE MODOC WAR

The Army's setbacks during the Modoc conflict prompted a musical chairs rotation of senior commanders into the fight. Although the war was of short duration, several commanders led forces during the major battles. The most notable included the following officers:

Lieutenant Colonel Frank Wheaton: A lieutenant colonel at the time he directed the first attacks on Captain Jack's stronghold, Wheaton would retire as a major general in 1897. A native of Providence, Rhode Island, at age 22 he was commissioned directly as first lieutenant in the 1st cavalry and was sent west for duty on the frontier. The Civil War found him as a lieutenant colonel in a Rhode Island infantry unit. During the fighting at First Bull Run, Wheaton assumed command when the regiment's colonel was killed. Wheaton served in the Peninsula Campaign and commanded a brigade at Fredericksburg, in actions around Chancellorsville, through the Wilderness, and during the siege of Petersburg. Promoted to division commander, he helped defeat Jubal Early's thrust towards Washington, D.C., and served under Philip Sheridan in the Shenandoah Valley. By the end of the war, he was a brevet major general in both the volunteer and regular corps.

Wheaton remained in the Army as a lieutenant colonel after the war, the outcome at the lava beds being one of the few blemishes on his record during the course of his long career.

Wheaton died in Washington, D.C. in 1903 and was buried at Arlington National Cemetery.

Major John Green: John Green led the largest attack force, the west wing, of the initial January 17, 1873, assault on Captain Jack's fortress. A German by birth, Green came to America at age six in 1831. At age 21, he enlisted in the Army and served as a sergeant in the U.S. Mounted Rifles during the war with Mexico. Commissioned as an officer at the start of the Civil War, he would eventually be brevetted to lieutenant colonel for his service, which included major actions at Antietam and Gettysburg. Green remained in the Army after the war, serving initially in the grade of major. Soon brevetted to colonel for commanding forces against the Apaches in Arizona, he was posted to the Pacific Northwest and was in command at Fort Klamath when the Modoc War began.

When forces under Lieutenant Colonel Frank Wheaton made the first assault against the lava beds, John Green commanded the "west force" in a planned pincer attack comprised of an overall total of about 400 men. Green's command consisted of an infantry company, a cavalry troop, two companies of Oregon militia, a company of California volunteers, and two 12-pounder mountain howitzers.

Wheaton's notion was to have Green's force, supported by the howitzers, carry the main attack from the west. Meanwhile, a smaller unit under Reuben F. Bernard would move from the east and close the Modoc's likely escape route. Once launched, the two wings would meet in the middle of the lava fields and trap the Modocs against Tule Lake.

When Green's force moved from the southwest corner in the early hours of January 17, a dense fog blanketed the area, preventing the howitzer crews from providing supporting fire. Green moved his force about a mile and a half into the heart of the lava beds, attempting to link up with Bernard's approach from the east. Confronted by difficult ground and increasingly heavy fire from Modocs hidden in the rocks and further concealed by fog, the advance slowed and eventually ground to a halt, stopped finally by a chasm too deep to cross.

To the east, Bernard's column met with a similar fate when initial progress was halted by an impassable ravine. Bernard had his men build a rudimentary fortification as a blocking position.

Wheaton abandoned the plan to close the pincer south of the stronghold. At Green's suggestion, an attempt was made to link up along the lake shore. Difficulties soon arose, however, when Bernard's forces were initially unable, or unwilling, to move. Green then attempted to shift his unit north along the edge of the lake. About 50 yards from the heart of the Modoc fortification, they were pinned down by withering fire. Green was wounded when he stood up, exposing himself to volleys from Modoc sharpshooters. The dismounted cavalry troops and half an infantry company struggled forward, eventually managing to connect with a portion of the Bernard's force. However, much of the infantry and the entire California volunteer force remained pinned down along the shore line and had to wait until darkness to withdraw.

The linkup between west and east forces was too thin and scattered to be of consequence. Late in the day, probably around 5 p.m., Wheaton realized the attack had failed and ordered Green and Bernard to retreat. It had been a horrific day for his command. Several dead were left on the battlefield along with rifles and ammunition quickly seized by the Modoc victors. So thick was the fog and so superb was the Indians' concealment that most soldiers had not glimpsed a Modoc warrior during the course of the battle.

Wheaton was subsequently relieved of command, replaced by Colonel

Alvan C. Gillem. John Green was later award the Medal of Honor for his gallantry in leading his men forward.

When Gillem replaced Wheaton as campaign commander after the first battle of the stronghold, Green remained Gillem's subordinate and commanded a mixed battalion of cavalry and infantry during the second, more successful, attack that followed.

Green remained in the Army until 1889, retiring as a colonel with a brevet promotion to brigadier general. He died in 1908 at Boise, Idaho, and was buried at Morris Hill Cemetery in that city.

Colonel Alvan C. Gillem: A native of Gainesboro, Tennessee, at age 21 Gillem graduated 11th in the West Point class of 1851. He was sent almost immediately to Florida where for a year he commanded a battery during the Seminole War. From Florida he was sent to Texas and served there on frontier duty for several years.

During the Civil War, Gillem's postings were initially in the western theater. Operating with the Army of the Ohio, he served as quartermaster, provost marshal, adjutant general, and troop commander in the 5th Infantry and in cavalry units. In September 1864, while shielding eastern Tennessee, troops under his command surprised and killed Confederate General John Hunt Morgan. As the conflict neared an end, he led forces involved in the capture of Salisbury, North Carolina. He was brevetted for bravery three times and ended the war as a brevet major general of volunteers and a brevet colonel in the Regular Army.

After the war, he served for two years as commander of the Fourth Military District, responsible for occupation forces in Arkansas and Mississippi. From there, he was posted again to Texas before being assigned to California.

Gillem's participation in the Modoc War had a checkered outcome. Although the April 15, 1873 attack, the second assault on Captain Jack's stronghold, was modestly successful in driving the Modocs out of their fortress, the ambush of one of his patrols 11 days later resulted in his being relieved of command. The so-called "Thomas-Wright Massacre" (named after the two officers who led the patrol) resulted in devastating losses to an ill-prepared unit. A week after the ambush at Sand Butte, the new commander of the Department of the Columbia, Brigadier General Jefferson C. Davis, relieved Gillem from command.

In 1875, at age 45, Gillem became seriously ill. He returned to his home in Tennessee to convalesce but died soon after while confined to a Soldier's Home. He was buried in Nashville at Mount Olivet Cemetery.

Brigadier General Jefferson C. Davis: Not to be confused with the Confederate President of the same name, Jefferson Columbus Davis was a Union general from Indiana who saw considerable action, and sparked considerable controversy, during the Civil War.

Davis was at Fort Sumter in April, 1861, when the war began. Quickly paroled, by August he was a colonel commanding an Indiana regiment which he led at the Battle of Wilson's Creek. In December, he became a brigadier general of volunteers and led divisions at Pea Ridge and Corinth. In August, 1864, Davis received a brevet promotion of major general for his service at the Battle of Kennesaw Mountain and was appointed commander of XIV Corps during the Atlanta Campaign. He served in that capacity as a member of Sherman's staff for the remainder of the war. He was brevetted to brigadier general in the Regular Army as the war drew to a close.

Though quite capable as a field commander, two controversial actions during the course of the war tarnished his legacy and possibly hindered his prospects for higher rank. On September 29, 1862, while recuperating from illness in Louisville, Kentucky, he shot and killed his superior officer, Major General William "Bull" Nelson. There was a history of bad blood between the men. Davis had long been offended by Nelson's public insults. When a bitter argument erupted, Davis shot and killed Nelson after Nelson slapped him in the face. Davis was initially arrested and imprisoned, but perhaps because the Union was in desperate need of competent field commanders, he was released after intervention by higher officials.

Davis's reputation was further clouded in December, 1864, when during Sherman's March to the Sea, he removed a pontoon bridge over Ebenezer Creek before African-Americans following Sherman's Army could cross. Hundreds were left to the vengeful mercies of Confederate cavalry.

Davis remained in the Army as a colonel in the regular establishment after the war. Notably, on March 15, 1868, he became the first American commander of the Department of Alaska after that territory was acquired from Russia. His treatment of Russian residents was sometimes questioned and his service there was not without controversy.

Davis received good marks for his leadership during the Modoc War. His presence in the field after replacing Alvan Gillem restored confidence after the shocks at the lava beds and the massacre of the Thomas-Wright patrol. His subsequent victory at Dry Lake devastated the Modocs and was the beginning of the end of the uprising.

In 1877, the final notable act of his extended military career was to lead a force of 300 men, equipped with two Gatling guns, to put down a general strike in St. Louis. Davis died in Chicago on November 30, 1879. He was buried in Crown Hill Cemetery in Indianapolis, Indiana. Ironically, that is also the burial place of General Edward R. S. Canby, whose murder prompted the Modoc conflagration.

Caleb Carlton

I t is doubtful that many of his Army colleagues saw duty at more frontier posts than did Colonel Caleb H. Carlton. From the time he was assigned to Camp Augur, Nebraska, in March 1867, his list of assignments over the next 30 years reads like a litany of the most historic posts of the Old West: Fort Laramie (twice); Fort Fetterman (twice); Fort Sill (three times); Fort McKavett, Texas; Fort D.A. Russell, Wyoming; Fort Sidney, Nebraska; Fort Sanders, Wyoming; Fort Lowell, Arizona; Fort Davis, Texas; Fort Elliott, Texas; Fort Brown, Texas; Camp Schofield, Indian Territory; and Fort Meade, South Dakota.

Carlton was post commander at Fort Sidney from January 1879 until May 1880, and at Fort Elliott from September 1886 to July 1887. In early 1892 he took command of the 8th Cavalry and held that position as well as post commander of Fort Meade until June 28, 1897.

Although his name is not attached in a major way to specific battles and campaigns, Carlton was on the periphery of many of the major events on the frontier. He was at Fort Fetterman in 1868-1869 at the close of Red Cloud's War. After Custer's defeat at the Little Bighorn in June 1876, he was sent from Fort McKavett, Texas, to Fort D.A. Russell at Cheyenne, Wyoming. He served there and at Forts Fetterman and Laramie through the Great Sioux War of 1876-1877.

Carlton took command of Fort Sidney, Nebraska, on January 27, 1879, arriving shortly after the Cheyenne Outbreak from nearby Fort Robinson. While at Fort Sanders, Wyoming, 1880, he led an expedition to North Park, Colorado, to help quell at threatened uprising. During July-October 1887, he led his battalion across Texas from Fort Elliott to Fort Brown.

In many ways, Carlton's career is representative of much of the officer corps of the frontier Army. He performed unheralded, routine duties leading scouts, fighting skirmishes, and handling a multitude of unglamorous tasks while living at austere posts far from civilization. Although fate did not assign Carlton and others like him major roles in great events, it is difficult to see how the Army could have functioned without officers like them.

Photos taken at the time Carlton began his frontier service show him as dark haired with a modest, but full, mustache. Side burns smaller than those typical of the time set off angular jaws, chin, and nose.

Carlton was a 30-year old veteran of Civil War combat when he reported to

Camp Augur on the Nebraska frontier. He was
born in Cleveland, Ohio, on September 1, 1836,
and graduated from West Point with the class of
1859.

Carlton saw extensive action during the Civil
War. During the first two years of the conflict he
fought in the Peninsula Campaign and at Gaines
Mill, Malvern Hill, Manassas, and Antietam.
After the latter battle he was assigned for a
time to staff duty in Washington, D.C., before
being posted to Rosecrans' army in the western
theater. In command of the 89th Ohio Volunteer
Infantry, his regiment was caught in the chaos of
the second day at Chickamauga. Engulfed by an
entire Confederate division, his unit was forced

Courtesy Ohio Museum Connection
Caleb Carlton

to surrender. Carlton was a prisoner of war from September 20, 1863, until May
7, 1864, when he was freed on a prisoner exchange. After his release he returned
to active duty and saw action at Kennesaw Mountain and during the siege of
Atlanta. In the closing days of the war he served as a regimental commander at
Chattanooga and as commander of the Western District of Kentucky.

The nation perhaps owes Carlton a unique, but little known, debt. In 1892, as
post commander at Fort Meade, South Dakota, he began the custom of playing
the "Star Spangled Banner" at military ceremonies and requested that those in
attendance stand, remove their hats, and show proper respect to the flag.

Carlton retired from the Army on June 30, 1897, after nearly 40 years of
service. He died March 21, 1923, at Atlantic City, New Jersey. He is buried near
his Cleveland, Ohio, birthplace.

Henry B. Carrington

Colonel Henry B. Carrington had the misfortune to command U.S. Army forces on the northern Plains during much of Red Cloud's War – a conflict some scholars have labeled as the only war other than Vietnam in which the U.S. did not achieve its primary objectives.

Carrington's area of responsibility covered an immense region of present-day Wyoming and Montana. His already onerous burden of pacifying and providing security over such a vast area was made more difficult, if not impossible, by circumstances that constrained his operations. Forces under Carrington's command were chronically undermanned, insufficiently equipped, and supplied only with great difficulty over extreme distances.

Carrington was unfairly blamed for the loss of an entire unit of 80 men sent to rescue a besieged wood-gathering detail. Other than the Little Bighorn, the Fetterman Fight, as the episode became known, was the Plains Indians' greatest victory. Although Carrington was relieved of his command after the Fetterman incident, testimony later revealed that Captain William J. Fetterman, the officer in charge of the relief force, had disobeyed Carrington's explicit orders.

Born in Wallingford, Connecticut, on March 2, 1824, Henry Carrington graduated from Yale in 1845 and attended law school there in 1847. After teaching for a brief time, he moved to Columbus, Ohio, to join in a law partnership. Multi-talented, with readily apparent administrative and organizational skills, at various times during his life he was a teacher, lawyer, writer, engineer, and senior Army officer.

Active in the anti-slavery movement, Carrington helped organize the Republican Party in Ohio. Carrington became a close friend and ally of Ohio Governor Salmon P. Chase, Abraham Lincoln's rival for the 1860 presidential nomination and later Secretary of Treasury in Lincoln's cabinet. In 1857, Governor Chase tasked Carrington with reorganizing the Ohio state militia. Soon after, Chase appointed him the state's adjutant general. By the outbreak of the Civil War, Carrington had created ten regiments of militia. He would eventually organize and equip 26 Ohio regiments. Carrington's administrative talents were widely recognized and in May 1861 he was commissioned as a colonel in the 18th U.S. Infantry.

Aware of Carrington's accomplishments in building Ohio's militia force, in 1862 Indiana's governor, Oliver A. Morton, asked for Carrington's help in organizing that state's military establishment. He succeeded in doing so, but drew criticism from some quarters for his zealous measures in support of Morton's efforts to gather intelligence on rebel sympathizers and break up groups favoring the secessionist cause. Nonetheless, in 1863 he was promoted to brigadier general and was placed in command of an Indiana-Ohio region eventually named the Northern Department.

Public Domain
Henry B. Carrington

Although some accounts have him accompanying the campaign that led to the Battle of Philippi early in the war, it is uncertain if Carrington ever heard a shot fired in anger. His superiors apparently regarded his recruiting and organizing talents so exceptional that he was kept in those duties.

Carrington remained in the Army when the conflict ended. In the summer of 1866 he was placed in command of a major, ostensibly peaceful, expedition bound from Fort Kearny, Nebraska, to Fort Laramie, Wyoming, where treaty talks were underway between the government and Sioux, Northern Cheyenne, and Arapaho tribesmen. The focus of the discussions was the Bozeman Trail, the shortest and easiest route from Fort Laramie and the Oregon Trail to the gold fields in Montana. The trail traversed the heart of Sioux and Cheyenne hunting grounds. Though the Natives regarded it as a threat to their way of life, there was little understanding among government officials, military or civilian, of the intensity of the Indians' opposition or of their ability to isolate and shut down the roadway.

A major area of contention was the government's intention to establish three military posts along the route to assist travelers and provide security. Several tribal leaders, Red Cloud foremost among them, objected to the military's presence on lands they regarded as their own. Lush with timber, water, and wildlife, the free-ranging tribes placed great value on the territory designed by the Army as the Montana District.

With talks already well underway, Carrington left Fort Kearny on May 14, 1866, with 700 men, four artillery pieces, and 226 wagons. Carrington had recognized his deficiencies in manpower and equipment. With the concurrence of his superiors he had delayed his departure until recruit levees were available to flesh out his depleted ranks and new Spencer carbines and fresh horses could be provided to a modest portion of his force. Initially, about 200 of his 700 soldiers were issued Spencer carbines and about the same number of his cavalry received mounts. Nonetheless, expecting an operating environment that government officials and senior military leaders had publically characterized as benign occupation duty, Carrington moved his inexperienced, marginally equipped force across the Plains toward Fort Laramie. The anticipated peaceful nature of the expedition was evidenced by the fact that several officers brought their wives along to accompany them during the march.

Seeking to reach Fort Laramie while the talks were still on-going so he could meet with the chiefs, participate in the discussions, and gain an appreciation of the treaty provisions, Carrington moved his column at a steady pace. After a march of 600 miles, he reached the fort on June 14. Carrington arrived at Fort Laramie only to find a shortage of officers, insufficient ammunition, and a lack of basic supplies including baking utensils.

During the latter stages of their trek across the Plains, Carrington's force had been frequently harassed by Indian raiders, an early indication that the recently concluded treaty was not holding. These first raids were precursors to the full blown uprising that would rage for the next two years.

Though most Sioux and Cheyenne leaders had agreed to the opening of the Bozeman Trail, or had not openly opposed it, the issue regarding the establishment of forts remained contentious. Still, the attacks by hostiles took government authorities by surprise – Carrington's expedition was intended as a peaceable march, not as a military campaign. Although officials minimized the seriousness of the raids for a considerable time, events would show that the size and composition of Carrington's force was inadequate to the task at hand.

It was typical of Carrington's ill-fortune that his move toward Fort Laramie and the timing of his arrival served to increase existing tensions. Word of Carrington's approach with his 700-man force prompted Red Cloud to quit the negotiations, asserting that the government had acted in bad faith by sending troops to take Sioux territory before the Indians had agreed to it. As the talks continued, government representatives maintained the position that safe transit of travelers and commerce could only be assured by the presence of three forts along the trail. Eventually, some chiefs came to favor that concession. Others did so only after gifts were provided. Red Cloud and several other leaders remained adamantly opposed, having told government negotiators that war was assured if the trail was opened and forts established. Small raids and thefts of livestock began immediately. By June 30, it became necessary for Carrington to provide escorts for all wagon trains moving up the trail.

Carrington's orders were to establish, organize, and command the Montana District. When he took over, the district had only one post, Fort Reno, about 160 miles distant from Fort Laramie, the region's major installation. Carrington's original instructions from senior commanders were to move Fort Reno 40 miles west, garrison it, and establish another post on the Bozeman Trail between the

Bighorn Mountains and the Powder River. Eventually two additional posts, one of the Bighorn River and a second on the Yellowstone, would also be built. The plan to relocate Fort Reno was immediately abandoned, overcome by the immediacy and scope of the existing threat. Rather than vacating and moving the post, Carrington instead felt compelled to repair and reinforce it. With repairs underway, Carrington left 200 of his initial force to man the post.

With his 500 remaining troops, Carrington moved up the trail toward the Bighorn Mountains. On July 13, the force made camp along Big Piney Creek, about four miles from the Bighorn range. Noting the favorable location, a few days later Carrington began building a fortification. The site, well chosen, was on a plateau abundant with grass and vegetation overlooking meadows rife with game. The sides sloped abruptly away in all directions, forming a natural perimeter. Timber from surrounding pine forests was plentiful as was clear water from nearby streams.

Carrington personally marked out the boundaries of the future Fort Phil Kearny and set up an extensive saw mill operation – a logging camp on Piney Island, about seven miles distant – to cut lumber for construction. As many as 90 wagons were used to haul the lumber from the mill location near present-day Story, Wyoming. Eventually, the fort would enclose a 600 by 800-foot area. Included inside it were separate quarters for infantry and cavalrymen, the unit's band, and the post commander; an officer's row, post headquarters, a sutler's shop which also doubled as a social club; a guard house, hospital, quartermaster and commissary buildings; a laundry facility and a powder magazine. The stockade that ringed the fort was formed of logs buried to a depth of three feet and extending eight feet above the ground. Firing notches were cut into it on every fifth log. There were gates on all sides. Five guard stands were manned at all times. Atop a 124-foot flagpole, an enormous 20 by 30 foot American flag was visible from a great distance by travelers coming up the trail.

Notably, though, the same features that attracted Carrington to the location also made it appealing to the local tribes. The area was a natural transit site and source of supply to hostile as well as non-hostile bands. Despite the fort's formidable appearance, a state of siege existed almost from the start. In one month, there were 35 attacks at or near the post. During the construction of the fort, it became difficult to cut and transport lumber except under heavy guard. Four blockhouses were built at the logging site and along the route to the fort. As the frequency and intensity of the raids increased, livestock were stampeded, wagon trains were repeatedly attacked, and movements outside the walls of the fort were impossible unless under heavy guard. Horse and cattle herds had to be protected around the clock. By one estimation, in the first six months after construction began on the fort and the sawmill site, 154 persons were killed, many of them wood-chopping teamsters and other civilian workers hired by the Army, and 700 head of cattle, mules, and horses were captured by the Indians.

Interspersed among the harassing raids were increasingly frequent major attacks on wagon trains – assaults that necessitated the commitment of large numbers of troops to rescue the besieged trains.

Despite his travails at Fort Phil Kearny, Carrington set out to fulfill his orders to establish a second post. In August, he sent two companies 90 miles north to the Little Bighorn. Named Fort C. F. Smith, the smaller post would be less consequential than Fort Phil Kearny. The third projected post would not be built. It was by then apparent to Carrington and others in the chain of command that there were not enough forces available to staff the existing posts, much less build another.

Meanwhile, conditions at Fort Phil Kearny continued to deteriorate. The constant peril gave lie to the authorities' misguided assumption that the Fort Laramie Treaty had resolved the "Indian problem" on the northern Plains.

Carrington recognized his obvious shortfalls in numbers and equipment. His correspondence makes it clear that he expected – indeed, believed he had been promised – that his units would be fully manned and equipped with the latest weaponry. Although he made his difficulties known, little help was initially forthcoming. Those supplies that did reach him had to be transported over great distances along a route that placed travelers in mortal danger.

Disaster in major form reached Carrington and Fort Phil Kearny on December 21, 1866. When a party of woodcutters came under attack a short distance from the post, Carrington sent Captain William J. Fetterman and 80 men to rescue the besieged party. Fetterman, an aggressive, self-confident officer who had seen extensive combat during the Civil War, apparently had little respect for Carrington whom he regarded as a Civil War paper pusher. Openly dismissive of Carrington, Fetterman had boasted that he and his cavalrymen could handle the entire group of Indians who were on the warpath. As events would show, it is quite possible that what Fetterman assessed as timidity on Carrington's part was in fact the colonel's more realistic appreciation of the threat and his unit's shortfalls in men, equipment, and capabilities.

Fetterman and his command rode out of Fort Phil Kearny at about 11 a.m. on a cold, wintery morning. Carrington's instructions to Fetterman were to "Support the wood train, relieve it, and report to me. Do not engage or pursue Indians at its expense. Under no circumstances pursue over the ridge." The ridge Carrington spoke of was slightly beyond the location where the woodcutters were embroiled, farther from the post. Passing over it would further endanger Fetterman's troops by taking them into rugged, ambush-prone terrain and making support from the fort more difficult. Possibly concerned by Fetterman's potential for recklessness, Carrington stopped Fetterman's column before it left the post and reiterated his orders.

Fetterman, though, either by design or oversight, or careless excitement, quickly advanced beyond the ridge. Led by Crazy Horse, the small group of attacking Sioux feigned a full out retreat from the struggle with the woodcutters. Crazy Horse's ploy was in fact the decoy phase of a well-executed trap. Fetterman took the bait; he and his 80 men followed Crazy Horse and his band over the ridge where he was ambushed by a thousand or more warriors. The "Fetterman Fight" started at about noon and was likely over within a half hour.

Carrington sent reinforcements as soon as heavy firing was heard at the fort. By the time the rescue party arrived, Fetterman and his entire force had been wiped out.

Fetterman was well-known with the small Regular Army establishment and popular among his officer contemporaries. As news of the battle along with reports of atrocities inflicted on the remains filtered out, newspapers and the general public placed initial blame on Carrington. Not having been a combat leader during the Civil War, Carrington was not well known among the Army's senior leadership. He found few supporters and received little sympathy from the general officer corps.

Carrington was immediately relieved of his command, as was his direct superior, Brigadier General Philip St. George Cooke. Along with his wife and a small party that included other officers' wives, Carrington set out on January 23, 1867, in the 30 below zero cold of a northern Plains winter, journeying first to Fort Caspar, Wyoming. Distraught, Carrington remained there for a short time until orders arrived assigning him to Fort McPherson, Nebraska.

Meanwhile, fallout from the disaster sparked a flurry of investigating committees and official inquiries, all chartered to examine circumstances surrounding the Fetterman Fight. Carrington personally testified at a hearing conducted at Fort McPherson. His explanation was supported by several witnesses, including the famed frontier scout Jim Bridger. Despite the supporting testimony and the conclusion of the senior investigator that Carrington had not been furnished with sufficient, troops, equipment, or supplies, public opinion remained generally unfavorable. The Army's inquiry reached no official conclusion. An investigation by the Department of the Interior exonerated Carrington.

Fate was never kind to Carrington in the timing of major events. In the weeks following his departure, Army forces along the trail were more fully equipped. Cavalry units received Spencer carbines while infantry companies were furnished new, Model 1866 Springfield rifles. In the summer of 1867, two battles evidenced the new weapons' lethality, particularly that of the Springfield rifle. On August 1, three miles from Fort C. F. Smith, 21 soldiers and nine civilians were working in a hayfield when they were attacked by several hundred Indians. Taking refuge behind logs and hastily dug rifle pits, the soldiers fought off an all-day attack. Two soldiers and one civilian were killed and three others were wounded in the Hayfield Fight. Indian losses were estimated at between eight and 23 killed.

Fort C. F. Smith had been reinforced in July with the addition of two more companies. The added strength, new weapons, and intelligence provided by Crow Indian allies greatly enhanced the security of the post.

August 2, the day after the Hayfield incident, brought further action several miles to the south near Fort Phil Kearny. In what came to be known as the Wagon Box Fight, 26 soldiers and six civilians under heavy attack took shelter inside an improvised stockade of wagon boxes. Using the new rapid-fire breach loading rifles, they held off a large body of attacking Sioux, inflicting numerous casualties.

Although the two battles were at best standoffs if not decisive losses for the Indians, the Sioux's continued harassments eventually forced the closing of the Bozeman Trail. With a new route – the Montana Trail – being opened and the Bozeman Trail rendered obsolescent by the advance of the transcontinental railroad, government officials negotiated a treaty ending the war and abandoning the forts (which were immediately burned by the Indians). The treaty held in general form for about eight years until further encroachments and the discovery of gold in the Black Hills caused the final, massive conflagration in 1876.

Carrington remained in the Army for three more years, retiring in 1870 after serving as commander of Fort McPherson. Thus ended Carrington's unfortunate experience on the frontier. Faced with shortages of men, modern weapons, and ammunition, he also lacked support from key members of his staff. From the outset he had not been well respected by the officers who served under him. To the general dissatisfaction of his officers, Carrington focused his initial efforts on building the formidable installation that became Fort Phil Kearny. While that was not an unreasonable decision given the anticipated long-duration occupancy and the severity of the soon to come northern Plains winter, the action infuriated many of his junior officers who, although inexperienced in Indian warfare, were eager to fight. Fetterman particularly disparaged Carrington's approach, regarding it as passive and ineffective. Confident that his troopers could prevail in any combat against Native warriors, he further believed that General Philip St. George Cooke had intended the garrison to wage a more aggressive campaign.

It remained Carrington's contention that he had been instructed, supplied, and equipped to build a garrison fort, not to fight a war against an aggressive, numerically superior foe. Anticipating a benign environment, shortly after his arrival he had issued an order instructing "Every soldier to treat all Indians with kindness."

Further confusing Carrington's situation was that – incredibly – he did not receive a copy of the Fort Laramie Treaty. Having arrived after the talks were concluded, he had little information on which chiefs had signed and which bands should be regarded as hostile. The combination of material and personal challenges led to eventual disaster.

Photographs taken of Carrington at the time of his service in the West show an angular face sporting a fuller version of a Van Dyke beard. His is pictured as dark-haired with a full head of hair along the sides and back, receding and graying a bit along a portion of his forehead. Ironically, after his first wife – a respected author, as was Carrington – died in 1870, he married the widow of an officer killed in the Fetterman Fight.

After leaving the Army, Carrington served for a time as professor of military science at Wabash College in Indiana. In 1878, he moved to Hyde Park, Massachusetts. His previous travails notwithstanding, Carrington's experiences in the West ended on a happier note when, in 1889, he helped draft a treaty with the Flathead Indians in Montana. The following year, he conducted an official census of Native populations encompassing the Six Nations and the Cherokee Indians.

Carrington was well regarded as an author, writing accounts of American history and Indian affairs. In 1908 the citizens of Sheridan, Wyoming, honored him for his service and at their request he spoke at the Fetterman massacre site memorial.

Carrington died in Boston on October 26, 1912, at age 88. He is buried at Hyde Park, Massachusetts.

Kit Carson

K it Carson's towering reputation as a scout, trapper, frontiersman, and mountain man overshadows the consequential portion of his life spent as commander of military forces in the American Southwest. Carson was, in fact, an able commander whose extensive service earned him a brevet promotion to brigadier general. Most notably, he served as General James H. Carleton's field commander during Carleton's extended campaigns to subdue Apache and Navajo bands in Arizona and New Mexico.

Carson's journeys took him throughout the American West guiding parties led by John C. Fremont on historic expeditions to the South Pass, the Columbia River into Oregon, and across California to the Pacific Ocean. Interspersed with years spent hunting and trapping – during which his paths intersected with frontiersmen such as Jim Bridger and William Bent – Carson led military forces during the war with Mexico and the Civil War as well as through several Indian campaigns.

The death of his father when Carson was a small boy terminated his brief formal education. Though functionally illiterate throughout his adult life Carson, abetted by his extensive travels and a keen intelligence, became fluent in Spanish, French, and several Native languages including Arapaho, Cheyenne, Navajo, Paiute, Ute, and Shoshone.

Of medium height and build, Carson was known for his personal honesty and integrity. Unlike many of his more boisterous mountain man contemporaries, he was self-effacing and unpretentious in his lifestyle.

Carson was born near Richmond, Kentucky, on Christmas Eve, 1809. His family moved west the following year, settling in a frontier region near Franklin, Missouri. When he was eight, his father was killed felling a tree while clearing the family's land. His father's death placed the family in dire economic straits, forcing the boy to quit school to work on the farm and engage in hunting to supplement the family's food supply.

Sometime around age 14, Carson was apprenticed to a saddle maker in the small village which at the time was near the eastern terminus of the newly opened Santa Fe Trail. After two years of disagreeable apprenticeship, Carson hired on with a large caravan bound for Santa Fe, taking care of the horses, oxen, and mules as the party moved west across the continent. Over the course of the next winter, and perhaps longer, he stayed in Taos, then in Mexican territory, with a noted trapper and explorer named Mathew Kinkaid who taught him trapping and frontier field craft.

Library of Congress
Kit Carson

For the next 11 years, roughly 1829-1840, Carson trapped and scouted for hunting and exploration parties. A notable trapping and trading expedition in 1829 took him through Apache territory all the way to Sacramento and Los Angeles before returning to Taos in the spring of 1830. During the journey Carson trapped extensively along the Colorado River and experienced his baptism under fire when the 40-man party was attacked by Apaches along the Gila River.

In 1835, while attending the annual rendezvous of mountain men held along the Green River in southeastern Wyoming, the 25-year old Carson met a young Arapaho woman whose name is translated as "Singing Grass." When Singing Grass expressed her preference for Carson's affections over those of another mountain man, the rejected suitor became belligerent, threatening others and disrupting the rendezvous.

Uncharacteristically, the mild mannered Carson was forced into a dual – fought on horseback – during which he wounded the aggrieved party with a pistol shot. Carson subsequently married Singing Grass who gave birth to two daughters before dying of a fever sometime before 1840.

During their years together, Carson trapped extensively through Colorado, Wyoming, Idaho, and Montana. Most often he was engaged in trapping beaver along the Yellowstone, Powder, and Big Horn rivers, usually in the employ of the Hudson Bay Company and sometimes accompanied by Jim Bridger.

By the end of the decade of the 1830s, the fur trade era was drawing to a close. Fashion tastes were changing – there was a new demand for silk – and in many places beavers had been hunted to near-extinction. Carson took employment as a hunter, working for William Bent at Bent's Fort, a civilian post near present day LaJunta, Colorado.

In 1841, Carson entered into a brief marriage with a Cheyenne woman who subsequently chose to remain with her family and accompany the tribe on its migrations. In 1842 he met Josefa Jaramillo, the daughter of a prominent Taos family, and married her early the following year. Eventually, they would have eight children together.

During an 1841 trip to visit his family in Missouri, Carson had a chance encounter that ultimately would change his life and secure his enduring reputation. John C. Fremont, a passenger with Carson on the same Missouri River steamboat, was at the time planning an expedition to South Pass on the Continental Divide. Learning of Carson's credentials, Fremont offered him a position as scout. Carson accepted and successfully led the 25-man party on a highly acclaimed five-month trek.

The success of the first expedition induced Fremont to quickly launch a second journey the following summer. The purpose of the 1843 exploration was to map the western portion of the Oregon Trail, following it from South Pass to the Columbia River. It would turn out to be an epic journey. Carson led the party along the Great Salt Lake into Oregon, mapping territory and describing flora and fauna along the way. When the assemblage became snowbound in the Sierra Nevadas, Carson's hunting skills and field craft saved the expedition. Moving south after the winter, the party pushed through the Mojave Desert, periodically attacked by Native bands. Pushed farther south by the threat from Mexican military units across whose territory they were transiting, the party eventually reached a small water hole around which would later grow the city of Las Vegas. After first returning to Bent's Fort, by April 1844, Fremont and Carson were in Washington, D.C., where Fremont reported on the journey. Published by Congress the following year, Fremont's journal further embellished the reputation of both men.

Carson's prestige was additionally enhanced when news of an adventure that had occurred during the expedition reached the American public. At one point in their travels the party came across a Mexican man and young boy, sole survivors of an attack by Navajos that had killed and butchered other men and women in the party and made off with 30 or more horses. Carson led a pursuit of the war party that found the raiders, killed two of them, and returned the stolen horses to the Mexicans.

Public acclaim and additional support and funding prompted a third Fremont expedition the following year. On June 1, 1845, Fremont with a party of 55 guided by Kit Carson left St. Louis, Missouri. Though not the stated purpose of the exploration, Fremont, perhaps anticipating war with Mexico, chose to move straight to California. With Carson leading the way, the cadre reached the Sacramento Valley in late 1846. There, Fremont tried without initial success to stir up a revolt among American settlers in the region. Threatened by far larger numbers of Mexican troops in the vicinity, Fremont left California and moved north into Oregon. Near Klamath Lake, Carson saved the party by alerting the group to a late-night surprise attack on the sleeping camp. After contentious and controversial squabbles with Natives, likely Modoc tribesmen, Fremont moved his party back to the

Sacramento Valley where he fomented and eventually led an uprising that became known as the Bear Flag Revolt.

With the valley reasonably secure, Fremont pushed farther south, reaching the provincial capital of Monterey in mid-July. There, his party met American naval forces under the command of Commodore Robert Stockton. With two warships, Stockton had wrested control of the harbor and the city. Having learned that the United States was now officially at war with Mexico, Stockton and Fremont joined forces in a prospective plan to capture Los Angeles and San Diego, thus securing most of California. Carson was appointed a lieutenant, formally launching his military career.

Rare in any conflict, events unfolded as anticipated. On July 29, disembarking from one of Stockton's vessels, a unit commanded by Fremont took San Diego without opposition. Soon after, Stockton captured Santa Barbara. Linking up again in San Diego, the combined force moved to the hamlet of Las Angeles and took it without resistance. On August 17, Stockton declared California to be United States territory.

The next day, August 18, Stephen W. Kearny, having moved from Bent's Fort, reached Santa Fe, New Mexico, and claimed the New Mexico region for the United States as well.

Eager to advise President James K. Polk of their conquest of California, Stockton and Fremont prevailed upon Carson to carry their correspondence overland across the continent and deliver it to the President. By many accounts, Carson believed he could make the journey in two months. On September 5, with a party of about 20 others, he set out from Los Angeles to do so.

A month into his journey Carson, moving east, happened to intersect with Kearny moving west toward the Pacific. Hearing from Carson that California was already in American hands, Kearny – with orders to capture New Mexico and California – sent 200 men, the bulk of his command, back to New Mexico. Kearny then ordered Carson to remain with him and guide his now much-reduced 100-man cadre to California. The mail to Washington was carried by another courier.

After advising Kearny to use pack mules and dispense with supply wagons, Carson guided Kearny and his dragoons across rivers, over mountains, through canyons along Gila River, and across the Mojave Desert. After numerous hardships, Carson brought Kearny and his men to within 25 miles of Los Angeles. There, on December 5, they learned that a revolt had broken out and much of Southern California had been retaken by Mexican authorities.

Soon after, a full-blown battle developed between Kearny's small force and a larger squadron of Mexican cavalry that blocked Kearny's path to Commodore Stockton's forces now holding out at San Diego. With their barely-trained mules weakened from the long journey and water and ammunition running low, Kearny was forced to retreat to a nearby hillock where he formed a defensive perimeter. There, his force was increasingly hard pressed in a fight that eventually lasted the better part of four days.

His situation becoming increasingly serious, on December 8 Kearny directed Carson and two others to slip away and attempt to reach Stockton and return with reinforcements. Using his frontier experience, discarding boots and canteens to reduce noise, Carson and his companions managed to sneak through. Carson returned on December 10 with about 200 troops and fresh mounts. The reinforcements fought through to Kearny's embattled troops, breaking the siege at what became known as the Battle of San Pasqual. Two days later, Kearny was in San Diego. Soon after, all of California was again in American hands.

After recapturing Los Angeles, Fremont again sent Carson to Washington, D.C., with news of the conquest. This time the journey was uninterrupted. After a trek across the continent Carson delivered his dispatches to Secretary of State James Buchanan and later met with Secretary of War William Marcy and President Polk as well.

After the war with Mexico, Carson experienced a few years of relative quiet as he and his wife Josefa worked to expand their ranching operations near Taos. Eventually, though, Indian troubles brought him back to government service. In 1853, James H. Carleton was assigned to command the cavalry unit at Albuquerque. Carleton's tour at that post began a long relationship between the two men with Carson initially serving as a scout for Carleton's cavalrymen and later as his primary commander in the field.

Carleton quickly launched a wide-ranging series of sorties in a relentless pursuit of Navajo and Apache bands that were raiding across Arizona and New Mexico. Carson, leading a company of New Mexico volunteers, contributed to an early success when a Jicarilla Apache camp was located in the Raton Mountains. In an attack jointly planned by Carleton and Carson, the cavalrymen struck the village in a surprise assault that routed the defenders and captured large quantities of food and weapons and most of the band's horses.

The following spring, Carson accompanied Philip St. George Cooke and 200 men of the 2nd Dragoons in an expedition against the Jicarillas. Leading a contingent of scouts, Carson guided the cavalrymen to a large band of raiders. On April 4, 1854, the dragoons prevailed in a battle at Ojo Caliente in north central New Mexico.

After an extended struggle, Carleton's ceaseless pressure induced the Navajos and Apaches to agree to peace settlements which brought a temporary respite to years of bloodshed. Carson contributed to the process by negotiating a pact – signed on January 23, 1858 – involving Arapahos and other bands around Taos.

After serving for a time as Indian agent for northern New Mexico, Carson joined a New Mexico volunteer unit at the outbreak of the Civil War. With a new rank and title as Colonel of Volunteers, Carson led a column under the overall command of Colonel Edward R. S. Canby. Carson's force was sizable for its time and place – about 500 men in two battalions, each with four companies.

Carson's first Civil War action occurred at Valverde, New Mexico, on February 24, 1862. Confederate General Henry Hopkins Sibley's invading rebels defeated Canby's Union forces in a day-long struggle. Carson's column, not initially engaged, was called into action early in the afternoon. The unit fought through the remainder of the day before Canby ordered Union forces to withdraw from the field. Though victorious at Valverde, the Confederate invasion soon collapsed and Carson and his men were subsequently engaged in putting down the multiple Native uprisings that flared up almost immediately.

When Canby was reassigned to other duties, he was replaced by James H. Carleton, Carson's colleague from years past. Carleton declared martial law throughout New Mexico Territory and launched a far-ranging resettlement plan aimed initially at the Mescalero Apaches in southeastern New Mexico. Determined that relocation was the only way to stop the Apaches' killing raids, Carleton ordered his commanders to strike hard with a scorched-earth program that would force the Apaches to move to the reservation. Villages were to be burned and crops and provisions destroyed. Carleton directed Carson to kill all male hostiles among the Mescaleros, an order the Carson refused to obey.

With Fort Stanton as his base, Carson moved his five companies of New Mexico volunteers against the Apaches. The resulting campaign took about two years. Finally, worn out and destitute, screened from their pastures and water holes, in the spring of 1863 the last of the Mescaleros surrendered.

When the Apaches were successfully placed at the Bosque Redondo reservation, Carleton turned his attention to the Navajos, intending to coerce the tribe into submission and move its members to Bosque Redondo as well. Carson objected, apparently sending a letter of resignation which Carleton refused to accept. Eventually, an accommodation was reached and Carson agreed to the assignment.

Under Carleton's overall direction, Carson initiated a relentless campaign through western New Mexico, capturing the Navajos' livestock and destroying crops, orchards, and villages. Carson received approval to employ members of tribes with long-standing enmity towards the Navajos.

His recruits approached their tasks with considerable zeal but were indignant when Carson prevented them from looting Navajo possessions.

It was a difficult time for Carson who also had to deal with less than stellar subordinates among his New Mexico volunteer units. Eventually, on January 12-14, 1864, at Canyon de Chelly in northwestern Arizona, forces under Carson defeated the last of the large Navajo war parties. The surrender of the Canyon de Chelly stronghold brought the closing chapter to the Carleton's resettlement program. Eventually, under great hardship, "the Long Walk" took the entire tribe – several thousand members – 300-400 miles to Bosque Redondo. Although Carson's promise to the Navajos that they would not be attacked or harassed during their exodus was apparently fulfilled, the physical hardships they encountered during the journey contributed to numerous deaths.

At the reservation they faced difficult circumstances compounded – much to Carson's displeasure – by the fact that initially not enough supplies were provided to accommodate their numbers. Four years later they were allowed to return to their homeland.

Tired and disgruntled, Carson left the Army for a short time, but returned at Carleton's request to help combat a bloody uprising by several tribes in western Texas. Leaving from Fort Bascom, New Mexico, on November 10, 1864, Carson's combined force consisted of 260 cavalry, 75 infantry, and 72 Ute and Apache scouts. He also took with him two mountain howitzers which would prove to be invaluable, an ambulance, and 27 wagons carrying 45 days of rations.

With his Indian scouts protecting his flanks, Carson's column made good progress until slowed by inclement weather a week and a half into the march. On November 24, his scouts reported the presence of a large Indian trail. Carson left his infantry at Mule Springs, about 30 miles west of the eventual battle site and with the rest of his command hurried to intersect the trail. Two hours after daybreak on November 25, Carson's cavalry found and attacked a large Kiowa village whose inhabitants fled, warning other camps nearby. Learning now that there were numerous hostile villages in the immediate area, Carson moved his force to Adobe Walls, a long-abandoned trading post about 17 miles west of present-day Stinnett, Texas, and dug in among the ruins.

Confronting him was a mixed assemblage of Apaches, Commanches, and Kiowas – well over a thousand warriors with additional numbers hurrying to the fight. Drastically outnumbered, Carson formed his defense around and inside the remnants of the desolate station. Shifting forces around the crumbling walls and building fragments and making excellent use of his mountain howitzers, Carson broke up repeated charges that lasted much of the day.

With much of his ammunition expended during the day-long fight, in late afternoon Carson slipped his troops away from the area, at one point setting the prairie on fire to delay the on-rushing pursuers. The withdrawal route took Carson's men past the Kiowa village they had attacked earlier in the day. Carson ordered it burned as they moved through the area.

Carson lost six killed and 25 wounded during the battle. Estimates of Indian losses are considerably higher, with some suggesting as many as 150 killed or wounded. Both sides claimed success – Carson because of the disproportionate number of casualties his cavalrymen had inflicted, and the Indians because they held the ground when the fighting ended.

Not long after the battle, news reached Carson of John Chivington's attack on a peaceful Cheyenne village at Sand Creek, Colorado. Carson, joined by several other military leaders, publically condemned the actions of Chivington and his men.

Later victories on the southern Plains induced the holdout bands of Commanches to sign a peace accord – the Little Rock Treaty – in 1865. At Carleton's recommendation, Carson was brevetted to brigadier general for his service during wars against the tribes of the Southwest.

The Adobe Walls campaign effectively closed Carson's career as an Indian fighter. After receiving his brevet promotion, he was appointed commander of Fort Garland, Colorado. Later mustered out of the Army, he took up ranching on territory familiar to him near the former location of Bent's Fort.

In 1867, Carson escorted four Ute chiefs to Washington, D.C., to meet with President Andrew Johnson. A few months after his return, on May 23, 1868, he died of a heart attack at Fort Lyon, Colorado, and was taken to Taos, New Mexico for burial. He was 58 years old.

William O. Collins

W illiam O. Collins was one of the few successful senior officers who did not have an extensive military background prior to assuming his duties in the American West. An able commander of volunteer cavalry units posted in the region of Ft. Laramie, Wyoming, Collins' military exploits are best remembered for his role in battles fought at Mud Springs and Rush Creek, Nebraska Territory, in early 1865. A few weeks after the encounters he was mustered out of service. Collins' humanity and common sense did much to keep large portions of the Sioux nation friendly or non-belligerent. As later events rather quickly revealed, his influence and steady hand would be sorely missed.

Collins was born in Somers, Conn., in August 1809. After acquiring a solid basic education at Wesleyan Academy at Wilbraham, Massachusetts, he graduated from Amherst College in 1833. When his young wife died that same year, he moved to Hillsboro, Ohio, a small town located on the plains and rolling hills in the southwestern part of the state. He would reside there for the rest of his life.

At Hillsboro, Collins studied law and became a successful prosecuting attorney. In 1843, he married Catharine Wever, a young woman from a prominent local family. Their union produced three children, only one of whom – a son named Caspar, who would also achieve military notoriety – lived to adulthood.

Collins was elected to the Ohio State Senate in 1859 and served one term before volunteering for military service at the outset of the Civil War. Granted a colonel's commission soon after his enlistment on December 19, 1861, he later accepted a commission as a lieutenant colonel when shortages of horses and equipment delayed the entry onto active duty of the battalion of volunteer cavalry he had recruited.

Collins quickly raised a regiment – the 6th Ohio Volunteer Cavalry – and remained with that unit until September 20, 1862, when he took command of a merged organization with whom his name is most closely linked, the 11th Ohio Volunteer Cavalry.

Soon after entering active service, Collins and the 6th Ohio were sent to St.

Louis, Missouri. The regiment remained there only a short time before being ordered to Fort Laramie in what was then Dakota Territory. Collins' entire remaining military career would be spent on the western frontier. His command encompassed an enormous region spanning east to west from the plains of present-day western Nebraska and eastern Colorado to South Pass in southwestern Wyoming, and south to north from the South Platte River in Colorado to the border of Montana.

After arriving at Fort Laramie, Collins quickly moved out, distributing and checking on forces at South Pass and other encampments scattered across his immense area of responsibility. He earned a reputation as an active commander, consistently on the move visiting his far-flung outposts.

Fort Collins Museum of Discovery
William O. Collins

Collins' varied duties at Fort Laramie were typical of those that confronted many post commanders in the west during this period. His soldiers, frequently with Collins in the lead, campaigned against renegade Indians; formed scouting parties; provided security for logging and stock herder encampments; escorted survey parties for the Union Pacific Railroad; protected wagon trains, mail routes and stage coaches during uprisings; established routes for improved roads; mapped the terrain, and repaired telegraph lines. Collins even provided reports on the region's flora, fauna, and weather to the Smithsonian Institution.

Tall, with an angular face framed by dark hair and beard, Collins was by most accounts a cheerful, well-liked officer remembered for his kindness and courtesy and respected by his officers and men. On one occasion he nearly lost his own life while staying behind in a raging blizzard to help two of his freezing cavalrymen. In his dealings with Native tribes, he evidenced more than the usual concern for their treatment and the handling of their grievances. Other than for the hostile bands, he maintained generally positive relations with local tribes and earned the respect of many tribal leaders.

The times were unsettled, however, and warfare on a major scale eventually touched Collins and his command. In early August 1864, Oglala Sioux destroyed a 12-wagon train near present-day Lexington, Nebraska, killing everyone except a woman and small boy. The so-called Plum Creek Massacre was the first episode in a prolonged period of violence that became known as the Sioux War of 1864. Within days, every stage station, wagon train, and road ranche between Fort Kearny, Nebraska, and Julesburg, Colorado, was under attack. Many were utterly destroyed, burned to the ground, as were numerous ranches and farmsteads. The loss of life was considerable. Among other losses, more than 100 people were killed along the Little Blue River in southern Nebraska. Soldiers set the prairie afire in an attempt to deny sustenance to the Indian ponies. For one of the few times on American soil, soldiers, ranchers, and settlers across the central Plains faced something very similar to total war.

On November 29, further fuel was added to the conflagration when Colonel John M. Chivington's Colorado volunteers attacked a Cheyenne village at Sand Creek, Colorado, and killed 150 or more men, women, and children. The actions of Chivington and his men provoked a further massive uprising that engulfed the region. The surviving Cheyennes became allies of the Sioux; the Sioux War became the War of the Plains Indians.

The Indians' vengeance for Sand Creek was not long in coming. On January 7, 1865, the town of Julesburg, Colorado, was sacked and soldiers from the nearby small outpost were killed. A futile twelve day chase did nothing to dissuade the Indians, who returned on the morning of February 2, further pillaging the town and leaving it in flames. The contraband taken by the Sioux and Cheyenne included thousands of sacks of corn and herds of livestock numbering in the hundreds. The raiding party was extremely large: 1,500 – 2,500 warriors were estimated to have participated in the second attack.

In the context of the time, the concentration of "hostiles" was almost unprecedented. So ominous was the situation that travel along the trail was limited to large caravans, usually escorted by soldiers. "In 1865 (a traveler's wagon train) was told that it could not start west from (Fort Kearny) 'without permission of the authorities,' who stipulated that before proceeding there would be 'no less than 100 wagons or a like number of armed men.'"

Julesburg would be the Indians southernmost raid. Apprehensive about the approach from Nebraska Territory of Colonel Robert R. Livingston with elements of the 1st Nebraska Cavalry and the 7th Iowa Cavalry, the Cheyenne and Sioux turned north toward the Tongue and Powder River regions of Montana. Their route led them over the emigrant road between the North and South Platte Rivers and placed the small outposts along the trail in immediate peril. On February 3, the first, a telegraph station at Lodgepole Creek, was quickly destroyed. The telegraph operator, the sole resident at the time, was away from the station when the attack occurred, saw the flames from a distance, and fled to safety.

Located on the trail in the vicinity of Courthouse Rock, Mud Springs was the next station up the line. The Indians reached it the following day.

For a long stretch of the Overland Trail known as the "Jules Cutoff" (a branch of the trail that provided a more direct route to Ft. Laramie for travelers coming up the South Platte), Mud Springs provided one of the few water sources. The availability of water made it an attractive location; in 1860, the Pony Express placed a home station on the site. The next year, on July 5, 1861, it became a telegraph post, one of the links in the nation's new transcontinental system.

The Mud Springs garrison consisted of only nine soldiers and a telegraph operator. Present also when the Indians appeared on the Fourth of February were four stock herders employed by Creighton and Hoel, a nearby cattle operation. The station facilities consisted of two log buildings. One, 35 by 16 feet, was divided almost in half with the telegraph office at one end and a squad room for the soldiers at the other. The second structure was a stable that measured about 40 by 20.

The tiny station was about to be set upon by 1,500 – 2,000 warriors fresh from attacks at Julesburg and the destruction of the station at Lodgepole Creek. In the words of one scholar, "(t)he little compound at Mud Springs was utterly indefensible, being surrounded by hills and knolls full of gullies, allowing attackers to creep up where they could not be seen or reached by cavalry charge."

The Indians wasted no time. Their first assault succeeded in capturing 15-20 horses belonging to the soldiers and cattlemen as well as almost the entire herd of cattle milling on the range close by.

At 4 o'clock that day, Collins, at Fort Laramie, received telegraphed information regarding the attack. Collins immediately wired Lieutenant William Ellsworth, posted at Camp Mitchell, Nebraska, directing him to leave immediately with 36 men of Company H, 11th Ohio Cavalry. Collins anticipated that by riding all night Ellsworth and his men could reach Mud Springs, about 50 miles distant, by sunrise the following morning.

Meanwhile, at 7 o'clock that same evening, Collins led 120 men out of Fort Laramie. Stopping only for short breaks through the night, Collins' force, comprised of members of Iowa and Ohio units, arrived at Camp Mitchell late the following morning. There they rested for eight hours, then resumed the march at 7 o'clock at night with Collins and 25 men speeding ahead of the main column.

Lieutenant Ellsworth's forced march brought his reinforcements to Mud Springs before dawn on February 5. Ellsworth ordered a bugle sounded to identify the group to the defenders at the besieged camp. Ellsworth's men were warmly greeted by the members of the small force holding out in the two buildings, but their presence did not prevent another successful raid just before sunrise when warriors captured more horses and mules, including some from Ellsworth's recently arrived party.

Daylight brought immediate action. A bluff at the rear of the buildings provided a vantage point for the Indians. As soon as the sun came up, 16 of Lieutenant Ellsworth's soldiers advanced up the height to push the raiders back. Firing as they moved forward, Ellsworth's men forced the Indians from one elevation to the next. Suddenly, from a nearby creek bank an enormous number of Indians – estimated at as many as 500 – rose up and opened fire in a barrage that one soldier described as like a "shower of hailstones."

The heavy fire, intense and increasingly accurate, caused the soldiers to fall back. As the detachment formed up to retreat, two soldiers (ironically, they were brothers) standing not far apart, were hit almost simultaneously. One received a shoulder wound that knocked him down. Struggling to regain his feet, he was able to stagger back to the station where he was placed in a bunk and eventually treated by a doctor who arrived with Collins' cadre later in the day.

The second casualty was shot in the hip. The shell lodged in his groin and made it difficult for him to move. He fell near a small crevasse and managed to roll over into it while drawing his revolver and preparing to defend himself. Soldiers observing from the station "could see the Indians jumping up, waving their scalping knives and yelling like demons," eager to finish off the trooper.

Watching from the squad building, Sergeant William Hall, a Civil War veteran new to the company, volunteered to try to reach the wounded man and bring him in. Others argued against the attempt, but Hall calmly hung his revolver belt on a nearby peg and stepped through the door. Running through a fusillade, he reached his wounded comrade, hoisted him on his shoulders, and carried him back to safety. Hall's act of heroism cheered his embattled colleagues who were hanging on against long odds, defending the station from firing positions in and around the two small buildings. Unfortunately, despite Sergeant Hall's valor, the wounded man later died of his wounds and was buried on a knoll near the station.

At sundown, the raiders pulled back temporarily, allowing the soldiers some much needed rest.

February 6 dawned cold and wintery. Still, to the defenders of Mud Springs, the daylight hours brought a welcome sight: Colonel Collins and his command from Fort Laramie reached the station. The men were exhausted, having marched two nights and a day with little rest. The long journey through the bitter cold had left several soldiers frostbitten; some had frozen ears and feet. The Indians, some of whom had broken away to steal cattle in the area around the station on February Fourth and Fifth, were taken by surprise by the arrival of additional reinforcements at Mud Springs. As Collins' men moved toward the station, the Indians returned en masse to the nearby heights, swarming over them and laying down a loose fire in an unsuccessful attempt to halt their advance.

Collins estimated that 500 – 1,000 Indians – he was inclined to favor the higher number – fought that day in the vicinity of Mud Springs. His report indicated that in addition to bows and arrows, the hostiles were armed with rifles and revolvers and appeared to have liberal amounts of ammunition. The heavy presence of American horses among the raiders led him to believe that non-Indians may have participated in the attack. The Civil War still raged at the time and rumors of Confederate soldiers or sympathizers aiding the Indians were not uncommon. The battle of Mud Springs yielded a similar story. Some enlisted men of the 11th Ohio reported seeing a white man with red hair and whiskers carrying a Texas Lone Star flag. The story has never been corroborated; thus, like other similar tales it must remain a subject for speculation.

When Collins' men fought their way into the Mud Springs compound, they quickly formed an improvised corral out of four overturned wagons and placed the horses and mules inside. The makeshift pen became the focus of several furious attacks throughout the day as the Indians attempted to stampede the cavalry mounts. Although some of the assaults carried up to the compound, none were successful as the now-reinforced garrison met them with heavy fire from their Spencer rifles.

Still, the defenders' situation remained precarious, vulnerable to warriors firing from sheltered gullies and ravines that bounded the station. Collins responded by telegraphing Fort Laramie to send an artillery piece which he intended to use to clear the vantage points that allowed the Indians to rake the compound with fire.

The fighting that continued around the station throughout the morning and early afternoon sometimes turned into one-on-one, hide-and-seek, pop-up-and-shoot encounters as soldiers attempted to move the Indians away from positions in the rugged terrain near the buildings. This was not an easy task, and at one point during the fighting two hundred Indians massed within 75 yards of the buildings. Gathering behind a sheltering hill and in sharp ravines that cut through it, they sent floods of high-arching arrows into the corral, wounding several animals.

The losses, which threatened to destroy the soldiers' mobility, could not be tolerated. Collins quickly put one squad of soldiers on horseback and sent another on foot to attack the position. A charge in the face of heavy fire eventually cleared the hillside. After gaining control of the terrain, the soldiers entrenched, dug a rifle pit, and fought off further threats from that portion of the battlefield.

The struggle swirled around the compound and heavy fighting continued for several hours until by mid-afternoon the soldiers' aggressiveness and concentrated fire began to wear on the attackers. Finally, pushed back in all directions, they withdrew.

The fight that day was violent and continuous. Army casualties from the action were seven wounded, three seriously. Those were in addition to the two casualties (one killed) the day before. Losses in horses and mules were also sustained during the course of repeated attacks. Collins estimated the Indians' losses at about 30, but acknowledged there was no way of confirming the number since the raiders immediately carried away their casualties. The Indians later asserted that no warriors had been killed.

During the night, the station was further fortified, and Collins, reinforced after dark by the arrival of Lieutenant William Brown – who, in 34 hours came all the way from Fort Laramie bringing 50 men and a twelve-pounder mountain howitzer – made plans to take the offensive. The next morning, February 7, as Collins' forces moved to the attack, a scouting party confirmed that the Indians had left the immediate area.

The Battle of Mud Springs was over. The Battle of Rush Creek was about to begin.

Located in Morrill County, Nebraska, in the valley of the North Platte River, the Rush Creek battle site is near the mouth of Cedar Creek (as Rush Creek is now called), not quite 20 miles northeast of Mud Springs. The series of violent clashes that would occur there on February 8-9, 1865, were a direct extension of the Mud Springs battle.

After scouts confirmed that the Indians had withdrawn from around Mud Springs on the morning of February 7, Collins rested much of his force through the day and made preparations for pursuit. Leaving one company behind to guard the station, Collins moved out early on February 8, traveling quickly with scouts in front and rear and on the flanks.

No Indians were immediately sighted but troopers found evidence of the great size of the war party and the general direction of its movement. The converging paths of the various Indian groups appeared to merge and flow toward Rush Creek. Scouts continued to follow the Indian "signs" and within a few miles discovered a recently abandoned village that covered several miles and contained the abandoned spoils of raids on ranches, outposts, and wagon trains. Collins pushed his column forward. Trailing the now concentrated assembly of warriors, Collins followed the traces left by thousands of travois and tipi poles.

The path led them to the North Platte River, frozen now by the bitter cold, where Indians were sighted grazing stock on the opposite embankment. As the troops tracked toward the river, enormous numbers of Sioux and Cheyenne – Collins thought perhaps as many as 2,000 – appeared on the hills behind the opposing bank and began moving in their direction.

The immense throng of hostiles advanced towards Collins' soldiers, lapping around the sides of the column. Crossing the river above and below both flanks, the warriors flowed around the entire command, surrounding Collins' force.

As the soldiers hurried to corral their wagons and dig in, Lieutenant

Brown's mountain howitzer bought them a few minutes of time, scattering the first groups of warriors who had bunched together crossing the frozen river. The respite was only momentary. The Indians quickly returned to the attack as the soldiers jabbed into the loose sand hills soil and built rudimentary breastworks that they steadily improved as the battle wore on.

Considering the urgency of the situation, the ground chosen for the defensive stand was generally good, although in Collins' words "there were many little sand ridges and hollows under cover of which (the Indians) could approach us."

Collins put sharpshooters on the knolls that overlooked the camp and had rifle pits dug on them. From these vantage points, the troops repulsed several probing attacks and for a time the battle regressed to move, pop up and shoot episodes like those that had occurred at Mud Springs.

Outnumbered and lacking sufficient forces to drive the Indians back en masse, Collins recognized that the struggle would be a defensive fight. As the battle took form, a crisis point soon developed when a large party of warriors penetrated to high ground about four hundred yards from the encircled soldiers. Taking cover in a long ravine overgrown by sagebrush and high clumps of fallen grass. "(w)arriors carried one another to the spot, two mounting a single horse, one of them slipping off while the other raced through the gully." The small hill overlooked Collins' position. From their vantage point, the Indians began pouring unrestricted fire into the encampment.

Realizing the threat, Collins ordered Lieutenant Robert Patton to take 16 men and assault the position. Patton's men, some from Company D, 7th Iowa Cavalry, the rest from the 1st Battalion of the Eleventh Ohio, mounted up and revolvers in hand, charged full speed at the Indians' stronghold.

Patton's men raced through the ravine, emptying the two revolvers that each carried and clearing the warriors from the hilltop. With orders to return immediately after scattering the Indians, Patton reformed his men, preparing to lead them back to the compound. As the company began to gather, they were suddenly attacked by an additional 150-200 warriors who came at them from sloping ground in back of the knoll. The Indians' attack carried them into the midst of Patton's men. For a brief time, desperate, hand-to-hand fighting spread across the hillside.

The route of the Indians' counter-attack made them visible to the men at the compound and exposed them to volleys from soldiers in excellent firing positions inside the breastworks. Concentrated fire from the soldier's barricade broke up the Indians' assault and enabled Patton and his men to struggle back to the fortification. Two men were lost during the furious charge. The body of one soldier was recovered before it could be captured and mutilated by the Indians. The other casualty was the victim of an unruly horse. Unable to regain control of the runaway animal, the soldier was surrounded by several warriors and killed; his body was carried away by the Indians before his companions could fight their way to it.

Collins' casualties for February 8 were two killed and nine wounded. Army participants believed that the Indians' losses were heavy, particularly during the course of Patton's charge and its immediate aftermath. Indians denied that claim, asserted that only one brave, a young Cheyenne, was wounded.

At sundown the Indians broke off their attacks and withdrew across the river. Collins took advantage of the respite, sending work details to Rush Creek to water horses and mules. One group mistakenly headed for the North Platte where they reported seeing the body of a warrior, apparently a casualty of the battle, lying on the ice. As the soldiers approached the river, they were placed under threat by a large party of Cheyennes and Sioux who moved toward them with apparent intent to resume their attack. Aware of the situation, Collins sounded recall, hurrying the soldiers back to the fortification.

During the night and early morning hours, soldiers labored to improve the breastworks, expecting a resumption of full-scale fighting when the sun came up. Sunrise instead brought four hundred warriors to some nearby bluffs. Some at first crossed the river provoking an initial short-lived exchange of fire. After a few minutes, the shooting terminated when the Indians withdrew and began moving away in a northerly direction.

Soon after, another group of warriors was sighted on high ground about a quarter-mile away, absorbed in some activity. Lieutenant Brown double-loaded the howitzer and the blast scattered the last group of Indians on the battlefield.

Eventually, a group of twenty soldiers scouted the location where the Indians had last been seen. There they discovered the horrifically mutilated body of the soldier killed in the previous day's charge.

By early morning, it was apparent that the Indians were gone. With his men exhausted and lacking sufficient supplies to fight a conclusive battle, Collins chose not to pursue. His men had marched nearly 400 miles in ten days and many were suffering greatly from the cold and the effects of two days and nights on a diet of hardtack and raw flesh. They had also lost significant numbers of horses and mules to their adversaries.

Collins' summary report for the combined Mud Springs-Rush Creek fights cited his total casualties at three killed, 16 wounded and seven disabled by frostbite. Collins estimated Indian losses from both engagements at 100-150. Contemporary Cheyenne and Sioux sources assert far fewer losses.

The encounters at Mud Springs and Rush Creek are significant in several ways. More than a decade ahead of the Little Bighorn, the size of the Indian assemblage – 2,000-2,500 warriors, predominately Cheyennes, Arapahos, Oglala and Brule Sioux, but perhaps, as Collins believed, also including some Kiowa, Apaches, and Comanches – was unprecedented for its time. The intensity of the combat itself, both at Mud Springs and at Rush Creek, was marked by sustained ferocity.

The long-term results of the two encounters were inconclusive. The Indians did not prevent the military from defending the trail or the telegraph, but neither did the military restrain the Indians from moving to Powder River, as was their goal all along. For the territorial and national governments, the twin battles were important because in combination Collins and his men had helped keep – although just barely – the trail and the telegraph lines open during a difficult time.

The massive Sioux outbreak along the nation's frontier caused the government to reorganize the command structure for the Plains. Ironically, included among the first troops ordered to the area were former Confederate prisoners. Called "Galvanized Yankees," they were freed from prison camps in return for their promise to fight Indians on the Plains. Collins used "Galvanized Yankees" to flesh out the strength of companies in the 11th Ohio.

Mud Springs and Rush Creek would be Collins' last major actions on the Plains. With the Civil War winding down, his services in the west ended in March, a month after the two battles. He was officially mustered out of service in Omaha, Nebraska Territory, on April 1, 1865.

Collins returned to Hillsboro after leaving the Army. For a time he served as Collector of Internal Revenue, appointed to that position by President Andrew Johnson. After a prolonged period of illness, he died of a stomach hemorrhage in Hillsboro on October 26, 1880.

While Collins was on active duty, a small outpost near the Poudre River was named in his honor. The city that grew up around that site – Fort Collins, Colorado – continues to carry his name.

After Collins left the Army, his son Caspar Collins, a second lieutenant in the cavalry – who had accompanied his father and fought at Mud Springs and Rush Creek – remained on active duty. Caspar was killed in action on July 24, 1865, when a small contingent of cavalrymen he was leading was ambushed near Platte Bridge (present-day Casper), Wyoming. The city of Casper (a misspelling of his name) is named after him.

Patrick E. Connor

B rigadier General Patrick Connor is best known for commanding American forces at the Battle of Bear River, Idaho, and leading the Powder River Expedition that included a significant encounter at Tongue River, Wyoming. While the Civil War raged in the East, Connor's services were entirely in the West. Although the assignment was not his preference – he strongly desired to be sent east to participate in the war's major engagements – he came to be one of the Army's preeminent Indian fighters. During the two and a half year interval between the Battle of Bear River (fought on January 29, 1863, near present-day Franklin, Idaho) and the final battle of the Powder River Expedition waged along the Tongue River in Sheridan County, Wyoming, on August 29, 1865, Connor's duties took him over a vast expanse of the continent from Utah and Montana to Nebraska.

The Powder River Expedition would form part of Connor's legacy; it was a campaign notable for having been one of the Army's earliest attempts to mount a multi-axis campaign against the Plains tribes. Connor's hopes of replenishing his forces after the bitter struggle at Tongue River and inflicting a major defeat on the Indians was foreclosed when the government decided instead to pursue a peace initiative – an effort that turned out to be a dismal failure. Disrupted by major difficulties with supplies, equipment, and personnel, as well as conflicting government policies, the expedition would achieve only limited success.

Patrick Edward O'Connor (he began signing his name P. Edward Connor at age 26), was born on St. Patrick's Day, 1820, in County Kerry, Ireland. His family immigrated to New York City when Connor was 12 years old. At 19, he began a five-year enlistment in the Army, seeing service in the Seminole War before being assigned to several posts on the Great Plains, including Fort Leavenworth. Honorably discharged in late 1844, Connor returned to New York City for two years before moving to Texas.

At the onset of the war with Mexico, Connor joined a unit of Texas volunteers – the Texas Foot Riflemen – and not long after was named the company's captain. Connor led the unit, part of General John E. Wool's Army of the Center, through several engagements including Palo Alto, Roseca

de Palma, and Buena Vista where he was
wounded and cited for bravery.

Honorably discharged in 1847, he
eventually arrived in California in January
1850, during the late stages of the gold
rush. In California he engaged in surveying,
contracting, construction, and road-building.
His marriage in 1854 to Johanna Connor (no
relation) produced three boys, only one of
whom lived to adulthood.

In May 1853, state authorities asked
Connor to serve as an officer in a company
of California State Rangers charged with
tracking down the bandit Joaquin Murrieta
and his renegade band. The successful effort

Mathew Brady, Library of Congress
Patrick E. Connor

broke up the outlaw group and ended with the death of four of the gang's
members, including Murrieta, and the capture of two others.

When the Civil War began, Connor was placed in command of the
Stockton Blues, a California militia unit. Over time, and with Connor's
effective recruiting, the unit evolved into the 3rd Regiment California
Volunteer Infantry. Once formed, the regiment was rather quickly called to
duty in Utah Territory to protect trails and telegraph lines from marauding
Indians and guard against possible uprisings by Mormon settlers and
Confederate sympathizers.

Connor's sojourn as commander of the District of Utah in the Department
of the Pacific began on August 6, 1862. The assignment would have several
consequences for Connor personally and for the history of the region. After
a time, Connor's discontent with his circumstance surfaced. He and his men
would have preferred to participate in the major battles then raging in the
East. Connor offered to withhold $30,000 from the regiment's pay to defray
costs of shipping the regiment to the East Coast. His request was turned
down by Federal authorities, including Union Army chief, General Henry W.
Halleck, who believed his presence was essential in the West.

When Halleck instead suggested a reconnaissance to the Salt Lake area,
Connor complied and established Fort Douglas, a citadel with a commanding
position above Salt Lake City. The creation of the fort greatly displeased
Brigham Young and other Mormon leaders, who tried unsuccessfully to have
Connor and his troops removed. Connor's soldiers eventually established a
newspaper that competed with the paper published by the Latter Day Saints
church, an action that further displeased Young, as did Connor's overt
protection and encouragement of non-Mormons in the area.

The persistent influx of settlers into the region led to periodic clashes between the immigrants and Native tribes. In early January 1863, an attack on a group of miners led authorities to call for a punitive expedition. Connor, the expedition commander, disguised the true size of his 300-man force by dispatching his troops in two increments. At the end of January, the two columns came together near present-day Franklin, Idaho.

After leading his unit 140 miles over terrain covered in deep snow and ice, on January 26, Connor's force located a sizable Shoshone village quartered along the Bear River near the Idaho-Utah border. The Indians were not totally unaware of Connor's approach and had dug rifle pits near the river and built willow barricades at the defensible areas.

After crossing the icy river, Connor's men struck the encampment and then feigned a retreat to induce the Indians to move and lower their vigilance. Connor then surrounded the village and launched a major assault, sending troops to block a ravine that formed the Shoshones' likely escape route. With the ravine sealed off, Connor ordered a flanking movement that placed the bulk of his troops along a ridge line. The elevated position allowed unrestricted fire on any warriors who attempted to escape by swimming across the frigid river.

The Bear River battle remains the subject of controversy. Nearly all of the 263 Indians in the village, including women and children, were killed. Other credible, though wide-ranging, estimates placed the numbers at from 200 to 400. Thus, some histories refer to the episode as the Bear River Massacre. Allegations surfaced that California militia members in particular engaged in indiscriminate firing, committed atrocities, and displayed a general absence of discipline.

As with other battles in the West, soldiers noted the similarity of wearing apparel between warriors and women and asserted that during the course of the melee, the tribe's women had also actively taken up arms. Connor's losses amounted to 21 killed and 46 wounded.

In the aftermath, material and war supplies found in the camp led Connor's men to contend that the Shoshones had perhaps been provisioned by Mormon authorities. One Indian survivor was reported to have stated that the band was planning an attack on the nearby town of Franklin.

Connor's victory at Bear River ended the long-standing threat to travel along the region's trails. By October 1863, Connor had concluded peace treaties with the area's remaining warring bands, closing out hostilities within the territory.

Connor's actions as District of Utah commander and while under fire at Bear River established his reputation as a blunt-spoken, forceful leader, unforgiving of his adversaries and relentless in pursuit. His colleagues saw him as quiet, unpretentious, taciturn – a red-haired Irishman who had risen through the ranks. (His red whiskers led his Indian enemies to label him Red

Chief.) A contemporary account described him as well-mannered, of medium size, square-shouldered, with reddish hair, blue eyes, and a prominent nose.

In March 1865, the District of Utah was merged into the District of the Plains, a vast region encompassing all or parts of the present states of Utah, Idaho, Montana, Wyoming, Colorado, and Nebraska. Connor was named commander of the new district, tasked with defending 2,600 miles of mail routes and telegraph lines while at the same time waging war on hostile tribes.

Connor's superiors, Generals John Pope and Grenville Dodge, envisioned a grand three-pronged attack aimed at warring tribes across the Plains. Ample troops, numerically at least, were initially available – 52,000 or more with the Civil War dying down and 5,000 on hand to guard stage depots and protect wagon trains. The numbers were misleading, however. Many of the troops were three-year enlistees whose terms of service were about to expire. Most, having enlisted to help put down a rebellion, had little inclination to go west and fight Indians. With troops eager to leave the Army and go home, discipline was a persistent problem. On at least one occasion, Connor had to admonish a group of officers for their lax conduct and poor example.

Among the chief malcontents was Colonel Thomas Moonlight, one of Connor's subordinate commanders, who railed at having been ordered to cross the Plains with his 11th Kansas regiment in the middle of winter to participate in the forthcoming campaign. Moonlight became one of Connor's most persistent critics.

The overall numbers allotted to Connor would swiftly dwindle. To help offset the losses, two regiments of "Galvanized Yankees" (former Confederate prisoners) were assigned to Connor's command.

Spring 1865 brought increased raiding throughout the region. In April, Connor ordered authorities at Fort Laramie to hang an Indian, Big Crow, who was charged with being a spy and with the murder of a white woman during a raid on settlers near the Little Blue River in Nebraska.

As raids increased in number, size, and lethality, Connor spent much of his early days as department commander working to suppress the burgeoning uprising – a task made more difficult by a shortage of supplies, lack of corn for his cavalry horses, and poor support from contractors. In official correspondence, Connor also complained of incompetence on the part of some of his subordinates – Colonel Moonlight foremost among them. After an especially egregious handling of an escort expedition, in early July Connor relieved Moonlight from command and sent him directly to Fort Kearny to be mustered out.

Meanwhile, plans for a major campaign progressed concurrently with increasing pressure from several groups for peace negotiations. Sparked in part by the public outcry over the Sand Creek Massacre – Colonel John Chivington's unprovoked attack on a peaceful Cheyenne village on

November 29, 1864 – the government's acquiescence to treaty discussions would eventually halt Connor's campaign before the complete set of results intended for it could be achieved.

The plan for the Powder River Expedition called for three columns to eventually converge in the vicinity of the Rosebud Creek. Colonel Nelson Cole, leaving from Nebraska Territory with the 12th Missouri Cavalry and the 2nd Missouri Light Artillery would turn west after skirting the Black Hills to the east and north. Lieutenant Colonel Samuel Walker, with six companies of the 16th Kansas Cavalry and other mixed units, was to move directly north from Fort Laramie. Cole's and Walker's forces were to merge near the headwaters of the Cheyenne River. Meanwhile, Connor would march northeast from Fort Laramie, skimming the eastern edge of the Bighorn Mountains. The wings were projected to rendezvous near the Rosebud on September 1.

As the expeditions formed during early and mid-summer, persistent large-scale, killing raids exploded across the region. One attack, at Platte Bridge Station, killed 28 soldiers and caused Connor to hurry a nine-company relief force to the scene. In the midst of growing public outrage, some newspapers openly advocated policy of extermination of the Plains Indians. Connor, frustrated by non-receipt of promised supplies and equipment and by generally inadequate support from contractors, chafed at the shortcomings and delays. Eventually, Connor ordered his quartermaster to contract and disburse money directly for supplies, wagons, and teamster support. The technical circumvention of regulations was seen by most as the necessary, forceful actions of a commander trying to keep a major expedition on track. Detractors saw it as an autocratic violation of the law. Further delays would disrupt the campaign timelines and almost assure that operations would run afoul of the Wyoming/Montana winter.

As the campaign began, Connor's guidance to his subordinate commanders was to prevent outrages of any kind on Indian women and children. They were to be taken prisoner and not harassed. Conversely, perhaps evidencing his frustrations or reflecting the popular sentiments of the time, Connor's initial orders to Cole and Walker directed them to not entertain any peace overtures from Indians and to kill every male Indian over age 12. General Pope, Connor's superior officer, immediately countermanded that portion of Connor's instructions.

On July 28, 1865, Connor put his force in motion moving west and north, eventually brushing against the Bighorn Mountains. Connor's column consisted of 558 soldiers and 179 Indian scouts (95 of them Pawnees led by Frank North). One hundred ninety-five teamsters and wagon masters drove 185 wagons and a herd of 226 beef cattle.

Of the three columns, Cole's was the largest with 1,168 officers and men from the 12th Missouri Cavalry and 2nd Missouri Light Artillery. Walker's contingent of Kansas companies consisted of about 600 officers and men. Altogether, 2,226 soldiers and 179 Indian scouts were committed to the campaign. During his march, the left wing of Connor's column opened a new route that linked with the Bozeman Trail and would be widely used by later travelers moving through the region.

As Connor's troops moved toward their rendezvous, they were periodically struck by raids of varying size and lethality. On August 14, about 175 miles north of Fort Laramie, after fighting several skirmishes, the force arrived at a low tableland on the west side of the Powder River. There, Connor decided to build a fort. The future Fort Connor, a stockade 120 feet square inside of which several buildings would be added over time, commanded a clear view in every direction. Action in the form of harassing raids began almost immediately. Frank North's Pawnees made several notably successful forays, chasing down attackers, taking scalps, and recovering horses, supplies, and mail stolen at other locations.

On August 17, North's Pawnees caught a party of 24 Cheyennes and in a running fight killed them all. Other than Connor's fight at the Tongue River later in the month, the Pawnees' victory accounted for the most hostiles killed during the expedition.

After a few days at the newly constructed post, Connor left much of the 6th Michigan Cavalry to garrison the installation and put the remainder of his force in motion. As Connor and his men tracked generally north, their route took them over terrain that was alternately desolate and sublime. Parched, near-treeless areas gave way to some of the most majestic landscapes in North America. Connor's troopers found fast-moving streams teeming with trout, and valleys abundant with game and grass. From timbered uplands they saw, in the far distance, the stunning, snow-capped peaks of the Bighorn Mountains. At times during the march, Connor's troops supplemented their Army rations, catching a seemingly endless supply of rainbow trout and feasting on deer, elk, and buffalo, all easily accessible as they moved through Wyoming and into Montana.

As depredations along the trail continued, Connor kept his column on the move. Guided by the legendary scout Jim Bridger, ably abetted by superb reconnaissance from Frank North's Pawnees and a group of Omaha scouts, the column pressed ahead, picking up increasing signs of the presence of hostiles in large numbers.

In the early evening of August 28, one of North's Pawnee scouts returned with information about an Arapaho camp. The Arapaho band was known to have been responsible for many of the attacks along the overland trail west of Denver. Their large village was located along the banks of the Tongue River about 35 miles to the west. After a quick supper, Connor rapidly assembled an attack force of about 300, consisting of 60 11th Ohio cavalrymen with good horses, 38 California volunteers, 100 artillerymen with two cannons, and 70 Pawnee and Omaha scouts.

Guided adeptly by Jim Bridger through a dark night, traversing terrain cut by defiles, fallen timber and underbrush, Connor's force reached the vicinity of the Indian encampment at daybreak. Their march up the valley of the Tongue River brought them to a mesa of about one square mile in size. There, they discovered hundreds of Indian ponies grazing and a large village about a half mile distant on the left side of the plateau.

Before breaking camp on the night of the 28th, Connor ordered that no one speak above a whisper and that horses that whinnied be quickly restrained. Now, as he readied his force for attack, he directed his troops create noise and confusion as they raced toward the village. They were to kill as many warriors as possible but to avoid harm to women and children. There was to be no scalping.

At about 8 o'clock in the morning of August 29, Connor aligned his troops, crossed over the crest of a ridge and ordered his bugler to sound the charge. Amid an incredible din – heavy firing, men and women shouting, horses whinnying, dogs barking, bugles sounding – Connor's men charged towards the camp, his troopers fanning out to the right and left, forming an arc that enfolded the village.

The extended run to the campsite allowed many Indian warriors time to get to their mounts. The camp had already begun preparations to leave that morning. Many of the Arapahos' 3,000 ponies were packed and ready to move and several tepees were down or partly disassembled. As the troopers swept towards them, women and children began moving quickly up the stream away from the camp.

After ordering a volley into the village, Connor and several cavalrymen raced ahead in pursuit of warriors preparing to escape. The scene inside the village was chaotic. Howitzers pounded the encampment, blowing apart tepees and inflicting casualties. Soldiers entering the village found themselves involved in hand to hand combat. In the midst of the melee, Connor's Indian scouts disregarded his orders, taking Arapaho scalps regardless of age or gender.

After a time, several Arapaho warriors reached and held a slice of elevated ground nearby, but were driven off by heavy fire as additional troops reached the area. Numerous others were killed by Omaha scouts who found Arapahos hiding behind stacks of buffalo robes near the riverbank.

Although caught momentarily in a crossfire Connor and about 30 others, including 15 Pawnee scouts, rode straight through the village, chasing a large party of fleeing Indians ten or more miles up Wolf Creek. After several miles of furious pursuit, Connor eventually called a halt when the cavalrymen's horses began to give out. Seeing their pursuers stop, the Arapahos used the moment to reform and attack Connor's small force. Connor ordered a fighting withdrawal, stopping periodically to collect stragglers and break the momentum of the pursuit. Eventually, they succeeded in rejoining the main force still engaged in a desperate struggle back at the Arapaho village.

At the camp, Indians shooting from rifle pits dug in the brush along the river bank kept the soldiers under fire. After holding for a considerable time, the Arapahos were eventually forced from their positions by skirmishers who edged cautiously towards them. Fighting in and near the village remained intense as Indian warriors, joined often by Arapaho women, continued to press their attacks, repeatedly charging Connor's men. Finally, at about noon the Indians broke off their assaults. A half hour later Connor brought his men together, ordering them to destroy the village and all its contents. All of the village's 220 or so lodges and their contents – robes, blankets, cooking utensils, and food supplies – were placed in an enormous pile and burned. The bodies of two soldiers killed in the battle were placed on the pyre to prevent their remains from being mutilated by the Arapahos.

At the outset of the fighting, Connor had directed Frank North to capture the Arapahos' pony herd. North did so, taking 500-600 horses (one contemporary sources places the number at 1,100). The Arapahos made repeated desperate attempts to retrieve their mounts but were beaten back by accurate fire from one of Connor's mountain howitzers. Connor sent North and his Pawnees ahead with the captured horses, and then pulled the remainder of his troops out of the village at about 2:30 in the afternoon.

The march back to the main base was fraught with danger. The Indians attacked Connor's column repeatedly throughout the late afternoon, evening, and night. Several of the Arapahos' forays carried to within a few yards of the rear guard, forcing frequent stops and defensive stands. Finally, near midnight the Arapahos made their final assault before vanishing in the night. Connor's troops reached their post at about 3 o'clock in the morning. By then they had marched almost a hundred miles with little food or rest.

After action reports cited 63 Arapahos killed, 250 lodges burned, 500 horses captured, and tons of Arapaho supplies destroyed. Connor's casualties included two cavalrymen killed. Of the several wounded, three or four later died of wounds as did two members of Frank North's Pawnee Scouts.

The following day Connor addressed his assembled force, specifically lauding a Winnebago chief and three Winnebago warriors as well as Frank North and fifteen of his Pawnee Scouts for their actions during the Tongue River battle. At the same time, he expressed his displeasure with the looting that had occurred while the battle was in progress and threatened to shoot future offenders.

Connor's victory was widely acclaimed. On September 21, he was honored with a large banquet in Denver. His respite was short-lived, however. The columns led by Colonel Cole and Lieutenant Colonel Walker were by this time in deep trouble. Like Connor's contingent, both units had experienced problems with supplies and near-mutinies from troops eager to be mustered out now that the Civil War was over. Their guides were generally incompetent; neither force had anyone the caliber of Jim Bridger.

In August, the two units came together about 40 miles north of Devil's Tower, Wyoming. After moving first north and then west, the combined force reached the Powder River on August 30. By that time their supplies were low and horses and mules were played out. Desperate to locate Connor, Cole sent a 20-man squad with his most reliable scout in an unsuccessful attempt to make contact. Cole was forced to place the column on half rations, only to find his problems compounded by frequent encounters with substantial groups of Sioux and Cheyennes. Casualties were forthcoming on both sides, sometimes in considerable numbers. One engagement involved an attack by 400-500 Indians and resulted in 25 warriors killed and numerous others wounded.

After a further attempt to move toward Connor's supposed location, Cole's increasingly dire circumstance caused him to reverse course and head toward Fort Laramie, Wyoming, a journey that began on September 3. During the march, several wagons and large quantities of unnecessary gear and equipment were destroyed. Debilitated by heat, exhaustion, and starvation, 225 horses and mules died or were shot. Scurvy became prevalent, particularly in Cole's camp. Indian attacks persisted almost on a daily basis. On September 7, six soldiers were lost in a skirmish. An engagement on September 8, perhaps involving 3,000 to 4,000 Sioux and Cheyennes was one of the largest battles ever fought against the Plains tribes. Cole's skillful use of artillery fought off repeated attacks, narrowly averting catastrophe on a scale that would have equaled the Little Bighorn a decade later. Freezing rain the night following the battle further compounded the troops' misery. Additional horses were lost and supplies were almost gone. By mid-September, the Cole-Walker command was in desperate need of assistance.

On September 15, Connor's scouts found the column after discovering 250 dead cavalry horses. After an exchange of messages, Connor directed Cole to turn towards Fort Connor, a much closer source of provisions than Fort Laramie, and provided directions to assist the column. In the meantime, Connor hurried food supplies to Cole whose men had been subsisting mainly on mule meat, berries, and rosebuds for three weeks. The main portion of the beleaguered column reached Fort Connor on September 19 and 20 where they received food and fresh clothing, and enjoyed the luxury of a bath in the river.

Walker reported one soldier killed and four wounded within his immediate command. Cole's losses numbered 12 killed and two missing along with hundreds of cavalry horses dead.

The dilemma regarding the Cole-Walker contingent was not the only issue that confronted Connor at this time. Two days after the fight at the Tongue River, a large survey party led by James Sawyers was attacked by several hundred Indians, some of whom were survivors of the battle with Connor. The expedition, chartered to explore and develop a more direct route from Sioux City, Iowa, to the Montana gold fields, consisted of 53 men and included 45 teams of oxen and 15 wagons. A military escort with 25 wagons, each driven by six mules, accompanied Sawyers as did five wagons of emigrant travelers and a private freight outfit with another 36 wagons pulled by 18 sets of oxen formed into six-yoke teams.

Harassed repeatedly by raiding parties large and small as they moved across Wyoming, by September 1 the expedition had struggled to the north bank of the Tongue River. A major attack that day forced Sawyers to form a defensive corral using the 60 wagons as a barricade. The attack evolved into a confused, prolonged episode that was part siege interspersed with multiple attacks and occasional parleys. The encounter lasted nearly two weeks. Early in the struggle Sawyers sent messages in an attempt to reach Connors. On September 13, conditions had deteriorated to the point that Sawyers had been forced to reverse his course and head toward Fort Connor. Soon after setting out, a cavalry company moving through the area and some of Connor's Omaha and Winnebago scouts found Sawyers and his party. They were the first of two companies sent by Connor to reach the scene and come to Sawyers' relief. Sawyers eventually continued to the Yellowstone River, finally reaching Virginia City before trekking down an existing portion of the Bozeman Trail.

For Patrick Connor, the Sawyer episode was more than just another in an extended series of distractions. Each had major consequences. The forces Connor allocated to rescue and escort Sawyers and his party had to be drawn from already scare manpower and equipment resources. Connors, who at the same time was trying to connect with Cole and Walker, missed the opportunity to consolidate his forces and fight what he planned as the final, conclusive battle of the war.

That had been Connor's intended plan: to rest Cole and Walker's men, replenish their supplies and horses, and along with his own command, renew the campaign. North and his Pawnees had discovered a large, particularly promising encampment of hostiles.

That operation would never take place. At about the same time Connor's expedition was forming, the government had launched an attempt to make peace with the belligerent tribes. On September 21, messengers arrived with orders to cease military operations. Soon after, a second dispatch came ordering General Connor to new duties in Utah.

The orders angered Connor, who thought his planned campaign would resolve the problems in the region. He, as well as his superior, General Grenville Dodge, believed – correctly, as it turned out – that the timing of the peace initiative was disastrously wrong and that the attempt was doomed to failure. Little could be done, however, as nearly all of Cole's and Walker's men soon received orders to muster out of service.

Thus ended the Powder River Expedition. While the grand design to devastate the hostile tribes had not been achieved, the presence of Fort Connor held war parties at greater risk enhancing security along the Bozeman Trail and momentarily restoring it for public use. Given the myriad of difficulties facing Connor, that perhaps was the best result any commander could have been expected to achieve.

Connor remained at Fort Connor until early October, finding in the meantime that he was under investigation for alleged contracting irregularities, having personally contracted for the provisions that were necessary in order to get the expedition underway. General Dodge defended Connor against the bizarre accusations and little became of them. Although no charges were filed, Connor was also criticized for the deaths of Native women during the battle at Tongue River. Connor returned to his duties in the District of Utah where in the spring of the following year, he was discharged from the military as a brevet major general.

The remaining years of his life were spent in Utah, mainly devoted to developing mining property. Successful at times – some called him the "father of Utah mining" – by the time of his death in 1891, much of his wealth and many of his mines had been lost. He ran unsuccessfully for statewide offices and expended considerable time and energy in confronting Mormon economic and political influence. He opposed polygamy and lived long enough to see it abolished. Much to his pleasure, non-Mormons had gained some political offices in the new state by the time he died.

Connor passed away at age 71 on December 17, 1891. He is buried in Salt Lake City.

Philip St. George Cooke

Although Philip St. George Cooke would have recoiled at the contention, many historians recall him primarily for having been the father-in-law of Confederate general J.E.B. Stuart. Cooke was a native Virginian who chose to remain with the Union when the Civil War began. That decision having been made, the two men never again spoke to each other.

The focus on the linkage to Stuart does a disservice to Cooke, whose nearly 50-year military career extended from the earliest days of western settlement in the 1820s through the Sioux wars of the 1860s and 1870s. His experience on the frontier exceeded that of most of his colleagues and the scope and variety of his contributions equaled those of many of his more renowned contemporaries.

Born June 13, 1809, at Leesburg, Virginia, Cooke entered West Point as a 14-year old and graduated in 1827 at age 18. Friends and biographers would alter recall him as a stern disciplinarian who set of high standard of personal honor. Though deeply religious, his language was "peppery." Many remembered also a keen sense of humor, perhaps most often displayed around young people for whom he had an abiding affection.

By 1828, Cooke was at Jefferson Barracks in St. Louis, posted there as a member of the 6th Infantry. His first acquaintance with the far west began almost immediately when he helped escort a trading party to Fort Gibson in present-day Oklahoma.

His first encounter under fire came soon after – a baptism considerably earlier than that experienced by most of his peers. On August 3, 1829, while escorting another group of traders along the Upper Arkansas River, Cooke's small force was attacked by several hundred Comanches. Cooke, with 36 men, broke up the momentum of the attack with a skillful enveloping maneuver and drove off the on-rushing mass with effective fire from a howitzer. Eight days later he led a company across a river under fire and helped defeat another assault on a nearby camp.

Assigned to Fort Leavenworth from 1830-1832, Cooke participated in the Black Hawk War against the Sac Indians. During one of the conflict's few major battles – the Battle of Bad Ax River, fought on August 2, 1832 – Cooke found Sac warriors on an island and successfully led three companies against them.

Back for a time at Jefferson Barracks, Cooke transferred to the 1st Dragoons and again led excursions to Fort Gibson and other sites in Indian Territory. The move to a cavalry unit was particularly apt for an officer who was known throughout the small army as a splendid horseman and for his soldierly appearance in the saddle.

In 1833, after a brief recruiting soiree, during which he was licensed to practice law, Cooke, with three dragoon companies, formed an advance guard for a caravan of about 50

Public Domain
Philip St. George Cooke

wagons bound all the way to Santa Fe in Mexican territory. At the Cimarron Crossing of the Arkansas River – which then formed the international boundary – he safely released his charges to the protection of Mexican army forces who met him there.

After several months of recruiting duty in 1835, Cooke was transferred in 1836 to Fort Gibson. His two years at the post would add to his already solid credentials as a frontier soldiers. Exploring, scouting, and escort duties took him north as far as Council Bluffs in present-day Iowa, and west all the way to the Rocky Mountains.

The year 1838 found him briefly in Washington, D.C., and then at Carlisle Barracks in Pennsylvania, where the Army established a cavalry school. After a brief stay at Fort Wayne in 1840, Cooke spent the next three years at Fort Leavenworth where his time was mainly consumed in escorting traders on the long, arduous journey to Santa Fe.

In June 1843, Cooke had a collision with a 180-man force from the new Republic of Texas. Led by Major Jacob Snively, the Texans apparently operated on both sides of the border, interfering with trade to and from Santa Fe. Cooke, on escort duty with a large merchant train, led a contingent of 190 soldiers in four dragoon companies, accompanied by 11 baggage wagons and two howitzers. Alerted by scouts to the Texans' presence, Cooke eventually met with Snively who greeted him with threats and belligerence. When Snively failed to comply with Cooke's request that he disarm his followers, (who Cooke believed – rightfully – were on American soil), Cooke moved his force across the river to a grove of trees where Snively's troops were sheltering. Cooke skillfully deployed his men in battle formation, positioning his two howitzers conspicuously in the middle of the line. After counseling among themselves, the Texans surrendered, piling their weapons in front of Cooke. Cooke gave the Texans ten rifles for protection, returned Snively's two pistols, and sent them home. Cooke's actions were upheld by a subsequent Court of Inquiry that determined he had acted properly and that the encounter had taken place in United States territory.

The summer of 1845 brought further experience in long-range campaigning. Beginning on May 18 and extending over the next 99 days, Cooke accompanied Colonel Stephen Watts Kearny and a force of 250 dragoons on a 2,000 march to the South Pass in Wyoming.

An even more notable journey was soon forthcoming. The spring of 1846 brought a declaration of war against Mexico and with it a plan by Kearny to occupy New Mexico and California. In October, Cooke assumed command of five companies of Mormon volunteers, called the Mormon Battalion. The unit had marched to Santa Fe from their initial campground in Iowa Territory under the leadership of a temporary commander. In the meantime, Kearny had marched on, taking 300 dragoons down the valley of the Rio Grande headed for California. Left behind were instructions for Cooke to cut a wagon road to the Pacific and take the Mormon Battalion with him.

It would turn out to be an epic journey. Cooke moved his 397-man force, under-equipped in almost every regard, from Santa Fe on October 19, making solid time despite obstacles imposed by landscape and climate. On at least one occasion, Cooke's column faced a 90-mile stretch in which water and grass were almost non-existent. Eventually, scouts found a mountain passage on a high plateau that led to water and pasture. As the unit approached Tucson, a fortified city under Mexican control, Cooke took a small force and, after negotiations failed, prepared to attack. As Cooke assembled his battle line, the Mexican commander abandoned the town, which Cooke occupied without further incident.

Reprovisioning from the ample supplies found there, Cooke resumed his march mapping the terrain along the way. Cutting through rock and mesquite under conditions so arduous that work crews were changed every hour, Cooke pushed the battalion west, cleaving a path suitable for wagon travel.

Cooke and the Mormon battalion reached San Diego on January 29, 1847. In a journey that had consumed the autumn and winter of 1846-1847, they had carved the first wagon road to the Pacific Ocean. Initial friction between Cooke and his Mormon soldiers had been overcome by the shared trials and hardships of the march. In later years, Mormon monuments commemorating the trek would give prominent mention to Cooke's leadership.

After a delay to testify at the court-martial of John C. Fremont, Cooke eventually joined the 2nd Dragoons in Mexico City at the conclusion of the war. As the U.S. forces were withdrawn, Cooke handled logistics and commanded the rear guard as Winfield Scott's army marched to the coast to re-embark at Vera Cruz.

Back in the States after the war, in October 1848, Cooke was assigned to a four-year tour as post commander and superintendent of cavalry recruiting at Carlisle Barracks. In November 1852, Cooke returned to the 2nd Dragoons, serving with the regiment in Texas. During the winter of 1852-1853, he drove Lipan Apaches and allied tribes across the Rio Grande. In 1854, by now a lieutenant colonel in command of Fort Union, New Mexico, Cooke led operations against the Jicarilla Apaches, skirmishing with a raiding party about six miles from the fort on March 5.

Later that month, he hurried a force of 200 men to the scene of a battle near Fort Burgwin, about ten miles from Taos, New Mexico, where a unit of dragoons from the post had been defeated by a party of Jicarillas and Utes. Twenty-two dragoons had been killed and 36 wounded during the three-hour battle. Cooke pursued the raiders relentlessly, chasing them more than 100 miles across severe terrain and through heavy snow. Nine days into the chase, he caught the war party at Agua Caliente and during the ensuing battle killed the chief and 20 other Apaches. Authorities later credited the action as having prevented the greater Ute nation from combining with the Jicarillas in a general war against the whites.

The year 1855 brought action against different adversaries in a far distant portion of the continent. In response to a public outcry, the administration of President Franklin Pierce launched a retaliatory expedition to avenge the killings of 29 soldiers near Fort Laramie, Wyoming the preceding year. The episode, known as the Grattan Massacre after the name of the officer in charge, Lieutenant John Grattan, prompted the government's first major campaign against the Plains Indians. The assemblage of 600 cavalry, infantry, and artillerymen led by General William S. Harney would be the largest force ever to enter Indian territory. Harney caught the group thought to be responsible for the Grattan incident near present-day Lewellen, Nebraska, not far from the historic Ash Hollow campground on the Oregon Trail.

The Indians, led most prominently by Chief Little Thunder, were camped along a stream called (at the time) Blue Water Creek, a small waterway that flowed into the nearby North Platte River. Arrayed in two villages, one of 41 Brule lodges and the second of 11 Oglala lodges, the camps were separated by a distance of three miles.

In the pre-dawn hours of September 3, 1855, Harney moved against the Brule encampment, the southern-most of the two villages. Harney, not knowing at the time of the presence of the Oglala lodges farther north, sent Cooke with a force of cavalry and mounted infantry on a large half-circle to position them on the reverse side of the Brule camp. During the march, Cooke's scout found the Oglala camp without being detected, preserving the element of surprise. Now aware of the combined encampments, Cooke took his force farther north, positioning them to the rear of both villages. In the meantime, Harney sent his infantry diagonally across the floor of the valley. After an attempted parley failed, Harney launched a full scale attack that drove the Brule into the narrow ravines, limestone caves, and coarse outcroppings that formed the high west wall of the valley. Cooke, moving at the first sound of firing, swept three companies in a column of fours across the bluffs to the hostiles' rear. A fourth company of mounted infantry was sent straight down the valley in an attempt to seal off the Indians' anticipated escape route.

Pressed between Harney's advancing infantry and Cooke's on-rushing cavalry, the Sioux attempt to make a stand proved futile and they began a panicked flight down the face of the bluffs toward open ground to the east. Cooke sent a company of cavalry down the hillside in an all-out pursuit that lasted several miles.

Called the Battle of the Blue Water, the encounter was a disaster for the Plains Indians. Harney's after action report cited 86 Indians killed at the scene and many more captured. Other accounts report as many as 50 more killed along the Indians' line of retreat. The encounter – the Sioux's first with a large, combined force of cavalry, infantry, and artillery – shocked the Plains tribes. For much of the next decade conditions along the trail remained generally quiescent.

Back in Kansas following the battle, in 1856 Cooke was called by the governor to lead a force from Fort Leavenworth to quell pro- and anti-slavery disturbances that threatened the fragile peace. Cooke's firm interventions, abetted by calm demeanor and good judgment, were credited with preventing widespread violence.

September-November 1857 found Cooke on another extended campaign, this time taking his regiment from Fort Leavenworth to Fort Bridger as part of the so-called Utah Expedition. After guarding livestock in the midst of a horrific winter and spring, Cooke moved through the Salt Lake City area to Camp Floyd, about 40 miles distant from the city. A friend of Brigham Young, Cooke donated material to the Mormon settlements in southern Utah.

The following year brought an extended leave of absence during which Cooke devoted much of his time to writing a manual of cavalry tactics. Though not without controversy, the manual was eventually adopted for use by the Army and remained its basic source of cavalry doctrine for more than 20 years. In 1859-1860, he traveled to Europe to observe the operations and training of European armies. When he returned the United States in the spring of 1860, he was named commander of the Department of Utah and was in that position when the Civil War began.

When Army units vacated Utah at the outset of the war, Cooke led his unit across the country for a final time. Sent east soon after Fort Sumter, Cooke was first assigned as commander of a cavalry regiment in Washington, D.C. In November 1861, he was promoted to brigadier general in the Regular Army. During George McClellan's ill-fated Peninsula Campaign, Cooke led cavalry at Yorktown, Williamsburg, Gaines Mill, and in other encounters, failing on one occasion to trap his son-in-law's troops behind Union lines. A charge led by Cooke at Gaines Mill met with disastrous consequences and not long after he was removed from field command. Cooke's supporters believed he had been scapegoated and he left with bitter complaints about the incompetence of senior leaders in the Army of the Potomac. Cooke spent the remainder of the war in various administrative functions – sitting on court-martial boards, commanding the District of Baton Rouge, and serving as Superintendent of Army Recruiting Service.

On April 1, 1865, he took command of the Department of the Platte. During the Red Cloud War, the deaths of 80 soldiers during the so-called Fetterman Fight in December 1866 caused Cooke as well as the local commander, Colonel Henry B. Carrington, to be reassigned. Cooke concluded his military career as commander of the District of the Cumberland and the Department of the Lakes. He retired from the Army in 1873 as a major general after almost five decades of service, having fought Indians, led expeditions into new territory, constructed posts, and built roads over which later legions would travel.

In addition to his volume on cavalry tactics, Cooke achieved some notoriety as an author of well-received works on military history, various memoirs, and an autobiography.

Cooke died in Michigan on March 20, 1895, at age 86. He is buried at Elmwood Cemetery in Detroit.

Samuel R. Curtis

I n the early months of the Civil War, Samuel Curtis was one of the more successful Union generals, winning a notable victory at Pea Ridge, Arkansas, and capturing the city of Helena. Despite those successes and a later victory at Westport, Missouri, he remains one of the least known senior generals on either side. Two factors like account for that irony. The first is that his triumphs took place in the trans-Mississippi region, a theater regarded at least initially as somewhat of a backwater. The second is that a disagreement with a political leader caused his removal from command and diminished the luster of his victories. Midway through the war, he was shunted off to to the central Plains where he found himself in the midst of a major Indian uprising.

Curtis was born February 3, 1805, in Clinton County, New York. The family eventually moved to Ohio from where, in 1827, Curtis received an appointment to West Point. He graduated in 1831 but served only a year, primarily at Fort Gibson in Indian Territory, before resigning effective June 30, 1832. Curtis returned to Ohio where he worked as a civil engineer and was admitted to the bar.

With the Mexican War began, Curtis served initially as Adjutant General of Ohio before being appointed to command an Ohio infantry regiment. Assigned to General John Wool's command in Zachary Taylor's army, Curtis did not see combat but as a member of the occupation force served as military governor of Matamoras, Camargo, Monterey, and Saltillo.

After the war, Curtis moved to Iowa where in 1856 he entered politics. An early supporter of Abraham Lincoln, he was first elected mayor of Keokuk and then won three successive elections to the U.S. Congress.

With the onset of the Civil War, Curtis resigned from Congress after being named colonel in command of the Second Iowa Infantry. Soon after, following a successful march and occupation of Hannibal, Missouri, in May 1861, he was appointed brigadier general. Curtis was then sent to the St. Louis area where for the rest of the year he restored general order to the divided, chaotic region and trained troops at Jefferson Barracks while organizing the city's defenses. After a time, a regiment known as the "Curtis Horse" was formed and named for him. The regiment was a polyglot unit comprised of soldiers from Nebraska, Iowa, Minnesota, Michigan, and Illinois. The regiment eventually joined Grant's campaign against Forts Henry and Donelson before later merging with other units.

In February 1862, as commander of the newly-formed Army of the Southwest, Curtis's forces pushed Confederate units under the command of General Sterling Price out of Missouri into Arkansas. On March 7 and 8, though outnumbered and under attack by separate columns, Curtis defeated General Earl Van Dorn at the Battle of Pea Ridge, near Bentonville, Arkansas. In a deft maneuver, Curtis turned around his entire army and repositioned it to fight the more numerous rebel forces. The victory was decisive and halted serious threats in the area for the next two years. Curtis was promoted to major general following the battle.

Public Domain
Samuel R. Curtis

After an arduous campaign made more difficult by poor logistics – low water on major streams hindered supply boats – ghastly roads, and poor communications, in July Curtis's army captured Helena, Arkansas. Meanwhile, Curtis found himself crosswise of Missouri's governor in a political controversy. During the Helena campaign, his troops had liberated hundreds of slaves and struggled to find ways to feed the legions who followed his army. Governor Gamble objected to Curtis's actions. (The Emancipation Proclamation freed slaves only in states in rebellion. Missouri, although popular sympathies were almost equally divided, had not seceded from the Union.) Lincoln, needing Gamble's continued support, removed Curtis from operational command.

Initially appointed to an administrative position as commander of the Department of Missouri, in January 1864 he was named commander of the Department of Kansas. Curtis's area of responsibility encompassed all of the present states of Kansas, Nebraska, and Colorado, and about half of Wyoming. Stationed at 29 mostly small posts, the 600 troops initially under his command guarded 2,300 miles of trails. Amiable and energetic, Curtis was 58 years old when he assumed command in a region where in a short time he would face conditions verging on total war. Beginning in southern Kansas, then shifting first north, then west, and back east all the way to the Missouri border, the central and western Plains were swept by a series of crises.

On July 21, Curtis moved from Fort Riley with 400 members of two

Kansas volunteer regiments. After establishing two new posts, Fort Zarah (near Great Bend, Kansas, named for Curtis's son killed earlier in the war by Quantrill's Raiders), and Fort Ellsworth (in present-day Ellsworth County between Fort Riley and Fort Larned), Curtis halted his march at Fort Larned in south central Kansas. Splitting his force into three columns, Curtis sent units north, south, and west across the Kansas Plains.

Though not much contact was made with the hostiles, the presence of Curtis's mobile columns cleared southern Kansas and the Santa Fe Trail of most of the Kiowa, Comanche, and mixed Kiowa-Apache bands whose raids had terrorized the region. Driven farther south, the hostiles began attacking Confederate outposts in Texas. To keep pressure on the Indians and police the border of southern Kansas, Curtis placed General James G. Blunt in command of a newly created District of Upper Arkansas, assigning him a 600-man force comprised mainly of militia units.

A bit farther north, a second cataclysm was about to erupt.

On August 7, the Plum Creek Massacre, near present-day Lexington, Nebraska, signaled the beginning of a massive Sioux uprising. For a time, travel along the overland trail was halted between Fort Kearny, Nebraska, and Julesburg, Colorado, and beyond. Raids, killings, and kidnappings occurred as far east as the Little Blue River in southeastern Nebraska. Dozens of settlers, travelers, and ranchers were slain. Within 48 hours almost all of the stage stations and road ranches along the trail were attacked. Wagon trains, some several miles long, filled with refugees fled eastward toward safety. For a time, central and western Nebraska were almost emptied of white population.

When the scope of the uprisings became apparent, Curtis left his headquarters in St. Louis and moved to take personal command in the field. Arriving in Omaha on August 16, he began assembling forces, mustering in militia units to complement the 1st Nebraska cavalry which by coincidence was home on leave after three years of combat. Quickly called back from furlough, the veteran unit was initially short of horses, guns, and equipment, all of which had been left at their previous post in anticipation of their return. At the outset only 60 horses were available for the regiment's 300 men. Nonetheless, on August 18, Curtis set out for Fort Kearny, accompanying the regiment and the newly assembled militia units.

Enroute to Fort Kearny, Curtis delivered weapons and a cannon to citizen defenders of Grand Island, who had erected fortifications in readiness for an attack on the city. When Curtis reached Fort Kearny on August 24, he began dispersing small contingents of troops, positioning them at several points along the trail. A week later, having on reflection decided that offensive operations held greater promise for a decisive outcome, Curtis launched a major expedition. On September 1, with several companies of the 1st

Nebraska Cavalry, Nebraska militia units, two companies of Iowa cavalry, a detachment of the 16th Kansas, and a company of Pawnee Scouts, Curtis left Fort Kearny, moving south and west toward the Kansas border.

A week of fruitless maneuvering followed. Curtis took his column across the Republican River and Prairie Dog Creek, finally camping on September 8 along the banks of the Solomon River. Not a single Indian had been sighted. It was a lesson numerous other western commanders would learn and relearn: for much of the year – until winter set in – campaigns launched with large bodies of troops seldom met with success. The formations were typically too unwieldy to catch the elusive, fast-moving bands.

While in camp along the Solomon Curtis split his district for the purpose of installing a more responsive command arrangement. As usual, there were not enough troops to cover the immense region and both sub-district commanders faced an almost chronic shortage of horses. Until more men and mounts were available, Curtis's forces assumed a defensive strategy aimed at protecting the overland trail.

Farther west, trouble was developing as well. Fed by a series of isolated clashes in Colorado between Indians and settlers, and further inflamed by the actions of Colorado Governor John Evans and Colonel John Chivington, commander of Colorado militia forces, Native bands in the region were growing increasingly restless. A somewhat confused series of communications between Curtis, Evans, and Chivington followed. Curtis wanted the warriors involved in killing raids to be punished and, at least initially, opposed general negotiations until the perpetrators were apprehended. Evans and Chivington actively manipulated the unsettled situation. Chivington advised the Cheyenne Chief Black Kettle and other peace-seeking Northern Cheyennes to shift their camp to an area near Fort Lyon. Presuming that location would provide sanctuary, the Indians moved as suggested, setting their village along Sand Creek, a few miles from the fort. A few weeks later, they were attacked and massacred by Colorado militia units led by Chivington.

In the interim, Evans dispatched a flow of near-hysterical messages to Curtis, Secretary of War Stanton, and others, demanding more troops – 10,000 was the figure cited in one message – to stem off what he described as an imminent attack by thousands of blood-thirsty renegades. In a precursor to his actions at Sand Creek, Chivington, ignoring instructions to the contrary, orchestrated the execution of five captured tribesmen. Curtis sent an investigator to determine the state of affairs and was informed that much of the perceived crisis had been self-generated by Colorado authorities.

Curtis has sometimes been criticized for not immediately taking action against Chivington. Those more sympathetic to him point out that confronted almost simultaneously with a major uprising along the overland trail, Bushwhacker violence in Kansas and Missouri, a campaign against Kiowas,

Comanches, and Apaches in southern Kansas, and the continuing obligation to confront renewed threats to the region by mainstream Confederate forces, the actions of a distant subordinate may have understandably not been at the forefront of his attention. Then too, it is not entirely certain how much Curtis initially knew of Chivington's misadventures. On December 21, 1864, three weeks after Sand Creek, Curtis relieved Chivington of his command.

In mid-October, having received word that Confederate General Sterling Price was again moving across Missouri toward the Kansas border, Curtis, acting in large measure on his own initiative, hurried to take command of Union forces in the field. Augmenting his few Regular Army units with Kansas militia regiments, Curtis threw together a self-named Army of the Border.

On October 23, at Westport, Missouri (near Kansas City), Curtis defeated Price, halting the invasion and driving rebel troops out of the area. Curtis's army chased the Confederates south of the Arkansas River Valley, an action that again sparked controversy. Although General McPherson complained that Curtis's troops had trespassed on his jurisdiction and General Grant complained that his pursuit had not been pushed far enough (Curtis had run out of supplies), the defeat was conclusive. Westport would mark the Confederacy's last large-scale action in the trans-Mississippi west.

Curtis's victory had eventual consequences for commanders farther west as well. With the rebel threat diminished, Curtis was able to shift forces to the Great Plains to bolster the thinly-spread units there.

On November 29, John Chivington attacked Black Kettle's Arapaho village at Sand Creek. Native outrage transformed a conflict with the Sioux into a war against the Plains tribes. Despite concerns about frigid weather, weakened ponies, and the effect on caches of food and supplies, Sioux, Cheyenne, and Arapaho warriors struck in the dead of winter. On January 7 and again on February 2, 1865, Julesburg, Colorado, and the adjacent military post, Fort Rankin, were attacked. Casualties were inflicted on both occasions and on the second raid the town was sacked and burned.

Colonel William O. Collins pursued the raiders and in early February fought substantial battles at Mud Springs and Rush Creek, Nebraska. Though casualties were sizable, Collins was unable to prevent the Indians from moving farther north and west into traditional ground in Dakota and Montana.

Curtis was gone by the time Collins fought his twin battles at Mud Springs and Rush Creek. On January 30, 1865, as part of a major reorganization, he moved to St. Paul, Minnesota, to assume command of the Department of the Northwest.

Although Curtis served only a short time as commander of the Department of Kansas, his brief tenure revealed an aggressive commander with a

235

willingness to innovate. In the summer of 1864, Curtis persuaded the Army hierarchy to engage the services of 70 Pawnee Indians as scouts and guides. Later, he suggested that Frank North form a company to be called the Pawnee Scouts. Soon mustered in, the Pawnee Scouts – implacable foes of the Sioux and Cheyennes – became legendary in the service to the frontier army.

In October, realizing that the present shortage of troops and the lateness of the season would prevent him from mounting a winter campaign, Curtis ordered that the prairie be set on fire. Attempting to achieve the same effect as winter conditions when shortage of forage weakened the pony herds and reduced the mobility of the hostile tribes, fires were set simultaneously (and later rekindled) from ten miles east of Fort Kearny to 20 miles west of Julesburg. The overall effect of Curtis's radical move is uncertain. There were indeed fewer attacks, but the tribes' preparations for the coming winter months may have also contributed to the declining numbers. Whatever the reason, the lull was momentary, interrupted by the widespread violence precipitated by the events at Sand Creek.

When Curtis took command of the Department of the Northwest, he found that actions of Generals Alfred Sully and Henry Sibley during the preceding two years had pushed the Indian threat farther to the west. In 1862, hundreds of citizens had been massacred when the area's Sioux suddenly struck settlements and farms from Acton and New Ulm to the Dakota border. Haunted by fears of a renewed uprising, the citizens of western Minnesota remained wary.

Believing correctly that the warring bands had been forced westward and were presently gathering near the Black Hills, General Sully, with Curtis's acquiescence, began preparing a campaign to that region. Sully's Black Hills expedition never came to pass. When both Curtis and his superior, John Pope, acceded to political pressure generated by Minnesota authorities, much to his displeasure Sully's efforts were instead vectored toward Devil's Lake. That region was much closer to Minnesota and in the past raiders had been known to strike from that location. Sully's rerouted expedition to Devil's Lake began on July 3. It accomplished very little. Few Indians were encountered and most of them were peaceful. In the meantime, Curtis struggled with problems in manning frontier posts at a time when volunteer units were being mustered out of service following the end of the Civil War.

In August, Curtis was named to a special commission to negotiate with the tribes. It would be his last substantive duty on the Plains. On October 6, along with other government commissioners, Curtis met with representatives from several bands at Fort Sully, near present-day Pierre, South Dakota. Beginning on October 10 several treaties were signed with Brule, Two Kettle, Sans Arcs, Blackfeet, Hunkpapa, Lower Yanktonnais, and Miniconjou elders. Provisions called for a cessation of hostilities and for the Indians' withdrawal from regions near the overland route. In return, the tribesmen were to receive $30 a year for each family. An extensive distribution of food, clothing, and presents followed the signings. Wagon loads of goods delivered hardtack, sugar, coffee, hams, coats, hats, blankets, powder, and bullets to the assembled bands.

In late 1865, Curtis left the Army and returned to Iowa. His work in Congress years before had helped prepare the way for a Pacific railway. Back in Iowa, he resumed his involvement with the railroad, serving as a government consultant as the tracks moved west. He was inspecting Union Pacific rails when he died near Council Bluffs on December 26, 1866.

Curtis was buried in Oakland Cemetery in Keokuk.

Grenville M. Dodge

G renville Dodge's military service comprised only a small niche in a long and productive life. Far better known as the driving force behind the transcontinental railway and specifically as the chief engineer of the Union Pacific, Dodge's time as an Indian fighter spanned a year and a half at the close and immediate aftermath of the Civil War. Though compressed, Dodge's tenure as commander of forces came at a time when fighting across the Plains grew significantly in scope and intensity.

An aggressive, offensive-minded commander, Dodge's intentions for a major campaign against the Indians' heartland were initially delayed and ultimately scaled back due to shortages of supplies, logistical delays, and the unexpectedly rapid demobilization of forces at the end of the war.

Dodge was born in Danvers, Massachusetts, in 1831. Educated at Norwich University as a civil engineer, he held a variety of railway surveying positions before settling in Council Bluffs, Iowa, in 1854. A second business, as a freight shipping agent, brought him familiarity with the Great Plains and transportation routes across the region. A third, as a banker, made him wealthy.

Dodge began the Civil War as a brigade commander of Iowa infantry and artillery units that he had helped raise. He quickly became known for his energy and aggressive scouting. In March 1862, at the Battle of Pea Ridge in central Arkansas, Dodge contributed significantly to the Union victory. Severely wounded, he was promoted to brigadier general of volunteers and returned to duty as commander of the District of Corinth and commander of the 2nd Division, XVI Corps in Grant's Army of the Tennessee.

In those dual positions, Dodge supported Grant's advance toward Vicksburg in several unique ways. He quickly earned a reputation for being able to repair railroad tracks almost as fast as Nathan Bedford Forest and other Confederate marauders could tear them up. He formed a select group of scouts and raiders that provided legendary service to Grant and later to Sherman on his March to the Sea.

One of the most intriguing, if little known, aspects of Dodge's military service concerned the highly effective network of intelligence agents –

perhaps 100 or more – that he put in place across parts of the Confederacy. Dodge's spies provided valuable information to General Sherman during the latter stages of the war. After aiding Grant's success at Vicksburg, Dodge was rewarded with command of the XVI Corps in Sherman's army. Calm, poised, with a genial demeanor, Dodge's colleagues would later recall him as being one of the few officers who could speak freely and forcefully to the volatile Sherman. Dodge was promoted to major general of volunteers in July 1864 and was wounded again during the Atlanta campaign in August. After recuperating, on December 9 Dodge was assigned as commander of the District of Missouri, the primary Indian fighting organization on the Plains.

Library of Congress
Grenville M. Dodge

Increasingly dissatisfied with conditions and personalities in the trans-Missouri region, General Henry W. Halleck, Chief of Staff of the Union Army, undertook a massive reorganization. Effective January 31, 1865, along with associated changes in leaders and territory, the Districts of Kansas and Missouri were merged. Dodge was named commander, presiding over a region that spanned a substantial portion of the central and western United States.

Thirty-four years old at the time of his appointment, Dodge was smart, forceful, and efficient, with a reputation as an exceptional organizer and manager. Photographs taken at the time reveal a handsome face with finely chiseled features, dark hair and short, carefully trimmed whiskers.

Dodge's primary adversaries on the Plains would be the Sioux, Cheyennes, and Arapahos. The nomadic warriors were skilled horsemen and hunters from cultures that celebrated warfare as a central feature of their existence. They made formidable adversaries. Dodge estimated the number of fighters at the time at about 25,000. Most recent scholarship places the likely combined strength closer to 11,000-15,000.

Within days of his arrival, Dodge met with General John Pope, new commander of the Division of the Missouri and Northwest. Together, they formulated plans for a major expedition into Indian territory. The campaign's design reflected the aggressive nature of both officers. Strong believers in offensive action, their blueprint called for cutting troops loose from guarding fixed posts and sending them against Indian strongholds across the region. Forces moving from several directions would converge on the Natives' historic sanctuaries, such as the one along the Powder River. The tribes were to be pursued, fought, and punished wherever they were found.

First though, Dodge had to deal with a more immediate problem. Deadly raids in January and February had again halted traffic along the overland trail. Dodge responded by ordering that wagon trains moving west from Fort Riley and Fort Kearny include the presence of at least 100 armed men. All government trains and most coaches would receive military escorts. The same system was applied to trains eastbound from Denver. Mail stations were to be sited within the protective distance of nearly military posts. By the end of March, Dodge was able to report that the trails were open and the mail was being delivered.

Although Pope and Dodge were eager to commence with their expedition, projected start dates were repeatedly moved back by a series of frustrating delays. Supply issues and inefficient support from quartermaster and government contractors plagued preparations. As was so often the case, the lack of horses posed acute problems. In some of Dodge's units not a single horse was serviceable for an extended campaign.

In preparing their grand scheme, Pope and Dodge had anticipated that additional forces in considerable numbers would become available when the Civil War ended. In reality, the Army's massive demobilization proceeded far more rapidly than expected. General Order 77, dated April 28, 1865, stopped all enlistments and Army purchases and established a process for an immediate reduction in the size of the military.

The troops Dodge had expected to be available to guard 2,600 miles of trails and telegraph lines while concurrently conducting major operations in the field were never to be forthcoming. Although two regiments of "Galvanized Yankees," former Confederate prisoners of war freed from captivity after consenting to fight on the Plains, helped ease the shortfall, the total manpower never approximated that initially anticipated by Pope and Dodge.

As campaign plans progressed, two further reorganizations influenced operations in the region. On March 28, Dodge established the District of the Plains with headquarters in Denver. The new organization combined the districts of Colorado, Nebraska, Utah, and Wyoming. On June 27, another massive restructuring took place. The old Military Division of the Missouri was abolished. Established in its place was a new Military Division of the Mississippi commanded by General William Tecumseh Sherman. John Pope was placed in command of the revised District of Missouri, covering Wisconsin, Minnesota, Iowa, Missouri, and Kansas, as well as the territories of Nebraska, Dakota, and Montana. Later, the territories of Colorado, Utah, and New Mexico were added to the department. Except for units under

General Alfred Sully operating mostly in northern Dakota and eastern Montana, Dodge was given operational command of other forces in the field.

Finally, in July, 2,500 troops in three strike forces led by General Patrick Connor began to take the field. Connor retained personal command of the column that left Fort Laramie on July 30, moving on a direct route into the Powder River region. On August 17, Connor's Pawnee Scouts killed a party of 24 Cheyennes. Eleven days later, Connor's main body of troops attacked and destroyed an Arapaho village along the Tongue River.

Meanwhile, two other columns were moving toward Connor. Led by colonels Samuel Walker and Nelson Cole, the units had joined together on the Little Missouri. Walker's contingent had left Fort Laramie on August 6, moving almost straight north. Cole's column had the most arduous task, leaving Omaha on July 1 and marching through the Nebraska sand hills and the Black Hills before connecting with Walker's troops. There, the plan was for the twin columns to move on to the Powder River area and, with Connor's troops, trap the hostiles inside the converging pincers. Neither Cole nor Walker reached the rendezvous with Connor. Plagued by stiff resistance, bitter weather, poor guides, and rugged terrain, after numerous tribulations both columns returned to their bases.

Their failure to link up with Connor would soon become a moot point. In yet another example of the bureaucratic infighting that would for years characterize government policy toward the Native tribes, Connor's expedition was called to a halt. A clash between the Interior Department, whose officials generally endorsed attempts at negotiated outcomes, and War Department representatives who mostly favored military action, had festered for months. Eventually, peace advocates gained the upper hand. Outraged by Chivington's actions at Sand Creek, concerned by the cost of operating military forces in remote areas, and tired after four years of Civil War, popular sentiment supported talks and troop cutbacks. On August 22, orders were published terminating the campaign (although the orders did not reach Connor in the field until after the attack on the Arapaho village). The District of the Plains was subsequently abolished and Connor was transferred to Salt Lake City.

Thus, the Indian War of 1865 fizzled to a close. The peace talks would ultimately prove to be unsuccessful. The Red Cloud War erupted the following year and would rage across the northern Plains until another attempt at a peaceful settlement – the Treaty of Fort Laramie – brought a pause in the fighting in 1868.

Dodge opposed the negotiations, believing that further military action held promise of an outcome more favorable to the government. Convinced that Washington did not appreciate the magnitude of the problem, he criticized the government's divided approach in assigning neither the Interior Department nor the War Department primacy in handling Indian affairs.

Often working at cross purposes, their shifting initiatives would frustrate military commanders for years to come.

Dodge's direct participation in military operations during this period was limited. On one occasion, while moving between posts in western Wyoming, he and his outriders were attacked by a sizable war party. Dodge's race to safety took him through a pass which he would later employ as part of the route for the transcontinental railway.

In May 1866, Dodge resigned from the Army to take the position as chief engineer of the Union Pacific Railroad. Dodge brought precision and extraordinary administrative talent to a project sufficiently vast that some have equated it to the digging of the Panama Canal and the lunar landing. His presence quickly made an impact. As the rails progressed steadily westward, travel on the system of overland trails came to an end. By the summer of 1867, the last stage coach jolted through the Platte Valley.

In 1866, Dodge was elected U.S. Representative from Iowa's Fifth District, splitting his time over the next two years between railroad work and congressional duties. He served only a single term before returning full-time to the Union Pacific.

On May 10, 1869, Dodge was one of the officials who drove the golden spike at Promontory Point, Utah. With the completion of the transcontinental line, Dodge resigned as the railroad's chief engineer. Although some of his contemporaries in the Union Pacific were implicated in the Credit Mobilier scandal, Dodge was not accused of being complicit. He later took positions with several rail systems in the West, Southwest, and Mexico, and served as on-scene consultant during construction of the Trans-Siberian Railway.

At the completion of the Spanish-American War, Dodge was appointed by President William McKinley to chair the commission that reviewed the performance of the U.S. military during the conflict. He later supervised construction of railroads in Cuba.

After moving to New York City for a time to oversee several business ventures, Dodge returned to Iowa where he devoted his later years to lobbying for railroads and veterans affairs. He died January 3, 1916. He is buried at Walnut Hill Cemetery in Council Bluffs.

John O. Gibbon

Counting his time as a West Point cadet, John Gibbon's military career spanned almost a half century. To the disappointment of many members of his North Carolina family, Gibbon chose to fight with the Union during the Civil War. Cool under fire – "steel cold" by one designation – he was a formidable combat commander who saw action in almost every major encounter in the eastern theater. Wounded both at Fredericksburg and Gettysburg, he was brevetted five times for promotion. As the war drew to a close Gibbon led the XXIV Corps of the Union's Army of the James in operations against Petersburg and in the pursuit of Lee's Army of Northern Virginia. At Appomattox, he was one of the three officers selected by General Ulysses S. Grant to arrange the details of the Confederate surrender.

Gibbon's substantive duties in the West began on December 1, 1866, when he took command of Fort Kearny, Nebraska. Except for a brief period spent on recruiting duty, from that time until the end of his career 25 years later he commanded posts and military departments throughout the West and Southwest.

John Gibbon was born on April 20, 1827, near Holmesburg, Pennsylvania, a village since swallowed by the city of Philadelphia. When he was nearing 11 years old, the family moved to Charlotte, North Carolina, where by most accounts they eventually acquired a few slaves. Gibbon, though, on duty in Utah Territory when the Civil War began, remained steadfast in his loyalty to the Union cause. During the course of the war his relationship with most of the Gibbon family in North Carolina was irretrievably broken.

As described by one of his aides at Gettysburg, Gibbon was of medium height, compactly built. He had a ruddy complexion, chestnut brown hair, deep blue eyes, and a mustache reddish in color. Photographs show a distinguished face with sharp brows, aquiline nose, full chin, and a composed, determined mouth. Anecdotes from colleagues suggest a calm but firm manner.

After graduating 20th of 38 in the West Point class of 1847, Gibbon was assigned to the 3rd Artillery. Sent to Mexico City and Toluca in the closing days of the war with Mexico, he arrived too late to see action. A brief posting

John O. Gibbon

to Fort Monroe, Virginia, was followed by service in Florida as the Army struggled to subdue the Seminoles.

Gibbon's first service on the frontier occurred in Texas in 1850. With a battery of light artillery, Gibbon was sent first to Ringgold Barracks near Rio Grande City and subsequently to Fort Brown, south of Brownsville near the Rio Grande. After an extended period sitting as a member of several court-martial boards, Gibbon was reassigned to Florida to assist in the removal of a group of Seminoles.

In September 1854, Gibbon began a new assignment as artillery instructor at West Point. Two years later, he took on additional duties as post quartermaster as well. When his instructor tour ended in July 1857, Gibbon revised his class notes into an artillery textbook. Published in 1859, *The Artillest's Manual* was adopted by the War Department and widely used for many years. Although his instructor duties were completed, Gibbon remained as post quartermaster until August 1859. In November of that year Gibbon, now a captain, was given command of Battery B, 4th Artillery and sent to Camp Floyd (later Fort Crittenden) at Fairfield, Utah, where the Army was maintaining a shaky relationship with the Mormon community.

In 1861, events following Fort Sumter took Gibbon and his soldiers on a 1,200-mile march to Fort Leavenworth, Kansas, and subsequently to St. Joseph, Missouri. There, the unit and its artillery pieces were loaded on trains and sent to Washington, D.C. Gibbon was immediately appointed chief of artillery for General Irwin McDowell. His obvious competence in organizing and training the raw units assigned to him eventually led, in May 1862, to promotion as brigadier general of volunteers and command of an infantry brigade. From that point forward, Gibbon's service reads like a chronology of the Civil War in the eastern theater. As a brigade commander, he fought at Brawner Farm, Second Bull Run, South Mountain, and Antietam. His unit's performance at South Mountain earned it the sobriquet "Iron Brigade."

In November 1862, Gibbon was promoted to division commander and led the unit during the fight at Fredericksburg. After convalescing from a wound sustained there, he returned to duty as commander of the 2nd Division of the II Corps led by General Winfield Scott Hancock. He led the division at Chancellorsville and Gettysburg. At Gettysburg, Gibbon assumed additional responsibilities when Hancock was ordered by General George Meade to assume command of both II and III Corps following the latter unit's near disaster on the second day of the battle.

On the final day, July 3, posted with Hancock in the center of the Union line strung along Cemetery Ridge, the II and III Corps bore the brunt of the fighting during the monumental assault that soon and forever after would be known as "Pickett's Charge." Posted near the famous copse of trees – the aiming point for Robert E. Lee's attack – and the "bloody angle" formed by an L shaped bend in the low stone wall that faced the advancing rebels, Gibbons' division was in the middle of the horrific struggle that followed. When in the face of heinous losses Confederate attacks carried over the wall and seemed for a brief time to place the outcome in balance, Gibbon rushed reinforcements to the scene to help beat back the threat. Severely wounded as he moved troops in the midst of the melee, Gibbon's injury, a bullet through the shoulder that broke his scapula, would disable him for the next four months.

Gibbon returned to administrative duty in mid-November, commanding a draft depot. When fully convalesced, his services were requested for field command. Gibbon rejoined his division and led it through battles at the Wilderness, Spotsylvania, North Anna, Topopotomy, Cold Harbor, and in the encounters around Petersburg.

Promoted to major general of volunteers in June 1864, Gibbon was appointed commander of the XXIV Corps in the Army of the James on January 15, 1865. He remained with that corps for the rest of the war, leading it to Appomattox in the final pursuit of Lee's army.

Gibbon reverted to his permanent rank of captain when the conflict ended. Soon after, following the Army's extensive reorganization of the artillery branch, he was advanced in grade to colonel on July 28, 1866. On December 1, Gibbon was ordered to take command at Fort Kearny, Nebraska. Except for one brief interlude, he would remain in the West until his retirement 25 years later.

Gibbon served at Fort Kearny until May 1867. Over the following years, assignments took him to Fort Sanders, near Laramie in what was then Dakota Territory, until December 1868; Camp Douglas, three miles east of Salt Lake City in Utah Territory, until 1870; and Fort Shaw, Montana, located on the Medicine River, 24 miles west of Great Falls, until 1872.

After duty as superintendent of the Army's recruiting service with headquarters in New York City during 1873, Gibbon returned to Fort Shaw where he remained for an extended six-year tour. Gibbon's career in the West is best known for two instances, both of which took place during the mid-1870s during his second tour at the fort.

The first, and most widely known, involved George Armstrong Custer and the Little Bighorn.

General Philip Sheridan's overall plan of operations for the summer of 1876 called for forces coming from three directions to meet in southeastern Montana where large numbers of hostiles were believed to be gathering. On June 17, General George Crook's column, the southern prong in Sheridan's scheme, was turned back after a fight at Rosebud Creek. Continuing the campaign were the Terry-Custer force with 1,200 men westbound from Fort Abraham Lincoln in Dakota Territory and a column of 440 soldiers led by Gibbon marching east from Fort Ellis, near present-day Bozeman, along the north bank of the Yellowstone River. Gibbon and Terry were to link up at a rendezvous point farther east along the Yellowstone.

On two occasions along the way, Gibbon's scouts brushed against the presence of Indians in sizable numbers. On the morning of May 16, Lt. John Bradley, scouting 35 miles down the Rosebud Creek, located an immense Lakota camp eight miles farther downstream. Bradley and his patrol raced to inform Gibbon who ordered his men to cross the Yellowstone and strike the encampment. The Yellowstone, an especially fast-flowing stream, hindered the passage of the small, improvised boats ferrying the cavalrymen. After an hour only ten horses had made it across. Four others had drowned in the attempt. With Lakota scouts now visible on high bluffs near the river, Gibbon called off the movement. Eleven days later, on May 27, Bradley reported that the village he had seen on the 16th had swelled significantly in size and had shifted farther to the west.

Gibbon chose not to attack. Why he did so is the subject of conjecture. He may have simply decided the numbers were too many for his modest-sized column to take on – a perhaps not unreasonable judgment given what happened not long after to Custer with a force half again as large. Thus, better in this analysis to wait until his forces were combined with Terry's before going after the hostiles. Communications between the columns being what they were – extremely difficult with Terry's and non-existent with Crook's – any battle he initialed would likely have to be fought alone, without prospect of assistance.

As with several aspects surrounding the Little Bighorn, it is unlikely that Gibbon's reasons will ever be fully known. Those sympathetic to his choice find it unlikely that an officer who had piled into the maelstrom of Pickett's Charge would decline a battle for any other than good reasons. In the same vein, others call attention to Gibbon's remarks to Custer – made on two occasions as Custer prepared to leave – to leave some of the Indians so his column could join in the battle. Those siding with Gibbon note that those comments hardly seem characteristic of a commander reluctant to fight.

Gibbon's report of the large village on the Rosebud reached Terry a week later. Gibbon, in the meantime, under previous orders from Terry, was moving east down the Yellowstone toward the Little Missouri. The day after Gibbon's courier reached Terry, Terry set out, riding south toward the Yellowstone to link up with Gibbon.

By the time the two columns met, Gibbon's command had been in the field for several weeks. As the campaign began, Terry had ordered Gibbon to move along the Yellowstone to the mouth of the Bighorn River, to prevent hostiles from scattering to the north. Given the comparatively small size of this contingent, Gibbon was to attack only if conditions were favorable.

Gibbon and his Montana column reached a point about 20 miles east of the Bighorn on April 20. There, they were advised by Terry to remain in place until the Dakota column, delayed by weather, could get away from Fort Abraham Lincoln. On May 21, five days after attempting to cross the Yellowstone in pursuit of hostiles, Gibbon shifted a bit downstream, establishing a new camp near the mouth of Rosebud Creek. Prompted by reports of a large number of hostiles moving towards him, Gibbon had marched to meet the potential threat but found no massed bands of Indians along the way. His unit was, however, harassed by small raiding parties bent mostly on stealing horses. A few days later Terry's note arrived directing him to move east from the Yellowstone toward the Little Missouri to meet the Dakota column. After couriers failed initially to connect, Terry, now about the steamer *Far West*, finally met Gibbon on June 9 about five miles downstream from Gibbon's camp. Learning from Gibbon of the large village sighted in late May, Terry ordered Gibbon back to his previous camp at the mouth of the Rosebud.

Although two weeks old, the latest information seemed to place the hostiles west of Terry's position, likely still on the Rosebud or somewhere along one of its neighboring rivers, the Bighorn or the Little Bighorn. To pinpoint their location before committing his full force, Terry sent Marcus Reno with six companies on an extended reconnaissance. Reno left on June 10. Deviating from Terry's instructions, and drawing his and Custer's wrath, Reno returned ten days later with more precise information regarding the hostiles' whereabouts.

Terry subsequently adjusted his plan, presenting it to Gibbon and Custer on board the *Far West* on June 21. Custer would move the following day, following the Rosebud to its source and then turning south past the point where Reno had picked up an immense trail. He was then to continue in that direction for a time to ensure that the Indians had not escaped in that direction before swinging west toward the valley of the Little Bighorn. Continuing on south would also allow Gibbon's slower moving infantry time to reach the Little Bighorn. Custer's larger, faster cavalry force would drive the Indians against Gibbon's column, which was expected to be in place at the mouth of the river on June 26.

Custer, however, chose to attack the massive encampment on June 25.

In the battle that followed, he and more than 200 of his men were killed. Four miles away in a separate engagement – Custer having split his forces – Marcus Reno and Frederick Benteen struggled to save the remainder of the regiment.

When Custer left on June 22, Gibbon and Terry moved west on the Yellowstone River aboard the *Far West*. After about 40 miles the river turned south and eventually brought them to the confluence of the Yellowstone and Bighorn where Gibbon's column was encamped. On June 23 the *Far West* transported Gibbon's men across the treacherous current to the east side of the river. Gibbon then marched his troops east and south for a day, crossing Tullock's Creek before moving back west and then farther south. Their route paralleled the Bighorn River, about a mile and half above the mouth of the Little Bighorn. They camped that night, June 25, unaware that about 20 miles away Custer's command had been wiped out earlier that day.

Although Terry and Gibbon hurried the column forward, the terrain, some of the most inhospitable either of them had ever experienced, slowed their progress. On the 26th, the column crossed from the Bighorn to the Little Bighorn, struggling along the west bank for several miles before camping as darkness fell. On the morning of June 27, farther south in the valley, an advance guard found the remains of the enormous, now abandoned village. Tepee poles and discarded utensils and gear littered the ground for more than three miles. Two standing lodges were ringed by dead ponies and filled with the corpses of slain warriors. Clothing from two or three cavalrymen was found. Farther ahead, Gibbon saw several people atop a tall bluff. After momentary uncertainty, they were identified as cavalrymen – Reno's and Benteen's soldiers who had fought off Sioux attacks for two days.

Custer's fate was initially uncertain. Soon, however, Lieutenant Bradley and his men, scouting along the hills that ran east of Reno's battlefield, discovered dozens of corpses strewn along the bluffs than ran down to the river. Bradley's initial count was 193; several more were discovered later. Custer had been found.

Burial parties from the 7th Cavalry's surviving companies assisted by Gibbon's men worked through the remainder of the 27th and much of the following day. Only three shovels could be found among the assembled force. Many of the sites were hollowed out with tin cups, knives, and spoons. Empty shell casings containing papers with the troopers' names were hammered into boards atop the graves.

Gibbon's men then assisted in transporting the wounded troopers from the Reno-Benteen battle to the *Far West*, using tepee poles from the abandoned village to construct litters. Material to bind the poles together was initially lacking. Gibbon's men subsequently dispatched several severely wounded horses and mules found disabled near the battlefield and used their skin to make rawhide thongs for litter ties.

Gibbon's men joined Terry in a consolidated force that included George Crook's men, newly arrived on scene from Fort Fetterman. The combined column was much too unwieldy to pursue the scattered and fast-moving Lakota and Cheyenne. Terry's units were in bad condition, and were withdrawn after a few days. Gibbon returned with his men to Fort Shaw.

The following year, still at Fort Shaw, his services were again called upon.

In early August 1877, Gibbon left the post with a force of 161 officers and men to take part in the campaign against the Nez Perce band making its way across the nation's northern frontier. Evading the pursuit of General O. O. Howard, who had trailed them all the way from their homeland in Oregon's Wallowa Valley, in late July the tribe crossed the present boundary of Idaho and Montana via the Lolo Pass. After a brief skirmish on July 28, the Nez Perce moved initially into the Bitterroot Valley and for a time traveled south, replenishing their supplies.

From the Bitterroot, the band crossed the mountains to Big Hole Basin in present-day Beaverhead County, Montana. Apparently convinced they had shed the pursuit of Howard and his cavalry, the Nez Perce took few precautions to defend their encampment, concerning themselves instead with cutting new poles for their tepees from the plentiful timber around the basin.

Howard, though, was not alone in the chase; he had drawn in other units, including Gibbon's, from posts throughout Montana Territory. As he followed the Nez Perce's trail through the Bitterroot Valley, Gibbon added 45 civilian volunteers to his column, bringing his total force to about 206 men.

During the daylight hours of August 8, scouts located the Nez Perce camp. Gibbon marched through the night, momentarily leaving behind his mountain howitzers and pack train. Gibbon's rapid pursuit brought his column to the vicinity of the camp by sunrise the following morning.

At dawn, Gibbon's men waded across the Big Hole River, waist deep and lined with willows where it flowed next to the village. The Indians were taken by surprise. Striking from the northwest, Gibbon's soldiers entered the sleeping village and opened fire at almost anything that moved in and out of the village's 89 tepees. Although the camp's 750-800 inhabitants fled immediately, the 200 warriors among them responded quickly and well. Early in the battle the officer leading Gibbon's left wing was killed while engaged in the fight at the north end of the village. When the men under his command did not continue their push, that portion of the camp was left unoccupied. The Nez Perce would later seek refuge there and use that sector to reassemble and counterattack.

A few minutes into what was already a heavy fight, Gibbon halted his men, not wishing to scatter his force in the face of stiff opposition. An attempt to burn the village met brought only marginal results. The cavalrymen were under steady fire and the Nez Perce used the interlude to further regroup. As the shooting grew in intensity, Gibbon's horse was hit and he was wounded in the leg. By this point, several soldiers had been killed and others wounded, victims of the Nez Perce's formidable marksmanship.

Gibbon realized his position was untenable. He pulled his forces back across the river, moving to a wooded area about 300 to 400 yards southwest of the village. There, out of sight of the camp, rifle pits were dug and rock and timber barricades were hastily thrown together.,

As Gibbon's men assembled their redoubt, the unit's mountain howitzer arrived on the field. The crew got off a few shots without noticeable effect before Nez Perce sharpshooters killed or wounded several members of the gun crew.

Although Gibbon was wary of an attack that might overrun his hastily built fortification, the battle settled into long distance sniping, with the soldiers shooting from inside their barricades and 50 to 60 Indians positioned in trees and rocks holding them at bay. Shielded by the warrior's fire, the village's women and children packed up, gathered the horse herd and moved 18 miles south where a fortified camp was built along Lake Creek. Later in the day, the Nez Perce attempted to burn the soldiers out of their fortification, but the wind shifted and extinguished the flames.

Throughout the following day, 20 or 30 Nez Perce riflemen kept the soldiers pinned inside their barricades. The warriors eventually withdrew that night, but Gibbon kept his force in place. The following morning, General Howard and his advance party arrived after a punishing 70-mile ride through the previous day and night. Howard then assumed responsibility for the pursuit, eventually clashing again with the Nez Perce nine days later at Camas Meadows. Finally, in early October the majority of the Nez Perce would surrender to the combined forces of Howard and Nelson Miles at Bear Paw Mountain.

Gibbon's battle at the Big Hole was bitterly fought and costly to both sides. Gibbon lost almost a third of his force – 23 soldiers and six civilians killed; 36 soldiers and four civilians wounded, two of whom later died – and was in no condition to continue chase.

The Nez Perce also suffered heavily. It is believed the tribe's total losses numbered 70 to 90 killed, of whom perhaps a third were warriors (sources vary between 12 and 33). Of all the clashes fought in the Nez Perce war, the battle with Gibbon was the most costly to the tribe.

On September 9, 1878, 353 Northern Cheyennes left their assigned reservation in Indian Territory and struggled hundreds of miles north, seeking to return to their homelands in Nebraska or move farther into southeastern Montana. Settler deaths, particularly in Kansas where 40 whites were killed, occurred along the way. Eventually, much of the strength of the United States Army – perhaps as many as 13,000 soldiers – assembled in a series of barriers to block the Cheyennes' route. A force commanded by Gibbon guarded the Yellowstone region.

In early October, having made it as far as Whitetail Creek, a secluded canyon north of the Platte River near present-day Ogallala, Nebraska, the Cheyennes split into two groups. One, a group of 149 led by Dull Knife, surrendered near Fort Robinson, Nebraska, on October 23. The second band under Little Wolf made it to Montana. In early 1879, the 114 survivors met one of Gibbon's officers, Lieutenant W.P. Clark, known to them as a friend. Clark promised and provided food and shelter and promised also that he would do everything possible to let them stay in the north country. That promise was also kept; Little Wolf's band was allowed to stay in the Fort Keogh area. The Cheyenne Outbreak was somewhat of an anomaly, however. Earlier in 1878, Gibbon, then serving as commander of the Department of Dakota, reported that the territory was remarkably quiet except for occasional small raids near the Black Hills.

After Fort Shaw, tours followed for Gibbon at Fort Snelling, Minnesota; Fort Laramie, Wyoming Territory; Fort Omaha, as commander of the Department of the Platte; Vancouver Barracks, as commander of the Department of Columbia; and San Francisco as commander of the Division of the Pacific.

Gibbon was promoted to brigadier general in the Regular Army on July 10, 1885. He retired at San Francisco on April 20, 1891.

Gibbon made his home in Baltimore, Maryland, following his retirement. He died there in the early morning of February 6, 1896. He is buried at Arlington National Cemetery.

John I. Gregg

On July 28, 1866, John Gregg was named first commander of the newly established 8th Cavalry regiment, with initial headquarters at Camp Whipple near present-day Prescott in Arizona Territory. Companies from the regiment saw service at military posts in Nevada, California, Arizona, Washington, New Mexico, Idaho, and Oregon. During its fabled history, units of the 8th were posted at some of the West's most famous installations, the Presidio of San Francisco, Fort Vancouver, and Fort Union, New Mexico, foremost amongst them.

Although Gregg and his cavalrymen fought dozens of skirmishes over the years – some of which Gregg led personally, others handled by subordinate commanders – his name is not intimately tied to a specific notable battle or campaign. Rather, he is remembered mostly for the scope of his stewardship. Much of the Southwest, Pacific Coast, and Pacific Northwest portions of the United States fell under his purview. With some exceptions, most of the actions fought by his horsemen were small unit, company-sized encounters waged in pursuit of Indian raiders.

John Irvin Gregg was born July 19, 1826, in Bellefonte, Centre County, Pennsylvania. Nicknamed "Long John" by his men for his towering 6 feet 4 inches in height, Gregg first saw service during the Mexican War. Appointed as an officer after having enlisted in the infantry as a private, he was promoted to captain prior to his discharge in 1848.

For the next 13 years Gregg worked in the iron industry in Pennsylvania, employed by a company owned by family members. Gregg volunteered for duty when the Civil War began and was initially commissioned as a captain in a Pennsylvania regiment. Soon after, he accepted a regular commission as a captain in the United States 6th Cavalry. By the end of 1862, he was a colonel. Gregg served in several different cavalry units and saw action in many of the Army of the Potomac's major fights including the Peninsula Campaign, Second Bull Run, Antietam, and Chancellorsville. He was a brigade commander at Brandy Station and Gettysburg. He compiled a notable record: he received Regular Army brevets to major for "gallant and meritorious service" at Kelly's Ford (March 1863); to lieutenant colonel after the battle of Sulphur Springs (October 1863); and to colonel after the second battle of Deep Bottom (October 1864). In August 1864 he received a brevet promotion to brigadier general in the volunteer army for his performance along Brock Turnpike during actions around Richmond and at the battle of Trevilian Station (August 1864). At the end of the war, Gregg became a brevet major general of volunteers and a brevet brigadier general in the Regular Army.

Gregg was wounded twice during the war, once in the second battle of Deep Bottom and again, slightly, at Sayler's Creek on April 7, 1865, a few days before the war ended. Captured by Confederate troops near Farmville, Virginia, the following day, he was

Courtesy House Divided Project, Dickinson College

John I. Gregg

held prisoner for two days and then released coincident with Lee's surrender at Appomattox.

Unlike many of his non-West Point contemporaries, Gregg chose to remain in the Army following the war. The assignment to Camp Whipple with the 8th Cavalry was his first substantive post-war duty. Over the coming months, Gregg led the newly formed units on expeditions into the Mojave Desert, chasing Native marauders who raided ranches and settlements in Arizona and New Mexico. The outcomes ranged from modest success to no contact, but the sequences of marches tired the raiders and kept them on the move. Gregg's impact, while consequential, did not equal the achievements of Crook and Miles, who followed him in command.

Gregg's duties were typical of those performed by commanders on the nation's frontier. He scouted; guarded wagon trains; attempted to keep trails open; chased, fought, and pacified hostile bands; and, to the extent possible tried to preserve law and order in regions where civil enforcement was minimal or lacking altogether.

Gregg kept his small units on the move. A sampling of reports from the time illustrates the nature of many of the encounters and the vast area in which they took place:

— Troop A (stationed at Camp Winfield Scott, Nevada), January 17, 1867: A 15-man squad engaged a band of Indians near Eden Valley, Nevada, killing two and destroying their rancheria and provisions. One enlisted man was wounded. February 11, 1867: the same unit found another war party near Independence Valley, Nevada, killing six raiders. April 29, 1868: While in pursuit of horse thieves, a three-man party was ambushed by a band of

Indians in a canyon east of Paradise Valley, Nevada. All of their horses were killed. The patrol leader was shot through the thigh and wrist, the other two members were severely wounded and died soon after.

— Troop B (headquartered in Camp Cadiz in San Bernadino County, California), April 16/17, 1867: In conjunction with Troop I, 8th Cavalry (stationed at Bernicia Barracks, California), the company engaged a band of Apaches in the Black Mountains of Arizona. One soldier and several Indians were killed. May 18, 1868: Troop B and a detachment of Troop L from Bernicia Barracks, engaged a band of Hualapais Indians on the Rio Solinas, in Arizona, killing six and destroying their provisions and Rancheria. August 23, 1868: While scouting in the vicinity of the Santa Maria River, in Arizona, the troop encountered a band of Indians, killing two and capturing one. September 9, 1868: A detachment of 17 men engaged a group of Hualapais Indians, killing two warriors and capturing four women. The following day the squad surprised a party of ten Indians, killing four braves and taking three women captive. On September 11, the same group was again in action against a band of Hualapais, killing five and destroying camp lodging and equipment. On the 13th, near the mouth of the Dragoon Fork or the Verde River, a ten-man patrol surprised a band of Tonto Apaches, killing two and capturing weapons and provisions. One soldier was wounded. November 9, 1868: A combined unit formed of detachments from Troop B and Troop L attacked a large band of Apaches, killing 11 warriors and destroying a large quantity of stores.

— Troop C (stationed at Fort Vancouver, Washington), April 5, 1868: Near the middle fork of the Malheur River in Oregon, a 48-man troop charged an Indian camp, killing 12 warriors, capturing three head of cattle and a horse and destroying 5,000 pounds of dried beef. June 11, 1868: Troop C in conjunction with Troop F (stationed at Camp Logan, Oregon), brought in 138 Indians who had surrendered to the cavalrymen. June 3, 1869: Scouting in the vicinity of Camp McDowell, Arizona, the troop (two officers and 57 men) surprised and destroyed an Indian Rancheria, killing several Indians, capturing horses and mules, and destroying stocks of bows and arrows. July 6, 1869: A 17-man detachment at Hacqualla, Arizona, was attacked by a large body of Indians. An intense fight followed before the attackers were driven away after having lost seven killed and two wounded. One soldier was killed.

From Washington to New Mexico, the same types of stories in almost countless number could be told of Troops A though M of the 8th Cavalry. Gregg kept his units actively employed across a vast landscape. It was a busy time.

In December 1867, Gregg began the process of moving his headquarters from Camp Whipple to Churchill Barracks, Nevada. In May 1868, a further move took the unit to Camp Halleck, Nevada. That move, too, was only temporary. Finally, on May 5, 1870, the 8th was permanently sited at Fort Union, New Mexico. During his two years as commander at Fort Union, Gregg had his forces – often deployed in company- or detachment-sized formations – in almost continuous duty in the field.

Before leaving Fort Union in late 1872, Gregg led a reconnaissance into the Texas Panhandle to survey and map a mostly uncharted region around the *Llano Estacado,* the Staked Plains. Gregg's exploration followed the Palo Duro Canyon eastward as far as the junction of Tierra Blanca and Palo Duro Creeks.

Gregg retired from the Army on April 2, 1879, and devoted much of the remainder of his life to veterans' affairs. He died in Washington, D.C., on January 6, 1892, and was buried at Arlington National Cemetery.

Ironically, when the 8th Cavalry regiment – the frontier unit John Gregg's name is most associated with – was formed, his cousin, David McMurtrie Gregg, also had expectations to command the new unit. Like John Gregg, David M. Gregg had been a Union cavalry commander during the Civil War. (It was David Gregg who was George Armstrong Custer's commander during the famous cavalry battle with Jeb Stuart at Gettysburg.) David Gregg had resigned from the Army prior to the end of the war, but when news of the formation of a new cavalry regiment reached him, he sought reinstatement. The assignment went instead to his cousin John.

Prior to the Civil War, David Gregg also had experience as a military commander in the American West. His time there as a young officer is most recalled for an extended march from California to Fort Vancouver, Washington Territory, and for a three-day encounter which pitted his 160-man cavalry company against several hundred Indian attackers. Gregg managed a successful fighting retreat with few casualties.

Benjamin H. Grierson

There are aspects of Ben Grierson's life that seem almost too noble, too far ahead of their time, to be true. Grierson organized the famed 10th U.S. Cavalry – the "Buffalo Soldiers" – and chose to remain with that unit of African-American soldiers despite near-ostracism by many of his fellow offers and repeated opportunities elsewhere that promised further and faster advancement. His support for a peace policy on the Kiowa-Comanche Reservation dampened tensions while outraging white residents on the Texas frontier. Though a relentless fighter, he dealt sympathetically and effectively with problems at the Jicarilla and Navajo agencies.

Indeed, portions of Grierson's story read like a work of fiction. Kicked and severely injured by a horse as a young boy, he grew up deathly afraid of horses – and became one of the Union's most outstanding cavalry commanders. A music teacher by profession, he had no previous acquaintance with military matters – and became renowned for his daring and inventiveness on the battlefield.

His post-war exploits in the American West and Southwest also left significant legacies. Grierson excelled at the unglamorous tasks that were necessary to the pacification and settlement of the West: protecting travelers, mapping and exploring, building roads, erecting telegraph lines, and handling relationships with restless tribes.

Grierson drew occasional criticism from contemporaries for a somewhat casual indifference toward discipline, an approach that sometimes created friction within the unit and difficulties off post. Nonetheless, on the trail and in the midst of battle there were few better. Grierson had an uncanny knack for anticipating the next moves of even the wiliest of his Native adversaries.

Born July 8, 1826, in Pittsburgh but raised and schooled in Youngstown, Ohio, Grierson was the unlikeliest military leader and cavalryman. At age eight he was nearly killed when kicked in the head by a horse. He regained his health but for much of his life retained an abiding fear of horses. Somewhat of a musical prodigy, at age 13 he was chosen as leader of Youngstown's band. At age 27, he was a music teacher and band leader in Jacksonville, Illinois. For a five-year period leading up to the Civil War, he complemented

256

his musical work by co-partnering in a mostly unsuccessful, and eventually bankrupt, mercantile business in Meredosia, Illinois. When the Civil War began, Grierson enlisted as a volunteer aide-de-camp. As his military talents became more evident, in October 1861, he was promoted to major and later to colonel and placed in command of the 6th Illinois Cavalry. After leading a number of small but successful raids and skirmishes, in November General William T. Sherman appointed him chief of cavalry for the 5th Division, Army of the Tennessee.

Library of Congress
Benjamin H. Grierson

Grierson's enduring niche in American military history took place in the spring of 1863 as Ulysses S. Grant was advancing on Vicksburg. Intended primarily as a diversion to pull Confederate attention and resources away from Grant's move up the east bank of the Mississippi, Grierson's Raid turned into an epic adventure. Leaving LaGrange, Tennessee, on April 17, Grierson took with him 1,700 men of the 6th and 7th Illinois and 2nd Iowa Cavalry regiments. For the next 17 days, Grierson's troops moved several hundred miles through parts of Tennessee, across the entire state of Mississippi north to south, and deep into Louisiana before uniting with Union forces at Baton Rouge. Along the way they repeatedly outfought, surprised, fooled, and slipped away from converging rebel forces – all the while taking prisoners and horses, destroying enormous quantities of war material, and ruining two railroads. A century later, Hollywood immortalized the event in Director John Ford's *The Horse Soldiers*, starring John Wayne.

In June Grierson was promoted to brigadier general of volunteers. A year later he commanded one of Sherman's cavalry divisions during the Meridian Campaign. He was subordinate to Samuel D. Sturgis when Nathan Bedford Forest defeated the latter at Brice's Crossroad. Subsequently, Grierson was made cavalry commander of the District of West Tennessee, and bested Forrest at Tupelo.

In late December 1864 and in early January 1865, Grierson led another memorable expedition, a two-brigade raid deep into Confederate territory. On Christmas Day he surprised and captured Forrest's camp at Verona, Mississippi. Three days later he attacked a train carrying 1,200 rebel troops at a station near Aberdeen. Grierson captured 500 prisoners and freed 253 Union soldiers who were being transported to prison camps. The exploit earned him another promotion – to brevet major general.

In one of the closing acts of the Civil War, Grierson led General Edward R. S. Canby's cavalry arm during the capture of Mobile, Alabama. Although not a West Point graduate and having had no acquaintance with the military prior to the war, to the surprise of many, Grierson chose to remain in the Army when the conflict ended. As were almost all officers, Grierson was reduced in rank after the war, but only to colonel. That is perhaps at least partly indicative of the value the Army saw in him and the institution's regard for his wartime accomplishments.

With the exception of a two-year stint (1873-1874) as Superintendent of the Mounted Recruiting Service in St. Louis, the remaining 24 years of Grierson's military career after the war were served in the West and Southwest. During the two decades prior to his retirement he commanded forts (Fort Leavenworth, and Fort Riley, Kansas, 1866-1867; Fort Gibson in present day Oklahoma, 1867-1869; Fort Sill, Oklahoma, 1869-1872; Fort Concho, Texas,1875-1878; Whipple Barracks and Fort Grant, Arizona, 1885-1886); districts (Indian Territory 1868-1869; Pecos 1878-1880; New Mexico, 1886-1888), and departments (Texas, 1883, and Arizona, 1888-1890).

One of Grierson's enduring legacies to the Army was his founding of the 10th Cavalry – the "Buffalo Soldiers." Grierson was one of the few officers who initially understood and supported the full implications of emancipation. He maintained an affiliation with the unit for much of his long career.

Through it all, he displayed complete faith in the capabilities and dedication of his African-American soldiers. On one occasion, he barely escaped court-martial when he protested a post commander's refusal to billet Grierson's black troops on the same installation with white soldiers. Grierson's immediate, forceful intervention upheld the honor of the unit and served notice that he expected equal treatment for his soldiers. Regarded as somewhat of a pariah by many of his contemporaries, Grierson turned down opportunities to transfer and accelerate his own advancement.

In May 1868, Department of Missouri commander General Philip Sheridan – preparing for a winter campaign to enforce the provisions of the Medicine Lodge Treaty – sent Grierson south from Fort Riley to Fort Gibson on the Arkansas River. Grierson scouted west and south of Fort Gibson, and wrote an exceptional report detailing road prospects, conditions at military posts, and an assessment of relationships with Native tribes in the region. Grierson selected the site for Fort Sill and supervised its construction while serving as post commander. General Sheridan thought the installation's stone buildings made it one of the best posts on the frontier.

Grierson's respect for Native cultures also placed him at odds with a large segment of the officer corps. Though occasionally embroiled in the typical disputes regarding the bounds of military and civilian jurisdiction over the tribes and reservations, Grierson was fully committed to the peace effort put forth by the Grant Administration. His support for a benign resolution of problems associated with the Kiowa-Comanche Reservation drew the ire of local residents.

Grierson worked extensively with Lawric Tatum, an Indian agent who arrived in mid-1869. Despite their efforts, their hopes for peace were less than successful. Kiowas in particular persisted in raids into Texas, fueled by a centuries-old warrior culture and disgruntlement with often late- arriving annuities promised by the government.

Grierson and Tatum attempted to quell the disturbances by demanding that captives and livestock taken by the Kiowas be returned. They withheld rations and annuities for the Indians off the reservation and attempted to stop traders from trafficking in weapons and ammunition. Their initiatives, though intensely pursued, had little impact. Authorities eventually adopted a harder line, allowing the military free rein to enter Indian Territory in pursuit of raiders and to recover property and captives.

In May 1871, Grierson may have saved General Sherman's life. Several Indians suspected of leading a raid on a wagon train in north Texas had been brought to Fort Sill for interrogation. When Sherman and Grierson met with the Kiowas, one of the chiefs leveled a carbine at Sherman. Grierson grabbed the barrel of the weapon and wrestled it from the Indian's hands.

In March 1872, Grierson was assigned to remove unauthorized settlers from the portion of the Missouri, Kansas, and Texas Railroad line that ran through the eastern portion of Indian Territory. Grierson moved his unit from Fort Gibson and succeeded without fanfare in extracting the trespassers. In September, he arranged a truce between rival factions of the Creek nation.

When Grierson returned in 1874 for his tour of recruiting duty, he found the companies of the 10th Cavalry scattered across West Texas. He quickly busied himself in rebuilding dilapidated installations. Fort Concho, in particular, received a complete makeover.

Continuing through much of 1877, a steady undertow of violence persisted along the Southwest frontier. Depredations increasing in severity and scope were perpetrated by both sides. Some Mescalero raids were launched in retaliation for horse stealing forays on reservations by white brigands – incidents that affirmed the Apaches' convictions that the government was unable or unwilling to protect the agencies.

During the same time, Victorio, one of the Mescalero's most vicious fighters, disavowed his earlier agreement to settle on a reservation and resumed his raids in West Texas and northern Mexico. In January 1878, Grierson's superior, General O. O. Ord, established a new organization, the Department of the Pecos, and placed Grierson in command. Grierson's area of responsibility encompassed the region from Fort Concho west to El Paso and from the Texas-New Mexico border south to the Rio Grande.

Ord's intention was to deny renegades access to the vital waterholes scattered across the arid landscape of West Texas. Grierson embraced the role with a passion, keeping patrols in constant motion through the region, mapping the area for the first time, opening roads, guarding mail routes and building telegraph lines. Grierson charged his company commanders with keeping journals that recorded distances and noted the region's topographical features and natural resources.

While Victorio remained on the loose, Grierson along with General Edward Hatch responded with a ceaseless campaign against the marauders that by early 1878 had succeeded in driving most of them back to the reservation. With Victorio forced across the Rio Grande, for a brief period extending into 1879, West Texas was relatively free from attack. Late that year, however, Victorio crossed the Rio Grande and again menaced the Big Bend area.

Grierson was at Eagle Springs in extreme West Texas when news of Victorio's attacks reached him. Grierson believed that the Apaches would eventually head for a watering hole at an isolated location known as Fresno Springs. With nearly a thousand men, Grierson laid a carefully planned ambush at the remote site. As Victorio's band approached unaware, a civilian wagon train blundered unknowingly into the ambush zone. Grierson had to quickly intervene, losing the element of surprise, to prevent members of the emigrant party from being slaughtered by Victorio and his 150 or so warriors. Seeing Grierson's cavalry rushing towards them, Victorio broke off the attack and fled back across the Rio Grande.

Wearying of continued raids and believing that at least a portion of the attacks were launched by reservation Indians, on March 24, 1880, Generals Pope and Ord, commanding respectively the departments of Missouri and Texas, ordered that the Mescaleros on the reservation near Fort Stanton in south central New Mexico Territory, be disarmed and their horses taken from them. Grierson and General Hatch were assigned to carry out the mission. Grierson, with 280 men of the 10th Cavalry and 25th Infantry, and Hatch with 400 soldiers from 9th Cavalry along with 60 infantrymen and 75 Indian scouts, converged on the reservation. An episode quickly followed that evidenced the difficulty in communications across the immense region as well as problems with the split chain of responsibility. As Grierson and Hatch were moving into the area, unknown to them a peaceful group of Mescaleros had been allowed by the Indian agent to temporarily leave the reservation – a request routinely approved – to hunt near Rio Tularosa, an area commonly used by the tribe.

Grierson and his cavalry were also prepared to employ standard practice. Raids were so common and disruptive at the time that any Indian found off the agency was presumed to be hostile. When scouts sighted a large band of well-armed Apaches, Grierson prepared to attack the following morning. Disaster was only narrowly averted when a messenger sent by the agent reached Grierson advising him that the Mescaleros had permission to hunt at Rio Tularosa. Grierson then met with the Indians and escorted them back to the reservation.

Under the overall command of General Hatch, the process of disarming the Mescaleros began on April 16. Judging the initial Indian response to be docile and non-threatening, Hatch released a number of troops, fanning them out to the west, leaving Grierson on the reservation with about 385 soldiers.

Before Hatch left with the bulk of the command, he and Grierson had devised a warning signal: three shots were to be fired in sequence if trouble developed and additional troops were needed. As the disarming process continued, the Mescaleros became sullen and belligerent. Already upset by an episode earlier in the day when Indians sent to retrieve cattle that had wandered away were attacked by a cavalry unit whose commander mistakenly believed the Indians were stealing them, the Mescaleros grew increasingly restless.

Sensing the growing disquiet and observing warriors creeping away from the assembly area, Grierson ordered the three warning shots to be fired. With tensions stretched to the breaking point, the shots fractured what little restraint remained. Chaos ensured. Mescaleros scattered in all directions. Racing to the scene, Hatch's troops added further to the disarray. In the confusion that followed, 10 Apaches were killed and 250 were captured. Sizable numbers escaped. Many eventually joined Victorio's raiders.

Effectively reinforced, Victorio resumed large-scale raids on each side of the border. Texas, in particular, was the scene of a concentrated series of attacks. With raids continuing north and south of the Rio Grande, an agreement was reached between U.S. General Ord, commander of the Department of Texas, and Mexican General Trevino, commander of troops in northern Chihuahau. Trevino advised Ord that 600 Mexican troops were available to go after Victorio's band and that additional numbers were on the way. On the American side, Grierson poured every soldier available from posts in Texas and New Mexico into the fray. Victorio was about to be hounded relentlessly.

On July 31, Grierson, with 20 men, was on an advance scout near the Rio Grande when he learned that Victorio was camped not far away. Grierson fortified his position and sent for help from nearby Fort Quitman. Victorio, meanwhile, had found Grierson's small redoubt. He moved against it with his band of 200 warriors, determined to envelop and destroy Grierson and his men. Unaware that help was on its way to the cavalrymen, Victorio apparently assumed that he could surround and kill the troopers at his leisure.

Grierson sent a small team of sharpshooters to delay Victorios's movements and waited for help to arrive.

Expert sniping by his riflemen brought Grierson an hour of time. As it turned out, that was just enough. Hurrying from Fort Quitman under a baking West Texas sun, a cavalry troop led by Captain Charles D. Viele reached Grierson's fortification. The fight immediately intensified. Victorio persisted in his attack, severely pressing Grierson and his newly-arrived cavalry.

As the fighting became heavier and more widespread, another cavalry company, this one led by Captain Malcolm Nolan, arrived at the scene from Fort Quitman. Now outnumbered and in danger of being surrounded, Victorio retreated. The bitter, four-hour fight had left seven Apaches killed. Numerous other casualties were carried away from the battlefield. The sizable losses were a difficult setback for Victorio's raiders. Grierson lost one cavalry lieutenant wounded and an enlisted man killed.

Victorio fled again to Mexico. Four days later he was back across the Rio Grande. Grierson again took up the pursuit. After Victorio initially eluded his main column near Bass's Canyon, Grierson anticipated that the Apaches would head toward Rattlesnake Springs where water and shelter were available. Grierson took his 10th Cavalry on an epic forced march – 65 miles in a single day in searing heat across some of the nation's most arid and inhospitable landscape – beating Victorio to the Rattlesnake Springs refuge.

Victorio and his band arrived at the springs at 2 o'clock the next morning, and found two cavalry companies under Captain Viele waiting in ambush. An initial heavy volley brought Grierson and the rest of his command, positioned nearby, racing into the fight. Their swift attack startled the Indians, causing heavy losses and sending Victorio into swift retreat.

Reeling from the setback, Victorio fell back toward Bowen's Springs in the Guadalupe Mountains. Again, though, Grierson anticipated his move. A cavalry troop led by Captain William B. Kennedy met him there, killing two warriors with the loss of one trooper.

Rebuffed again, Victorio moved in the direction of the Sacramento Mountains, where they were met by yet another of Grierson's swarming patrols, this one led by Captain Thomas Lebo. As Grierson continued to push more troops into the region, on August 18, Victorio retreated into Mexico, giving up his attempt to remain north of the border.

Grierson, meanwhile, was tracking a band of young warriors who had split off from Victorio. One of his 10th Cavalry companies pursued the renegades and brought them to battle at Ojo Caliente, Texas. The clash prevented the band from moving farther into the state, but more importantly, delayed them from rejoining Victorio, who was waiting for them at Tres Castillos, in northern Chihuahua.

Pursued initially by a combined U.S.-Mexican force augmented by friendly Apache scouts, Victorio had taken his warriors to that location, a long-favored refuge for the Mescaleros. The site, a large basin accessible only though a box canyon, offered shelter, water, grass, and game.

Unknown to the Apaches, a large column of Mexican soldiers, irregulars patterned after the Texas Rangers, and Tarahumari Indian scouts, led by Colonel Joaquin Terrazas, had stealthily positioned themselves near the canyon entrance. As Victorio's band attempted to leave their campground, Terrazas attacked and pinned them inside the walls of the narrow canyon. The fighting lasted the entire day, tapering off only when darkness fell before resuming again at dawn the following day. About an hour after sunrise, sensing that the Indians were nearly out of ammunition, Mexican soldiers charged into the canyon, killing Victorio and his remaining warriors in a final fusillade.

The campaign against Victorio was significant. Notoriously cruel, he was a deadly and implacable foe. Initially angered, it is thought, by his relocation to the San Carlos Reservation, his attacks had likely killed 200 New Mexicans, 100 soldiers, a large but uncertain number of Texans, and at least 200 citizens of Mexico. Although raids of varying severity continued for a time on both sides of the border, the Apaches were deprived of one of their most capable and charismatic leaders.

Eventually, in large measure due to Grierson's efforts, peace came to West Texas. Along with it, aided by the mapping of thousands of square miles of territory, secure travel, mail and telegraph service, came increased settlement and two transcontinental rail lines.

In 1882, the more benign conditions along the frontier allowed the Army to close forts and consolidate units at fewer locations. The 10th Cavalry was posted to Fort Concho and Fort Davis, Grierson's headquarters in West Texas. Grierson enjoyed his time there and would have preferred to remain, but in April 1885, the 10th was ordered to duty in Arizona. The move was likely prompted at least in part by internal dissension within the unit, an environment attributable in some measure to Grierson's loose style of command. Never a hands-on disciplinarian, at Fort Davis Grierson's attention was further diverted by his day-to-day ranching activities.

In Arizona, the department commander, General George Crook, again scattered the regiment's companies across several posts in the southern part of the territory. Grierson established his headquarters at Whipple Barracks near Prescott.

In April 1886, a change in departmental leadership brought Nelson Miles to Arizona to replace Crook, who had requested a transfer after a disagreement with General Sheridan, the division commander. Miles and Grierson would work well together. In June, Miles sent Grierson to adjudicate a quarrel between settlers and Hualapai Indians along the Colorado River. Grierson handled the clash calmly and fairly, impressing Miles who increasingly relied on him for diplomatic missions. In July, Miles transferred Grierson and his headquarters to Fort Grant and in November gave him command of the District of New Mexico.

In New Mexico, Grierson became the champion of the Jicarilla tribe, successfully supporting their cause in contentious issues involving reservation locations, the movement of the tribe, and antagonisms with local settlers and cattlemen. Grierson assisted the tribe on their move to a new location. He took personal responsibility for reimbursing a surveyor and directly supervised the removal of fraudulent settlers from reservation grounds.

Soon after, he defused a similar situation on the Navajo reservation which stretched across northeastern Arizona and northwestern New Mexico. In August 1887, settlers blocked the Navajo's access to water on the San Juan River. Grierson went to the scene and restored passage to the tribe. In the meantime, he investigated four violent confrontations that had occurred on the reservation between Navajos and whites.subsequently, Grierson's adept handling of difficulties on the Jicarilla and Navajo reservations earned him the gratitude of both tribes.

In November 1888, Grierson succeeded Miles as commander of the Department of Arizona. He was promoted to brigadier general in the Regular Army on April 5, 1890. He retired three months later, on July 8, while serving as departmental commander.

Grierson died August 31, 1911, in Omena, Michigan. He was interred at Jacksonville East Cemetery in Jacksonville, Illinois.

Winfield Scott Hancock

Winfield Scott Hancock was one of the Union Army's most renowned combat leaders. Highly successful as a division commander, he was promoted to corps commander not long before the titanic clash at Gettysburg.

If, as it is sometimes said, one or two special days during the course of a lifetime can determine a person's legacy, then surely Gettysburg was Hancock's defining moment. Leading a corps for the first time, his performance was so extraordinary that forever after it shaped history's assessment of his life. At Gettysburg on the second and third days of July 1863, Hancock saved the battle, and perhaps the war, for the Union.

His performance in the American West was less memorable. Although he was posted to positions on the frontier on no less than five occasions during the course of his career, his combined time in those duties was relatively brief. During an abbreviated tour as commander of the Department of the Missouri, he led one major expedition that is recalled mainly for its lack of consequence.

Hancock's various tours of duty on the frontier were marked by differences in circumstances, locations, and responsibilities. His first, immediately following graduation from West Point in June 1844, took him to the 6th Infantry, first at Fort Towson in Indian Territory on the Red River in present-day Choctaw County, Oklahoma, and later to Fort Washita. It was a relatively calm period in the soldiers' over-watch of the tribes of the southern Plains. Hancock used it to learn his trade, mastering the intricacies of moving, training, and supplying a military unit.

His second, following notable service in the war with Mexico, initially brought him back to St. Louis, again with the 6th Infantry. The stay was a brief one, however, and the unit was soon posted to Fort Crawford at Prairie du Chien, Wisconsin. By then regimental quartermaster, Hancock's adept handling of the move drew favorable notice from his superiors. On October 1, 1849, he was named regimental adjutant and aide-de-camp to the 6th Infantry commander, Newman S. Clarke.

Although Hancock did not particularly enjoy his assigned quartermaster duties, he quickly earned a reputation within the tiny army for his mastery of those tasks, a skill that was aided by a generous nature and, in Ulysses S. Grant's description, a "genial disposition." It was his prowess as a quartermaster that promoted his assignment to Florida in February 1856, where the Army was fighting a third and final war with the Seminole tribe. Under trying conditions, Hancock tended his duties with apparent ease and exceptional competence.

His tour at Fort Myers completed, at the personal request of General William S. Harney, Hancock was assigned to accompany Harney to Fort Leavenworth, his third time in the

Public Domain

Winfield S. Hancock

West. Hancock remained at Leavenworth for nine months as the Army tried with mixed success to cope with increasing violence in "Bleeding Kansas" and keep the region under control.

In late 1857, President James Buchanan sent General Albert Sidney Johnston with a force of 1,500 men to Utah to chastise Brigham Young for his failure to recognize a non-Mormon governor appointed by Buchanan. After Johnston's unit suffered from horrific winter weather, in mid-1858 Harney was sent west with reinforcements. Hancock accompanied him as quartermaster, responsible for a 128-wagon train, several ambulances, and 1,000 mules. When the difficulty with Young was quickly resolved, Hancock was sent to Fort Bridger in the southwest corner of present-day Wyoming. There, he rejoined the 6th Infantry, the entire regiment having been brought together for a march to the West Coast. As regimental quartermaster, Hancock organized the expedition, assembling provisions, equipment, and draft animals. By August 31, the regiment was on its way to California. Hancock's conduct of the extended trek across inhospitable terrain again drew compliments from his colleagues and praise from his superiors. When the regiment reached the coast, Hancock was diverted south to the pueblo of Los Angeles to assume duties there as chief quartermaster of the Southern District of California.

Hancock's fourth position in the West occurred after he had gained notoriety and two-star rank during the Civil War. His tour would not last long, but during the course of it Hancock led a major campaign against the Plains Indians for the first and only time.

In the summer of 1866, General William T. Sherman, commander of the Military Division of the Missouri, received approval from President Andrew

Johnson to assign Hancock as commander of the Military Department of the Missouri, a position subordinate to Sherman.

At the time, Hancock's department comprised Missouri, Kansas, and the territories of Colorado and New Mexico. For the most part, Hancock's tasks paralleled those of other departmental commanders in the Far West – protecting emigrants, manning posts, and keeping overland trails, mail routes, and telegraph lines open. One unique obligation, though, on-going at the time of his arrival, effected Hancock's organization: the Kansas Pacific Railroad was under construction and advancing westward.

Conditions in the department were relatively placid when Hancock took command. The outrage following the Sand Creek Massacre in November 1864 had largely, momentarily, settled into a sort of wary, unsettled truce. In mid-November 1866, peace commissioners sent by the U.S. government negotiated a shaky pact – the Treaty of the Little Arkansas – with tribal representatives.

As would be a recurring theme throughout the frontier era, two circumstances provoked the ire of military commanders responsible for dealing with the Native tribes. The first, and major, issue was that the Bureau of Indian Affairs, in the Department of the Interior – not the Army – was responsible for handling tribal affairs, administering to their needs, and setting policy. The second concern was an off-shoot of the first. In conducting its business with the tribes, the Bureau of Indian Affairs often licensed unscrupulous traders who trafficked in arms, ammunition, and liquor.

When Sherman began receiving reports of increasing restlessness among the tribes from commanders of western posts, and with railroad construction progressing steadily in that direction, he asked the newly appointed Hancock to join him at a conference in St. Louis. During a March 8, 1867 meeting, Sherman decided to respond to the threatening undertones with what amounted to a show of force – a preventative display of might that would hopefully awe the tribes before deeper trouble developed. Sherman directed Hancock to journey through the tribal grounds of the Cheyennes, Arapahos, and Kiowas. Hancock was to inform Indian leaders to cease their threats and marauding and to tell them also that if they wanted a war, the Army would surely provide them with one.

With Sherman's concurrence, Hancock assembled a force of 1,400 men composed of members of the 37th Infantry, the recently formed 7th Cavalry under the field command of Lieutenant Colonel George Armstrong Custer, an artillery battery, and equipment to assemble pontoon bridges. As a force to chase mobile, nomadic Plains Indians, it was a highly unwieldy column. That, however, was not the primary purpose: Sherman and Hancock held out hope that the display of strength and firepower would have the desired effect of intimidating the tribesmen.

Hancock launched the expedition of March 22 with a force concentrated at Fort Riley, near Junction City, the railhead of the Kansas Pacific. Hancock was one of the Army's most gifted commanders at conducting a march; indeed, over the next several weeks the trek itself went exceptionally well. Hancock's plan was to move from outpost to outpost across the region. In addition to meeting Indian leaders along the way, the itinerary would allow him to inspect installations and show the flag. At one of his first stops, at Fort Zarah, near a bend of the Arkansas River in the center of Kansas, he ordered major improvements to the installation and its defenses.

Trouble began to surface on April 12 at Fort Larned, six miles west of the present-day city of Larned, Kansas, when a planned meeting with tribal representatives fell apart due to weather, the tribe's diversion to conduct a buffalo hunt, and general confusion. Hancock, impatient with the delay, decided not to wait. The following day, he moved 21 miles to Pawnee Forks, a branch off the Arkansas River.

The chiefs, by now also disgruntled by Hancock's departure, set fires along the way to delay the advance. Eventually a tentative agreement was reached to meet again at a Native village along Pawnee Forks. Again, misinterpretation and confusion disrupted the proposed conference. As Hancock's force approached, the Indians sent their women and children away from the camp. Hancock, dealing with Plains tribes for the first time, apparently took their departure as a sign of distrust or disrespect, or preparation for battle, and ordered Custer's cavalry to prevent their escape and return them to the village.

Custer trailed the Indians to a newly established campsite, surrounded it, and found it empty. The women and children had fled farther north. Custer attempted to follow the trail the next morning, but the Indians had disguised their tracks masterfully and disappeared.

As he attempted to track the Natives, Custer found depredations along the trail. At one location, three men had been killed at a stage station. Custer initially reported that the deaths had come at the hands of the band of Indians he was chasing. Later, it was discovered that the men had been killed by a different group of marauders.

Nonetheless, when Hancock received the initial, erroneous, report he considered the killings as justification for destroying the abandoned village at Pawnee Forks. On April 17, as punishment for the attack on the stage station, Hancock's soldiers burned the camp's 250 lodges and all provisions in it, including 1,000 buffalo robes.

The destruction of the village prompted flare-ups around Kansas, particularly along the stage route, as Indian bands retaliated. In a skirmish near the Cimarron Crossing of the Arkansas, six Cheyenne braves fleeing from the Pawnee Forks village were discovered and attacked by a detachment of the 7th Cavalry. One soldier was wounded and two Cheyennes were killed during the fight. Those would be the campaign's only casualties on either side.

Later at Fort Dodge, Hancock met with Kiowa and Arapaho representatives. The session was one of the few quasi-substantive meetings that occurred during the expedition.

Hancock's campaign ended later in the summer. He had maneuvered his force hundreds of miles across a landscape encased in a sea of prairie grass, mostly flat with only a few undulating hills, rising imperceptibly toward the foothills of the Rockies. The results of the campaign were decidedly mixed. The expedition had afforded Hancock the opportunity to inspect the posts under his jurisdiction and the march itself had contributed to the training of his troops, many of whom were inexperienced. In terms of achieving one of its stated objectives, however – the intimidation of the Plains tribes – the campaign was an exercise in futility. Eruptions, mostly hit and run attacks on civilians, continued.

Soon after Hancock returned to his headquarters, he found another problem to deal with: George Armstrong Custer. After Hancock's Kansas expedition, Custer had been detailed to Fort McPherson, near present-day North Platte, Nebraska. At Fort McPherson, Custer met with William T. Sherman and was dispatched on an extended campaign that took him first to the forks of the Republican River in southeastern Nebraska where he fought an encounter with the Sioux, then west to Fort Sedgwick near Julesburg, Colorado, and finally back southeast to Fort Wallace, Kansas.

At Fort Wallace, for reasons that remain uncertain – perhaps on a whim as he was prone to do, or, as some speculated, reacting to rumors that an officer had been flirting with his wife Libby – Custer left without leave or authorization and raced across Kansas to Fort Riley to see his wife. Hancock ordered him court-martialed for that act as well as several others including abuse of his troops during their extended march. The court found Custer guilty on all eight counts and suspended him for a year. Custer responded by writing magazine articles critical of Hancock's handling of the Kansas expedition, asserting that the court-martial action was an attempt by Hancock to divert blame for the campaign's modest outcome.

In the meantime, Hancock suspended offensive operations in order to given yet another peace commission a chance to negotiate with the Plains tribes. The result, the Medicine Lodge Treaty, signed on October 27, 1867, brought another short-lived respite to the region. Hancock, though, was not there to see the result. On August 26, President Johnson ordered him to New Orleans to take on Reconstruction duty, a service that by most accounts he performed admirably over the next year and a half.

On March 4, 1869, Ulysses S. Grant took office as President of the

United States. Grant regarded Hancock as a political rival and apparently believed that he was handling the defeated Southerners with too light a touch. Hancock found himself reassigned to the Plains, this time as commander of the Department of Dakota with headquarters in St. Paul, Minnesota. It would be Hancock's fifth, and final, assignment in the West. Hancock's purview extended 1,200 miles from east to west, taking in all of Minnesota, Dakota Territory, and Montana Territory. West of the Minnesota-Dakota border the vast expanse remained mostly untamed, traversed by buffalo herds of immense size and cut by broad rivers that defined the landscape. Inside the departmental boundaries lived Sioux, Northern Cheyenne, Crows, Mandan, Chippewa, Ponca, Assiniboine, Flathead, Blackfeet, Gros Ventres, and Arikara tribesmen – altogether, more than a quarter of all the Natives in the continental United States. To administer to them and keep the peace, he had 1,682 soldiers scattered in tiny, mostly one- and two-company outposts, across the region.

Immediately after taking command, Hancock set out to inspect his enormous department. Over the next several weeks, traveling by boat, horseback, and stage, he traveled 6,800 miles inspecting all 15 posts, visiting troops, and meeting with tribal leaders. Having learned from his Kansas experience, thoroughly prepared for each session, he listened to the chiefs, heard their tales of starvation and disease, and did what he could to address their hardships.

Though routine duties – repair and construction of facilities, guarding trails, and providing general security – occupied much of his time, Hancock was also confronted with several challenges unique to the department. Fort Buford, an isolated post 22 miles southwest of present-day Williston, North Dakota, was under almost constant threat. Survey crews from the Northern Pacific Railroad, cutting across Sioux territory, demanded protection, as did Indian agencies in the relatively more settled regions along the Missouri River and inhabitants of far-flung mining settlements in remote areas of Montana. Lastly, white incursions into the Black Hills region – given by treaty to the Sioux after the Red Cloud War of 1868 – posed a persisting problem.

Hancock began by bolstering, as much as he could, Fort Buford, sustaining it as bulwark against tribesmen still elated after burning Forts C. F. Smith and Phil Kearny, abandoned by the Army after the Red Cloud War. He built an additional temporary camp to protect the Montana mining settlements. When violence in Fort Garry (now Winnipeg), Canada, threated to spill across the border and bring large numbers of hostile Sioux back into the United States, he constructed a new post as a defensive measure. The presence of Fort Pembina, two miles south of the U.S.-Canada border in the extreme northeast corner of North Dakota, induced the warring Sioux to remain in Canada. In

1870, he established temporary posts at six agencies to protect Indian Bureau employees and guard friendly Indians from attacks by hostiles.

In the winter that followed, Hancock and other regional commanders supplied forces in support of an expedition against the Blackfoot tribe. Planned by General Philip Sheridan, on January 6, an expedition led by Major Eugene S. Baker moved from Fort Ellis at the bend of the Gallatin River, to Fort Shaw on the Sun River near present-day Great Falls, reaching that location on January 14. After a brief rest and reinforcement, Baker continued north toward the Marins River. In the early morning hours of January 23, his soldiers found and attacked a large camp situated along the banks of the stream. Baker's assault took the village totally by surprise. One hundred seventy-three members of the tribe were killed – 53 of them women and children caught in the confused melee as fighting raged from lodge to lodge through the camp. One hundred more women and children were captured and subsequently released. After the fight, Baker returned to Fort Ellis, reaching there on February 6 after a march of 600 miles in the midst of bitter weather.

Almost alone among senior Army commanders, Hancock took steps to forcibly uphold provisions of the Treaty of Fort Laramie (1868) that assigned the Black Hills to the Sioux and prohibited white incursions into the territory. In the face of unremitting pressure from mining interests and groups of prospectors already assembled and ready to push into the area, Hancock held firm. Threatening to use force against parties moving to encroach on or occupy the region, Hancock stated that he would employ troops to "uphold the faith of the government." Hancock's actions dissuaded some prospective expeditions from making the attempt. There can be little doubt of Hancock's convictions regarding the treaty. On one occasion, 18 Army deserters trekked toward the hills intending to pan for gold there. Hancock's men ran them down and captured them all.

For the length of his tenure as commander of the Department of Dakota, Hancock kept the Black Hills inviolate. In 1874, two years after his departure, Custer, acting under the authority of General Sheridan, led an expedition into the hills. The following year an attempt by the government to buy the Black Hills from the Sioux failed. Conditions continued to deteriorate. Finally, outraged by events, the war chiefs of the Sioux nation began to assemble. By the spring of 1876, the last of the Great Sioux Wars had begun. By mid-summer, Custer was dead at the Little Bighorn.

Before leaving the Department of Dakota, Hancock proposed changes to the reservation system and, along with others, criticized the government's continued supply of weapons to the warlike tribes. He cautioned also that building a railway across traditional Sioux hunting grounds would surely provoke a response.

Hancock performed one final act of service prior to his departure. When the report of Lieutenant Gustavus C. Doane's expedition to the Yellowstone region reached him with descriptions of geysers, mud pots, and scenic canyons, Hancock forwarded the document to the Adjutant General of the Army, indorsing it for publication. In February 1871, Secretary of War William W. Belknap sent it to the United States Senate. The report influenced Congress's decision the following year to establish Yellowstone as the first of the nation's national parks.

In November 1872, General George G. Meade, the Army's ranking major general, died. As per long-standing custom, Hancock was assigned to New York City to command the Division of the Atlantic, the billet traditionally occupied by the Army's senior two-star general. He would remain in the post, with headquarters at Fort Columbus on Governors Island, for the rest of his life.

Hancock's time in the West had ended. His service to the country had not.

Hancock's military career had begun three decades earlier when he entered West Point as a scrawny, 5 feet 5 inches tall 16-year old. (He was born February 24, 1824, in Montgomeryville, Pennsylvania.) By the time he graduated with the class of 1844, he had sprouted into a tall, well-proportioned young man, slightly over 6 feet tall and weighing about 170 pounds. Described by a contemporary as "the handsomest man in the United States Army," Hancock had light brown hair, a firm jaw, and deep blue eyes. A moustache and small chin tuft set off otherwise clean cut features.

Hancock's fine appearance was further distinguished by an innate command "presence." He was cordial, gracious, and generous with acquaintances. On duty, he was at times more severe; meticulous and thorough, after years as a quartermaster and adjutant he did not countenance shoddy staff work. Hancock was known for taking pains to care for his men. Almost universally recalled for his warmth and friendliness, his soldiers liked him, contemporaries and subordinates trusted him, and superiors relied on him.

In later life, West Point roommate and lifelong friend, Henry Heth, (ironically later a Confederate general who fought at Gettysburg), commented on Hancock's good looks and told humorous bachelor tales of trailing along on evening soirees and taking the "left overs" from among the young belles who fawned after the dashing Hancock.

Hancock married Almira ("Allie") Russell, a vivacious, blond-haired beauty. In the tiny, pre-war military they became one of the Army's favorite couples. Allie accompanied Hancock even on his most Spartan assignments. Their daughter Ada was probably the first white child born at Fort Myers, Florida. Wherever they were posted, their quarters became a welcoming oasis for other couples and single officers.

When the Civil War began, Hancock, Allie, and their children left Los Angeles and returned to the East Coast. Hancock was given a command billet in the Army of the Potomac and rather quickly became known to the American public. After a battle in the Peninsula Campaign, General George McClellan – seldom known to compliment anyone other than himself— wrote that "Hancock was superb today." The sobriquet stuck: "Hancock the Superb" stayed with Hancock for the rest of his life.

As the war progressed, Hancock saw action in most of the major battles fought by the Army of the Potomac: Antietam, Fredericksburg, and Chancellorsville. It would be Gettysburg, though, that brought him lasting notoriety.

When initial contact was made by the armies converging on the small town not far across the Pennsylvania border from Hagerstown, Maryland, General George G. Meade, newly appointed commander of the Army of the Potomac, sent Hancock racing ahead to the battlefield. The Union's on-scene commander, General John Reynolds, had been killed early in the fighting. Although Hancock was not the senior Union officer on the field, Meade ordered him to take command and access the situation. In the chaos of the first day, with Union forces pushed back through town, Hancock and General O. O. Howard fought off attacks, hastily putting forces together on Cemetery Hill and building a defensive line. Hancock perhaps made the most momentous decision of the battle: he determined that the Union Army should stay and fight at Gettysburg. When Meade arrived at midnight, he concurred with Hancock's decision.

On the second day, July 2, Hancock and his II Corps were posted in the middle of Cemetery Ridge, the long shank of the Union's fish hook-shaped defensive line. When General Dan Sickles inexplicably pulled his III Corps off the ridge and advanced it into a wheat field some distance to the west, a portion of the Union front was left uncovered. In horrific fighting, rebel forces engulfed Sickles' command and began moving toward the area Sickles had vacated, threatening to split the Union line. Hancock saw the danger and sent a nearby unit racing toward the on-coming mass of Confederates, seeking to buy enough time to plug the gap with other forces. Hancock's actions essentially sacrificed the 1st Minnesota. The regiment lost more than 200 of its 289 men, but delayed the rebel advance long enough for Hancock to pull other units to the area and reestablish the defensive line.

On July 3, the final day of the battle, Hancock and his corps again held the middle of the Union line on Cemetery Ridge. Again, they were fated to be in the midst of the action. Robert E. Lee had aimed the spear of his vast, rolling attack at a copse of trees in the center of the Union line. Pickett's Charge would come straight at Win Hancock and his II Corps.

As Confederate shells tore at Union positions on Cemetery Ridge, Hancock rode calmly along the line. Seemingly impervious to danger as always during a battle or on the march, he wore a clean, well-pressed white shirt under his uniform jacket. When the shelling ceased, thousands of Confederate soldiers in a line a mile long stepped out of woods along Seminary Ridge and began moving the three-quarters of a mile toward the copse of trees.

Torn into by cannon fire and later by the massed rifles of the II Corps, the rebels paid a terrible price. Still they came. Perhaps 2,500-3,000 made it over a stone wall and into the Union forces and massed cannon behind it. One Union regiment retreated and another for a moment threatened to break. Rallied by Hancock's officers, and with additional forces streaming into the fight, the rebel attack faltered. Pushed back over the low wall, they began a slow retreat across the field that had brought them into the fight less than an hour before. They left behind 5.032 wounded. Another 1,123 were killed and several hundred more were captured. During the fight, Hancock, in the midst of the action as usual, was badly wounded when a Confederate shell struck the pommel of this saddle. Shell fragments, pieces of wood, and a bent nail from the saddle were driven into his inner thigh.

The wound troubled him periodically for the rest of his life. He recovered after a long recuperation but never fully regained his mobility or restless energy in combat. He performed well leading his corps during the Overland Campaign, the Battle of the Wilderness and Spotsylvania Court House, lost (for the only time) at Ream's Station during the siege of Petersburg and won again at Hatcher's Run. Eventually, plagued by recurring problems with the wound, Hancock asked to be removed from field command. He handled recruiting and administrative chores for the rest of the war. In the public's mind, though, he remained "Hancock the Superb."

Hancock maintained a lifelong interest in Democratic Party politics. Prestige from his wartime service and a reputation for candor and integrity propelled him to the party's 1880 presidential nomination. In a close election, Hancock and Republican opponent James A. Garfield both carried 19 states, but Garfield won the electoral college vote 214-155.

Hancock remained in his job as commander, Department of the Atlantic. He died in his quarters on Governors Island on February 9, 1886. He was buried at Montgomery Cemetery, Norristown, Pennsylvania.

Stephen W. Kearny

Stephen Watts Kearny is best known as a trail blazer and as the leader of an epic expedition during the Mexican War. His death, in 1848, occurred before major Native conflicts erupted across the American West. Nonetheless, his explorations, mapping endeavors, and councils with Plains tribes added much to the government's early knowledge of the region and its people. Kearny was a mentor to several officers – James W. Carleton, Edwin V. Sumner, Philip St. George Cooke, and others – whose names are linked inseparably with the history of western expansion. Known as the "Father of the United States Cavalry," Kearny's employment of mounted troops to escort wagon trains established the precedent that continued until the closing of the frontier.

Kearny was born in Newark, New Jersey, on August 30, 1794. He attended Kings College (Columbia University) for a time before withdrawing to take a commission with the 13th Infantry when war was declared against Great Britain on June 18, 1812. In April 1813, he distinguished himself at the battle of Queenston, fought slightly north of the Canadian border along the Niagara River. Wounded during the encounter, he was captured and later released in a prisoner exchange. Kearny transferred to the 2nd Infantry in 1815 and chose to remain in the Army after the war ended.

Following three years of recruiting duty, in 1819, Kearny first experienced the American West as a member of the Yellowstone Expedition. In command of an infantry battalion, Kearny and his men helped construct Fort Atkinson, an impressive log fortification on the banks of the Missouri River, nine miles north of present-day Omaha, Nebraska. For a time in the 1820s, the fort was America's largest military post and the only military installation west of the Missouri.

Twelve months later, Kearny accompanied an overland expedition to Fort Snelling in present-day Minnesota, helping blaze a route to the post on the Upper Mississippi. In 1825 – now a major assigned to the 1st Infantry – he was part of an expedition led by General Henry Atkinson charged by President James Monroe to stabilize the region and open it to commerce – most especially the fur trade. Traveling by keel boat, the 476-man company journeyed far north up the Missouri River and a hundred miles farther west past the mouth of the Yellowstone, making contact with Ponca, Sioux, Mandan, Cheyenne, Arikara, Hidatsa and Crow tribesmen along the way.

Public Domain
Stephen W. Kearny

Kearny kept extensive journals noting in considerable detail routes, terrain features, and interactions with Native tribes. After reaching their farthest point west on August 17, the column returned to Fort Atkinson, reaching the post on September 19 without the loss of a single man or boat.

In 1826, the government opened Jefferson Barracks, a short distance south of St. Louis. Kearny helped with the construction and was named the first commander of the new installation, the Army's principal western depot.

Kearny's tenure at Jefferson Barracks bracketed a busy, eventful time. Called away temporarily from post construction, Kearny took his unit, part of an 800-man contingent led by General Atkinson, on a campaign against the Winnebago tribe that at the time was causing friction in northeastern Minnesota. Moving his force up the Mississippi and the Wisconsin River, Atkinson coerced the tribe into a settlement.

On September 10, 1828, Kearny's battalion moved for a time to Fort Crawford, an old, dilapidated installation near Prairie du Chien at the confluence of the Mississippi and Wisconsin Rivers. Kearny relocated the post, rebuilding it on higher, healthier ground before returning to Jefferson Barracks in June 1829.

During the spring and summer of 1831, Kearny and the 3rd Infantry moved south rebuilding Fort Towson on the Red River in the southeastern portion of present-day Oklahoma. Sent there to police the eastern tribes relocated to the area by government policy, Kearny remained at the post until reassigned to Fort Leavenworth where an organization entirely new to the U.S. Army was about to be formed.

In March 1833, after the repeated urgings of several military leaders, Congress at long last approved the formation of the 1st Regiment of United States Dragoons. The new unit consisted of 1,832 officers and men in ten companies. Kearny, promoted to lieutenant colonel and now second in command to Colonel Henry Dodge, ran the unit's day to day operations. Kearny faced initial frustrations in organizing and equipping the unit and complained about the qualifications of some of the officers assigned to it. Training techniques and tactical doctrine were non-existent. Kearny struggled to create them from scratch. Nonetheless, sooner than he would have preferred, on November 20, 1833, five companies were ordered west.

Sent to Fort Gibson in Indian Territory, the transfer of the mounted unit responded to public pressure to deal with the tribes – primarily Commanches, Pawnees, and Kiowas – that were causing disruptions in the area. On May 31, 1834, Kearny joined the force with the remaining five companies, now more fully equipped, trained, and supplied.

In mid-June, nine companies of 500 dragoons under the shared overall command of Henry Leavenworth and Henry Dodge moved across the Arkansas River into the heartland of the southern Plains tribes. The expedition impressed the Native leaders and led to a major meeting with representatives from nearly all of the region's tribes later in the year.

While the Leavenworth-Dodge endeavor was generally successful in its diplomatic efforts, the actual orchestration of the campaign was almost catastrophic. Operating at times in 115 degree heat, 88 dragoons died and a dozen others, including Kearny, fell ill. One hundred cavalry mounts perished. Leavenworth died during the course of a buffalo hunt. The enormous losses in men and material led to questions regarding Dodge's competence and eventually, during the summer of 1835, he resigned his position. Kearny, now a colonel, took command of the 1st Dragoons.

When the expedition returned, the War Department divided the unit, sending portions to Forts Gibson, Leavenworth, and Des Moines. In early September, Kearny took 113 troopers north on a three-week march to Fort Des Moines in Iowa Territory. Kearny completed construction of a post there while shielding nearby settlers from Sac and Fox tribesmen. In June of the following summer he took 150 men, draught animals and wagons farther northeast on a long trek to Minnesota where he parleyed with Sioux and Sac tribal leaders. In late August, the column returned to Fort Des Moines after a 1,100-mile journey during which not a man or an animal was lost – a sterling compliment to Kearny's field craft.

Shortly after assuming command of the 1st Dragoons, Kearny established three new posts along a line momentarily conceived as a loose separation between Native territory and Anglo settlements. In late 1836, under Kearny's supervision, a team of officers led by Captain Edwin V. Sumner drafted a comprehensive manual for dragoon operations. Two years later, he orchestrated Sumner's appointment as commandant of a new cavalry school at Carlisle Barracks, Pennsylvania. The six-week course of instruction, the first of its kind in the U.S. military, operated with exceptional success before eventually being terminated due in large measure to competing demands for manpower during the Seminole War.

Beginning in the mid-1830s, over the next decade Kearny's dragoons in

277

packets ranging in size from squads to battalions touched almost every corner of the frontier as it then existed east of the Rockies. In successive years, the 1st's troopers journeyed to Green Bay, Wisconsin, and Council Bluffs, Iowa; went south to the Canadian River in Texas; moved west along the Platte River, and trekked north through both Dakotas to the Canadian border.

Concurrent with his 1st Dragoon duties, Kearny was also given command of what was then called the Army's Third Military Department, a vast region that encompassed much of the Plains and Far West. Tasked with protecting the frontier and keeping the peace among the tribes, Kearny took over at a time when the flow of settlers along the Oregon Trail was beginning to surge. With travel continuing to increase in the early 1840s, Kearny ordered his troops to begin escorting wagon trains, a practice that the Army ingrained as a near-standard procedure. The mounted escorts complemented the generally more benign relationship between the tribes and the government that existed at the time and successfully preserved the peace – albeit at times an uneasy one – over much of the next two decades.

In 1845, Kearny led a 250-man, 99-day expedition with five dragoon companies along the overland trail from Fort Leavenworth into Wyoming. Near Fort Laramie he held a major council with Sioux chiefs, urging them to refrain from attacking emigrant wagon trains. Taking a southern route, he returned to Fort Leavenworth via Bent's Fort (near present-day La Junta, Colorado) and the Arkansas River, Kearny met with Cheyenne and Arapaho tribesmen during the course of the journey.

During this time Kearny became the military's "troubleshooter," He believed westward expansion brought inevitable friction with the Native tribes. His experience had taught him that violence was often preventable if military presence was timely and negotiations were properly handled. Each summer, he sent dragoon battalions into the heartlands of the Plains tribes, seeking with general success to impress the tribes with government power, dissuade them from violence, and induce them to negotiate grievances. On several occasions, Kearny was personally called upon to mediate differences between settlers and tribes and between tribal factions.

To help protect the overland trail and those who traveled along it, in 1846, Kearny established a new post near present-day Nebraska City, Nebraska. Over time, however, the most heavily traveled portion of the route shifted north and west. Two years later, the post – which became the legendary Fort Kearny – was moved to a location along the Platte River astride the trail in central Nebraska.

The year 1846 brought war with Mexico. The conflict would make Kearny a nationally-known figure. With a force of about 2,500 men labeled the Army of the West, Kearny, now a brigadier general, led an epic campaign that gained control of New Mexico and helped in the final pacification of California.

Organized in May and June of 1846, the Army of the West consisted of about 1,600 soldiers in two volunteer infantry regiments, a mounted cavalry regiment, artillery and infantry battalions, 300 cavalrymen of the 1st Dragoons, and, eventually, 500 members of the Mormon Battalion.

Advancing from Bent's Fort, Kearny's troopers arrived in Las Vegas, New Mexico, on August 15, meeting no serious opposition along the way. Aided by the preparatory work of Philip St. George Cooke and James W. Magoffin, a local merchant, sent ahead with an advance cadre, Mexican military units withdrew from the area, ceding control of the territory to Kearny's troops.

On August 18, Kearny and his column took possession of Santa Fe, the territorial capital. Kearny quickly established civil and military authorities to govern the region. After assigning about 800 men to occupy the territory and dispatching the same number to join other forces fighting in Mexico, he moved on toward California with his remaining force. On September 25, Kearny left Santa Fe with about 300 dragoons, mounted mostly on ill-trained mules, his cavalry horses having played out on the hundreds miles of trail on the way to New Mexico. Philip St. George Cooke was directed to follow with the Mormon Battalion and construct a wagon road to the Pacific. Cooke's journey would in itself form a legendary chapter in the story of the overall campaign.

Leaving Santa Fe, Kearny followed the Rio Grande on a difficult journey through arid, desolate terrain. Several days into the journey near Socorro, he met scout Kit Carson with a small party carrying dispatches east from California. Carson siad California was already in U.S. hands, seized by a force of Marines and sailors under the command of Commodore Robert F. Stockton, of the Navy's Pacific Squadron, assisted by a California battalion led by John C. Fremont.

Believing California was secure, Kearny sent 200 of his dragoons back to Santa Fe. Taking Carson with him as a guide, he continued on west with a depleted force of 100 men. As he pushed on towards San Diego, he learned from an intercepted Mexican courier of an on-going uprising – a "counter-revolution" – with fighting in and near Los Angeles. Stockton had been forced to retreat to San Diego. Soon after, Kearny's column was joined by Marine Major Archibald H. Gillespie accompanied by about 30 men, part of Stockton's force operating in the area.

On December 6, in the midst of fog and rain, Kearny's ragged unit encountered a large force of Mexican lancers. Kearny attacked but wet powder and the lack of trained mounts soon placed him on the defensive. Kearny's small force of dragoons, Gillespie's Marines, and a few local militia were forced into retreat. Driven to a nearby hilltop, surrounded, they fought of several attacks. Meanwhile, couriers led by Kit Carson slipped through enemy lines and hurried to San Diego where Commodore Stockton dispatched a company of Marines and sailors to lift the four-day siege of Kearny's embattled troops. The relief force quickly drove off the attackers, but not before Kearny's unit had suffered heavily. Sources vary as to the number of Americans killed, but some place the figure as high as 22. Kearny himself was slightly injured, one of 13 others wounded in action. Altogether, almost a third of the entire force became casualties in what became known as the Battle of San Pasqual.

American commanders rallied quickly. In late December, a combined force consisting of Kearny's dragoons, Stockton's Marines and sailors, and two companies of Fremont's California battalion won battles at San Gabriel and La Mesa. On January 10, 1847, Los Angeles was recaptured. Soon after, the Treaty of Cahuenga, signed near San Fernando, ended the fighting in California.

The close of the fighting brought on an extended, bitter dispute between Stockton and Kearny, each claiming authority to administer the territory. Fremont's role was also contentious. He was eventually court-martialed and given a dishonorable discharge, a sentence quickly commuted by President Polk. Fremont resigned his commission, was later elected senator from California and, in 1856, was the Republican Party's first candidate for president.

In March and April 650 additional soldiers arrived and took over garrison duties from Stockton's Marines and sailors. Kearny was named commander-in-chief of land forces and civil governor, For a short time he served as military governor before appointing other territorial officials. His administrative duties attended to, Kearny returned east accompanied by Fremont, who upon arrival at Fort Leavenworth was placed in custody and subsequently court-martialed in Washington, D.C.

Sent to Mexico in the spring of 1848, Kearny served briefly in administrative duties during the closing days of the conflict as governor of Vera Cruz. Later, after contracting a tropical disease described variously as malaria or yellow fever, he was sent to Mexico City for a time to serve as governor there. The increasing severity of his illness necessitated his return to St. Louis, where he died on October 31 at age 54. Kearny's death cut short a career that, given his already extensive experience in the region, would almost surely have witnessed his deep involvement in the later history of the West.

Kearny is buried in Bellefontaine Cemetery in St. Louis.

Robert R. Livingston

T he military career of Robert Ramsay Livingston may serve to represent the contributions and experiences of numerous other volunteer, non-regular officers, whose service on the frontier encompassed only the duration of the Civil War. Called by circumstances to fight Indians in the midst of the conflict, Livingston proved a highly capable commander who led forces under daunting conditions.

Not all volunteer, short-term officers were successful as Indian fighters. Some, like Thomas Moonlight, failed miserably. Others, John Chivington for example, failed in ways that transcend the battlefield. Nor was failure the sole province of non-regulars, as the examples of Custer, Joseph Reynolds, and several others so vividly illustrate.

Livingston, though, exemplifies the best of the legions of volunteer, non-professional soldiers who filled the Union Army's ranks and fought its battles in the American West.

Given his background it seems a bit implausible that Robert Livingston would turn out to be an adept, successful military leader. An acclaimed physician by profession, he had no military training prior to enlisting as a private in the first volunteer company formed in Nebraska Territory.

Livingston was born in Montreal, Canada, in 1827. He attended medical school at McGill University in that city and later took additional training at the College of Physicians and Surgeons in New York City.

Livingston's wide-ranging intellect led him shortly after to an interest in copper mining in the Lake Superior region. For a time, he was superintendent of a mining exploration firm headquartered in Boston. When a financial panic struck the country in 1857, the consequences were disastrous for the nation's mining industry. Livingston left the company and resumed his medical practice in Plattsmouth, Nebraska. For a time he was also editor of the Plattsmouth newspaper.

Citizens in the Plattsmouth area formed a volunteer company after news of Fort Sumter reached the city (indeed, the unit was raised even before the official call for volunteers from the national government). Livingston enlisted as a private and was immediately elected as captain and commander of the unit that eventually became Company A of the 1st Nebraska Infantry. The company was mustered into service on June 19, 1861. By October 4, 1862, after actions at Fort Donelson, Shiloh, and Corinth, Livingston had advanced through a series of promotions to colonel and was given command of the regiment.

In October 1863, the 1st Nebraska was converted from infantry to cavalry. Livingston oversaw the extensive re-equipping and training made necessary by the changeover. The importance of the conversion became apparent with the announcement of the regiment's new mission: to destroy or drive out guerilla bands operating in northeastern Arkansas in the general area from Pilot Knob to DeVall's Bluff. In five months of sometimes sharp skirmishes extending through early 1864, Livingston reported 800 rebels killed or captured and several bands broken up.

Nebraska State Historical Society
Robert R. Livingston

By the summer of 1864, the regiment had been away from home for three years. Finally, in June, the unit was granted furlough. The bulk of the command arrived via steamer in Omaha on June 28.

When the troopers arrived home they fully anticipated being returned to their former duties in Arkansas when their furloughs were over. That was not to be the case. Nine days later, on August 7, a massive Sioux uprising exploded across the central Plains. Within 24 hours, every stage station and road ranche between Fort Kearny, Nebraska Territory, and Julesburg in present-day Colorado, were attacked. Hundreds of settlers were killed and many others, mostly women and children, were taken captive. The overland trail was shut down from the Big Sandy in Nebraska to Denver and miles of telegraph lines were destroyed.

With the Civil War raging and titanic battles being fought that would determine the survival of the country, the Federal government allocated few resources to the perceived frontier backwater. The forces in the region were ill-prepared to combat the enormous assault that rolled over the Great Plains. At Fort Kearny in central Nebraska, only a single company of cavalry was available to protect countless miles of trail and telegraph lines. Now, with travel cut on the road, mail disrupted, and telegraph service destroyed, the national authorities took notice of the threat. New units were sent to the area and the 1st Nebraska was hastily recalled from leave. Livingston designated Omaha as the rendezvous point for the unit to reassemble. By the 1st of September, most of the regiment was back in the field.

The department commander, General Samuel Curtis, believed that a major expedition against the Sioux, rather than protecting the overland road and telegraph lines via a string of small outposts, would have a decisive effect. Taking Livingston and several companies of the 1st Nebraska, a militia company, two companies of the 7th Iowa Cavalry, a detachment of the 16th Kansas Cavalry, and a squad of Pawnee Scouts, Curtis set out after the Sioux. By September 8, he had taken his column south across the Republican River and Prairie Dog Creek to a camp near the Solomon River in north central Kansas. They had not sighted a single Indian.

At that point, Curtis split his large force. After a circuitous trek, Livingston and his troops arrived back at Fort Kearny on September 26. Curtis's experience illustrated the difficulty of chasing fast-moving nomadic bands with large formations of less mobile troopers. Curtis's lack of success prompted a change in tactics. At least for the time being – until the Civil War ended and additional forces were available – the Army would adopt a generally defensive posture aimed at keeping the 600 miles of trail open.

On September 29, Curtis divided the District of Nebraska, placing Livingston in command of the east sub-district. Livingston's area of responsibility ran east to west from the Missouri River to Julesburg, Colorado. To keep the trail open over that distance, he had 971 men of the 1st Nebraska, 7th Iowa, a volunteer cavalry company and four small militia companies. Their duties were to protect stage coach and telegraph stations and escort trains of emigrants and freight wagons. His force was spread out over the entire distance, the smallest unit being 23 men at Mullally's Road Ranche, near present-day Cozad, Nebraska, and largest at Fort Kearny with 112 soldiers.

By October 5, Livingston had repositioned his forces, posting them every 15 miles along the trail from Plum Creek Station, near present-day Lexington, Nebraska, to Julesburg. Most of Livingston's mini forts were established at existing road ranches, many of which were already well fortified. (Road ranches were lodging and mercantile facilities sited along the trail. They provided meals, merchandise, and feed for livestock; sold wood, liquor, playing cards, cheese and garden vegetables. Some had blacksmith and horseshoeing capability. At others, spent horses, later rehabilitated, could be traded for fresh ones.)

From these locations, cavalry troops moved up and down the trail, patrolling, policing telegraph lines, and escorting wagon trains. Livingston ordered the commanders of these small posts to hold trains at their locations until sufficient numbers of armed men were accumulated to provide effective defense on the trail. Livingston set the threshold at no less than 50 to 60 armed members of emigrant freight trains. Though with considerable difficulty, the trail was kept open.

Livingston realized that his picket line of outposts provided only a partial answer to the threat along the trail. Like other commanders then and later – Mackenzie, Crook, Miles, among them – he believed the ultimate solution would be to attack the Indians while they were encamped in their winter quarters when the tribes were relatively sedentary and their ponies were weakened by lack of forage.

While others recognized the same opportunity, it was already too late to mount a winter campaign in 1864. Instead, on October 17, General Curtis ordered Livingston to set a massive prairie fire as soon as the grass was dry and prevailing wind conditions were favorable. The idea was to destroy the prairie grass the Sioux and Cheyenne depended upon to sustain their pony herds. On October 22, Livingston ordered post commanders to set fires simultaneously on a line from ten miles east of Fort Kearny to 20 miles west of Julesburg. When the initial fires died down, Livingston instructed commanders to rekindle them. The effectiveness of the program is difficult to gauge. The fires did not totally stop the attacks, but the scorched earth in combination with a severe winter did apparently reduce them in number.

Livingston's problems consisted of more than a shortage of manpower. From the beginning he lacked, in both numbers and quality, sufficient horses to properly equip his cavalry regiment. The 1st Nebraska, having left its mounts in Arkansas when it departed on furlough, now had to requisition, scrounge, and plead for replacement horses. The condition of many of the early-arriving mounts was extremely poor. For a time in order to conserve the strength of the horses, Livingston ordered his enlisted men not to ride their mounts except when engaged on official duty.

The lull in the action induced by the measures taken by Curtis and Livingston was short-lived. On November 29, Colonel John M. Chivington with a force of Colorado militia attacked a peaceful Cheyenne camp at Sand Creek, Colorado, killing large numbers of villagers, the majority of whom were women and children. Chivington's massacre re-ignited the war. Outraged tribesmen launched killing raids across the Plains, attacking Julesburg and its nearby military post on January 7, 1865, and returning on February 2 to sack and burn the town.

Learning about the attack on Julesburg, Livingston hurried up the overland trail with two companies of cavalry, gathering additional forces from the mini forts along the way. After receiving reports and viewing the destruction of the city, he warned his superiors that this war would be different – far larger and more severe than the usual hit and run episodes in the past.

The Indian bands that struck Julesburg were aware that Livingston was advancing towards them. After the second attack they moved away to the north, fighting forces led by Colonel William O. Collins at Mud Springs (February 4-6) and Rush Creek (February 8-9) along the way.

They left behind scenes of devastation. For a time, traffic along the trail was non-existent, stopped by the widespread attacks. With characteristic energy, Livingston set about repairing the telegraph lines that had been cut for scores of miles. He formed three large repair crews and worked them in shifts day and night. By February 12, he had restored service to Denver and by February 17 to Fort Laramie. He instructed military units escorting stage coaches and wagon trains to stop and repair any breaks they saw in telegraphs lines before moving on.

Responding to renewed orders that all government trains and overland mail coaches were to be provided with military escorts, Livingston reshuffled his forces. Posts were established so escorts of east- and west-bound stages would have to travel less than 20 miles, reducing the fatigue on horses and men. By March 1865, stages were again running regularly.

In the meantime, events outside the frontier were catching up with Livingston's military career. With the Civil War at last at an end, massive demobilization and reorganization programs were quickly launched. The 1st Nebraska found itself combined with another cavalry unit. At the same time, the end of the war had freed up large numbers of regular officers for duty elsewhere. Livingston was mustered out of service on July 1, 1865. In recognition of his contributions, he was brevetted to brigadier general the same day. The members of the 1st Nebraska protested his departure to no avail. (The full regiment was not released from service until July 1, 1866.)

Livingston returned to this medical practice in Plattsmouth. In 1869, President Grant appointed him Surveyor General of Iowa and Nebraska. Two years later he became medical director of the Burlington and Missouri Railroad, a position he held until his death.

Livingston was the first president of the Nebraska State Historical Society and served as president of the faculty, and professor of surgery, at Omaha Medical College. Always active in civic affairs, he rose to prominent positions in the Masonic Order.

Livingston died September 28, 1888. He is buried at Oak Hill Cemetery in Plattsmouth.

Robert B. Mitchell

R obert Mitchell commanded the District of Nebraska from February 24, 1864, until March 28, 1865. For a short time thereafter (until August 22, 1865), he led the Department of Kansas. Although Mitchell's tenure was relatively brief, it encompassed an especially difficult period in the settlement of the West. In the summer and fall of 1864, a massive Native uprising exploded across the central Plains. Months of raids, killings, kidnappings, thefts of livestock and other depredations followed, culminating with the burning of an entire town.

While he held an important command position during an extraordinary time, Mitchell's performance was somewhat uneven and generally unexceptional. His most enduring legacy is perhaps the city of Mitchell, Nebraska, located not far from a long-vanished frontier post – Fort Mitchell – that was also named after him.

Mitchell was born in Richland County, Ohio, on April 4, 1823. A lawyer by profession, he practiced law in Mansfield from 1844-46 before leaving for service in the Mexican War where he saw action as a junior officer in an Ohio regiment. Mitchell resumed his law practice after the war, maintaining an office in Mansfield for nine years before moving west in 1856.

Mitchell eventually settled in Kansas where he quickly became active in politics and by the following year was elected to the territorial legislature as a free-state advocate. He served as territorial treasurer from 1858-1861. In 1860, he was a delegate to the Democratic National Convention.

At the outset of the Civil War, Mitchell was appointed colonel in the newly-formed 2nd Kansas Infantry regiment after first serving briefly as Adjutant General of Kansas. On August 10, 1861, at Wilson's Creek, Mitchell was severely wounded while leading the 2nd Kansas in battle. After a lengthy convalescence and promotion to brigadier general of volunteers, he was given command of a brigade at Fort Riley, Kansas. He later led a division at the Battle of Perryville and for a time commanded General George H. Thomas's cavalry corps in the Army of the Cumberland – duties which took him with Thomas to Chickamauga. Mitchell was subsequently called to

Washington, D.C. He was serving on court-
martial duty when appointed to command the
District of Nebraska in February 1864.

Mitchell was regarded a strict, severe
officer. Shortly after assuming command of
the District of Nebraska, he dismissed several
officers at Fort Laramie who frequented the
"squaw camps" near the post and admonished
others to set good examples for their men. His
leadership, though, seems to have inspired
loyalty. Although a strong Democrat in a
Republican community, early in the Civil War
his contemporaries elected him to command
positions in the volunteer unit.

Conditions in Mitchell's district were fairly
benign. That changed, however, as general
restlessness and the machinations of Colorado

Public Domain
Robert B. Mitchell

militia commander John Chivington and governor John Evans began to raise
the passions of the Plains tribes. By mid-summer, Mitchell was advising his
superior, General Samuel Curtis, to expect a major uprising.

Like others who held positions of responsibility on the Plains, Mitchell
initially had scant resources – as few as 600 troops – to police a region that
extended from the Missouri River into central Wyoming and parts of eastern
Colorado. Mitchell's request for additional troops was disapproved by Curtis
who could not spare any from the demands of the Civil War and a threatened
invasion of Missouri and Kansas. After the major outbreak in August 1864,
with commerce halted and depredations widespread, Mitchell received
reinforcements. Composed mainly of the 7th Iowa, 11th Ohio, 1st Nebraska,
and associated militia units, the numbers – 1,500-2,000 – while welcome,
were small considering the vastness of the territory. Major contingents were
initially posted in Omaha, Camp Collins in Colorado Territory, and near the
Sweetwater River in Wyoming.

From the time he became commander, Mitchell was almost constantly
in the saddle, shifting between Omaha, Julesburg, Fort Laramie, and points
beyond. Like his colleagues, he lacked manpower, horses, and equipment.

By April and May 1864, reports began to trickle in that powerful
combinations of Indian tribes were congregating on the Smoky Hill and
Republican Rivers in northern Kansas and near the forks of the Platte in
Nebraska. Sensing the growing danger, on three occasions Mitchell tried to
reach accommodations with Native leaders. Though Mitchell assessed the
outcome of an early meeting as being productive, in fact none of the sessions
met with a positive outcome. An attempt in June, after signals suggested that

that the Cheyennes were assembling in large numbers and planning attacks, brought tribal leaders to Fort Cottonwood (later re-named Fort Mcpherson) near present-day North Platte, Nebraska. The talks, though, quickly reached an impasse. Mitchell demanded that the chiefs exert greater control over their rebellious young warriors and that the bands stay out of the Platte Valley. Most particularly, he requested that they distance themselves from the overland trail. The chiefs insisted that the whites stay out of their tribes' traditional hunting grounds between the Niobrara River and the Upper Missouri. The talks broke up in anger and attacks grew in intensity.

Mitchell had no previous background in dealing with the tribes. Indian recollections indicate that during the talks he may have spoken to the chiefs in an offensive, condescending manner. If that is true, an attempt to resolve the historic enmity between the Sioux and Pawnee may be further evidence of his inexperience and naiveté. Mitchell brought considerable numbers of both tribes together at Fort Cottonwood. Separating the groups by a line of cavalry interspersed between them, he sought to foster, if not reconciliation, then at least a negotiated truce. With each side in close proximity to their ancient enemy, violence was only narrowly averted.

Peace talks having failed, Mitchell parceled out small units along key points on the trail, complementing a larger plan installed by General Curtis. One of the tiny posts, at Mud Springs, Nebraska, staffed initially by only nine soldiers, would later be the scene of a major fight between 200 troopers led by Colonel William O. Collins and 1,500-2,000 Indian attackers.

In August 1864, widespread attacks brought a flurry of activity to the district. A new post was established along the trail about 12 miles west of present-day Scottsbluff, Nebraska. The small, post, originally known as Camp Shuman and later renamed Fort Mitchell, was home to a company of the 11th Ohio Volunteer Cavalry and 70 or so Pawnee Scouts. The magnitude of the attacks brought General Curtis personally into the field along with some desperately needed reinforcements. After putting in place the beginning of a string of linked outposts, Curtis and Mitchell decided that a major expedition against the tribes held better promise of shielding the trail. Neither officer fully appreciated the elusiveness and mobility of the Plains warriors, who easily evaded larger masses of cavalry and rarely offered battle in a set-piece fashion.

On September 1, Curtis left Fort Kearny, accompanied by Mitchell and a mixed command of cavalry companies, militia units, and Pawnee Scouts. The column pushed south and west, reaching the Solomon River in north central Kansas a week later without sighting any hostiles.

Curtis split his force at that point, returning east to Fort Kearny with Colonel Robert Livingston while sending Mitchell west to Fort Cottonwood and then north to Ash Hollow, a famed location on the Oregon Trail near present-day Lewellen, Nebraska. Mitchell's extensive reconnaissance – 212 miles during a week in the saddle – eventually brought him back to Fort Cottonwood on September 24. No contact was made with the warring bands. Their presence, however, was evident. Attacks continued on a wide scale including two raids that killed soldiers not far from Fort Cottonwood.

The large expedition having achieved few results, Curtis and Mitchell then reverted to their initial plan, stationing clusters of troops along the trail, opting for a defensive strategy until more manpower and horses became available.

Meanwhile, fueled by Chivington's wanton attack on a Cheyenne village in late November, Indian raids increased in size and intensity. On January 7, 1865, raiders attacked Julesburg, Colorado and Camp Rankin, a small sod-walled military post nearby. Fourteen soldiers and five civilians were killed while simultaneous raids struck ranches and stage stations nearby.

Believing that the hostiles were camped along the Republican River and its tributaries near the intersection of the borders of Nebraska, Kansas, and Colorado, Mitchell stripped nearby posts of manpower and assembled a second major expedition. With 640 men composed of elements of the 1st Nebraska, 7th Iowa, and Nebraska militia companies along with 100 wagons, tents, 50 extra horses, four 12-pounder mountain howitzers and two 3-inch Parrot guns, Mitchell moved from Fort Cottonwood on January 15. Over the next 12 days, in a giant 350-mile arc, the column scouted southwest Nebraska and northwest Kansas before circling back to Fort Cottonwood. The expedition found a few abandoned camps and sighted distant smoke signals and scouts but made no contact.

Mitchell's men suffered horribly during the march. The column moved in weather that sometimes reached 23 degrees below zero accompanied by high winds and snow pellets. Almost every trooper sustained some degree of frostbite, with ears and fingers being the most commonly afflicted. Fifty soldiers were so completely disabled from frozen limbs or other injuries that they were subsequently discharged from service. One hundred horses were ruined and six wagons were broken and abandoned. Distraught by the outcome of the expedition, and himself suffering from frost bite, Mitchell requested a reassignment, preferably to fight rebels, or acceptance of his resignation. Neither was forthcoming.

Meanwhile, raids in the Platte Valley continued. Even while Mitchell's expedition was in the field, attacks were launched on ranches, stage stations, and telegraph operations. During the last week of January, raids extended by as much as 80 miles west of Julesburg, an area left generally unscathed in previous uprisings. The multiple attacks involved kidnappings and considerable loss of lives, including women and children. Thefts of horses, burning and looting of homes and ranches and other depredations struck every part of the district.

Mitchell sought to respond using Curtis's earlier-tried technique of setting fire to the prairie, although it would appear that the winter weather mitigated the effect. On January 27, he ordered fires set from Fort Kearny to Denver, aiming to create a fast-moving 300-mile line of fire that would destroy forage for the Indians' pony herds and drive away the game the tribes depended on for sustenance. Employing, in many cases, bales of hay bound by chains, using horses and ropes, troopers towed blazing bundles across the prairie.

Mitchell's effort did seem to drive away much of game in the area. The Indians, however, were little affected, having moved away from the fire zone. The large scale raids continued unabated.

The devastation reached its peak on February 2 when Julesburg was again subjected to a second, massive attack. Combinations of three tribal groups, perhaps as many as 1,500-2,000 warriors, struck the town at 10 o'clock in the morning, this time destroying it totally. Businesses were sacked and looted, and several buildings, including the stage station and telegraph office, were burned to the ground. Raiders ran off hundreds of head of livestock, stole stocks of flour and corn, and destroyed telegraph lines for miles around – at least 10 miles west towards Denver and 34 miles north in the direction of Fort Laramie. The approach of Colonel Robert Livingston with a 300-man force caused the Indians to depart later that day.

After the battle, Mitchell believed correctly that the raiders would move to join other hostile Northern Cheyennes and Ogalas in their stronghold in the Powder River region. Within a week after the destruction of Julesburg, Colonel William O. Collins had fought major battles at Mud Springs and Rush Creek with perhaps as many as 2,000 warriors as the band moved north and west into Wyoming and Montana.

Rebuked by Curtis for having left Julesburg relatively undefended, Mitchell asked to be reassigned. On March 25, 1865, he was relieved as commander of the District of Nebraska and posted to Fort Leavenworth as commander of the Department of Kansas.

Mitchell was mustered out of the Army on January 15, 1866. Appointed by President Andrew Johnson, he was immediately confirmed as governor of New Mexico Territory. He stayed on as governor through 1869, when he resigned and returned to Kansas. Reentering politics, he lost a congressional bid in 1872. Mitchell later moved to Washington, D.C., where he died on January 26, 1882, a few weeks short of his 59th birthday. Buried initially at the Congressional Cemetery, he was later reinterred at Arlington.

Thomas Moonlight

The officer with the most intriguing name was one of the least successful of the commanders who led forces against Native tribesmen on the western frontier. Thomas Moonlight performed capably during his Civil War service where his colleagues generally judged him to be a loyal subordinate and a tenacious fighter. He earned special plaudits for his performance at the Battle of Westport. As others of his contemporaries would also learn, however, fighting Indians was a different matter altogether. In the West his repeated failures caused him to be removed from command.

Moonlight's dismissal from the Army did not harm his later political career. Aided no doubt by his skill as an orator, after returning to his home in Kansas he was elected and appointed to a series of high offices.

Moonlight was born in Scotland on September 30, 1833. At the age of 13 he immigrated to the United States after earning passage as a deck hand. For the next seven years he worked as a laborer on farms and in mills and factories near Philadelphia. Solidly built, with a full, dark beard, Moonlight would develop a reputation for being headstrong and impetuous with a special fondness for strong drink.

At age 20, Moonlight enlisted in the Army. Assigned to the 4th Cavalry, he advanced to the rank of sergeant and saw service in Texas, the Seminole War, and the Mormon Campaign. In 1858, he was honorably discharged at Fort Leavenworth, Kansas, but remained on that station as chief clerk in the commissary department.

At the outset of the Civil War, Moonlight raised a light artillery battery. The unit never completed mobilization, however, its members having been assigned to another newly forming regiment. Moonlight later joined a Kansas infantry regiment (soon converted to cavalry) and received an eventual appointment to colonel.

Serving mostly with the Kansas Cavalry, Moonlight's war was mainly fought against bushwhackers and rebel guerillas in Kansas and Missouri. When Quantrill's Raiders attacked Lawrence, Kansas, in August 1863, it was Moonlight's forces who formed the pursuit. The highlight of Moonlight's service came at the Battle of Westport on October 23, 1864. Commanding

a brigade of General Samuel Curtis's Army
of the Border, Moonlight held the invading
Confederate Army until Curtis's main force
arrived and sent them into headlong flight.
Moonlight was brevetted to brigadier general
of volunteers in February 1865.

In the early days of that year, Moonlight
and the 11th Kansas were sent west to help
confront the massive attacks that had erupted
across the Plains. What had begun in August
1864 as predominately a Sioux uprising
had been transformed into a war against
several Plains tribes enraged by the atrocities
committed by John Chivington and the
Colorado militia at Sand Creek, Colorado, in
late November 1864.

Brady/Handy, Public Domain
Thomas Moonlight

After a difficult march the unit arrived in
Denver where Moonlight had been assigned as commander of the District
of Colorado replacing the discredited Chivington. He found that Chivington
had left him with multiple problems to deal with. Administratively, the
district was a shambles. There was a shortage of men, weapons, and horses.
Moonlight soon discovered that he had little control of six new militia
companies recently formed by Governor John Evans.

Given the immense territory he had to police, Moonlight found the initial
lack of horses particularly vexing. Earlier, more than a thousand horses had
been purchased for Chivington's 100-day volunteers. When the volunteers
mustered out only 400 animals were returned and nearly all of those were
unserviceable. Chivington had captured 600 Indian ponies at Sand Creek,
but only about 100 were turned over to the government and none of those
was fit to ride.

When word reached Moonlight in his Denver headquarters that Julesburg
had been sacked and burned on February 2, he declared martial law. He
followed with a series of bloodthirsty, inflammatory speeches that did little
but excite the already tense conditions in the frontier settlements.

On March 28, General Grenville Dodge, overall commander for the
region, established the Department of the Platte, a new administrative unit
the combined the territories of Utah, Colorado, Nebraska, and Wyoming.
General Patrick Connor, commander of the new organization, divided the
region into four sub-districts. In April, Moonlight took command of the
northern sub-district, consisting mainly of western Dakota Territory and a
slice of Colorado that included Julesburg.

Moonlight and the 11th Kansas arrived at Fort Laramie, headquarters of the northern sub-district, on April 9, acting on orders by General Connor to move the unit from Denver to the Wyoming post. Moonlight complained bitterly about being forced to make the march in harsh conditions.

At Fort Laramie, the 11th Kansas took on a primary role of providing security between the fort and Platte Bridge (near present-day Casper, Wyoming). Faced with increasing raids which killed several cavalrymen, on May 3 Moonlight took his first offensive action. Leading a force of about 500 troopers from the 11th Kansas, 11th Ohio, and 7th Iowa regiments, he moved his column through snow flurries and bitter cold. Moonlight's destination was the Wind River Valley where it was believed that the Cheyenne raiders were encamped in a village containing perhaps as many as 300 lodges.

No contact was made as the soldiers moved east, although there was momentary excitement on one occasion when a large herd of antelope was mistaken for a party of Indians. Moonlight's expedition returned to Fort Laramie empty-handed a week later. Moonlight suggested that a major campaign farther north and west into the heart of the Powder River region might produce decisive results.

Back at Fort Laramie, events were forthcoming that revealed Moonlight's impetuousness and lack of insight. On May 26, in retaliation for continued raids along the trail and the mistreatment of two white women captives, Moonlight publically hanged two Oglala Sioux chiefs. The women, Lucinda Eubanks and Laura Roper, had been taken captive the prior August during raids along the Little Blue River in Nebraska. Both had been physically and sexually abused before their releases were secured. Irate, Moonlight ordered the execution of the two chiefs, although there is some testimony that one of them may have assisted in freeing the two women. Moonlight then directed that the two bodies be left hanging, untouched, as an example to the tribes.

The corpses remained on the gallows for weeks, further infuriating the Indians. Depredations increased after the hangings with attacks on military posts, wagon trains, and telegraph lines. Horses, mules, and livestock were stolen. Soldiers taken captive were horrifically mutilated.

Within his command, Moonlight alienated members of the 11th Ohio, who perceived his statements and actions as favoring his parent unit, the 11th Kansas. Moonlight, like other commanders, was already faced with morale and disciplinary problems from members of volunteer regiments eager to return home now that victory had been won in the Civil War. The internal strife induced by Moonlight further detracted from the efficiency of the forces under his command.

Meanwhile, an event occurred near Horse Creek in the extreme western panhandle of present-day Nebraska that would eventually lead to Moonlight's downfall. Earlier in the summer, the decision had been made to move the large numbers of Sioux camped near Fort Laramie to a location near Fort Kearny,

Nebraska. The large size of the encampment – perhaps as many as 1,500 to 2,000 or more Indians – was becoming a hindrance. Called by soldiers and settlers the "Laramie Loafers," the Indians were generally peaceful and subsisted on government rations. There was a shortage of provisions, though, and feeding them was becoming an issue. Secretary of War Edwin Stanton resolved to move them to Fort Kearny where it was thought subsistence might be easier until the Office of Indian Affairs took responsibility for their care. The Sioux were most reluctant; the Fort Kearny location would place them in near proximity to their ancient blood-enemies, the Pawnees.

Nonetheless, on June 11, the move began with Captain William D. Fouts leading an escort that included four officers and 135 cavalrymen. The action was mishandled from the start. Fouts did not disarm the Sioux although it was known that many of the more aggressive leaders were opposed to the move. The tribesmen were allowed to congregate as a group at the rear of the column, separated from troopers who might otherwise have observed them. Ironically, Fouts had posted a distant rear guard but did not allow them to carry cartridges for their weapons. In camp during the first nights of the movement, some of the troopers mistreated Sioux women.

In the late evening of June 13, camp was made on Horse Creek, about two miles below its mouth on the North Platte River and 12 miles west of Fort Mitchell in the Nebraska Panhandle. Although some tribesmen refused to go along with the plan, in the early hours of June 14, the Sioux made their break from the column after slaying tribal elders who were opposed to the rebellion. In the fighting that followed, Fouts was killed immediately. Four other cavalrymen were slain and four more wounded in the struggle. The Indians, although suffering an estimated 30 casualties, successfully broke away taking 400 horses with them.

News of the fight reached Fort Laramie the same afternoon. Moonlight quickly gathered a force of 234 cavalrymen from California, Ohio, and Kansas units and set out after the Sioux. Moving rapidly across the North Platte, Moonlight pursued with an ill-considered haste that within three days caused 103 of his troopers to turn back because of spent horses.

On the morning of the 17th, 120 miles northeast of Fort Laramie along Dead Man's Fork of Warbonnet Creek in extreme northwest Nebraska, Moonlight halted the remainder of his command for a rest.

The place he chose was a deep ravine about 80 yards wide. One bank was particularly steep, stretching perhaps as much as 60 feet above the ravine floor. Moonlight ordered the horses turned loose to graze. Although some of his officers urged him to do so, he declined to post a guard detail to secure the mounts.

Not long after, 200 or more Sioux surprised Moonlight's bivouac and made off with 75 horses. The veteran units responded quickly and eventually succeeded in recovering about half of those taken. Shooting continued for a half hour until the Indians moved out of range. Cavalrymen claimed several Sioux killed, shot at long distance. One trooper was wounded. After burning saddles and other gear no longer needed, the cavalrymen began the 120-day trek back to Fort Laramie, many of them walking the entire distance.

When news of the debacle – along with reports that Moonlight had been drinking almost constantly during the march – reached department headquarters, Connor removed Moonlight from command. Connor had earlier expressed his exasperation with Moonlight, criticizing his handling of duties and labeling him as incompetent. Now, on July 7, Connor wrote to his superior, General Grenville Dodge, informing him that he had ordered Moonlight to Fort Kearny to be mustered out. By some accounts, Connor then met Moonlight near Court House Rock in western Nebraska and provided him personally and directly with the reasons for his dismissal.

Moonlight later tried to finesse his removal by attributing his departure from the Army to a reduction in force, part of the military's massive demobilization after the war. There is little doubt, though, that he was summarily dismissed.

Moonlight's departure did not end his influence on conditions inside his unit. At some point before he left, Moonlight told several companies of the 11th Kansas that they were entitled to be mustered out. While his speech undoubtedly represented his personal feelings and certainly reflected the desires of the cavalrymen, no orders had been received allowing the 11th's release from service. In a unit already troubled by low morale, Moonlight's statements fostered further insubordination and disobedience, creating a state of near-rebelliousness for his successor to deal with.

Still only 31 years old, Moonlight returned to Kansas and embarked on a successful political career. He was elected Kansas's Secretary of State in 1868 and state senator in 1872. He later served for two years as the state's adjutant general.

In 1887, President Grover Cleveland appointed him governor of Wyoming Territory, a post he held for two years. In 1893, a further appointment from President Cleveland made him minister to Bolivia. After relinquishing that position in 1897, he again returned to Kansas.

Moonlight died February 7, 1899, at Leavenworth at age 65. He is buried at Mount Muncie Cemetery in Leavenworth County.

Edward O. C. Ord

Although Edward Ord had a long and distinguished career in the American West, his name is seldom linked with specific notable episodes or campaigns. As commander of two of the most active and significant departments on the frontier – the Department of the Platte and the Department of Texas – Ord supervised operations within enormous geographic areas, but seldom led troops in the field.

He was, though, a highly capable combat leader as evidenced by his service in the Civil War.

Edward Ord was born on October 18, 1818, in Cumberland, Maryland, but within a year of his birth his family moved to Washington, D.C., where they maintained a home for many years. Considered by some to be a mathematical genius, Ord received an appointment to West Point at age 16. He graduated with the class of 1839, ranked 17th in a class of 31, the roommate of William T. Sherman.

Commissioned as an artillery lieutenant, soon after graduation Ord was assigned to Florida where the Second Seminole War was underway. Ord served an extended three-year tour in the war zone, working under General William T. Harney. After four subsequent years of garrison duty in the East, Ord began a notable assignment on the West Coast.

With the outbreak of the Mexican War, Ord, along with Sherman and Henry W. Halleck, was sent to California, sailing by way of Cape Horn. Conditions in the region were unsettled. The territory still officially belonged to Mexico, although heavy fighting in the Mexican heartland against Santa Anna's government had begun the preceding year.

Ord's ship arrived off Monterey in February 1847. For an extended period he commanded the American garrison in that city. His administration was well-regarded; he was lauded for his successful personal initiatives to preserve the peace and restore law and order within his large, restless jurisdiction. On one occasion along with two other men, he tracked three accused murderers to Santa Barbara. When one attempted to escape, Ord shot him. The other two were taken to a Spanish court, where they were convicted and hanged.

During the course of his career Ord would play a major role in the design and construction of several major military installations. The first instance occurred at Monterey, where Ord and his subordinate, William T. Sherman, completed work on a post that after several name changes became the Presidio of Monterey.

Public Domain
Edward O. C. Ord

At the conclusion of the war, Ord remained for a time in the West, heavily involved in survey duties across the territory that was soon to become American's 31st state. Ord assisted in the plating of Sacramento, produced several district maps, and surveyed the public lands in and around Los Angeles – an effort that a colleague used to create the first map of the city. After two years (1850-1852) in the East at Fort Independence, Maryland, Ord returned to the West and for the next three years participated in a major survey of the Pacific Coast.

Ord's most direct participation in Indian warfare occurred as a junior officer during what turned out to be an exceptionally long tour in the Pacific Northwest. In the mid- to late-1850s, units to which he was assigned saw action in the Rogue River War and in operations against the Spokane Indians. In 1858, he was placed in command of Fort Miller, near present-day Fresno.

After a year spent attending the Army's artillery school at Fort Monroe, Virginia, Ord was sent back to the Pacific Coast, first to Fort Vancouver, Washington Territory, and subsequently to the Presidio of San Francisco where he was posted when the Civil War began.

With two artillery companies, Ord was ordered back to the East Coast as fighting grew in intensity. Quickly made a brigade commander, he led Union forces to victory at the Battle of Dranesville on December 20, 1861, defeating forces led by Confederate General J. E. B. Stuart. Dranesville was one of the first Union victories of the war.

In May 1862, Ord was promoted to major general of volunteers and after a few brief intervening assignments, assumed command of the 2nd Division of the Army of the Tennessee. At the Battle of Hatchie's Bridge in southern Tennessee on October 5, Ord adroitly led his division in a fight against rebel forces retreating from Corinth, Mississippi. Ord was wounded late in the fight but left field command only for a short time. In the summer of 1863, Ulysses S. Grant assigned him to command the Union Army's XIII Corps, a force that Ord led at Vicksburg during the latter stages of the siege of that city. In 1864, Ord returned to the eastern theater where he took command of the XVIII

Corps. Late that fall, he was seriously wounded in the successful assault on Fort Harrison, one of the fortifications guarding Petersburg, Virginia.

Ord's most notable achievement in the Civil War occurred during the final hours of the conflict. On April 9, 1865, Ord, now promoted to commander of the Army of the James, pushed his troops on a superbly conducted march to Appomattox Court House. There, his divisions relieved Philip Sheridan's cavalry and blocked the Confederate line of advance. Sherman lauded Ord's "skillful, hard march the night before" as being one of the chief causes of Robert E. Lee's surrender. Ord was present with Grant and other notables in the parlor of the McLean house when the formal surrender document was signed.

Following the assassination of Abraham Lincoln, Ord led an investigation that determined the Confederate government was not complicit in the conspiracy plot. After Reconstruction duty with the Army of Occupation and other departmental command assignments, on November 18, 1871, Ord was named commander of the Department of the Platte, headquartered in Omaha, Nebraska. The oddly shaped department encompassed all of Iowa, Nebraska, Wyoming, Utah, and a portion of Idaho.

Ord presided over the Department of the Platte until April 1875. In that position, and in the job that would follow as commander of the Department of Texas, Ord's troopers performed tasks that while seemingly mundane were essential to nation-building and the taming of the frontier: surveying, mapping trails, patrolling, manning outposts, and escorting emigrant trains. Ord's tenure with the Department of the Platte was fairly quiescent by the standards of the time. Native outrage over the Black Hills Treaty was yet to come, as was the Black Hills Expedition and the Little Bighorn. Still, there was probably no "typical" day in Ord's life during this time. The duties were varied and his responsibilities spread over a sizable portion of the middle section of Western America. A snapshot of events within only a small segment of the vast territory illustrates the scope and diversity of the challenges that faced him.

Inside the new state of Nebraska, the early- to mid-1870s brought a series of clashes as the frontier moved inexorably westward. On April 26, 1872, William F. "Buffalo Bill" Cody, chief of scouts, and three members of Company B, Third United States Cavalry, were awarded Medals of Honor for actions during an encounter with a raiding party of Minneconjou Sioux along the banks of the South Loup River near present-day Stapleton.

Flare-ups, usually small, between settlers and Indians in central and northwestern Nebraska were frequent. Sioux warriors striking from Dakota Territory raided ranches and farmsteads, stealing livestock and sometimes venturing farther south to attack the Pawnee reservation near Genoa. After small but vicious clashes between settlers and tribesmen at Sioux Creek

(March 1873) and Pebble Creek (January 1874), Fort Hartsuff, near Elyria, was constructed and manned by the end of 1874.

The region's sometimes extreme weather often had a direct effect on military operations. After the battle with Indians along Sioux Creek in early 1873, settlers in the North Loup Valley petitioned the government to send a military expedition though the area. Ord responded immediately, and in April a cavalry company from Fort Omaha scouted the North and Middle Loup regions. As they reached Loup City on their return, they were caught in a horrific blizzard. All 60 cavalrymen took shelter in a tiny store building (one of two structures in Loup City at the time), hunkering down through the massive storm that began on April 13 and continued in full, unabated fury for three days. Although they attempted to protect their animals by placing them in bushes on the lee side of a river bank, when the storm was over the troopers found that 25 horses and four pack mules had been suffocated by the snow.

Two extraordinary events marked Ord's service with the Department of the Platte. In January 1872, along with General Philip Sheridan, George Armstrong Custer and William F. Cody, he participated in the famous buffalo hunt held on behalf of visiting Russian Grand Duke Alexei Alexandrovich.

A year later, Ord was in command when the intertribal bloodbath known as Massacre Canyon took place near Trenton, Nebraska. On August 5, 1873, a thousand or more Sioux warriors surprised a party of 400 Pawnees on a buffalo hunt and killed dozens of men, women, and children. The proximity of a patrolling cavalry company may have prevented a later continuation of the struggle. The clash between the ancient enemies was the country's last major battle between Native tribes.

In the summer of 1875, Ord was reassigned to the Department of Texas. Although the Native adversaries would be different in the Southwest – Apaches and Comanches instead of Sioux, Cheyennes, and Arapahos that his troopers had confronted on the Great Plains – his activities were much the same as those that had engaged him during his time with the Department of the Platte. Over the next five years, soldiers under his command quieted uprisings, chased raiding bands and cattle rustlers, scouted, helped construct telegraph lines, and pacified hostile territory. Ord's troopers identified additional grazing land and found deposits of minerals and precious metals.

Two notable events highlighted Ord's time in Texas. In the spring of 1880, in concert with General John Pope, commander of the Department of the Missouri, troops were ordered to a Mescalero reservation to disarm Apaches thought to have been involved in recent killing raids. In the confused and mishandled operation that followed, 250 Apaches surrendered but scores got away and joined Victorio, implacable leader of the most violent warring band.

Over the next several months, events escalated into one of the largest manhunts in the history of the Southwest frontier – a relentless, two-nation pursuit of Victorio and his raiders. With the Apaches marauding on both sides of the Rio Grande, Ord negotiated an agreement with the Mexican commander in northern Chihuahua that provided for a cooperative campaign to pursue the renegades.

When in mid-summer Victorio crossed the border into Texas, Ord sent a cavalry force under the command of Colonel Benjamin Grierson to track him down. In a July 31 encounter, Grierson soundly defeated Victorio who again fled across the border. He returned four days later, but Grierson, anticipating his moves, surprised and defeated him at Rattlesnake Springs, Bowen's Springs, and near the Sacramento Mountains. Finally, on about August 18, Victorio retreated again into Mexico. Tired and dispirited, he took shelter at a favorite hideaway. A Mexican force led by Colonel Joaquin Terrazas located Victorio and his remaining followers in the Tres Castillos Mountains. In bitter fighting that lasted through the day of October 15 and the following morning, Victorio and several others were killed. Apache raids would continue for a few more years, but few of the remaining or emerging leaders were of Victorio's caliber.

Ord also oversaw the building of Fort Sam Houston, a huge installation that graces a suburb of San Antonio and remains an active Army post in the 21st century.

Ord was serving as departmental commander when he retired from the Army as a brevet major general in December 1880. The following year he accepted an appointment to build a railroad from Texas to Mexico City. While working in Mexico in 1883 he contracted yellow fever. On his way by ship from Vera Cruz to New York City, he was taken seriously ill and put ashore for treatment at Havana, Cuba. He died there on July 22, 1883. He is buried at Arlington National Cemetery.

Ord was known as a "soldier's officer." Concerned for the well-being of his enlisted troopers, he paid special heed to rations, equipment, and medical support with notable attention to care of sick and wounded soldiers. Contemporaries admired his courage under fire. In later years none could recall him ever losing his self-control or conducting himself as anything other than a gentleman.

John Pope

Ohn Pope is mostly remembered in American military history as the losing general at the Second Battle of Bull Run. The decisiveness of that defeat cost him command of his army. On taking command, Pope had boasted loudly of his earlier triumphs and ambitious intentions. While his words may have been intended to inspire his troops, they succeeded mainly in alienating soldiers already embittered by his having replaced George McClellan, their popular favorite. As a result, he was regarded by his army and by much of the public as being a windy braggart. At times he was openly jeered by troops who regarded his comments as a slur on their abilities and an indictment of their previous commander. There is truth, or at least a measure of it, in many of the criticisms of Pope. At times and in varying degrees, he was arrogant, verbose, and boastful. He was also at times and in varying degrees, opinionated, loudly profane, and a man of volcanic temper. As his later service would show, in the American West he was also one of the very best of the Army's departmental commanders.

Pope graduated 17th of 56 from the West Point class of 1842. A topographical engineer by training, his varied career had taken him first to Florida for two years. He then served two years surveying the border of the northern United States before being sent to Mexico where he was brevetted twice for service at Monterey and Buena Vista. Pope's first, brief introduction to Minnesota, where duty would return him more than a decade later, took place as a member of a survey expedition soon after returning from the war. A tour in the Southwest, as chief topographical engineer for the Department of New Mexico, followed. In 1853, he surveyed a potential southwest route for a Pacific railroad.

Controversy first enveloped Pope in 1860 when he made a speech criticizing the policies of President James Buchanan. The uproar nearly cost him his commission. Court-martial proceedings were initiated but eventually dropped. Pope served as a member of President Lincoln's presidential escort. After brief duty in Chicago as a recruiting officer, at the outset of the war he received a commission as brigadier general of volunteers.

Transferred to Missouri in July, he cleared the state of Sterling Price's forces and pushed the rebels south into Arkansas. Named commander of the

Army of the Mississippi, he led Union forces to victory at the Battle of New Madrid – for which he received a promotion to brevet major general. In a deft maneuver he then captured Island Number 10. Serving next under General Halleck, Pope participated in the siege of Corinth, Mississippi.

Public Domain

John Pope

In June 1862 he was transferred east, taking over a corps command. In September, following his atrocious introductory speech and thrashing at the Second Battle of Bull Run, he was sent to Minnesota to command the Department of the Northwest.

After his humiliating defeat, Pope was viewed by most as having been banished to the Northwest, a supposedly quiet theater. True, a war was on-going there, but compared to what was happening elsewhere in the country, it was judged to be a "small" one.

In the Northwest, though, John Pope wrote a second chapter to his story, albeit a much lesser known one. At a time when the nation was beset by its deepest crisis, his achievements there were especially timely and valuable. While Pope certainly was subject to the flaws mentioned earlier, he would also prove to be an aggressive leader, a capable planner of major expeditions, an adroit handler of civil affairs, and perhaps the most capable administrator of any of the Union's departmental commanders.

The Dakota War of 1862 (1862-1865) brought Pope to the Department of the Northwest, an enormous jurisdiction covering the states of Wisconsin, Iowa, and Minnesota and the territories of Dakota and Nebraska. Like many of the conflicts with the Native tribes, the war had multiple roots. Two were common to almost all of the disputes. Alleged ill-treatment by government agents and unscrupulous traders was the first irritant. Growing pressures for land from ever-increasing numbers of white immigrants was the second.

Added to these global factors were issues specific to time and place. The Civil War caused military forces to be withdrawn from the frontier garrisons, a fact of which the Indians were well aware. At the same time, word was reaching the tribes that the war was going badly for the Union. These two factors apparently provoked seemingly contradictory emotions among the tribes. One prevailing sentiment was to strike while the Army forces were weak and reeling. The second was a fear that the rebels might invade and enslave the Indians as they had the blacks. Additionally, there was considerable apprehension that the war was costing so much that there would be no money left to pay the tribes' promised annuities.

The most direct cause occurred on April 17, 1862, when four young braves, acting on a dare, killed five white settlers near Acton, Minnesota. Though the action was not premeditated, the assembled bands, believing that the killings would disrupt already frayed relations past the point of no return, decided on a pre-emptive war. The full scale uprisings that followed fostered one of the worst massacres in U.S. history. Before the rampage was quelled between 450 and 800 settlers were killed, with a figure of 757 being the most commonly cited estimate.

At the outset of the war, there were about 6,500 Sioux living in scattered groups along the Minnesota River. Another related band, 3,000-4,000 Yankton Sioux, roamed farther west in Dakota Territory. The combined assemblage was presumed to have about 1,500-2,000 warriors. All were under the overall leadership of Chief Little Crow. The organization was loose, however, and the bands operated semi-independently.

As the war commenced, Sioux forces were primarily divided into two war parties. One, operating furthest south, would attack major posts at Fort Ridgely and New Ulm. That force would eventually be involved in a series of raids and skirmishes such as a noted encounter at Birch Coulie. The second band would raid Minnesota's northern counties and attack Fort Abercrombie. Other raids were launched by independent groups operating all along the frontier. Their goal was to exterminate white settlers in the area between the Dakota border and the Mississippi River.

When the uprising began, Army forces in the region – many of whom would soon be withdrawn for Civil War duty and replaced by local volunteers – were garrisoned at four locations. Two were in Dakota Territory: Fort Abercrombie, located on the Red River a half mile east of present-day Abercrombie, North Dakota; and Fort Randall, on the southwest side of the Missouri River about 45 miles west of present-day Yankton, South Dakota. The remaining posts were in the new state of Minnesota. Fort Ridgely was 12 miles northwest of New Ulm on the north branch of the Minnesota River. Fort Ripley was located on the Mississippi River about 40 miles north of St. Cloud. Altogether, the combined garrisons housed 879 soldiers.

John Pope was a proud, vain, sensitive man. He was disheartened, if not embittered, by the assignment to the Northwest. Nonetheless, during the ten days it took him to settle his affairs, leave Washington, D.C., and travel to St. Paul, he apparently steeled himself to the inevitable. When he took command on September 16, 1862, his exceptional energy and aggressiveness were immediately apparent.

He faced a daunting task. There was at first no staff or organization to assist him and no functioning quartermaster organization to buy mules and requisition materials and supplies. The only experienced troops in his entire department were the 3rd Minnesota and a small portion of the 10th

Minnesota. One of his major component commanders, General Henry Sibley, had only 27 horses. There were almost no wagons, although there was an immediately identified need for 500 or more.

Despite the formidable challenges, Pope pitched in with characteristic vigor, one of his first steps being to order 2,500 horses. He eventually received about 2,000, using them to convert his veteran units to mounted infantry and organize a regiment of rangers. By January 1863, General Sibley had 1,046 cavalrymen under his command. To strengthen his thinly manned garrisons, Pope found additional forces – first among them four regiments from Wisconsin – and quickly pulled them into the region. Unwilling to remain on the defensive, he advised Sibley to continue with his plans to go after the Sioux, telling him that he (Pope) would push forward everything he could to assist him as soon as men and supplies became available. With Sibley's initial concept as a basis, Pope moved forward, establishing and garrisoning a chain of posts across the frontier. At a time when there was not a single soldier or military post in the hundreds of miles from Fort Randall to Fort Benton, Montana, in February 1863, Pope began planning a campaign aimed at ending terror attacks and driving the hostiles from Minnesota.

Pope's plan was two-fold. General Sibley, with a force of 1,400 men would move west and north from southern Minnesota, driving the Sioux into Dakota Territory. Meanwhile, General Alfred Sully with 1, 900 men would travel north up the Missouri River from Sioux City, Iowa. Ideally, the Sioux would be trapped between the converging columns. Even if not, the hostiles would be pushed west, away from the Minnesota frontier. Sibley would eventually fight engagements at Big Mound, Dead Buffalo Lake, and Stony Lake, attaining a decisive victory at Big Mound, near Devil's Lake, North Dakota. Sully's force, slated for travel on steamers, was delayed by low water on the Missouri, preventing the planned junction from taking place.

Pope acknowledged that the campaign did not achieve its objective of snaring the Sioux. While the results were not all that he had hoped for, there were scattered signs of progress. Sibley's string of victories in the summer of 1863 pushed the warring groups farther west. Most significant, perhaps, was a later triumph at Wood Lake on September 23, that resulted in the release of captives held by the Sioux and further scattered the hostile bands. The following year, Sully's victory at Whitestone Hill in central South Dakota inflicted heavy casualties, destroyed equipment, and dispersed the warriors who confronted him. The net effect of Sibley's and Sully's actions was to push the hostiles away from Minnesota and take the immediate pressure off the frontier settlements. Sibley's win at Wood Lake marked the end of major clashes in Minnesota. The defeat evidenced an inter-tribal riff; white captives were released and large numbers of Sioux subsequently surrendered or were taken prisoner.

Soon after, a five-person military tribunal was appointed to try the Sioux who had participated in the uprising. Some modern scholars have questioned the panel's proceedings, particularly the seeming haste in which some of the sessions were conducted. Eventually, 392 prisoners were tried. Sixteen were given prison terms and 303 were sentenced to death.

When the results were transmitted to Washington, President Lincoln asked the newly-arrived Pope, who had not been involved in the tribunal, to send the full trial records of all those convicted. Pope immediately complied and Lincoln set two legal scholars to the task of reviewing them. Lincoln's intention was to make a distinction between military belligerents – those who had fought on the battlefield – and those who had raped and murdered. Eventually, 38 – those convicted of rape and wanton murder – were hanged at Mankato on December 20, 1862. The event remains the largest mass hanging in American history.

Little Crow, the Sioux leader of the rebellion, initially escaped to Canada. After sneaking back across the border on a horse-stealing raid, he was shot and killed by a settler.

While Sibley's victory at Wood Lake brought major fighting within the borders of Minnesota to a close, the power of the Sioux nation had not been broken. Ominous news of buildups of Sioux tribesmen southwest of the Missouri River in Dakota Territory brought the promise of renewed fighting in the spring. Rumors of Sioux plans to block river traffic and attack emigrant trains and settlements further abetted the underlying fears.

Pope responded by requesting more cavalry to go after the nomadic bands and by planning a campaign that would take the battle to the Sioux. The 1864 expeditions would again send Henry Sibley and Alfred Sully deep into Indian territory.

Sully would traverse farthest west, moving across present-day North Dakota and, for a time, into eastern Montana. On July 28, 1864, at Killdeer Mountain in western North Dakota, his highly innovative tactics thoroughly defeated the Sioux in what may have been the largest single engagement between U.S. Army forces and Native tribes ever fought on American soil. Sully then pursued the Sioux bands, forcing them farther west and beating them again in a three-day running skirmish called the Battle of the Badlands. By the end of 1864, the threat to Minnesota and much of eastern Dakota Territory, and along with it the apprehension of renewed major uprisings in the region, had been generally dispelled.

The Sioux problem was only one of a myriad of difficulties Pope faced during his tenure in the Department of the Northwest. At times unrest surfaced among the Winnebagos as well. Pope dealt with those with diplomacy and threats of force. Violence was averted.

Squabbles with the Indian Bureau over jurisdictional issues and contractor practices were frequent. Those irritants were compounded by a troublesome cross-border issue. Unscrupulous traders venturing from British America (Canada) sold weapons and liquor to the tribes. At the same time, warring bands could flow back and forth across the border, seeking sanctuary when under threat. Pope sought permission to engage in "hot pursuit," a request not acted upon by British authorities.

Perhaps the most vexing problem, though, was the continuing demand by national authorities to pull troops to fight in the "big" war. Pope's forces, already thin, were periodically drained of experienced fighters by seemingly perpetual requests for more troops to oppose the rebels. Pope, to his credit, complied as faithfully as he could, keeping only minimally essential forces. Even General Henry W. Halleck the Army's administrative chief, an officer not noted for fulsome praise, found Pope to be the most ready of all department commanders to provide assistance when asked. Pope's willingness to help on a national level often came at a price – confrontations with local politicians outraged over the withdrawing of troops from frontier outposts.

The manpower issue was further exacerbated by requests for soldiers to accompany emigrant wagon trains across the Plains. The discovery of gold in Dakota and Montana brought further demands for security details and escort duty as miners and families pressed into the region.

When conscription laws were enacted, Pope was called upon periodically to assist in putting down riots and quelling unrest associated with the draft. A stickler for upholding the tenets of civil law, he was generally unwilling to provide forces in situations that might cause soldiers to collide with civil authorities or the general public. While he sometimes kept forces in reserve in event of a major draft emergency, he believed local and municipal police were best and most properly suited to handling the issue. He shunned military actions unless all legal procedures were exhausted and local authorities were incapable of effective response.

"Copperhead" (Northern supporters of a peace movement and/or the Southern cause) activities further demonstrated Pope's convictions toward civil law. When a subordinate commander confiscated a suspected Copperhead's arms and property, the items were returned. The officer was severely reprimanded by Pope who asserted that the commander had no right to seize property on the claim that it might later be used to resist the government. Pope's consistent focus was on military-specific matters. When he could, he avoided issues that he believed were more properly the purview of state and local officials.

That balancing act was not always easy to perform and the demarcations were not always clear. When a Confederate force under General Sterling Price moved north in 1864 and guerilla activity threated to again explode, pleas for assistance came from city officials as distant as Keokuk, Iowa.

Along with numerous others, the mayor of that city feared his community was about to be overrun by what he believed to be enormous numbers of rebels moving rapidly in his direction. Pope responded in a tone that in a later day would probably be labeled "tough love." He saw no threat from Price, believing, correctly, that the rebel force was small and could be dealt with by Union forces farther south. As for guerilla activities, also small and scattered in his opinion, those could be handled by local militia units. Pope did send an official to investigate the extent of the potential threat and later left an officer to advise the local home guard commander.

By the time Pope's tour as department commander ended, all but a few Indians had been expelled from the state of Minnesota and relocated 250 miles west. Their forced exodus was in response to the demands of a terrorized public and requests from government officials. Pope's views, by contrast, had shifted considerably over the 29 months he had been in charge. From supporting calls for extermination – fairly common during that period – when he first arrived, by the time he left he was one of the few officials advocating a plan for long-term resolution of the "Indian problem." Articulated on February 1, 1865, in his last dispatch as departmental commander Pope proposed several interesting notions. One called for returning the peaceable bands back east, assisting with food, shelter, and provisions while weaning them away from annuity payments. Warring bands would be promised peace and kind treatment in return for good behavior. Pope was convinced that sales of whiskey and swindles by traders had contributed to the general unrest. Trouble would be greatly reduced, he thought, if the government made it impossible for white men to profit from commerce with Indians. Thus, trade would be regulated, extended only by authorized representatives at specific locations. Officers and soldiers would be prohibited from trading with the tribes.

Pope's sojourn in the Northwest earned him a promotion to brigadier general in the Regular Army. A short time later, on March 13, 1865, he would receive a brevet to major general given in retrospect for his victory at Island Number 10 three years earlier.

In late 1864, General Grant offered Pope command of a proposed organization that would include all of the former Department of the Northwest plus the states of Kansas and Missouri. The proffer recognized Pope's success in command of the Department of the Northwest as well as changing conditions on the battlefield. Minnesota and portions of Dakota had been generally pacified but new problems had erupted across the Plains in a massive uprising that began in August. Dealing with the issue would be easier if handled by a single commander located more convenient to the action at St. Louis, Missouri. The new organization was officially established on January 30, 1865. Pope formally took command five days later, on February 3.

Pope had served well in an "orphan" department. Starting without aides, quartermaster, or other staff, he had quelled the major uprisings and managed to stretch his thin forces to protect settlements, escort wagon trains and guard against Confederate guerillas – all in the face of repeated demands for his troops from national authorities. Far more than most of his contemporaries, he was responsive to civil rights and rather astutely handled civil affairs within his department. Rare among military officers, he sought measures to solve the "Indian problem," not just manage it.

Pope handled civilian complaints and interferences roughly, but honestly. He dealt with those worked for him in much the same way. In the Department of the Northwest, Pope was blessed with two capable subordinates – Henry Sibley and Alfred Sully. On occasion, he scolded, preached to, and lectured them. On less frequent occasions, he praised them.

Pope served in Missouri until October 1, 1866. After six months leave, on April 1, 1867, he took command of the Third Military District performing Reconstruction duty in Georgia, Florida, and Alabama. A series of departmental commands followed: Department of the Lakes (1868); Department of the Missouri (1870); and finally, Department of California and District of the Pacific (1883). On October 26, 1882, he was promoted to major general.

Pope's reputation – pompous, arrogant, boastful – followed him throughout his career. No one, though, ever accused him of being reluctant to fight; his accomplishments in the Northwest served the Army and the country very well.

Pope retired from the Army in 1886. A Kentuckian by birth (in Louisville on March 16, 1822), Pope died September 23, 1892, at age 70. He was buried in Bellefontaine Cemetery in St. Louis.

Joseph Reynolds

Although Joseph J. Reynolds commanded forces along the western frontier for a decade, he is most remembered for a single episode – a horrifically mismanaged battle fought along the Powder River in southeastern Montana on March 17, 1876.

Reynolds was born at Flemingsburg, Kentucky, on January 4, 1822. His family moved to Lafayette, Indiana, when he was in his mid-teens and that city remained his home of residence through much of his military career.

Reynolds attended Wabash College for a year before receiving an appointment to West Point, where he graduated in 1843 (10th in a class of 39), a friend and classmate of Ulysses S. Grant.

After receiving his commission, Reynolds moved quickly through active duty tours at Fort Monroe, Virginia, and Carlisle Barracks, Pennsylvania. He served briefly with Zachary Taylor's occupation army in Texas, returning to West Point as war broke out with Mexico. At the Military Academy, he taught geography, history, and ethics for two years and natural and experimental philosophy for the next six. Following another brief tour of duty in Indian Territory, in 1857 he resigned his commission. For the next four years, Reynolds taught mechanics and engineering at Washington University in St. Louis while assisting with the family grocery business in Lafayette.

When the Civil War erupted in the spring of 1861, Reynolds was appointed to an Indiana regiment and was quickly promoted to brigadier general of volunteers. In September, he successfully led forces at Cheat Mountain in western Virginia, assisting General William S. Rosecrans in repulsing Robert E. Lee. Following the death of his brother – with whom he partnered in the grocery business – Reynolds again resigned his commission, leaving the service in January 1862.

Although Reynolds held no official position after returning to Indiana, he helped organize and train the state's military units. On September 17, 1862, he returned to active duty and two months later was appointed major general of volunteers.

Reynolds held responsible positions through the remainder of the war. He commanded a division at Hoover's Gap and at Chickamauga (though his performance there was undistinguished); served as Chief of Staff for the Army of the Cumberland; fought at Chattanooga; led forces around New Orleans, and organized the campaign against Mobile. By the close of the war, he was a corps commander and commander of the District of Arkansas.

Public Domain

Joseph J. Reynolds

Civil War service was followed by a series of assignments in Texas. Initially posted as commander of the Sub-District of the Rio Grande, he was named soon after as commander of the District of Texas, and then subsequently served as commander of the Fifth Military District and eventually as commander of the Department of Texas. While in that duty, he was involved in an ambiguous contest for a U.S. Senate seat which eventually went to another candidate. Reynolds' time in the Southwest was also marked by his brevet promotion to major general in the Regular Army (1867) and his transfer to the 3rd Cavalry late in 1870.

In 1873, he assumed command of Fort McPherson, Nebraska, and the following year took command of Fort D. A. Russell in Wyoming Territory with concurrent posting as commander of the District of the South Platte.

Reynolds was serving in that duty when, early in 1876, he and his command were tabbed to participate in a campaign devised by Lieutenant General Philip H. Sheridan. Sheridan's aim was to strike villages through the winter months, before hundreds of additional warriors left reservations to join the hostile bands in the spring.

Accompanied by expedition commander General George Crook, commander of the Department of the Platte, Reynolds and his troops left Fort Fetterman, Wyoming Territory, on March 1, 1876. Pushing through deep snow and wind chill factors well below zero – at times soldiers had to break up their morning bacon with an ax – Crook's goal was to surprise the hostile bands, catching them unprepared for battle inside their winter lodges.

Crook's force consisted of 10 companies of cavalry and two companies of infantry, altogether numbering 30 officers, 662 enlisted men, 35 Indian scouts, 62 employees managing five pack trains, 89 wagon train workers and five ambulance attendants. As always with Crook, mule pack trains played a featured role in his operations. On the Powder River campaign, he used 892 mules in addition to 65 wagons and 656 draft horses.

Crook also took with him 70 head of cattle to be used as fresh meat for the troopers during the march. However, at 2 o'clock in the morning on the second night on the trail, Indians attacked the sleeping column and stampeded the herd. When an early morning attempt by scouts to track and recover the cattle failed, Crook decided to press on without them.

At the outset, Crook and Reynolds hoped to cover 20 to 30 miles a day and reach Montana by March 9. Slowed by bitter cold and heavy snowfall, the column did not cross into Montana Territory until late in the afternoon of March 11.

From the time the cattle herd was scattered, the column was under constant surveillance by hostile trackers. Still hoping to achieve surprise, on March 7, Crook hid his cavalry in a valley and sent much of his infantry back to their post. The ruse, which gave the appearance of the entire column abandoning the campaign, succeeded in fooling the Indians. For the next 10 days, the cavalry remained unseen as it moved into Montana.

On March 16, scouts reported the presence of Sioux hunters in the vicinity, a possible indication that a camp was nearby. Crook split his force, assigning six companies of cavalry – about 400 men – to Reynolds. Crook kept the remaining companies and the pack train. Crook's directions to Reynolds were to find the camp, attack it, defeat the warriors, destroy the village, and capture or kill as much of the pony herd as possible. Although the testimony is sometimes debated, by almost all accounts he also instructed Reynolds to carry away meat and other food provisions which could be used to sustain the troopers during the campaign.

Led by the legendary scout Frank "the Grabber" Grouard, the troops set out late in the afternoon from near Otter Creek and trailed the Indians through a bitter cold night. Grouard managed to stay on the trail through the fury of a Montana blizzard, tracking across rugged ground covered in places with ice and drifted snow.

Eventually, near sunrise the following day, he discovered a village of about 65 lodges – various estimates place the number between 50 and 100 – sheltered along the west bank of the Powder River in southeastern Montana near the present-day city of Moorhead. The scouts' initial report to Reynolds said that Crazy Horse was in the camp, but in actuality the village consisted of about 50 Cheyenne lodges led by Old Bear and 15 Oglala lodges housing He Dog's band as well as a few Minneconjous. Altogether, there were possibly 150-200 warriors in the encampment.

Reynolds halted his column on high ground cut by a deep, narrow ravine where his troops took shelter while he planned his attack. Conditions were especially difficult. Temperatures were extreme and a thick ice fog blanketed the river bottom. Reynolds could not see the village and, as would soon be evident, directions provided by his scouts were less than clear.

Reynolds intended his main attack to be launched from the south. While that assault was in progress, a company would split off from it and capture the Cheyennes' pony herd. In the meantime, a second unit would cordon off a line northwest of the camp to preclude Indians from fleeing in that direction, their most likely escape route. A third wing would be held in reserve, available to strengthen the assault if necessary or move elsewhere on the field as conditions dictated.

Plans having been made, Reynolds divided his command into three columns and ordered them to their positions. Things quickly went awry. Daylight revealed troublesome terrain features. Indeed, the village was not at the location where Reynolds and one of the strike columns thought it to be. Communications between scouts and commanders and between commanders of the strike units became confused. Two columns inadvertently clustered together along the same small ridge. Eventually, one was ordered to support the other. At one location, an undetected ravine obstructed a direct route into the village. To increase mobility while moving across the rugged terrain, members of one unit shed their overcoats, intending to recover them after the battle. In the confused aftermath of the subsequent fight, the overcoats were left behind. They were sorely missed during the remainder of the expedition as temperatures stayed below zero. At Reynolds' court-martial the company commander testified that Reynolds had refused to allow him to recover the coats, believing it was too dangerous for his troops to return to the area where they had been discarded.

Deep snow and sharp gullies slowed the columns as they moved to their start lines. Several horses slipped and fell – one broke its neck – as the cavalrymen struggled across a hostile landscape layered with ice. All was held in abeyance until the southern-most unit, the force that would spearhead the attack, reached its position.

Finally, shortly after 9 a.m., with the sun already having been up for an hour and the village by now wide awake, arrangements were sufficiently in place to begin the attack.

About two hundred yards from the south end of the village, orders were given to mount up and move toward the encampment. The attack began as a brisk walk with troops aligned 50 abreast. Once discovered by the Indians they were to charge initially at a trot and keep cohesion as long as possible.

Poor reconnaissance quickly forced an adjustment in the plan. The orientation of the village was not as anticipated and the assault had to be launched from the southwest instead of from the southeast as was the original intention.

Farther south, confused by the terrain, the blocking force of 100 soldiers was in the wrong place. Instead, of posting within 150 yards of the village as the commander believed they were – a position that would have allowed him to support the attack with aimed rifle fire from high ground – he was in fact almost a thousand yards distant. Reynolds, moving between units to coordinate the attack, was informed incorrectly that the screening force was properly placed.

The Indians' campsite had been well-selected. Spread out among trees and ravines tracing down the hillside, the lodges were pressed against bluffs on the west side of the river, sheltering them from the bitter wind. The majority of tepees were nestled in a group of cottonwoods; others nearer the river were cloistered amidst a dense growth of willows.

About five minutes after opening the attack, troopers reached the outer ring of tepees and began moving through the village. By all accounts, the Indians were taken by surprise. Though warriors swarmed out of their lodges, the camp was quickly overrun. Shocked by the charging cavalry, the Cheyennes began to take flight. Pressed toward bluffs and ravines west and northwest of the village, the retreating warriors used timber and the fractured terrain to regroup. Contrary to Reynolds' expectations, the Indians made a fighting withdrawal. From thickets of willows and plums in high ground northwest of the village, initially in small groups of three to five, they began returning heavy fire.

For a considerable time the company fighting its way through the village received little help from the blocking force. Still positioned at too great a distance, their supporting fire was weak and ineffective. After about 25 minutes into the fight the assault company was joined by a second unit that moved against the north edge of the village. Tying itself to the flank of the initial attackers, the combined force, now dismounted, continued the sweep through the camp. By this time, casualties had been taken by both sides. One soldier had been killed and three others wounded as the troops moved through the village. Six cavalry horses had been shot down as well.

By about 9:30, nearly all of the Indians had been driven from the village. A screen of troops had been established at the edge of the camp facing north and west where most of the Indians had fled and from where return fire was most intense. While the fight in the village was in progress, a small company of cavalry had captured the village's pony herd, estimated at 700 or more colts, yearlings, and war ponies.

With the village cleared and a firing line established, Reynolds supervised the destruction of the lodges. Although the troops continued to receive fire from high bluffs along the west side of the camp, by about 11 o'clock most of the encampment had been destroyed. Tons of dried and fresh meat, dried fruit, ammunition, clothing, cooking utensils, and other camp paraphernalia were consumed in the flames.

As shooting from the bluffs continued, Reynolds' troops eventually wrapped a horseshoe-shaped defensive line around the encampment although the effort suffered from initial miscommunication between commanders and one commander's misinterpretation of movements on the field. With his units under persistent fire, Reynolds stripped the company guarding the pony herd to bare essentials, leaving only scouts and a few soldiers while the rest were ordered to join the firing lines in and around the village. The orders reached them at a time when – inexplicably – they were eating lunch and their horses were unsaddled. After a considerable delay reaching the action, they skirmished until the battle ended.

By mid-day, three soldiers had been killed and another mortally wounded as the Cheyennes' counter-fire continued to grow in intensity. Six other men were injured. Two of the dead were brought off the field and placed in a makeshift hospital at the base of a nearby bluff. Two other casualties were left where they fell along the skirmish line. One was dead. The other, though seriously wounded, was still alive.

The wounded man, part of a four-man squad positioned in a ravine in front of the skirmish line, was abandoned when the rest of the company was withdrawn and his squad mates could not carry him to safety through the heavy fire. Much to the distress of his colleagues, Indians were seen mutilating the trooper.

By 2 o'clock in the afternoon, the destruction of the village was essentially complete. After torching the lodges, Reynolds hastily reformed his force near the bluff where the field hospital had been established. Still under fire, Reynolds, apparently shaken, asked the doctor to hurry the movement of the wounded men to safety. The doctor later testified that Reynolds ordered him to leave the two dead troopers at the hospital site. Their remains, as well as those of the third fatality and the trooper wounded near the skirmish line, would be left on the battlefield.

Altogether, Reynolds' casualties from the fight were four dead and six wounded although several others suffered from frostbite, hunger, and exhaustion. Indian sources asserted that Native losses numbered only one Sioux and one Cheyenne warrior. Reynolds' cavalrymen estimated the number of Indian casualties at 30 to 50.

Reynolds pulled his force from the battle area at mid-afternoon, seeking to link up with Crook on the way back to Fort Fetterman. Though he had destroyed the village, he left almost devoid of other results.

Specific responsibility to herd the captured ponies and secure them to the column was not assigned. Eventually, a loose arrangement evolved and directions were given to follow the column with the herd and shoot any ponies that could not keep up. Tracked by Indians throughout the day, the main column reached camp at the mouth of Lodgepole Creek at sundown. After great difficulties with inhospitable terrain and wandering animals, the pony herd was brought in at about 9 p.m. The horses were placed under minimal guard, or by some reckonings no guard at all, in an area south of the main camp.

At 8 o'clock the next morning it was discovered that most of the herd, plus some cavalry horses, were missing. The presumption was that they were taken by Cheyennes who had trailed Reynolds deep into the night, following him to the campsite. It is possible, though, that at least some of the horses may have simply wandered off or been lost of the way to the camp. Whatever the combination of reasons, the size of the pony herd had dwindled from an estimated 700 in the immediate aftermath of the battle to less than 200 the following morning. Reynolds sent scouts to search for the ponies but only a few were eventually recovered and many of those were found by Crook's column as it moved to rejoin Reynolds.

Reynolds linked up with Crook the following day. His men had been without sufficient rations for two days and their horses had last been fed prior to the attack. Once joined, the columns were harassed on the way back to the fort by Cheyennes attempting to recover additional ponies. Eventually, many of the horses were shot in a successful effort to dissuade the Indians from further raids.

On March 26, a week after meeting at Lodgepole Creek, the beleaguered column arrived back at Fort Fetterman. The troopers had marched 465 miles during their 26-day deployment, much of it through difficult terrain in the midst of merciless weather. Over the 190 miles from the battle site to the fort, they had lost 90 cavalry horses and mules and another 100 or so Indian ponies abandoned or killed along the way to relieve their suffering.

On March 27, the expedition was officially dissolved.

Crook was incensed with Reynolds' performance and subsequently filed charges against him. Reynolds was confined to Fort Russell, Wyoming Territory, until the court-martial trial in January 1877. He was found guilty of three charges: leaving his dead and wounded on the battlefield; allowing the Indians to recapture the pony herd, and disobeying Crook's orders to keep the supplies that were destroyed at the village. Reynolds was suspended from rank and command for a year; however, his friend and West Point classmate, Ulysses S. Grant, remitted the sentence. Reynolds resigned from the Army on June 15, 1877.

Reynolds' critics had much to find fault with. Rushing to prepare his attack, his initial reconnaissance was hasty and incomplete. Darkness, initially, combined with dense fog and intruding landscape prevented him from identifying the specific location and layout of the camp. Key terrain features were obscured as well. Attack plans as relayed to his commanders were confusingly vague. His retreat from the battlefield was unduly rushed – panicked, by some accounts – and leaving his wounded and dead on the battlefield violated one of the most sacrosanct tenets of combat leadership. In addition to problems of his own making, Reynolds was poorly served by some of his subordinate commanders, two of whom were also court-martialed. Miscommunication between company commanders inhibited the effectiveness of the attack. At least one unit was misplaced on the field and another was mishandled during the fight.

All battles have consequences. For Reynolds personally, Powder River wrecked his career. But, there was a larger, indirect effect as well. The attack induced warring tribes to band together in larger groups as a protective measure. In the aftermath, General Philip H. Sheridan devised a multi-axis of attack strategy that later that year resulted in Crook's clash at Rosebud Creek and Custer's defeat at the Little Big Horn.

After leaving the military, Reynolds took up residence in Washington, D.C. He died February 15, 1899, and was buried at Arlington National Cemetery.

Henry H. Sibley

enry Hastings Sibley (not to be confused with Confederate General Henry Hopkins Sibley), was a man of many talents: businessman, fur trader, congressman, first governor of the state of Minnesota, civic leader, and, as the Dakota War of 1862 would demonstrate, a competent military commander.

It is the Dakota War that brings Sibley to these pages. Though a relatively brief episode in a life filled with several diverse accomplishments, Sibley's generalship along with that of Alfred Sully, pacified the near-frontier at a time when the nation's resources and attention were focused almost entirely on the on-going larger conflict that threatened to dismember the Union.

Sibley's successes, both as a battlefield leader and as an expedition manager, contributed significantly to achieving the government's objectives. The hostiles were driven from Minnesota and a follow-up "punitive expedition" pushed them farther west across the Plains.

Sibley was born in Detroit, Michigan in 1811. He was described by a contemporary as a robust, athletic man who spoke French and understood the Dakota language. After beginning as a clerk in a mercantile business, as a 23-year old he became a partner in the American Fur Company with headquarters in what is now called Mendota, Minnesota. For a time he entered into a de facto marriage with a Native American woman, the granddaughter of a Dakota chief. He later married the daughter of the commanding officer at Fort Snelling, Minnesota.

At age 27, Sibley began a long and successful political career. Commencing with an appointment as justice of the peace, Sibley subsequently served as congressional delegate from Wisconsin Territory, congressional representative from the Territory of Minnesota, representative in the Minnesota territorial legislature, member of the state constitutional convention, and, finally, as first governor of the state of Minnesota, serving one term (1858-1860).

When the massive Sioux uprising began near Acton in August 1862, Sibley's successor as governor, Alexander Ramsey, asked Sibley to serve as colonel of the state militia. It was not an appointment that Sibley requested or welcomed, believing others more qualified. Sibley did in fact lack military

experience, but he was conscientious, an
effective handler of people and organizations
and was well known and respected throughout
the new state. He also knew the Sioux very
well having lived among them or traded
with them for 28 years. Thus, as Governor
Ramsey anticipated, Sibley's appointment was
accepted without controversy by the public.

The murder of five settlers, including two
women, at Acton in Mercer County on August
17, 1862, was the first act in a bloody rampage
that may have killed as many as 800 settlers
in towns, fields, and farms across southern
Minnesota. The following day 20 civilians
were killed in an ambush near Redwood Ferry.

Minnesota Historical Society
Henry H. Sibley

Later on the 18th, at Milford Township, a short
distance west of New Ulm, Sioux raiders swept down on an unsuspecting
community, slaying 50 initially and then four more members of a small
wagon train soon after. Still, the day's depredations were not over. Upriver
from New Ulm another wagon party was attacked. All of the men were killed
and the women were taken prisoner.

Terror spread through the settlements. The following day brought mixed
news of horrific deaths, mutilations, fleeing families, miraculous escapes, and
burning towns and farms. Isolated homesteads were especially vulnerable.
Most were struck without warning. Gristly tales abetted the panic. Near Lake
Shetek in Murray County, the Sioux caught settler families seeking shelter in
a swamp – a place forever after called "Slaughter Slough" – killing at least
15 and wounding several more. Altogether, more than 20 communities were
attacked before the destruction ended.

Throughout the horrific night of August 18 the settlers fled to Fort Ridgely
in the northeast corner of Nicollet County. In the afternoon of August 20, 400
Sioux warriors led by Chief Little Crow, one of the principal leaders of the
uprising, attacked the fort which did not have an enclosed stockade. Bitter
fighting lasted until nightfall when, aided by effective use of two artillery
pieces, the Indians were driven back and broke off the attack.

Two days later, on August 22, the Sioux returned with a force of nearly
800 warriors. Hours of combat ensued with several attacks pushed back
with the aid of double-loaded canister shot from the fort's artillery pieces.
The extent of Sioux casualties is not known. Among the soldier and settler
defenders, three were killed and 13 wounded.

It was at this point that Henry Sibley entered the scene. Offered a colonel's
commission by Governor Ramsay, he reluctantly accepted. After waiting for

a time for supplies and reinforcements, on August 26, he moved toward Fort Ridgely sending an advance force ahead to sustain the garrison until he and the remainder of this 1,400 man-force arrived the following day.

Meanwhile, the town of New Ulm was attacked twice, the first time at 3 p.m. on August 19. Aided by a heavy thunderstorm, hastily constructed barricades, and late-arriving settler reinforcements, the townspeople drove back the attackers. The Sioux returned in larger numbers four days later, enveloping the town. The morning of August 23 brought the beginning of a seesaw battle that raged through the city. The Sioux, with far greater numbers, launched repeated attacks. At one point, amidst burning buildings, an Indian charge was met by a counter-charge led by Charles E. Flandrau, the commander of the area's militia forces. Eventually, after a day of carnage the Indians broke off the attack.

In all, 190 buildings were destroyed in the fighting. Losses among New Ulm's defenders numbered 34 dead and 60 wounded. Sioux losses were unknown but believed to be considerable.

Henry Sibley would fight the war with ill-trained, ill-equipped militia forces soon to be further handicapped by a shortage of horses as volunteers began returning home to harvest the year's crops. The few weapons among them that were initially available were mostly old and antiquated. Ammunition was so short that at one point, water pipes were melted and turned into bullets.

Sibley quickly launched into a training program for his 1,400 inexperienced troopers. A few days into it the regimen was interrupted by the need for forces to respond to a crisis at a place called Birch Coulee. At 10 o'clock in the morning on August 31, a detail party had departed Fort Ridgely to bury bodies at nearby homesteads – at least 16 were soon found – and gather information on Sioux movements. The following day several more, including the remains of 20 soldiers ambushed on the first day of the war, were discovered as the party temporarily divided to search both the north and south sides of the Minnesota River.

The campsite selected that night by the patrol commander was not well suited for defense. The site was easily approachable under cover. Shielded by a large ravine (Birch Coulee) to the east, a knoll to the west, tall grass to the east, and a draw to the south, the camp was vulnerable from all sides, although the heaviest attacks would come from the north and south.

Just before dawn on September 2, the Sioux attacked, driving in the camp's 10 pickets, killing at least one while pouring fire into the tents and wagons in the bivouac area. Thirty soldiers were wounded or killed in the first few minutes. Survivors first attempted an ineffective skirmish line, then sought shelter in hastily dug rifle pits, behind overturned wagons and the carcasses of the company's horses, almost all of which had been killed in the early moments of the battle.

Heavy fighting lasted for almost an hour. Reports of the battle carried to Fort Ridgely, 16 miles away where Sibley immediately sent out a 240-man rescue party led by Colonel Samuel McPhail. As McPhail approached the Birch Coulee battlefield, he was duped by a small party of Indians into thinking he was surrounded by a larger force. McPhail stopped, set up a defense, and send for additional help.

Sibley responded quickly with his entire remaining force, reaching McPhail's position near midnight. At dawn, he moved on, shelling the area as he progressed. Near Birch Coulee concentrated artillery fire scattered the Sioux, lifting the siege. Sibley rode into the battle site at about 11 o'clock in the morning on September 3. He found a scene of destruction. Thirteen soldiers were dead and 47 were severely wounded – four would die in the days that followed – and several others had sustained minor wounds. The carcasses of 87 horses littered the encampment.

More casualties were sustained at Birch Coulee than during any battle of the war. Sibley drew a lesson from the conduct of the battle and its outcome: his forces had to be more adequately trained.

As attacks and pillaging continued over a widespread area, hastily constructed fortifications were thrown up at several settlements. Fort Abercrombie, a tiny three-building outpost on the west bank of the Red River was attacked on August 30, September 3, and, most heavily, on September 6. Devoid of stockade or blockhouses, the small fort survived under quasi-siege conditions until September 23 when reinforcements arrived, although skirmishes continued nearby for another six days. Five soldiers were killed and five wounded during the repeated assaults. Indian losses – inflicted by soldiers, settlers, and artillery fire – were later reported by Native sources as being unusually heavy.

On the evening of September 22, Sibley's force encamped on a roughly triangular perimeter formed by ravines and the east shore of Lone Tree Lake, about five miles north of present-day Echo, Minnesota. (The forthcoming fight, known as the Battle of Wood Lake, is somewhat misnamed. Wood Lake is, in fact, about three and a half miles west of the site of the encounter.)

During the night, Little Crow led 700-1,000 warriors to the bivouac area and positioned them in tall grass near the camp. His plan to attack as the soldiers were breaking camp was foiled by members of the 3rd Minnesota who rose early in a quest to supplement their food rations. As the shooting grew more intense and Sioux in large numbers threatened to overwhelm the small unit, Sibley ordered them back. A hastily put together skirmish line stopped the Indians' frontal charge. Soon after, the Sioux launched a heavy strike along the ravine on the right of Sibley's defenses. He countered it with concentrated artillery fire and by shifting an additional unit to the threatened site. As the attackers retreated, Sibley sent six companies to clear the area. Soon after, he dispatched another company to a section of the perimeter under pressure near the lake.

After two hours of heavy fighting the Sioux broke off the assault and withdrew. Sibley had gained a decisive victory, although one not without cost. Losses among soldiers were seven killed (another source claims only four) and 33 wounded. Indian losses were thought to be especially heavy, with perhaps as many as 30 killed. Rare for them, the Sioux had left the bodies of warriors – at least 14 of them – on the battlefield. Mankato, one of the Sioux's most prominent chiefs, was among those killed. For the Sioux, the heavy losses at Wood Lake marked the end of major organized warfare in Minnesota, and set the stage for the subsequent release of captives.

Sibley remained in camp for two days making plans and tending the wounded. Due to a lack of cavalry he chose not to engage in a close pursuit. He perhaps also feared that doing so might lead to the deaths of the more than 200 captives held by the Indians.

For the Sioux, the catastrophe at Wood Lake changed the dynamic of the war. Dissension inside the tribe had already been growing; a sizable contingent led by influential chiefs advocated peace. While Little Crow and his warriors were engaged at Wood Lake, members of the peace party took control of the captives and moved them to their own camp. Prepared to defend against Little Crow's men, instead peace advocates watched the defeated hostiles flee to the west, seeking safety on the open prairie beyond Sibley's reach.

Sibley arrived at the camp near Lac qui Parle at about 2 p.m. on September 26 and entered into negotiations. Two hundred forty-one captives were immediately set free at the site that immediately became known as Camp Release. An additional 28 held elsewhere were turned loose the following day.

With the release of the captives, Sibley asked to be relieved of his command. In a letter to General Pope, he stated that the objectives of his campaign – to defeat the Indians and free the captives – had been attained. His request was not granted. Instead, on September 29, President Lincoln approved his promotion to brigadier general of volunteers.

When Sibley's troops occupied the Indian village that had held the captives, about 1,200 tribesmen were taken into custody. In the days that followed, additional parties came to surrender under flags of truce. Eventually, Sibley's forces held about 2,000 prisoners. Food supplies soon became a problem and on October 4, he sent 1,250 Sioux under guard to gather corn and potatoes from nearby fields. Eventually, he moved 1,700 men, women, and children to Fort Snelling where provisioning was easier. There, and at Mankato where punishments were carried out, soldiers guarding the Indians sometimes had to shield them from attacks by vengeful citizens.

Sibley's triumph at Wood Lake ended major outbreaks in Minnesota. A military tribunal later found more than 300 Sioux guilty. At President Lincoln's behest, an attempt was made to distinguish warriors who had engaged in battle from those who had perpetrated criminal actions. On December 20, 1862, those adjudged to have committed rape and wanton murder were hanged at Mankato.

The demands of outraged citizens, frightened by the hundreds of deaths and appalled by stories of atrocities, fueled pressure to remove Natives from Minnesota. During the coming weeks, almost all, including non-Sioux, were sent west to Dakota Territory. Only 102 "friendlies" were allowed to remain. Several became scouts for Sibley on his later campaigns.

Little Crow, the primary leader of the uprising, escaped capture and fled across the border to Fort Garry (present-day Winnipeg, Manitoba). On July 3, 1863, while back in Minnesota on a horse-stealing foray, he was shot and killed by a settler.

Sibley established posts along two crescent-shaped defense lines arcing from Fort Abercrombie east and south to the Iowa border. Shock from the cataclysms of the previous year persisted, however. The thought of the banished tribesmen joining other thousands of free-ranging hostiles in Dakota Territory in further attacks was more than citizens and political leaders cared to contemplate.

To counter an anticipated summer attack along the Minnesota frontier, General Pope, the departmental commander, planned a two-pronged "punitive expedition" into Dakota Territory. Sibley would lead one column, mostly infantry, north from Fort Ridgely to Devil's Lake in present-day North Dakota. Alfred Sully would take a cavalry-dominated wing up the Missouri River Valley before swinging north to meet Sully.

Sibley left on June 16, 1863, moving in a column five miles long. Traveling at times from 2 o'clock in the morning until noon to avoid the blistering heat, the difficult, month-long trek took Sibley to a point about 40 miles southeast of Devil's Lake. There, scouts advised him that assemblage of Sioux had recently left Devil's Lake and headed generally west toward the Missouri River. Early on July 20, Sibley set out after them with a force of about 2,000 infantry, 800 cavalry, 150 artillerymen and associated scouts. Sibley took with him 225 mule-drawn wagons carrying supplies for three months and 100 wagons filled with ammunition and equipment. It was the largest body of troops ever sent against the Indians in the Upper Missouri River region. Four days later a patrol sighted Indians moving across the prairie toward a large village not far away.

Sibley halted and made camp while Sioux tribesmen watched from a range of hills about a mile distant. The largest band was positioned on the highest knoll, called Big Mound, in present-day Kidder County, North Dakota. The battle commenced when from the midst of warriors riding towards Sibley's camp, a young warrior shot one of the surgeons accompanying the column.

The Sioux attacked in considerable numbers – perhaps as many as 1,500 – and fought until late afternoon, before Sibley's numbers and firepower forced them to break off the battle. Their retreat took them westward, followed immediately by Sibley whose close pursuit resulted in a running fight that lasted until darkness set in. Two days later he caught the Sioux again, and making effective use of cannon to disperse large clusters of Sioux horsemen, beat them again at an encounter near Dead Buffalo Lake. On July 28, two days after the Dead Buffalo Lake engagement, Sibley inflicted a major defeat on the Sioux at Stony Lake, northwest of present-day Driscoll, North Dakota. At Stony Lake, Sioux in enormous numbers attacked Sibley's force as it was breaking camp. Arrayed in a vast semicircle, a mounted column five to six miles across faced Sibley's troopers. Shifting forces and using cannon until his wagons were laagered, Sibley routed the attackers, forcing them across the Missouri. The hasty withdrawal and Sibley's unremitting pressure caused the Sioux to abandon many of their carts and travois, as well as dried meat, tallow, robes, cooking utensils, and camp paraphernalia.

Sibley lost three killed and four wounded, one of whom died later. Sioux losses are uncertain. The tribe's oral history mentions 24 warriors killed in the three battles. Conversely, one Minnesota regiment alone claimed as many as 31 slain out of a possible total of 150.

Sibley pressed on the following day, July 29, reaching the east bank of the Missouri in the vicinity of present-day Bismarck. He waited for a time without result for Sully's column to join him. Then, with supplies running low, he turned toward Fort Snelling, reaching there on September 13.

Sully, meanwhile, delayed by low water in the Missouri, had not begun his part of the planned pincer movement until August 21. He reached the area near Bismarck about a week later and learned that Sibley was on his way back to Minnesota. Sully then turned southeast and after a rapid three-day march fought and decisively defeated a large mass of Indians at Whitestone Hill. Over the next two days spent scouring the countryside, 156 Sioux were taken prisoner and tons of the tribe's supplies and equipment were destroyed.

In August 1864, rumors of unrest among the Chippewas, perhaps incited by disaffected Sioux, reached Sibley at this headquarters in St. Paul. Sibley sent a small contingent of soldiers to calm settlers near the tribal region along the Wisconsin-Minnesota border. At the same time, he denied military protection to whiskey traders. In combination, those measures eased the restiveness.

Sibley remained on active duty until August 1866. For the remaining quarter century of his life he was active in business and civic affairs. He served as president of a variety of corporations associated with railroads and financial institutions. His civic endeavors were notable for their number and diversity: president of the chamber of commerce, president of the Minnesota Historical Society, member of the Board of Visitors at the United States Military Academy, president of the Board of Regents of the University of Minnesota, and president of the Board of Indian Commissioners.

Sibley died in St. Paul, where he had made his home for three decades, on February 18, 1891. He was buried in Oakland Cemetery in that city.

David S. Stanley

D avid Stanley had a solid, if unspectacular, career in the West both before and after the Civil War. He is perhaps best remembered for being the commander of the Yellowstone Expedition in 1873. That campaign, which featured George Armstrong Custer and the 7th Cavalry, characterized much of Stanley's later career. As a department commander and sometime leader of expeditions, during his service on the Plains he did not often lead forces in direct combat. That circumstance was due mainly to the nature of the positions he held and to local conditions at the time. There could be no doubting of Stanley's personal courage: he was awarded the Medal of Honor for service during the Civil War battle of Franklin, Tennessee.

David Sloane Stanley was born in Cedar Valley, Wayne County, Ohio, on June 1, 1828. After graduating ninth in his West Point class of 1852, he was sent to the West for the first time. For an extended period as a young lieutenant in the 2nd Dragoons, he served as quartermaster for a survey party that mapped a southern railway route from Arkansas to San Diego. For a short time he was posted at Fort Chadbourne, 11 miles northwest of present-day Bronte on the Texas frontier. Duty on the central Plains followed in support of Harney's expedition sent to punish the Sioux for the so-called Grattan Massacre.

After Harney defeated the Brule and Oglala Sioux at the Battle of the Blue Water, near Lewellen, Nebraska, on September 3, 1855, Stanley remained with other forces kept in the region for a time as Harney negotiated with the Native tribes. In mid-March 1856, the mission having been completed, most of Harney's troops were ordered back to Fort Leavenworth. Stanley and a small company were exceptions. A new post, Fort Randall, three miles southwest of present-day Pickstown, South Dakota, was planned for construction.

In late June, Stanley and another lieutenant, George Paige, landed 84 troops of the 2nd Infantry at a place called Handy's Point on the Missouri. There, a half mile from the river, they constructed the new post on a plateau about 150 feet high. The site was well-chosen. The river near the fort was

almost a thousand yards wide and provided
an easily accessible landing for steamboats
which for several years after – until the
coming of the railroads – were the major form
of large transport into the region. Fort Randall
remained an active post until 1892.

Mathew Brady, Public Domain
David S. Stanley

Later, Stanley joined his regiment at Fort
Leavenworth where in addition to Indian
patrols the unit was engaged in keeping the
peace between pro-slavery forces and free
soil advocates. As assignment to Fort Smith,
Arkansas, and along with it a transfer to the
4th Cavalry followed in 1860.

By some accounts, when the Civil War
began, Stanley turned down a colonel's
commission in the Confederate Army,
choosing instead to remain with Union forces. In late September 1861, he
was appointed brigadier general of volunteers. Stanley was involved in many
of the major battles in the western theater: Wilson's Creek, New Madrid,
Island Number 10, and Corinth, where he commanded a division. In October
1862, he was promoted to major general of volunteers and appointed chief
of cavalry of the Army of the Cumberland. His contributions at the battles
of Stones River, Tennessee; Resaca, Georgia; and Ruff's Station, Georgia,
resulted in brevet promotions in the Regular Army to the grades of lieutenant
colonel, colonel, and brigadier general. In 1864, he was given command of
the Army of the Cumberland's IV Corps and sent to Tennessee to form part
of George Thomas's army, hurriedly pulled together to confront the rebel
invasion of the state led by John Bell Hood. His actions during the Battle of
Franklin on November 30, 1864, during which he was severely wounded,
would later earn him the Medal of Honor.

While recovering from the wound to his neck, in mid-January 1865,
Stanley was posted to Texas. Now with the 5th Cavalry, Stanley provided a
military presence to counter the uncertain ambitions of Emperor Maxmilian's
forces in Mexico. In October 1865, he established his headquarters in San
Antonio and remained there until the last of his units were mustered out early
in 1866. The duty was sometimes less than pleasant. His men were volunteers
anxious to get home after having served in a conflict that had been now over
for the better part of a year. As Stanley acknowledged, morale was low and
discipline was difficult to maintain.

Stanley's time in San Antonio was marked by one other episode that
earned him a footnote place in American history. While in Texas, he ended
the Army's experiment with camels (a program initiated by then-Secretary

of War Jefferson Davis in the 1850s), selling the remaining animals from the camel corps to a circus company.

Stanley was mustered out of volunteer service on February 1, 1866. A short time later he was promoted to colonel in the Regular Army and assigned as commander of the 22nd Infantry. That posting brought a return to the Plains region later in the year. By 1868, Stanley was in command of Fort Sully, about 20 miles northwest of present-day Pierre, South Dakota. While violence persisted in parts of the frontier, Fort Sully was a mostly pleasant assignment. The post was garrisoned by 300 troops and although surrounded by 500 or so lodges of Brule and Yankton Sioux, the tribes were generally benign.

Stanley shared Winfield Scott Hancock's convictions regarding restricting incursions into treaty-bound areas and on land set aside for use of the military. In 1869, when a settler named Tomkins established a residence on prohibited ground, Stanley ordered it burned. Stanley's action caused a considerable outcry in the local press but succeeded in dampening the enthusiasm of others who contemplated trespassing on treaty territory.

In the spring of 1872, Stanley led a force of 600 infantry with a strong artillery component from Fort Rice to the Powder River. The move, made in concert with another 400-man unit led by Major E. M. Baker, was intended to put units in place in preparation for violence anticipated as Northern Pacific Railroad construction reached the area. Stanley's unit generally fared well. Baker's contingent, patrolling farther west, was withdrawn in the face of overwhelming numbers of hostile tribesmen.

The Baker episode signaled the powerful opposition that would face soldiers and survey crews as the railroad pushed west and convinced Philip Sheridan that further help was needed. In the spring of the following year, Sheridan transferred the 7th Cavalry to Dakota Territory. Not only did the 7th's manpower bulk up military strength in the area, but the influx of cavalry allowed the Army to more effectively pursue and run down hostile bands.

The regiment's arrival in the area coincided with the railroad's plans to continue building west from Bismarck into Montana Territory. Under Stanley's overall command, the Yellowstone Expedition was formed to escort the railroad's survey parties along the north bank of the Yellowstone River. Stanley assembled a column of 1,700 men with Custer's 7th Cavalry forming the main striking force.

The two men clashed almost immediately. Custer, a difficult subordinate as always, attempted to handle the 7th as a separate entity from the remainder of the expedition. His behavior, described as petulant and capricious by other members of the force, provoked antagonisms between the two officers and between Custer and others in the party. Custer, a teetotaler, blamed Stanley's drinking for their difficulties. Over time, the two of them generally smoothed over their difficulties. Stanley eventually ceded Custer near-complete independence. Two later fights with the Sioux temporarily restored Custer's reputation, which still suffered from the lingering effects of his 1867 court-martial. Although in one of the encounters along the Yellowstone on August 4, the arrival of Stanley's artillery rescued Custer, he later boasted that he had "swung free" of Stanley during the campaign. As is so often the case with Custer's story, the picture is mixed. On one occasion, his superb scouting marked the expedition's path through tortuous terrain in the Badlands.

For a three-year period beginning in 1879, Stanley was back in Texas, overseeing operations against marauding tribes primarily in the western part of the state. In 1882, he was ordered to Santa Fe as commander of the District of New Mexico. When General Ranald Mackenzie retired in 1884, Stanley was promoted to brigadier general in the Regular Army and named commander of the Department of Texas.

Stanley retired from the Army on June 1, 1892. From September 1893 until April 1898, he served as commander of the Soldiers' Home in Washington, D.C. Stanley died in Washington on March 13, 1902 and was buried in what is now known as the United States Soldiers' and Airmen's Home National Cemetery.

Samuel D. Sturgis

The answer to the trivia question "Who was the commander of the 7th Cavalry at the time of the Little Bighorn?" is ... Samuel D. Sturgis. Sturgis was the overall organization commander who at the time was exercising that role in an administrative capacity. Custer was the operational commander in the field. That arrangement was a fairly common pattern in the frontier army.

After the Little Bighorn, Sturgis assumed operational command of the 7th and led it in the field during the Nez Perce War. It is a bit uncertain whether his earlier status – serving only as administrative commander – reflected his preference at the time, was a result of being away on extended detached service, or some combination of both. His son, recent West Point graduate James Sturgis, was one of Custer's officers killed at the Little Bighorn. Sturgis's tenure with the 7th Cavalry, which extended from May 6, 1869, until his retirement on June 11, 1886, formed only a portion of a forty-year career that encompassed extended periods of duty in the West before and after the Civil War.

Sturgis was born June 11, 1822 in Shippensburg, Pennsylvania. He received an appointment to West Point at age 20 and graduated in 1846 as a second lieutenant in the 2nd U.S. Dragoons. Wartime service in Mexico followed almost immediately. Sturgis was assigned to the 1st Dragoons under Zachary Taylor's overall command, when he was captured at Buena Vista while making a reconnaissance. He was held prisoner for eight days before being released.

After the war, Sturgis was sent to the American West for the first time and took part in several Indian campaigns. His name first surfaced in a major way for an action in 1860. That year, Sturgis led a column of 1st Cavalry on a reconnaissance through the Republican River Valley, a stronghold of the Plains Indians. Near present-day Cambridge, Nebraska, Sturgis fought a 15-mile running battle with large groups of Northern Cheyennes. Sturgis's clash was one of the first recorded instances of significant combat in the region and was the precursor to three later major campaigns through the valley – one led by Custer and two by Eugene Asa Carr – that followed after the Civil War.

At the time of Fort Sumter, Sturgis was in command of Fort Smith, Arkansas. When much of his unit – a portion of the U.S. 1st Cavalry – defected to the Confederacy, Sturgis, acting on his own initiative, marched his remaining troops to Fort Leavenworth, Kansas, saving much of their equipment in the process.

Sturgis was a captain at the outset of the war. Photos taken at the time reveal a solidly built, ruggedly handsome man with an open face framed by a full head of dark, wavy hair, modest mustache, and chin whiskers.

Mathew Brady, Public Domain
Samuel D. Sturgis

He was promoted to major soon after and was serving in that grade at the Battle of Wilson's Creek, Missouri, when he took command of Union forces after the commander, Brigadier General Nathaniel Lyon, was killed. He was appointed brigadier general of volunteers as of August 10, 1861, the date of the battle.

A brief, inconsequential tour in charge of fortifications around Washington, D.C., followed. When the Confederates threatened the area in August 1862, Sturgis was assigned to support General John Pope, then in command of what was then called the Army of Virginia (later the Army of the Potomac). To Sturgis's great consternation, battlefield snafus precluded his troops from weighing in effectively during the Second Battle of Bull Run.

Sturgis was subsequently given command of the 2nd Division of the IX Corps and led that unit at South Mountain, Antietam, and Fredericksburg. His leadership at South Mountain was exemplary and would later earn him another brevet promotion. At Antietam on September 17, 1862, after a series of piecemeal attacks, his division eventually took Burnside Bridge, a key objective in the fight, but was unable to push the rebels away or prevent them from reconstructing their line. At Fredericksburg on December 13, the 2nd Division was part of the bloody frontal assault on Marye's Heights. The unit, along with other Union divisions, was driven back with heavy loss. Sturgis's performance, however, was a rare bright spot and earned him a brevet promotion to major general.

After Fredericksburg, Sturgis's division was assigned to the western theater where he held a series of brief commands in Tennessee and Mississippi. For a time he was Chief of Cavalry for the Department of the Ohio. As Sherman's forces moved against Atlanta, Sturgis's cavalry was assigned to protect Union supply lines. Seeking to shield the routes from Confederate raiders led by Nathan Bedford Forrest, Sturgis moved to Tupelo, Mississippi, to confront the marauders. In June 1864, at the Battle of Brier's Crossroads near Guntown, Mississippi, he was badly beaten by Forrest's

Samuel D. Sturgis

troopers. The severe losses and large numbers of prisoners taken by rebels effectively ended Sturgis's active role as a commander for the duration of the war. At the conclusion of hostilities, he was a brevet major general. When the conflict was over, he reverted to his permanent rank of lieutenant colonel.

On May 6, 1869, Sturgis was promoted to colonel in the Regular Army and assigned as commander of the 7th Cavalry. His subordinate was George Armstrong Custer, who for much of the next seven years was the regiment's de facto commander in the field. The relationship between the two men was not a comfortable one.

On detached duty in St. Louis at the time, Sturgis did not accompany the 7th on the Little Bighorn expedition. His son, Lieutenant James G. "Jack" Sturgis, was killed during the battle. Jack Sturgis's body was never identified. By one account his severed head, by another, an article of his clothing, was found in the abandoned Indian village along the river. Samuel Sturgis never forgave Custer for the loss of his young son, believing his boy had been needlessly sacrificed, a victim of Custer's ego, during a mishandled battle. When the remnants of the 7th Cavalry returned to Fort Abraham Lincoln after the fight, Sturgis assumed operational command of the unit.

September 1877 saw General O. O. Howard, commander of the Department of the Columbia, three months into his pursuit of the Nez Perce on their near-mythical journey across the northern quarter of the continental United States. Sturgis joined the chase after the Nez Perce passed through a portion of Yellowstone Park. General Howard, having tracked the Nez Perce since mid-June through some of the most rugged terrain in North America, directed Sturgis to maintain the pursuit while Howard rested his force.

After supplementing Sturgis's 360 horsemen with an extra company of cavalry, two mountain howitzers, and a contingent of scouts that included Bannocks and Crows, Howard set Sturgis on the trail. The Nez Perce had ventured into the Yellowstone region seeking assistance and asylum from friendly Crow tribesmen. However, the Crows, realizing that helping the Nez Perce would risk retribution from the Army, rejected the appeal.

Rebuffed by their erstwhile allies, the Nez Perce turned north toward Canada, their one remaining hope for sanctuary. Although the Nez Perce trek was not noted for its depredations, as the band moved along Clark's Fork of the Yellowstone, they killed several prospectors and ranchers while raiding for food, horses, and provisions.

On September 12, the tribe camped near the opening of series of narrow defiles along Canyon Creek. The ground was especially rugged. Walls along each of the small canyons towered 300 to 500 feet, crested by ridges with mostly flat tops. Small streams, forks of Canyon Creek, coursed along the floors of dwarf canyons that extended for about six miles.

The following morning while several warriors were absent raiding

331

nearby ranches, Sturgis's cavalry was detected moving towards the camp. His approach was unexpected. Sturgis had pushed his force severely for a month since taking the trail on August 12. Within the past two days they had barely missed the Nez Perce along Clark's Fork before riding 60 miles in a downpour and then swimming their horses across the Yellowstone River near present-day Laurel, Montana.

Although his men were exhausted, when scouts reported that the tribe had broken camp about six miles distant Sturgis moved swiftly to intercept them. He sent a battalion commanded by Major Lewis Merrill north along a high ridge line in an attempt to cut off the Nez Perce who were moving along the floor of a shallow canyon. Sturgis kept a second battalion (led by Captain Frederick Benteen, a survivor of Custer's battle at the Little Bighorn), momentarily in reserve a short distance behind the first wave.

When Merrill's unit of about 150 men crested the ridge overlooking the valley floor, he chose to dismount his cavalrymen and form a skirmish line. Why he did so instead of mounting a charge is uncertain; he later drew criticism for the decision. In the meantime, the Nez Perce marksmen, sheltering behind rocks and in trees, brought Merrill's line under fire, holding up the advance.

With the attack slowed, Sturgis, seeking to close the exit to the canyon, sent Benteen on a sweep to the left, moving first west then north, in an attempt to trap the horse herd and capture Nez Perce women and children. In the meantime, Merrill was ordered to move into the canyon to threaten the rear of the column as the Nez Perce retreated along the valley floor.

Neither effort was particularly successful. Both were held up by accurate fire from Nez Perce warriors posted on high ground. Merrill's men were eventually able to push the warriors down the northeast portion of the ridge, but little else was accomplished. Benteen captured a few horses, but further efforts were futile as a Nez Perce rear guard skillfully held off additional attempts until nightfall. The fighting, which had commenced at about noon, continued until dusk. When darkness fell, the village and the horse herd escaped through nearby rocks and timber.

Replenished the following day by the arrival of additional large number of Crow scouts (variously estimated at between 50 and 200) on fresh horses, Sturgis immediately sent the Crows as well as some Bannocks after the Nez Perce.

Sturgis and his cavalry followed, but the grueling 37-mile pursuit further wore down his exhausted mounts, forcing some of his troopers to walk before the day was over. The Crows, however, managed to catch the tail of the Nez Perce column and in the skirmish that followed made off with about 400 of the Nez Perce's 2,000 horses. Sturgis resumed the chase the following day but was unable to catch the fleeing band. Out of supplies and with his horses in no shape to travel, Sturgis waited at a camp along the Musselshell River where two days later he was resupplied and joined by General Howard and his command.

Sturgis's casualties during the running fight along Canyon Creek totaled three killed and 11 wounded, one of whom died later. Sturgis claimed 16 Nez Perce killed, but tribal sources insisted that only three, one warrior and two old men, were killed and three more were wounded.

The delay caused by Sturgis's unexpected attack and the loss of horses slowed the Nez Perce's flight toward Canada. Though not in themselves deciding factors, in combination they likely contributed to the tribe's decision to rest at Bear Paw Mountain before proceeding on to Canada.

Howard's arrival at the Musselshell River bivouac ended Sturgis's senior command responsibilities with the expedition. Howard continued the pursuit, bringing Colonel Nelson Miles from Fort Keogh to join in the chase. On September 30, Miles caught the Nez Perce while they were encamped near Bear Paw Mountain. An initial bloody encounter placed the village under siege. Howard joined Miles three days later. On October 5, Chief Joseph with the majority of the Nez Perce tribe surrendered.

Sturgis retired from the Army in 1886. He died September 28, 1889, at St. Paul, Minnesota. He was buried at Arlington National Cemetery.

Sturgis's son and grandson, both named Samuel D. Sturgis, achieved general officer rank in the U.S. Army.

Alfred H. Sully

lfred Sully's career is unusual in several respects. Most prominent among them is that while his accomplishments equaled those of several more renowned contemporaries, his name and his achievements are less well remembered. Indeed, at Killdeer Mountain, North Dakota, on July 28, 1864, he led Army forces to victory in perhaps the largest pitched battle in the history of Plains warfare – an encounter that surpassed the numbers who fought on both sides at the Little Bighorn. During the Civil War, Sully saw action in some of the early major battles in the East, but rare among senior officers, spent the bulk of the conflict fighting Indians on the frontier. Lastly, in addition to being a competent military commander, he was a gifted artist. The son of a nationally-known portrait painter, Sully's water colors – many of them painted while serving on duty stations on the Great Plains and Pacific Northwest – grace the displays of galleries throughout the country.

It is perhaps understandable that Sully's legacy has gone relatively unnoticed because the conflict his name is most prominently linked with remains one of the nation's lesser known conflagrations. The Dakota War of 1862 was fought at the time when the nation's collective attention was riveted by some of the bitterest battles of the Civil War. Although the death count was large by Indian war standards, as the nation tore itself apart the titanic clashes in the East and along the Mississippi dwarfed all other events in the public's consciousness.

Alfred Sully was a slender officer of medium height. His distinguished appearance was made notable by a thin face framed by dark hair and a long, narrow beard that extended to the top buttons on his tunic. In his later years the "salt and pepper" in his beard added further character to his looks.

Sully was born in Philadelphia in 1821. After graduating from West Point in 1841, he was sent to Florida with the 2nd Infantry Regiment to quell the Seminole uprising. Sully spent a year at Fort Russell on Key Biscayne before being posted to Sackett's Harbor, New York. He remained there on an extended tour until the conflict with Mexico absorbed most of the nation's tiny army.

In 1846, Sully joined Winfield Scott's forces in the early fighting and participated in the siege of Vera Cruz. In 1848, along with the 2nd Infantry, Sully was sent to California, newly acquired in the aftermath of the Mexican War. He was posted at Monterey primarily but spent some time at Bernicia as well. Assigned chiefly to quartermaster duties, Sully's tour in California lasted until 1854. For the next seven years he commanded forces across the central Plains at Fort Pierre, Fort Kearny, and Fort Ridgely in Dakota Territory, Nebraska Territory, and Minnesota, respectively. His responsibilities were standard fare for most frontier officers: building forts, patrolling trails, and escorting emigrant wagon trains. Clashes with Sioux and Northern Cheyennes added to the Indian-fighting experience gained in campaigns in California and Oregon during his service in the Pacific Northwest.

Public Domain
Alfred H. Sully

A different sort of warfare would soon occupy Sully's attention. Within a month after Fort Sumter, the U.S. flag was torn from the roof of the post office in St. Joseph, Missouri, and trampled by a secessionist mob. Later in the summer of 1861, Confederate militia took control of the town. Sully led Union forces from Fort Leavenworth, Kansas, and in September occupied the city, declared martial law, and put down persisting violence.

Along with many other veteran officers based on the Plains, Sully was called east as the fighting intensified. Appointed colonel in the 1st Minnesota Volunteer Infantry in March 1862, he served for a brief time manning defenses around Washington, D.C., and then led units during the Seven Days Battle, Antietam, and Fredericksburg. His performance at Antietam on September 17 earned him command of a brigade and promotion to brigadier general of volunteers. In December he led a brigade at Fredericksburg.

In the spring of 1863 Sully was removed from command and returned to duty in the West. The stated reason for his dismissal was an alleged inability to control a near-mutinous regiment of New York infantry. There was, however, also speculation that his identification as a "McClellan man" – sympathetic to, if not supportive of, General George McClellan – may have contributed to his removed by superiors wary of officers with known linkages to the controversial former commander of the Army of the Potomac.

Sully was disheartened by the transfer. Nonetheless, the timing and location of his new posting were propitious. Sent to the District of Dakota, Sully was immediately engaged in combatting a major Sioux uprising fought on grounds familiar to him in Minnesota and Dakota. The assignment was militarily sound as well: Sully's experience with Plains Indians exceeded that of most of his contemporaries.

The Dakota War of 1862 was a bloodbath that eventually killed hundreds of settlers, soldiers and a large but uncertain number of Native Americans. General John Pope's campaign plan for 1863 called for Sully's command to move north up the Missouri River while forces under General Henry Sibley pushed from southwest Minnesota into Dakota Territory. Pope, commander of the Department of the Northwest, intended that the two converging wings would form a pincer, trapping the Sioux. While the full plan never reached fruition, a series of successful clashes led by Sibley near Devil's Lake, North Dakota, and a triumph by Sully at Whitestone Hill reduced the immediate threat to the Minnesota frontier.

Much to the displeasure of General Pope, Sully's departure was delayed by low water levels on the Missouri that prevented travel by steamboat. Prodded by Pope, Sully began his expedition on August 21, 1863, initially moving north along the Missouri River with a force of about 1,900 men. The bulk of Sully's striking power was supplied by the 6th Iowa Cavalry commanded by Colonel David Wilson and the 2nd Nebraska Cavalry led by Colonel Robert Furnas, plus assorted scouts and artillery. After leaving one company of the 2nd Nebraska at Fort Randall, the first in a chain of forts on the Upper Missouri just north of the Dakota-Nebraska border, Sully followed the river angling west and north until the column reached Fort Pierre in August.

At Fort Pierre, located almost in the center of present-day South Dakota, Sully rested and replenished his force. On the 13th, he again took the field moving generally north. He took with him about 1,200 men, the remainder having been left to garrison outposts along the way or placed on patrol duty. Sully was a prudent officer, known for security and discipline while on the march. On September 3, scouts discovered a large Sioux village of about 400 lodges housing 2,000 – 4,000 Indians, at Whitestone Hill, 23 miles southeast of present-day Kulm, North Dakota.

The encampment housed Indians from several Sioux tribal groups – Santee, Yankton, Teton – some of whom had fled the fighting in Minnesota or had been pushed to the region by General Sibley's column. It was late afternoon when the scouts' report reached Sully who was riding with the main column about 10 miles away. Sully quickly dispatched an advance force of about 300 men, directing their commander, Major A. E. House, to surround the camp and, if possible, prevent the Sioux from scattering. After assigning four companies to guard his supply train, Sully then hurried toward the village with his main force of 600-700 cavalrymen.

At about 6 o'clock, Sully reached high ground overlooking the Indian camp. The large, dispersed village spread out on the prairie before him. Seeing movement in the village and tepees being torn down, he sent the 6th Iowa to the right and the 2nd Nebraska to the left to close off ravines which afforded concealment and escape routes for the Sioux. After both flanks were covered, Sully, with three companies and artillery, moved straight into the village. Because of the close-in chaotic nature of the fighting that later followed, Sully's artillery was never used. Initial resistance was scattered and considerable numbers of Sioux surrendered as Sully advanced.

Fighting flared up on the flanks, however, and grew in violence as Sioux warriors were caught between the Iowans on one side and the Nebraskans on the other. Advancing on foot, the Iowa unit pressed the Sioux towards the 2nd Nebraska, a unit Sully later complimented for its marksmanship. Both cavalry regiments were equipped with infantry rifles rather than their normal carbines, thus increasing the range and lethality of their weapons. Firing from as close as 60 yards, the cavalrymen exacted a heavy toll on their attackers.

As darkness approached, in a poorly conducted charge led by Colonel Wilson the Iowa regiment was beaten back and both sides hunkered down for the night. Wary of friendly fire prospects and losing communication with his soldiers in the dark, Colonel Furnas pulled his Nebraska troops back slightly to a more favorable defensive position in the rolling terrain.

During the night, most of the Indians abandoned the camp. The Sioux did not entirely flee the area, however, and for the next two days skirmishes, sometimes heavy, continued as they fought to retake the village or regain their possessions. On September 5, a 27-man patrol collided with 300 or more Sioux about 15 miles from the battle site. The cavalrymen were forced into a fighting retreat, losing six killed and one wounded. Meanwhile, Sully's troops destroyed the village and its contents, burning perhaps as much as a half million pounds of dried buffalo meat, the Indians' cache of winter provisions.

Altogether, Sully's casualties probably amounted to 20-22 killed and 38 wounded. Estimates of Sioux losses varied widely, ranging from 100-300 with another 150 or more captured. Rare in frontier casualty reports, the Indians' estimates of their own casualties were as high or higher than those suggested by the cavalrymen. Some tribesmen guessed that as many as 300 had been killed or wounded and another 250 taken prisoner. Clearly, it was a devastating loss for the Sioux.

Native losses included an unknown number of women and children, prompting some participants and many critics to label the battle as a massacre. Dissenters argued that most were killed in the chaotic jumble of the fight inside the village and that large number of cavalry losses (although some may have resulted from friendly fire) did not bespeak of a massacre.

Their extended time in the field had left Sully and his troopers low on supplies. With wounded to care for and horses and mules played out, he left Whitestone Hill on September 6 and returned to Fort Pierre. Nearby, he built a new fort, Fort Sully, and quartered there with much of his command through the winter of 1863-64.

Operations resumed in the spring. Sully's victory at Whitestone Hill and Sibley's successes elsewhere in North Dakota had reduced, but not eliminated, the threat to settlers in the region. Pope's 1864 campaign was intended to shield them from attacks that persisted, although in Minnesota the raids were neither of the size nor the frequency of previous years. Ordered by General Pope to establish a string of forts along the Missouri River, Sully pushed a sizable force west across North Dakota into the area of the Little Yellowstone.

A second purpose of Sully's expedition was to protect lines of communication to gold fields newly discovered in Montana and Idaho. Badly needed by the Union, the most direct route for the ore was via steamboat on the Missouri River through Sioux territory. On June 28, as Sully's forces were on the march, three Indians killed a topographical engineer who was collecting specimens while accompanying Sully's column. After an advance element of troopers chased and killed the three warriors, Sully, a man of considerable temper, had the corpses decapitated and the heads mounted on stakes as a warning to other hostile tribesmen.

The full campaign came together the following day, June 29, when a 1,700-man contingent having followed the Missouri River from Sioux City, Iowa, joined a second column of 1,550 soldiers who marched overland from Fort Ridgely, Minnesota. Eight days after the units joined, Sully established a new post, Fort Rice, 30 miles south of present-day Mandan, North Dakota, as a base for the expedition. Steamboats were chartered to transport supplies and support the expedition as it moved. Alerted by scouts to the presence of a massive encampment 130 miles northwest, Sully left Fort Rice on July 19. Forced to devote some of his manpower to convoy a wagon train of 200 miners and families, Sully took with him about 2,200 men supported by two artillery batteries and eight howitzers. On July 26, a week into the march, Sully's scouts skirmished with a large party of Sioux near present-day Richardton, North Dakota. One scout was wounded in the struggle. Convinced that the Sioux now knew of his presence, Sully moved quickly, covering as much as 47 miles on the day before the battle. In the early morning hours of July 28, Sully's chief scout reported sighting an immense Sioux village with perhaps as many as 1,600 lodges, about ten miles away.

The site of the encampment was along the east rim of the Dakota Badlands. Aptly named, the landscape was cleft by sharp crevasses, dry washes, and jagged outcroppings. Realizing that the fractured ground was not conducive to cavalry, Sully devised a marvelously innovative tactic: he dismounted his cavalrymen and formed them into a massive hollow square, a mile and a quarter long on each side. Sheltered inside the square were his horses and artillery, giving the latter freedom to shift inside the moving formation to cover areas most under threat. As standard practice, one trooper out of every four moved in back of the line, holding mounts for his squad mates. Making effect use of his rifles, which out-ranged the Indians' weapons, Sully moved the enormous square toward the village.

Shots were first exchanged at long range before the Sioux began probing the sides of the formation, singly at the outset, then in small groups, and finally in larger contingents. All such threats were beaten back, helped by effective artillery fire that broke up the larger masses of warriors.

As the square pushed inexorably forward, a Sioux attempt to shatter the formation with an attack on the trailing edge was blown apart by an artillery shell that exploded in the midst of several on-rushing warriors. Charges followed against both the left and right sides of the square. Both were defeated with losses. On the right, Sully's men leaped into saddles and mounted a counter-charge. Supported by fire from a battery of howitzers, the tactic scattered the Yankton and Santee attackers. The cavalrymen chased and caught a band of fleeing warriors, piling into them with sabers and side arms. One trooper was killed in the melee.

It was late afternoon, nearly dark, when Sully reached the village. He broke off the attack but ringed the village with artillery and bombarded it through the night. Some warriors fought delaying actions, but most of the camp's inhabitants fled, leaving tepees and possessions behind.

The next day Sully ordered the destruction of the contents of the village. Tepees, buffalo meat, blankets and other possessions were burned. Weapons were destroyed and holes were punched in cooking pots and pans. Other utensils were damaged beyond repair. Perhaps as many as 3,000 dogs, used to pull travois as well as for food by the Sioux, were shot. Some contemporary reports suggest that before they could be stopped, early arriving Winnebagos, bitter enemies of the Sioux, killed an unknown number of adults and children who had been left behind.

The majority of the Sioux fled west from Killdeer Mountain deeper into the Badlands. Some remained behind, though, and for a few days harassed the column. The night after the battle two of Sully's pickets were killed and another wounded by a small party of raiders. The following night another was killed by friendly fire, likely induced by frayed nerves.

The battle and its immediate aftermath cost Sully five dead and ten wounded. Sully estimated Sioux casualties at 100-150 killed. The Indians acknowledged 31 dead.

Killdeer Mountain was a massive encounter waged over a landscape covering several miles. The engagement likely involved the largest number of combatants – 2,200 soldiers and an estimated 1,600 or more Indian warriors – of any battle in the American West. Perhaps because of the relatively small number of casualties and the fact that it was not decisive in the long-term, neither the battle itself nor Sully's exceptional tactics are well remembered.

Sully was subsequently joined on the march by the 800 soldiers he had earlier left to guard the civilian wagon train. With his command now bulked up to 3,000 soldiers, Sully pushed west through the Badlands' innumerable gullies and clay ridges. On August 7, his column was attacked deep in the Badlands near present-day Medora, North Dakota, by large numbers of Sioux. What later became known as the Battle of the Badlands was really a three-day running skirmish – a series of attacks, charges, counter-charges, and spasm exchanges – that left 13 troopers dead or wounded. Sully later estimated that the Sioux suffered 100 casualties or more, but most modern scholars believe the tribe's losses were considerably less.

The battle began in earnest in the early morning hours of August 7 when Sioux raiders attempted to capture or scatter the 7th Iowa Cavalry's horse herd. Soon after, one of the regiment's companies was ambushed. Later in the day, hundreds of warriors lined hilltops near Sully's main camp before being dispersed by artillery fire.

On August 8, terrain features forced the column into narrow defiles, stretching it out over three or four miles. At times during the day, an estimated 1,000 Sioux showered arrows on the cavalrymen, firing from bluffs at the front and along the sides of the constricted passages. Sully defended successfully, using cannon fire and cavalry charges to push back the attackers. Despite the opposition from warriors swirling around the flanks, the column moved about ten miles during the day.

August 9 began with a reprise of the previous days' activities. This time the action was focused near the front of the column where masses of Indians on high ground unsuccessfully attempted to disrupt Sully's advance. At mid-day, the column finally cleared the Badlands, breaking out into a broad, level plain. The open expanse gave Sully room to maneuver. Free to deploy his artillery and with his cavalry now unobstructed, Sully quickly dispersed the tribesmen. Soon after, scouts found the remainder of a large, recently occupied village. The Sioux had scattered in all directions. The battle was over.

On August 12, the column reached the Yellowstone River where two steamboats were waiting with 50 tons of supplies. Convinced that he had pushed most of the hostiles into Montana, Sully dispatched 900 troops – 600 infantry and dismounted cavalry and 300 cavalry – from Fort Rice to rescue a cavalry unit and members of an emigrant train trapped 160 miles away near present-day Marmarth, North Dakota. A Hunkpapa Sioux war party that included Sitting Bull, who was wounded in the fight, had attacked and surrounded the dug-in troopers. Sully's relief force arrived in time to break the siege, although not before casualties had been sustained by both sides.

In the latter stages of the conflict, Sully suggested an unusual peace plan. Believing that much of the Indian problem emanated from unscrupulous traders and agents, he advocated that the military take direct charge of Indian affairs. He believed the large annuity payments intended for the tribes' use provided an incentive for fraud and abuse by the agents and contractors who handled them. Treating the tribes fairly, he thought, would reduce many of the causes for dispute. These views were generally shared by Generals Pope and Sibley. Like those officers also, Sully was frustrated by the presence of British traders who crossed the border and supplied weapons, liquor, and other goods to the Plains tribes.

In 1865, Sully and his troops were slated to assist Colonel Patrick Connor on the ill-fated Powder River Expedition. However, public pressure associated with continuing threats against Dakota and Minnesota caused his force to be diverted from the campaign. Sully and a large force were sent instead toward the Devil's Lake region where few hostiles were seen and little was accomplished.

After the so-called Fetterman Massacre in December 1866, Sully chaired a commission that convened to investigate the circumstances surrounding the loss of Captain William J. Fetterman and his 80 men. As events transpired, that would become a familiar role for Sully. His experience as a military commander and his acquaintance with tribes across the central and northern Plains caused him to be called often for duty on special panels. Two years later, he served as commissioner during the talks which ended Red Cloud's War. In the following decade he chaired investigations related to the conflict with the Nez Perce as well.

Sully's Civil War service had earned him brevet promotions to brigadier general and major general in the Regular Army. After the war, he reverted to his permanent grade of lieutenant colonel. He served initially as commander of the 3rd U.S. Infantry. After a subsequent promotion to colonel he assumed command of the 21st U.S. Infantry.

Sully died in 1879 while in command of Fort Vancouver in Washington Territory. He was buried in Laurel Hill Cemetery in his hometown of Philadelphia.

Edwin V. Sumner

In western annals, Edwin V. Sumner's name surfaces less frequently than those of many of his colleagues. By the time frontier expansion began to take root in a major way in the mid-1850s, Sumner had already been a military officer for 35 years. His substantive service on the Plains was cut short by the Civil War, where he was the oldest officer on either side to command forces in combat. Sumner died in 1863, before the major uprisings that inflamed the Western and Southwestern regions of the United States for the next two decades – conflicts that drew much of the assembled strength of the U.S. Army and made, or destroyed, the reputations of officers who had been his contemporaries.

Nonetheless, although his time on the central Plains was fairly brief, Sumner's contributions, while not large in number, were significant in their consequences.

Sumner was "old school Army:" rugged, stern, austere, conscientious, and loyal – perhaps to a fault – to his superiors. He was renowned for his courage and honesty but not highly regarded as a tactician or as a leader of large forces in the field. He was known throughout the Army as "Bull" for his booming voice or, sometimes, "Bull head," after allegedly having had a bullet ricochet off his skull during the war with Mexico.

Sumner was born in Boston on January 30, 1797. As a young man in Troy, New York, he pursued a business career for a time before entering the Army in 1819. His 44 years of service encompassed the Black Hawk War, various Indian campaigns, the War with Mexico, and the Civil War.

When the United States Dragoons were created by an act of Congress in 1833, Sumner was one of the first officers assigned to the new organization. In 1838, he established the Cavalry School of Practice at Carlisle Barracks, Pennsylvania, and served as its commandant.

Sumner's first acquaintance with the Far West occurred in the early stages of the Mexican War when he accompanied Stephen W. Kearny's Army of the West on its epic trek through the Southwest. Sent later to serve under General Winfield Scott, Sumner fought at Cerro Gordo and was brevetted to colonel for his performance at Molina del Rey. Sumner was wounded once and brevetted twice for his service in Mexico.

By the end of the war, Sumner was commander of the 1st Dragoons. Soon assigned as commander of the Ninth Military District in the newly acquired territory of New Mexico, for a three and a half month period he was the acting territorial governor. He served as military governor of the territory for two years beginning in 1851 before being sent, in 1853, to Europe to study cavalry tactics in the European armies

Promoted to full colonel in March of 1855, he was posted to Fort Leavenworth, Kansas, as commander of the 1st U.S. Cavalry Regiment. The assignment would be his most prolonged and consequential period of duty on the Plains.

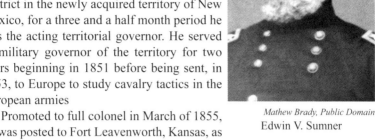

Mathew Brady, Public Domain
Edwin V. Sumner

The Plains Indians were not the only problem confronting Sumner during his time at Fort Leavenworth. The passage of the Kansas-Nebraska Act in 1854 turned Kansas into a cauldron. In the eastern part of the territory, pro-slavery "Bushwhackers" and free-soil "Jayhawkers" battled for supremacy. The doctrine of "popular sovereignty," ostensibly meant to allow citizens to choose free state or slave state status, brought legions of armed outsiders into the territory. Sumner and the 1st Cavalry were quickly caught up in attempting to keep peace between factions and arbitrating their often violent disputes. "Free soil towns" and "slave towns"– little more than armed camps – sprang up, sustained by the flood of belligerents pouring into "Bleeding Kansas." In May 1855, a pro-slavery band comprised mostly of Missourians attacked the free soil town of Lawrence, provoking the "Wakarusa War" (named after a nearby river). Sumner's intervention and the arrival of additional cavalry troops eventually stabilized the area.

During the Battle of Black Jack in the summer of 1856, free state forces under John Brown and Samuel Shore captured a pro-slavery commander named Henry C. Pate and several of his men. Sumner was ordered by Governor Wilson Shannon to secure the release of the hostages and restore peace to the region around Baldwin City. Sumner, with elements of the 1st Cavalry, went to the site in present-day Douglas County to meet with the belligerents. A brief standoff between cavalry troopers and John Brown's irregulars preceded a prolonged period of negotiations. After extended discussions, Sumner secured the freedom of the prisoners and for a time reestablished order in a region seething with unrest.

The period of calm did not last long. On July 4, the governor ordered

Sumner to disperse the free state legislators meeting at the time in Topeka. Both Governor Shannon and Sumner believed they were adhering to the somewhat fuzzy intentions of President Franklin Pierce and Secretary of War Jefferson Davis. Both men believed that a civil war might erupt in Kansas if the legislature was allowed to meet. Claiming it to be the most painful duty he ever had to perform, Sumner nonetheless obeyed orders. When local authorities were unable to take effective action, as a last resort Sumner, with a show of force by the 1st Cavalry, induced the free staters to disband. For the next few months an uneasy peace prevailed in the eastern portion of Kansas.

The same was not true in western Kansas and farther north in Nebraska Territory, where Sioux and Northern Cheyennes were increasingly restless. In 1857, Sumner led dragoons from Fort Leavenworth on a wide-ranging scout through the Republican River Valley all the way to Fort Kearny in mid-Nebraska. The region was understood to be a bastion of the Plains Indians. In the years ahead, the tribes would bitterly contest Army and settler movements into the area. Sumner's contingent included names that would soon appear in the nation's headlines. Future Union generals James Sedgwick and Samuel Sturgis were members of the reconnaissance party as was a promising but difficult to handle young officer named J. E. B. Stuart.

Sumner's scout foreshadowed events to come. Samuel Sturgis's reconnaissance in 1860 brought the first significant clashes. After the Civil War ended, three major campaigns over successive years – 1867 (Custer), 1868 (Carr), and 1869 (Carr) – eventually cleared the valley of Cheyenne Dog Soldiers.

Sumner was one of the first commanders on the Plains to experiment with the use of Native scouts, using a small cadre of Pawnees during the expedition. The outcome was less than positive, however, and it would be left to Frank North a few years later to fully develop and exploit the Pawnees' abilities.

In 1858, Sumner assumed command of the Department of the West with headquarters in St. Louis. When Lincoln was elected president, Sumner was one of the officers who escorted him to Washington, D.C. After Fort Sumter, Lincoln sent Sumner west to take command of the Pacific Coast region after his predecessor, Albert Sidney Johnston, resigned to accept a generalship in the Confederate Army. Sumner's efforts over the next several months are sometimes credited with helping keep California in the Union in the face of considerable rebel sentiment, particularly in the Los Angeles area. He was promoted to brigadier general, U.S. Volunteers, in March, 1861.

Sumner was called back east in the fall of 1861 to take command first of a division, and soon after, a corps in the Army of the Potomac. Sumner trained II Corps very hard, promising its soldiers that he would ratchet down the intensity when they were better prepared for combat. He led the corps through the Peninsula Campaign and was wounded during the Seven Days Battle and again at Antietam. He was promoted to major general of volunteers in July 1862 and later brevetted to major general in the Regular Army for his actions at Fair Oaks in May 1862.

When Ambrose Burnside succeeded George B. McClellan as commander of the Army of the Potomac, he grouped corps into "grand divisions" and appointed Sumner to command the Right Grand Division on the Army's flank. Sumner led that force during the bloody, failed attack on Fredericksburg in December 1862.

When Joseph Hooker subsequently replaced Burnside, Sumner, tired of the infighting among his general officer colleagues, asked to be relieved of his command. Reassigned as commander of the Department of the Pacific, he took leave in Syracuse, New York, before traveling on to his new post. He died of a heart attack on March 21, 1863, while at this home in Syracuse. He was buried in Oakwood Cemetery in that city.

Alfred H. Terry

L ike his contemporary Winfield Scott Hancock, Alfred Terry is known
far more for his Civil War exploits than for his accomplishments
on the western frontier. In the latter stages of the Civil War, Terry
led the Army component of the combined land-sea operation that captured
Fort Fisher, the bastion that guarded Wilmington, North Carolina, the last
remaining rebel port on the Atlantic seaboard. With an invasion force of
9,600 men supported by Admiral David D. Porter's 56-ship armada, Terry's
victory at Fort Fisher – the so-called "Gibralter of the Confederacy" – led to
the rapid capture of Wilmington, completing the blockade of the Confederate
States.

Although he commanded departments in the West for a combined total
of 17 years, Terry seldom led forces in the field. The one notable exception
occurred in 1876, when a combination of circumstances resulted in his being
named to lead a major campaign, though his is not the name most associated
with it. Indeed, history has relegated Alfred Terry to a footnote status. He
was, in fact, the overall commander of the expedition that led to the Little
Bighorn. George Armstrong Custer was his principal, difficult, subordinate.

Terry was born in 1827 in Hartford, Connecticut, and grew up in New
Haven. A lawyer by training, much of his professional life prior to the Civil
War was spent as clerk of state courts.

At 6 feet 2 inches, Terry was a tall, gaunt man with a long face, bushy
beard and kind disposition. In later years, he was principally known for
his administrative skills. Widely read, Terry had a long-standing interest in
military history and tactics. At the outset of the war, he raised a regiment of
volunteers and led it through early clashes. In April 1862, he was appointed
brigadier general of volunteers. Given command of a division, he commanded
the unit through a series of engagements in the East including the siege of
Charleston; Morris Island, South Carolina, and the associated capture of Fort
Wagner in September 1863.

In 1864, Terry's division was sent north to Virginia to join the Army of
the James, led at the time by General Benjamin Butler. Terry and his men
were involved in numerous engagements around Richmond, including the

Mathew Brady, Public Domain
Alfred H. Terry

Bermuda Hundred Campaign. During the siege of Petersburg, the division saw action at the Battle of New Market.

Terry's Civil War reputation derives mostly from his masterful leadership of the combined arms offensive that captured Fort Fisher, the portal to Wilmington, North Carolina, the South's last remaining seaport. After David Farragut's triumph at Mobile Bay, Wilmington became the Confederacy's blockade-running port and, indeed, its only major port available to commerce from the outside world. Home to vital railroads and shipyards, the city was sheltered by a peninsula and surrounded by fortifications. Fort Fisher anchored the area's formidable defenses. Over four years of war, Confederate commanders had built the place into a citadel protected by minefields and layers of interlocking gun emplacements.

In December 1864, General Grant assigned General Benjamin Butler to command the Army portion of the land-sea operation intended to take Fort Fisher or place it under siege. Butler failed miserably. Defeated in the attempt to take the bastion, he then neglected to besiege it as instructed. Grant, irate, relieved him of command and directed Terry to make a second attempt.

Working successfully with Admiral Porter, Terry's men stormed ashore on January 15, 1865. In some of the fiercest hand-to-hand fighting of the war, Terry sent one wing against the fort while another blocked Confederate reinforcements from reaching it. Terry's victory at Fort Fisher opened the way to Wilmington, which fell on February 22. The loss deprived Lee of his army's most valuable supply line. With Terry's 9,000 men and Porter's fleet, the Fort Fisher expedition was the largest combined Army-Navy operation of the Civil War.

Terry was regarded as one of the most capable officers with no previous military experience to emerge from the war. He was one of the few volunteer officers promoted to brigadier general during the conflict. He would also be one of the few to remain in the Army when the war ended.

Sent west after Lee's surrender, in 1867, as commander of the Department of Dakota, Terry foresaw the benefits of constructing a chain of forts stretching across Minnesota to the Sun River in Montana. The following year he helped negotiate the Treaty of Fort Laramie that ended Red Cloud's War and ceded the Black Hills and most of the western portion of present-day South Dakota to the Sioux tribe. In the years ahead, the Army would make use of Terry's legal background, employing him often in similar roles.

Terry opposed the incursions of miners and settlers into the prohibited region, arguing with Sherman that once the intruders had established footholds, too often they subsequently demanded protection from the military – an appeal inevitably granted in response to the resulting public outcry.

Unsettled conditions marked much of Terry's tenure in the department. Fed by antagonisms over events in the Black Hills, the tribes' restlessness kept tensions high. Soon after taking command, Terry provided military escorts for parties surveying the Yellowstone area and regions along the international boundary with Canada. The next year, 1873, brought the 7th Cavalry and its flamboyant field commander, George Armstrong Custer, into Dakota Territory to garrison Fort Abraham Lincoln and other posts along the Missouri River.

In 1874, Terry, bowing to the wishes of his superiors – the Grant Administration had decided to allow miners into the treaty grounds – directed Custer to lead a major expedition into the Black Hills. The Army's presence there was a technical violation of the Laramie Treaty that Terry had helped negotiate six years earlier. Terry may have believed that survey parties were permissible under the treaty, but strongly objected to land claims on the territory.

The discovery of gold brought increasing numbers of miners to the area along with added pressure from commercial interests to open the region to settlement. Eventually, the small frontier army was unable – and increasingly less willing – to turn away the flood of prospectors and settlers that swept into *Paha Sapa*, the Lakota's sacred ground.

In 1875, having given up the futile attempt to bar intrusions into the hills, the government made an effort to buy the region from the Sioux. Terry served as a member of the Allison Committee during its unsuccessful attempt to purchase the Black Hills area. Continued incursions and the Army's presence in *Paha Sapa* inflamed the tribes. Eventually, fed by growing outrage, the Great Sioux War of 1876 erupted early in the year.

Aided by their Northern Cheyenne and Arapaho allies the Sioux nation – the largest and most warlike tribe on the Plains – waged war across an enormous landscape that covered much of the north central region of the United States. From clashes in northern Montana to the Battle of the Blowout in north central Nebraska, the struggle that began in early 1876 and ended 19 months later with the death of Crazy Horse at Fort Robinson was the climactic phase of the long, bitter conflict with the Plains Indians.

As violence exploded across the frontier, General Philip Sheridan, commander of the Military Division of the Missouri, put in motion a grand strategy intended to crush the Plains tribes once and for all. As conceived by Sheridan, three columns moving from different directions would come together in the Yellowstone-Powder River area where large numbers of "non-treaty Sioux" and other bands that had left reservations were believed to be massing. Caught inside the closing pincers, the hostiles would either be destroyed or hammered into submission.

As events began to play out, the 1,100-man column led by General George Crook was fought to a standstill at Rosebud Creek on July 17, 1876. Crook temporarily returned to Fort Fetterman to replenish, taking his unit away from the prospective rendezvous. Meanwhile, Colonel John Gibbon with a mixed force of 440 cavalry and infantry, moved from Fort Ellis, Montana, east along the Yellowstone River. Eventually, in early June, Gibbon linked up with Alfred Terry's column which had begun its westward march from Fort Abraham Lincoln in Dakota Territory on May 17.

Terry's 1,200-man column included 150 wagons, three infantry companies and an artillery detachment with four guns. The main striking power came from 12 companies of the 7th Cavalry led by Custer.

Custer owed his presence on the expedition in part to Alfred Terry. A few months before, Custer's testimony to a Congressional Committee investigating graft on Army posts in Dakota Territory had alienated the Grant Administration. As plans for the campaign were being formulated, Grant initially prohibited Custer's participation in it. Citing the need for Custer's Indian-fighting experience to enhance the expedition's prospects for success, Terry, along with Generals Sherman and Sheridan, urged Grant to reconsider. He eventually did so but only under the stipulation that Custer would not have a leadership role.

For reasons not entirely clear, Terry was named to lead the Dakota column. The 7th's nominal commander, Colonel Samuel Sturgis, was assigned at the time to recruiting duty. It is possible that these responsibilities persuaded the Army hierarchy to look elsewhere for a field commander. Additionally, they may have believed that given Sturgis's long absence from the frontier, there would not be sufficient time for him to adequately prepare for the campaign. Terry suggested the names of other colonels as prospective commanders, but Sheridan eventually decided that Terry himself should take the lead.

Although Terry had intervened to help assure that Custer was part of the campaign, their relationship on the march was not altogether a comfortable one. Custer, as was almost always the case, chafed at this subordinate role, He told one contemporary that he would "swing free of Terry" when the occasion allowed. On the trail, he drew Terry's ire by wide-ranging excursions away from the main column.

When Terry met Gibbon on the Yellowstone in early June, he adjusted his plans based on information regarding a large Indian encampment Gibbon's scouts had sighted on May 26. The immense village was at the time on Rosebud Creek, a bit farther west than anticipated.

To locate the hostile camp more precisely, Terry dispatched Major Marcus Reno on a reconnaissance in force. Reno found a large trail, followed it for a time, and identified the likely location of the village in the valley of the Little Bighorn.

Terry's choice of Reno to lead the reconnaissance was probably a signal of his displeasure with Custer's antics during the march. Custer was a far more experienced frontier officer than Reno; Terry's decision may have been a reminder to Custer about who was really in charge.

Although Reno's scout had not gone without misadventures along the way, information from it gave the now combined columns of Terry and Gibbon a clearer view of the placement of the village. Fearing the Natives would scatter, Terry reacted quickly outlining his intentions to Gibbon and Custer in a June 21 meeting aboard the steamer *Far West.*

Terry's plan called for Custer to leave the following day, taking the entire 7th Cavalry south along Rosebud Creek. Custer was to follow that stream and assess the large Indian trail that Reno had found a few days earlier. Conditions permitting, Custer was to continue past that point, moving farther south towards the Tongue River headwaters as a final assurance that the Indians had not fled in that direction. Having made that determination, Custer and the 7th were then to turn west toward the Little Bighorn. The extra time on the Rosebud would allow Gibbon to move along the Yellowstone, cross over to the Bighorn and reach the north end of the valley of the Little Bighorn where it was expected to arrive in the morning hours of June 26. Once in position, Gibbon's command – four companies of cavalry, five of infantry, and an artillery detachment – would form a blocking force. Custer and the 7th Cavalry would drive the hostiles into Gibbon's barrier, smashing them in between.

Terry directed Custer to move past the intersection of the trail Reno had found, thus delaying sufficiently for Gibbon's column to move into position. Custer chose not to do that, turning instead west toward the Little Bighorn at the junction of the Indian trail. Critics have sometimes faulted Terry for his orders – which allowed Custer discretion if he felt an attack was justified by circumstances. Those who question the orders argue that Terry, a lawyer by training, crafted his words in a skillful way that would defer potential blame whatever happened; or, alternately, that they were written with the recognition that Custer would do as he pleased regardless of conditions. Those more sympathetic to Terry believe Custer's nature was such that whatever the directions on paper, he would attempt to interpret them in a way that would take the 7th Cavalry unilaterally into a fight. His closing words to Gibbon (about not waiting for Gibbon's arrival before launching an attack) would seem to support that view, as does another consideration. Custer was given the veteran frontiersman George Henderson to act as liaison between his and Gibbon's columns. Terry's intention was for Custer to send Henderson to Gibbon to keep him advised when Custer turned west or when contact with hostiles was foreseen. Custer never released Henderson to go to Gibbon. By not sending him when, contrary to instructions, the 7th turned west on Reno's trail, Custer seems to have made a clear choice to fight the Indians alone. Even the surviving members of the regiment recognized that when the column turned west early and Henderson remained with it, the die was cast: Custer was determined that the 7th Cavalry – alone – would fight the battle.

As Custer left, Terry, perhaps mindful of Custer's actions at Washita eight years prior, cautioned him not to abandon his wounded. That Terry was aware of Custer's preference for unsupervised action and knowledgeable of his recent personal trials – i.e., his issues with the Grant Administration – is certain. Terry advised a subordinate that he would keep Custer on a loose rein so he would have a chance to redeem himself in the eyes of the public. Then too, Terry recognized that Custer was the more experienced Indian fighter; indeed, he was one the Army's veteran commanders of combat with the Plains tribes. For all of these reasons, Terry seemed willing to give Custer considerable latitude. Custer, by most accounts, would likely have taken it anyway.

Atrocious terrain kept the Terry-Gibbon column from reaching the Little Bighorn as planned on the morning of June 26. Instead, they reached the valley later in the day, traveled part way through it and camped for the night with lines shaped for defense in a hollow square. By then, Custer and more than 200 of his men had already been dead, lying on a nearby hillside, for more than a day.

On the way to the Little Bighorn, advance scouts had been puzzled to see blue-shirted riders in the distance. Initially assumed to be members of Custer's command, they quickly scattered after being identified as Lakota warriors wearing cavalrymen's jackets. On the morning of the 27th, the column reached the abandoned village stretched three or more miles along the valley floor. Indian corpses and cavalry accoutrements were found in the debris. Soon after, Lieutenant Nolan Bradley, chief of Gibbon's scouts, reported finding numerous remains along the bluffs east of the river. Terry was shaken by the news and was weeping openly when the column made contact with Reno and Benteen, holding out on what is now called Reno Hill at the southeast end of the battlefield.

Terry's command remained in camp on the Yellowstone until the end of the month before moving to the mouth of Rosebud Creek. On August 8, now replenished, they began moving up the Rosebud Valley. Two days later they made contact with Crook's force marching towards them from Fort Fetterman. For a brief time, with Terry in overall command as the senior officer, the two columns moved in concert, a mass assemblage of cavalry and infantry. Too large to be effective, the units soon split. The separation was likely welcomed by both Terry and Crook whose relationship was known to be uncomfortable.

At the end of the month, Crook began operations in present-day South Dakota. After experiencing severe hardships during the march, his force prevailed at the Battle of Slim Buttes on September 9-10.

Terry, meanwhile, scouted with his command north and south of the Yellowstone before ordering his units back to their posts on September 5. Terry accompanied the shattered remnants of the 7th Cavalry back to Fort Abraham Lincoln. After a brief stop there, he continued on to his headquarters in St. Paul, Minnesota. In the days ahead, forces dispatched by Terry and Sheridan under the command of George Crook, Nelson Miles, and Ranald Mackenzie defeated the Sioux and their allies in a series of encounters throughout Montana, Wyoming, and Dakota. When Crazy Horse surrendered at Fort Robinson on May 6, 1877, the Great Sioux War was effectively ended. Though later critical of Custer's actions in private correspondence, Terry was magnanimous in his public comments declining to cast blame on him or the 7th Cavalry.

In 1877, Terry, responsible for military affairs in the Montana region, provided forces to assist in the Nez Perce War. At the request of General O. O. Howard, who had pursued the Nez Perce all the way from the Pacific Coast, Terry sent units under John Gibbon from Fort Shaw and Nelson Miles from Fort Keogh to intercept the Nez Perce as they attempted to reach sanctuary in Canada. Gibbon fought the Nez Perce at Big Hole River on August 9. Miles, joined in the fighting by Howard, waged the siege that concluded the war at Bear Paw Mountain on September 30 – October 5.

Later in October, Terry was sent to Canada to negotiate with Sitting Bull, who with a group of followers had crossed the border, fleeing relentless pursuit by Nelson Miles. Sitting Bull refused at the time to return. When in 1881 he decided to come back and live on a reservation, it was Alfred Terry to whom he surrendered.

On March 3, 1886, Terry was promoted to major general in the Regular Army and appointed commander of the Department of Missouri. He retired from the Army in April 1888, disabled after a long illness. Terry died at his home in New Haven, Connecticut, on December 16, 1890. He was buried in Grove Street Cemetery in New Haven.

George Wright

eorge Wright was a veteran of the "Old Army." An 1822 graduate of West Point, by the time the Mexican War began he already had 24 years of military service. At the outset of the Civil War, he had been in uniform 37 years. Before each of those wars, he had fought Indians; Seminoles in Florida in the 1840s and Yakima (or Yakama), Coeur d'Alene, Palouse, Spokane, and other Pacific Coast tribes in the mid- to late-1850s.

Wright was a tough, decisive commander. His harsh methods succeeded in permanently pacifying the region but as Wright himself acknowledged, " … our route has been marked by slaughter and devastation."

Wright was a Vermonter, born at Norwich on October 22, 1803. Frank, genial, dignified in manner, he would earn a reputation for intelligence and reliability. After graduating from West Point at age 21, he served initially with the 3rd U.S. Infantry in Wisconsin and Maine, parts of which were still relatively raw and untamed at the time. At Jefferson Barracks in St. Louis, Wright was sent as a young officer 150 miles into Indian country to gauge the climate of the Pawnee tribe. He returned without incident and submitted an insightful report on Pawnee grievances. In 1838, Wright transferred to the 8th Infantry and spent several years on the Canadian border before leaving for duty in the Seminole War where he was brevetted to major.

Promotions to major and lieutenant colonel in the Regular Army followed in the years after the war. In 1852, Wright was assigned to Pacific Division headquarters and placed in command of the Northern California District. For the next two and a half years he maintained the fragile peace with general success. Although criticized at times in the press for too often siding with the tribes' viewpoint, he was highly respected by whites and Natives.

In 1855, Wright was promoted to colonel and assigned to command the 9th Infantry. The regiment was stationed in Virginia when alerted for duty in Washington Territory. Wright travelled east to join the unit and moved with them by steamboat to Panama. The 9th crossed the isthmus by train and linked up on the Pacific side with two ships that carried them to their final destination at Fort Vancouver where they disembarked on January 21-22, 1856. Wright's movement of the 700-man unit was masterfully done,

handled in the words of one of his soldiers "without worry, doubt, or confusion."

As in California, Wright's expressed views were initially sympathetic to the plight of the Native tribes. To the chagrin of territorial authorities, he protested that the militia units were little more than armed gangs that often preyed upon peaceable tribes. He lamented the Natives' susceptibility to white diseases. It is uncertain whether Wright's later severe measures against the tribes represented a change of heart on his part or whether in his mind they were necessary as dictated by circumstances.

Public Domain
George Wright

Wright arrived at a time of general disquiet. By mid-decade two Rogue River Wars had already been fought and conditions remained unsettled. As had been the case in California, Wright found himself caught in the middle of an organizational dispute. Washington Territorial Governor Isaac Stevens took a hard line toward the tribes, seeking to place them on reservations, thereby freeing their land for settlement and access to the area's resources. Though Governor Stevens negotiated several treaties, the tribes by and large regarded them as unfair, depriving them of considerable parts of their historic homelands. In contrast to Stevens' position, Wright's immediate military superior, General John Wool, Commander of the Department of the Pacific, advocated a more benign approach, less focused on placing the tribes on reservations.

As tensions mounted, March 26 brought news of an Indian attack on Fort Cascades, built near Cascades Rapids on the Columbia River. The attack killed 14 civilians and three soldiers. Twelve others were wounded. Wright took 250 men, gathered additional troops along the way, and managed to clear the area of attacking bands of Yakimas, Klickitats, and Cascades. Leaders of the attacks were identified and caught. In a pattern that he would continue to employ, nine of the alleged perpetrators were hanged and few more were imprisoned.

Wool, alarmed at the uprising and the depredations that continued, sent Wright directly into the Yakima homeland. Leaving on June 17, Wright took a force of 450 men and moved against the tribe whose warriors were believed to be preparing for battle. An early attempt to negotiate a truce in return for the Yakima's promise to return stolen goods was broken off by the Indians.

As Wright continued to move his force toward the Yakima villages, he learned that most of the Indians were busy fishing – attempting to lay in a supply of salmon before leaving the area. Wright received assurances that when the salmon run was over, the Indians would comply with his orders. To insure compliance, Wright took a chief and his family hostage. As events turned out, most of the band's men, women, and children, along with their livestock, followed Wright back to Fort Naches. Some stolen horses and cattle were returned as well.

Though initially conceived as a reprisal expedition, in the end Wright had managed a peaceful resolution. His troopers had marched 300 miles into areas previously uncharted by white men. Fort Naches, where the tribesmen were taken, would soon be abandoned. Wright subsequently ordered the construction of a new post – Fort Simcoe – in Kittitas Valley.

In the meantime, another episode with a considerable backstory influenced events in the region. When Governor Stevens attempted to travel to Fort Walla Walla to meet with several chiefs outraged by multiple grievances including the attempted killings of Indian women and children by undisciplined volunteer militia units, General Wright refused to provide Stevens with a military escort. Wright's refusal was perhaps indicative of the bitter personal relationship between the two men. When Stevens' party was attacked in route, Wright sent Colonel Edward Steptoe to his rescue.

One of the alleged perpetrators of the attack on Stevens was an Indian leader named Leschi, who was either captured or gave himself up. Government authorities sentenced Leschi to be hanged. Wright, who perhaps had promised the chief that he would assure his personal safety, argued forcefully against the execution, expressing his strong opposition in a letter to his superiors. Despite Wright's intervention, Leschi was eventually hanged. Wright's open advocacy may have won him momentary respect from some of the tribal leaders.

In May, Colonel Steptoe reentered Wright's story. Sent by General Wool to investigate the killing of two settlers and thefts of horses and mules near Colville, Steptoe left Fort Walla Walla on May 6, 1858, with a modest force of 158 soldiers. On May 17 the column was attacked by an overwhelming mass of Indians, perhaps a thousand or more warriors from several comingled groups. Seeing the blocking force, Steptoe had time to avoid battle and begin a measured retreat. Not content with turning the soldiers around, the Indians attacked heavily along Steptoe's route of march. The troopers found momentary refuge on a hillock; surrounded and under fire they fought off repeated assaults. Nearly out of ammunition, they managed to slip through the tightening ring under cover of darkness and make a successful dash to safety, perhaps helped along the way by friendly Nez Perce. Called the Battle of Tohotominne (fought near present-day Rosalia, Washington), the battle cost the lives of five soldiers, one civilian and two Nez Perce scouts. The losses were fairly substantial given the standards of the time. Authorities, including President James Buchanan, were outraged. General Wool resigned his position and was replaced by General Newman S. Clarke.

Two weeks later Wright wrote to his new commander suggesting that a sizable body of soldiers launched at the warrior's heartland might chasten the tribe sufficiently to cause them the cease their struggle. Clarke responded immediately to Wright's note, essentially giving him free rein, telling him to attack the Indians wherever he found them, punish them severely and remain in the field until success was complete.

It took Wright two months to assemble and organize the expedition to his satisfaction. On August 28, 1858, Wright moved into generally uncharted territory with a force of about 680 men – 190 cavalry, 450 infantry, a 90-man rifle unit, 100 civilian support personnel and 33 friendly Nez Perce scouts (all dressed in blue uniforms to prevent friendly fire incidents in the heat of battle). More than 700 horses and mules completed the caravan which Wright pushed steadily into the steep, dry hills of eastern Washington. Troops and animals struggled through intense heat and dust occasionally seasoned by violent thunderstorms.

Within two or three days, large groups of Indians began shadowing the column, at times setting the native grass on fire in an attempt to stampede the pack train. On the night of August 31, about 15 miles southwest of present-day Spokane, Wright made camp for the night. As the troops settled in, pickets noticed warriors assembled on elevated ground about two miles away. Separated from Wright's camp by one large lake and three small ones, the hostiles' numbers grew larger with each passing hour. Wright's Nez Perce scouts told him that the original large body of Palouses had been reinforced by Spokanes, Coeur d'Alenes, and perhaps other bands as well.

At about 9:30 the next morning, September 1, Wright moved against the still-growing war party, leaving only a few troops and the howitzer company behind to protect the pack train. As the troopers approached the heights, Wright sent his cavalry sweeping around the north and east sides of the hill while he moved straight from the west with his main force. Eager to get to the top of the hill so he could see the full panorama and better command the battle, Wright drove his soldiers up the steep slope. Pushed by Wright's on-rushing troopers, the Indians fell back, descending the reverse flank of the hill before taking cover in thick timber and scrambled rocks near the bottom.

Firing from positions inside stands of pine trees near the lake and sheltered in ravines and gullies that cross-crossed the landscape, the Indians struggled to hold back their blue-clad attackers. Slowed only momentarily, Wright dispatched a skirmish line. Accurate fire from the advancing troopers scattered the Indian defenders who broke and ran in confusion. As the Indians raced away, Wright sent his cavalry charging after them, cutting down additional large numbers. In a fight that lasted for about four hours,

Indian losses were estimated at 50-100 with perhaps the same number of horses killed as well.

Quickly named the Battle of Four Lakes, the struggle was a debacle for the assembled tribes who fled northeast into a pine forest about four miles away. Later conjecture was that the tribes may have underestimated the range and lethality of the troopers' weapons. Wright's infantry used new Springfield .58 rifled muskets, firing minie balls for the first or one of the first times in American warfare. His cavalry was armed with Sharps carbines. Both weapons out-ranged the Indians' smooth bore muskets and bows and arrows.

Four days later, on September 5, Wright moved north toward the Spokane River. Within an hour groups of Indians, increasing in number as the day progressed, began moving parallel to the pack train. Eventually perhaps as many as 500 warriors, more than had faced Wright at Four Lakes, threatened the column. Once again the Indians set fire to the prairie grass in an attempt to spook the pack train. In heavy smoke that obscured vision, Wright ordered a charge. Surprised by the wall of troopers that seemed to burst out of the smoke and flames, the Indians broke and ran, stopping periodically to make brief stands amidst the chaos of a running battle. When the Indians clustered for defense or prepared for a counterattack, Wright made effective use of his howitzers, breaking up the groups, killing several, and wounding a war chief.

In spurts and rushes, attempted stands, charges and counter-charges, the battle flowed for 14 miles and lasted much of the day. Sharp firing continued until about 5 o'clock in the afternoon. In the aftermath, Wright's column moved on to the Spokane River and camped alongside it for the night. Called the Battle of Spokane Plains, the fight inflicted significant numbers of casualties on the tribes. As at Four Lakes, Wright's column again sustained no losses. The battle site became the location of the future Fort George Wright.

Believing that he had demonstrated the superiority of his force, Wright now launched a course intended to coerce the tribes into permanent submission. On September 7, he met with a prominent Spokane chief and told him that the tribes must submit to government authority. Wright admonished the chief with words to the effect that resistance is futile and if attempted "war will be made on you this year and next, until your nations shall be exterminated." He then ordered the chief to spread the word to other tribes in the region.

On the same day, nine Indians came in to parley. Soldiers identified one warrior suspected of being involved in killing civilians near Colville. Wright ordered him to be hanged – on the spot, immediately. Another brave who was recognized by troopers as having been a leader during the two battles over the past week was taken into custody.

The day was not yet over. As Wright moved his force upriver toward the present border with Idaho, his soldiers set fire to lodges and grain storehouses in Indian encampments discovered along the way. Estimates vary, but perhaps as many as 900 Indian ponies, most belonging to the Palouse tribe, were captured during the march. Wright ordered them shot. Probably about 650 were eventually killed after Wright's soldiers built a corral to contain them. The process consumed much of two days as Indians watched from a distance. To further reinforce his intended lesson, Wright ordered the carcasses stacked and left to rot. Troopers named the location – near present-day Aturdee, east of Spokane – "Horse Slaughter Camp."

Wright's policy was clearly intended to intimidate the tribes into submission. On September 15, he wrote to the department commander, advising General Clarke that 900 horses and cattle had been killed or captured for the soldiers' use. He reported large caches of wheat, camas roots, vegetables, and dried berries destroyed. Wright believed, he reported to Clarke, that he had "struck a blow from which the Natives could not recover."

His assessment, as it turned out, was correct. The cumulative effect on the Native economy was devastating. Wright had correctly gauged the shock effect on the region's tribes.

A few days later, on September 15, Wright pushed east 40 miles toward a small mission at Cataldo in northern Idaho, where he rendezvoused with Coeur d'Alene tribesmen. To the surprise and relief of the local tribe, on September 17 an agreement – rather lenient for its time – was quickly reached. The tribe agreed to return stolen property and turn over the tribesmen who had attacked Steptoe. Settlers and white travelers were to be given safe passage across tribal territory. Wright took one chief and four other prominent tribesmen and their families to serve as hostages and help assure that the provisions of the pact were adhered to. If no violations occurred, the hostages would be set free in a year. As the conclave continued, Wright urged his soldiers to exercise restraint toward the assembled warriors and their family groups. Before the gathering broke up, there was considerable trading of clothing, blankets, and other military items in return for moccasins, bows and arrows, and other Native gear.

On September 22, Wright met with a large assemblage of Indian leaders at a location along Latah Creek, about 25 miles south of Spokane. Over the next day or two, 107 chiefs from several tribal groups agreed to essentially the same provisions hammered out with the Coeur d'Alenes a few days before.

On the morning of the 24th, while Wright's forces were still bivouacked at Latah Creek, Qunchan, a fearsome warrior known to have led attacks on settlers showed up looking for his father who Wright had arrested the day before. After a brief struggle Qunchan was captured and hanged within a half hour of his arrival.

Later that day nine additional braves were put in irons. Six were identified as participants in the attack on Steptoe and were promptly hanged as well. The site of the executions was rather quickly named "Hangman Creek." Wright left the area on September 26, taking hostages with him on the way back to Fort Walla Walla. Collecting additional Palouse prisoners along the way, he hanged at least four more suspected of attacks and killings. Clearly intended to intimidate, the executions took place in front of Indian onlookers. Wright's coercion was successful; the Palouses caused no more trouble.

After 60 days on the march, the column arrived back at Fort Walla Walla on October 5, accompanied by 33 hostages. Wright apparently lost only two men during the eventful expedition – both died of eating hemlock along the trail.

On October 9, Wright held a council with Walla Walla Indian leaders. During the meeting he asked the assembled chiefs if any had participated in attacks on soldiers or miners. About 35 in the large gathering stood up. Wright collected four, perhaps in his judgment the most severe offenders, and ordered them hanged.

Wright's carefully planned campaign, executed with brutal precision, pacified the region. Broken and battered, deprived of land, animals, and food supplies, the Indians acquiesced to Wright's terms rather than face continued depredation or annihilation. Wright had chosen to fight terror with terror and in this instance the stratagem worked.

While acknowledging his iron-handedness, Wright justified his actions commenting that "(I have) treated the Indians severely, but they deserved it all. They will remember it." During the remainder of his tenure there were no further Indian uprisings on the Columbia Plateau.

While controversial, Wright's strategy in the Pacific Northwest resulted in (from the government's viewpoint) one of the most successful Indian campaigns waged in the West. The shock of overwhelming firepower combined with the intimidation from widespread hangings of suspects defeated the tribes psychologically as well as physically. Wright's apparent intent was to make war horrific, brutal, and *short* – and perhaps save lives on both sides over the long run.

Interestingly, one of the junior officers accompanying Wright on his expedition was a young lieutenant named Philip H. Sheridan. If indeed those were the lessons intended by Wright, his protégé would apply them in full measure in the years to come.

Sheridan was only one of the exceptionally able group of officers Wright surrounded himself with on the campaign. Sixteen of those who rode with him would later become general officers (11 Union, five Confederate) during the Civil War.

Wright was commander of the Department of Oregon when the Civil War began. After serving briefly as commander of the Department of Southern

California, in October 1861 he was promoted to brigadier general of volunteers. Although his clear preference was to return to the East Coast and lead Union forces fighting there, Army authorities kept him in the West where his success in pacifying Indians, safeguarding the region from Confederate sympathizers, and sending trained troops to the larger conflict was readily acknowledged. By 1862, he had assembled a force of 6,000 men – the largest troop contingent yet seen in the Far West.

In June 1864, Wright became commander of the District of California. In 1865, as part of an extensive post-war restructuring, the Army created a new Department of the Columbia encompassing Washington and Idaho Territories and the state of Oregon. On July 30, Wright was on his way to Fort Vancouver when his ship, the steamer *Brother Jonathan*, was wrecked at sea off the coast of southern Oregon. Wright, his wife, and others were lost. His body was recovered six weeks later. He was buried at Sacramento Historic Cemetery.

Closing thoughts

A marvelous aspect of the battlefields of the American West is that most of them remain remarkably unspoiled. Because of their locations in sparsely settled areas distant from urban centers, nearly all of them have escaped the sprawl and commercial development that threaten historic sites elsewhere in the nation. The military leaders who led forces across those grounds, and the war chiefs who opposed them, would recognize them still.

Indeed, the most famous of all battlefields in the West, the Little Bighorn, remains almost as it was on that sultry June day in 1876. Rifle pits dug by embattled troopers are still visible on Reno Hill. Along the banks where the immense Native village once stood, the Little Bighorn River rolls unvexed and unaltered across the Montana Plains.

In addition to considerations of distance and isolation, far-sighted federal and state legislation, often complemented by local programs, have successfully shielded most of the West's major battlegrounds from incursion. Among scores of possible examples, in California the Lava Beds National Monument conserves the terrain so ably defended by Captain Jack's Modoc warriors. In Colorado, the Sand Creek National Monument marks the location of the horrific event that precipitated so much bloodshed. In Oklahoma, the Washita Battlefield National Historic Site protects the grounds where Custer's 7th Cavalry surprised Black Kettle's sleeping village. In Texas, Ranald Mackenzie and his cavalrymen would find Palo Duro Canyon, a National Historic Site, as recognizable as when they eased their way down its steep walls to strike the villages scattered along the canyon floor. The list goes on: Montana has a plethora of national and state monuments and no western state is without plaques or roadside markers commemorating this unique period in our nation's history.

Some sites reside on privately owned farms and ranches. Fortunately, most are tended by dedicated stewards who have preserved the hallowed grounds entrusted to their care. At Warbonnet Creek, on hauntingly beautiful private ranchland in northwest Nebraska, the two conical hills behind which Wesley Merritt hid his troopers before attacking Little Wolf and his Northern Cheyennes still dominate the landscape. Sweeping from around those hills three companies of the 5th Cavalry launched the last great cavalry charge in

American history. Here, as at other places, the site remains so pristine that with little effort the fascinated visitor can almost hear the bugles sound and see the guidons unfurled in the morning air.

Thus by enormous good fortune the great battlefields of the American West remain essentially unchanged, available to all who wish to learn, reflect, and be enthralled. And touching and inspiring all who hear them, the stories of the military leaders who fought on them reach to us across the decades.

References

Preface
"the finest light cavalry in history"
Leckie, Robert, *The Wars of America.* New York: Harper & Row, Publishers, 1968, p.12

"They never loved him ..."
Robinson, Charles M. III, *Bad Hand: A Biography of General Ranald S. Mackenzie.* Austin, TX: State House Press, 1993, p. xvi

"and have the right of habeas corpus"
Dundy, Judge Elmer J., *United States ex rel. Standing Bear v. Crook*, U.S. District Court, Omaha, Nebraska, 1879

Notes
"Between 1865 and 1891 ..."
Sauers, Richard, *America's Battlegrounds.* San Diego, CA: Tehabi Books, 2005, p. 59

"During the twenty-five year period ..."
McDermott, John D., *A Guide to the Indian Wars of the West.* Lincoln, NE: University of Nebraska Press, 1998, p. 28

"total number of Civil War books ..."
Eicher, David J., *The Civil War in Books: An Analytical Biography,* Champaign, IL: University of Illinois Press, 1996

Eugene A. Carr
"... a particularly sharp conflict"
Paul, Eli R. (ed), *The Nebraska Indian Wars Reader, 1865-1877.* Lincoln, NE: University of Nebraska Press, 1998, p. 5

"skill, fighting, and marksmanship"
King, James T., "The Republican River Expedition, June-July 1869," *Nebraska History,* September 1960, p. 170

"those whose horses are fit for service"
King, James T., "The Republican River Expedition, June-July 1869," p. 198

John M. Chivington
"I love to kill Indians"
www.buffalosoldier.net/Sand_CreekMassacre.htm. Retrieved October 16, 2012

"It is not possible ..."
www.buffalosoldier.net/Sand_CreekMassacre.htm Retrieved October 16, 2012

363

"extermination of the red devils"
www.pbs.org/weta/thewest/people/a_c/chivington.htm Retrieved October 16, 2012

"deliberately planned and executed …"
United States Joint Committee on the Conduct of the War, Massacre of Cheyenne Indians, 38th Congress, Second Session, Washington D.C., 1865 and *Report of the Secretary of War,* 39th Congress, Second Session, Senate Executive Documents No. 26, Washington D.C., 1867

"a cowardly and cold-blooded slaughter"
www.pbs.org/weta/thewest/people/a-c/chivington.htm Retrieved October 16, 2012

"I stand by Sand Creek"
Becher, Ronald, *Massacre Along the Medicine Road,* Caldwell, ID: Caxton Press, 1999, p. 406

George R. Crook
"plain as an old stick"
Greene, Jerome A. in Hutton, Paul Andrew and Durwood Ball (eds.) *Soldiers West: Biographies from the Military Frontier.* Norman, OK: University of Oklahoma Press, 2009, p. 246

"an Indian is a person …"
Dundy, Judge Elmer J., *United States ex rel. Standing Bear v. Crook,* U.S. District Court, Omaha, Nebraska, 1879

"never lied to us"
www.thelatinlibrary.com/chron/civilwarnotes/Crook.html Retrieved February 22, 2013

George Armstrong Custer
"to finish us at their leisure"
Custer, George Armstrong, *My Life on the Plains.* Lincoln, NE: University of Nebraska Press, 1998, p. 135

"particularly sharp conflict"
Paul, Eli R. (ed.), *The Nebraska Indian Wars Reader, 1865-1867.* p.5

"Lying in irregular order …"
Custer, George Armstrong, *My Life on the Plains.* p. 188

"destroy the villages and ponies …"
Donovan, James, *A Terrible Glory: Custer and the Little Bighorn.* New York: Little, Brown, and Company, 2008, p. 63

"selfishly indifferent to others …"
Dippie, Brian W. in Hutton, Paul Andrew and Durwood Ball (eds.), *Soldiers West: Biographies from the Military Frontier.* Norman, OK: University of Oklahoma Press, 2009, p. 232

"We are goading …"
Connell, Evan S., *Son of the Morning Star: Custer and the Little Bighorn.* San

Francisco: North Point Press, 1984, p. 242

"cut loose"
Donovan, James, *A Terrible Glory: Custer and the Little Bighorn*. P.115

"the great hero of the battle"
Donovan, James, *A Terrible Glory: Custer and the Little Bighorn*. P.372

"a sad and terrible blunder"
Donovan, James, *A Terrible Glory: Custer and the Little Bighorn*. P. 313

William S. Harney
"Man who kept his word"
en.wikipedia.org/wiki/William_S._Harney.htm Retrieved June 10, 2011

"a sickly half-starved cow"
Dobson, Geoffrey B., *Indian Wars, Wyoming Tales and Trails*. http://www.
wyomingtalesandtrails.com/Custer Retrieved June 22, 2011

"about 20 feet wide …", "abrupt and 3 to 4 feet high"
Journal of Lieutenant G.K. Warren in Mattes, Merrill J., *The Great Platte River Road*. Lincoln, NE: The Nebraska State Historical Society, 1969, p.318

"in order to gain time and learn something of the disposition …"
Journal of Lieutenant G.K. Warren in Mattes, Merrill J., *The Great Platte River Road*. p. 320

"the cavalry made its appearance …"
Werner, Fred H., *With Harney on the Blue Water: Battle of Ash Hollow, September 3, 1855*. Greeley, CO: Werner Publications, 1988, p. 67,70

"nearest practicable descent …"
Mattes, Merrill J., *The Great Platte River Road*. p. 323

"there was much slaughter in pursuit."
Werner, Fred H., *With Harney on the Blue Water: Battle of Ash Hollow, September 3, 1855*. Greeley, CO: Werner Publications, 1988. p. 58

"The casualties of my command …"
Official report of General William S. Harney in Werner, Fred H., *With Harney on the Blue Water: Battle of Ash Hollow, September 3, 1855*. p. 50-53

"We passed the graves …"
Mattes, Merrill J., *The Great Platte River Road*. p.331

"fought with great intensity …", "when distance and strangeness of dress …"
Mattes, Merrill J., *The Great Platte River Road*. p. 325

"in pursuit, women if recognized …", "with such intensity of high emotion …"
Official report of Lieutenant Colonel Philip St. George Cooke in Werner, Fred H. *With Harney on the Blue Water: Battle of Ash Hollow, September 3, 1855*. P. 56-59

365

"indefatigable in his attention to the suffering …"
Mattes, Merrill J., *The Great Platte River Road.* P. 325

Ranald S. Mackenzie
"think like an Indian …"
Robinson, Charles M. III, *Bad Hand.* p. 108

"most promising young officer"
Grant, Ulysses S. *Personal Memoirs.* New York: The Library of America, 1990, p. 772

"alone and aloof, cold and efficient"
Robinson, Charles M. III, *Bad Hand.* p. 20

Wesley Merritt
"timely, professionally executed, and desperately needed."
Hedron, Paul, *First Scalp for Custer, The Skirmish at Warbonnet Creek, Nebraska, July 17, 1876.* Lincoln, NE: University of Nebraska Press, 1980. p. 84

Nelson A. Miles
"From where the sun now sits, I will fight no more forever."
Wellman, Paul I., *Indian Wars of the West.* Garden City, NY: Doubleday & Company, 1956. p. 186

"fought with almost scientific skill."
Josephy, Alvin M., Jr., *The Nez Perce Indians and the Opening of the Northwest.* New Haven: CT: Yale University Press,1965. p. 632

Frank J. North
"Organized at Columbus, Nebraska …"
Information courtesy of Margaret E. Wagner, Editor, Publications Office, the Library of Congress in Phillips, Thomas D., *Battlefields of Nebraska.* Caldwell, ID: Caxton Press, 2009, p. 278

Philip H. Sheridan
"a brown, chunky little chap …"
Robertson, James I. Jr., *For Us The Living.* New York: Fall River Press, 2010, p.207

"crows flying over it …"
www.encylopediavirginia.org/Hard_War_in_Virginia_During_the_Civil_War
Retrieved December 18, 2012

Henry B. Carrington
"Support the wood train …"
Thackery, Lorna, "The Next Generation in the Study of Custer's Last Stand," *Billings Gazette,* June 23, 2004

"every soldier to treat all Indians with kindness"
"Records Relating to Investigations of the Ft. Philip Kearney (or Fetterman) Massacre. Testimony of Colonel Henry B. Carrington. Special Orders No. 7, June 13, 1866." National Archives and Records Administration, Washington D.C.

William O. Collins
"In 1865 (a traveler's wagon train) was told …"
Mattes, Merrill J., *The Great Platte River Road.* p. 233

"(t)he little compound at Mud Springs …"
Phillips, Thomas D., *Battlefields of Nebraska. p. 67*

"shower of hailstones", "could see Indians jumping up …"
McDermott, John D., *Circle of Fire: The Indian War of 1865.* Mechanicsburg, PA: Stackpole Books, 2003. p. 37

"there were many little sand ridges …"
McDermott, John D., "The Battles of Mud Springs and Rush Creek," *Nebraska History,* Summer, 1996, p. 83.

"warriors carried one another …"
McDermott, John D., "The Battles of Mud Springs and Rush Creek," *Nebraska History,* p. 83

John O. Gibbon
"steel cold"
http://www.friendsnezpercebattlefields.org/General-John-Gibbon.htm p. 10. Retrieved September 26, 2012

"Troop A (stationed at) …" (summary of activities)
O'Connor, Lt. Charles M., "The Eighth Regiment of Cavalry" in http://www.history.army/mil/books/R&H/R&H-8CV.htm Retrieved June 14, 2013

Winfield S. Hancock
"genial disposition"
Grant, Ulysses S., *Personal Memoirs.* New York: Library Classics of the United States, 1990, p. 771

"uphold the faith of the government"
Jordan, David M., *Winfield Scott Hancock: A Soldier's Life.* Bloomington, IN: Indiana University Press, 1998, p. 234

"handsomest man in the United States Army"
de Trobiand, Regis, in www.civilwar.org/education/history/biographies/winfield-scott-hancock.html Retrieved August 30, 2013

"Hancock was superb today …"
Eicher, John H. and David J. Eicher, *Civil War High Commands.* Stanford, CA: Stanford University Press, 2001, p 277-278

Stephen W. Kearny
"Father of the United States Cavalry"
En.wikipedia.org/wiki/Stephen-W-Kearny Retrieved October 15, 2013

Edward O.C. Ord
"skillful, hard march the night before"
Arlington National Cemetery website. "Biography of Edward Otho Cresap Ord"

David S. Stanley
"swung clear"
Donovan, James, *A Terrible Glory: Custer and the Little Bighorn.* p. 115

Edwin V. Sumner
"old school Army"
Claiborne, Thomas, *The Warrior Generals: Combat Leadership in the Civil War.*
New York: Crown Publishers, 1997. p. 59

Alfred H. Terry
"swing free of Terry"
Philbrick, Nathaniel, *The Last Stand.* New York: Viking, 2010. p. 17

George Wright
"our route has been marked by slaughter and devastation;" "without worry, doubt,
or confusion …;" "war will be made on you this year and next …:" "struck a blow
from which the Natives ….;" "(I have) treated the Indians severely …"
Cutler, Don, "Your Nations Shall Be Exterminated," *MHQ: The Quarterly Journal
of Military History,* Spring 2010

BIBLIOGRAPHY

General References: Indian Wars
Greene, Jerome A., *Battles and Skirmishes of the Great Sioux War, 1876-77: The Military View*. Norman, OK: University of Oklahoma Press, 1998
Josephy, Alvin M., *War on the Frontier*. New York: Time-Life Books, 1986
McDermott, John D., *A Guide to the Indian Wars of the West*. Lincoln, NE and London:University of Nebraska Press, 1998
McDermott, John D., *Circle of Fire: The Indian War of 1865*. Mechanicsburg, MD: Stackpole Books, 2003
Michno, Gregory F., *Encyclopedia of Indian Wars*. Missoula, MT: Mountain Press Publishing Company, 2003
Michno, Gregory F., *Dakota Dawn: The Decisive First Week of the Sioux Uprising, August 1862*. El Dorado Hills, CA: Savas Beatie, 2011
Robinson, Charles M. III, *A Good Year to Die: The Story of the Great Sioux War*. Norman, OK: University of Oklahoma Press, 1996
Sauers, Richard Allen, *America's Battlegrounds*. San Diego, CA: Tehabi Books, 2005
Utley, Robert et al., *Indian Wars*. New York: Mariner Books, 2002
Wellman, Paul I., *Indian Wars of the West*. Garden City, NY: Doubleday & Company, Inc., 1956

Reuben F. Bernard
Arlington National Cemetery Website, http://www.artlingtoncemetery.net/rfbernard. htm, Extracted June 11, 2013
Ontko, Gale, *Thunder over the Ochoco, Vol IV Rain of Tears*. Bend, OR: Maverick Publications, Inc., 1998
Russell, Don and Edwin Sweeney, *One Hundred and Three Fights: The Story of General Reuben F. Bernard*. Mechanicsburg, PA: Stackpole Books, 2003
Saunders, Arthur C., *The History of Bannock County, Idaho*. Pocatello, ID: The Tribune Company, 1915
Utley, Robert F., *Indian Wars*

Edward R.S. Canby
Eicher, John H. and David J. Eicher, *Civil War High Commands*. Stanford, CA: Stanford University Press, 2001
Heyman, Max L., Jr., *Prudent Soldier: A Biography of Major General E.R.S. Canby*. Glendale, CA: The Arthur H. Clark Co., 1958
Johnston, Terry A., *Devil's Backbone: The Modoc War 1872-3*. New York: St. Martin's Paperbacks, 2012
Murray, Keith A., *The Modocs and their War*. Norman, OK: Oklahoma University Press, 1976
Riddle, Jeff C. Davis, *Indian History of the Modoc War*. Charleston, SC; Nabu Press, 2010
Utley, Robert Marshall, *Frontier Regulars: The United States Army and the Indians,*

1866-1891. Lincoln, NE: Bison Books, 1984

(Other Commanders in the Modoc War)

Jefferson C. Davis
Eicher, John H. and David J. Eicher, *Civil War High Commands*
Hughes, Nathaniel Cheairs, Jr., and Gordon H. Whitney, *Jefferson Davis in Blue: The Life of Sherman's Relentless Warrior.* Baton Rouge, LA: Louisiana State University Press, 2002
Levstik, Frank R., "Jefferson Columbus Davis" in *Encyclopedia of the American Civil War: A Political, Social, and Military History.* New York: W.W. Norton & Company, 2002

Alvan C. Gillem
Johnston, Terry A., *Devil's Backbone: The Modoc War 1872-3*
Report of Colonel Alvan C. Gillem, 1ST Cavalry, Modoc War, 1873 to the Assistant Adjutant General, Headquarters Department of the Columbia. Amazon.com: Forgotten Books, 2012

John Green
Quinn, Arthur, *Hell with the fire out, a history of the Modoc War.* London: Faber & Faber, 1998
Riddle, Jeff C. Davis, *Indian History of the Modoc War.*
Thompson, Edwin N., *"Modoc War, Its Military History & Topography.* Sacramento, CA: Argus Books, 1971

Frank Wheaton
Eicher, John H. and David J. Eicher, *Civil War High Commands*
Murray, Keith A., *The Modocs and their War*
"Wheaton, Frank," in *The Encyclopedia Americana,* 1920

James H. Carleton
Hunt, Aurora, *Major General James Henry Carleton 1814-1873: Western Frontier Dragoon.* Glendale, CA: Arthur H. Clark, Co., 1958
Hutton, Paul A. (ed.), *Soldiers West: Biographies from the Military Frontier.* Lincoln, NE: University of Nebraska Press, 1987
Pettis, George H., *The California Column: Its Campaigns and Services in New Mexico, Arizona, and Texas during the Civil War, with Sketches of Brigadier General James H. Carleton, its Commander and other Officers and Soldiers.* Santa Fe, NM: New Mexico Printing Co., 1908
Wellman, Paul I., *Indian Wars of the West*

Caleb H. Carlton
"Behind the Lines: True Stories of the Ohio Battle Flags," Ohio Historical Society Exhibits. Extracted January 18, 2013
Carlton, Colonel Caleb H., 89th Ohio Volunteer Infantry, "Papers of Caleb Henry Carlton." Library of Congress Manuscript Division, Washington, D.C.

"National Anthem's roots reach to Fort Meade," South Dakota Public Broadcasting. "Dakota Digest," July 31, 2012

Weaver, Bryan P., and H. Lee Feuner., *Sacrifice at Chickamauga: A History of the 89th Volunteer Infantry Regiment.* Palos Verges Peninsula, CA: Moyweave Boooks, 2003

West Point. Class of 1859: Cullum's Register, July 9, 2011

Eugene A. Carr

"Battle of Cibecue Creek." http://en.wikipedia.org/wiki/Battle_of_Cibecue_Creek Extracted February 28, 2010

"Battle of Fort Apache." http://en.wikipedia.org/wiki/Battle_of_Fort_Apache Extracted February 28, 2010

"Carr, Eugene A.", *The Handbook of Texas Online.* www.tshaonline.org.handbook/online/articles/CC/fcadd.html. Extracted March 1, 2010

Eicher, John H. and David J. Eicher., *Civil War High Commands*

King, James T., "The Republican River Expedition June-July 1869," *Nebraska History,* September, 1960

King, James T., *War Eagle: A Life of General Eugene A. Carr.* Lincoln, NE: University of Nebraska Press, 1963

Phillips, Thomas D., *Battlefields of Nebraska.* Caldwell, ID: Caxton Press, 2009.

Henry B. Carrington

Brady, Cyrus Townshend, *The Sioux Indian War.* New York: Barnes & Noble, 1992

Brown, Dee, *The Fetterman Massacre.* Lincoln, NE: University of Nebraska Press, 1984

Calitri, Shannon Smith, "Give Me Eighty Men: Shattering the Myth of the Fetterman Massacre." *Montana: Magazine of Western History,* 2004

Carrington, Frances Courteney, *My Army Life and the Fort Phil Kearny Massacre, With an Account of 'Wyoming Opened.* Lincoln, NE: Bison Books, 2004

Finerty, John F., *War-Path and Bivouac.* Lincoln, NE: University of Nebraska Press, 1968

"Records Relating to Investigations of Ft. Philip Kearny (or Fetterman) Massacre. Testimony of Col. Henry B. Carrington" Washington, D.C.: National Archives & Records Administration

Wellman, Paul I., *Indian Wars of the West.*

Kit Carson

Carson, Kit and Milo Milton Quaife, *Kit Carson's Autobiography.* Lincoln, NE: Bison Books, 2013

Carter, Henry Lewis, *Dear Old Kit: The Historical Christopher Carson.* Norman, OK: University of Oklahoma Press, 1968

Dunlay, Tom, *Kit Carson and the Indians.* Lincoln, NE: University of Nebraska Press, 2000

Ellis, Edward S., *The Life of Kit Carson Hunter, Trapper, Guide, Indian Agent and Colonel U.S.A.* Amazon Digital Services, 2012

Hutton, Paul Andrew and Durwood Ball (eds.). *Soldiers West: Biographies from the Military Frontier*

Roberts, David, *A Newer World, Kit Carson, John C. Fremont, and the Claiming of the American West.* New York: Simon & Schuster, 2002
Sides, Hampton, *Blood and Thunder: An Epic Story of Kit Carson and the Conquest of the American West.* New York: Anchor, 2007

John M. Chivington
Becher, Ronald, *Massacre Along the Medicine Road.* Caldwell, ID: Caxton Press, 1999
Hoig, Stan, *The Sand Creek Massacre.* Norman, OK: University of Oklahoma Press, 1974
McDermott, John D., *Circle of Fire: The Indian War of 1865*
Michno, Gregory F., *Battle at Sand Creek.* El Segundo, CA: Upton & Sons, 2004
Michno, Gregory F., *Encyclopedia of Indian Wars: Western Battles and Skirmishes.* Missoula, MT: Mountain Press Publishing Co., 2003
Potter, James, *Standing Firmly by the Flag: Nebraska Territory and the Civil War, 1861-1867.* Lincoln, NE: Bison Books, 2012
"Report of the Joint Committee on the Conduct of the War," Senate Report No. 142, 38th Congress, Second Session, Washington, D.C.: Government Printing Office
Smiley, B., "Sand Creek Massacre," *Archeology Magazine,* Vol. 52, Number 6, November/December 1999

William O. Collins
McDermott, John D., "The Battles of Mud Springs and Rush Creek." *Nebraska History.* Summer 1996
Phillips, Thomas D., *Battlefields of Nebraska.*
Springs, Agnes Wright, "Colonel William O. Collins for Whom Our City is Named." *Fort Collins Express,* May 20, 1923
Ware, Eugene F., *The Indian War of 1864.* Lincoln, NE: University of Nebraska Press, 1960
Watrous, Ansel, *History of Larimer County, Colorado.* (Classic Reprint). Leicester, UK: Forgotten Books, 2012.

Patrick E. Connor
Madsen, Brigham D., *Glory Hunter: A Biography of Patrick Edward Connor.* Salt Lake City, UT: University of Utah Press, 1990
McDermott, John D., *Circle of Fire: The Indian War of 1865*
Miller, Rod, *The Massacre at Bear River.* Caldwell, ID: Caxton Printers, Ltd, 1990
Potter, James D., *Standing Firmly by the Flag: Nebraska Territory and the Civil War, 1861-1867*
Rogers, Fred B., *Soldiers of the Overland: Being some account of the services of General Patrick Edward Connor and the volunteers of the Old West.* San Francisco: Grabhorn Press, 1938
Wagner, David E., *Patrick Connor's War: The 1865 Powder River Expedition.* Norman, OK: The Arthur H. Clark Company, 2010

Philip St. George Cooke
Bearss, Edwin C., and Sara B. Bearss (ed.), *Dictionary of Virginia Biography.* Richmond, VA: Library of Virginia, 2006

Foreman, Carolyn Thomas, *General Philip St. George Cooke.*
digital.library.okstate.edu/chroniclesv032/v032p195.pdf. Extracted October 8, 2013
Hutton, Paul Andrew and Durwood Ball, *Soldiers West: Biographies from the Military Frontier*
Longacre, Edward G., *Lincoln's Cavalrymen: A History of the Mounted Force of the Army of the Potomac.* Mechanicsburg, PA: Stackpole Books, 2000
Warner, Ezra J., *Generals in Blue: Lives of the Union Commanders.* Baton Rouge, LA: Louisiana State University Press, 1964
Young, Otis E., *The West of Philip St. George Cooke, 1809-1895.* Norman, OK: The Arthur H. Clark Company, 1955

George Crook
Brady, Cyrus Townsend, *The Sioux Indians Wars.* New York: Barnes & Noble, 1992
Crook, George and Martin F. Schmitt (ed.), *General George Crook: An Autobiography* Norman. OK: University of Oklahoma Press, 1946
Greene, Jerome A., *Battles and Skirmishes of the Great Sioux War, 1876-1877*
Robinson, Charles M. III, *A Good Year to Die: The Story of the Great Sioux War*
Robinson, Charles M. III, *George Crook and the Western Frontier.* Norman, OK: The University of Oklahoma Press, 2001
Wellman, Paul I., *The Indian Wars of the West.*

Samuel R. Curtis
Atherne, Robert G., *Forts of the Upper Missouri.* Lincoln, NE: University of Nebraska Press, 1967
Becher, Ronald, *Massacre along the Medicine Road*
Gallaher, Ruth, "Samuel Ryan Curtis." *The Iowa Journal of History and Politics 25,* July 1927
Holst, David L., "General Samuel Curtis and the Civil War in the West." Master's Thesis, Illinois State University, 1974
Josephy, Alvin M. Jr., *The Civil War in the American West.* New York: Alfred A. Knopf, 1991
Potter, James B., *Standing Firmly by the Flag: Nebraska Territory and the Civil War, 1861-1867*

George Armstrong Custer
Connell, Evan S., *Son of the Morning Star: Custer and the Little Bighorn.* New York: North American Press, 1984
Custer, George Armstrong, *My Life on the Plains.* Lincoln, NE: University of Nebraska Press, 1952
Dippie, Brian W., *Custer's Last Stand: The Anatomy of an American Myth.* Lincoln, NE: University of Nebraska Press, 1994
Donovan, James, *A Terrible Glory: Custer and the Little Bighorn.* New York: Little, Brown, and Company, 2008
Egan, Timothy, *Short Nights of the Shadow Catcher.* New York: Houghton Mifflin Harcourt, 2012
Macdonald, John, *Great Battlefields of the World.* New York: Macmillan Publishing Company, 1984
McMurtry, Larry, *Custer.* New York: Simon & Shuster, 2012

Philbrick, Nathaniel, *The Last Stand.* New York: Viking, 2010
Scott, Douglas D., Peter Bleed and Stephen Damm, *Custer, Cody, and Grand Duke Alexis: Historical Archaeology of the Royal Buffalo Hunt.* Norman, OK: University of Oklahoma Press, 2013

(Custer's Lieutenants)

Frederick Benteen
Donovan, James, *A Terrible Glory: Custer and the Little Bighorn*
Hammer, Kenneth, *Men with Custer: Biographies of the 7th Cavalry June 25, 1876.* Hardin, MT: Custer Battlefield Historical and Museum Association, 2000
Mills, Charles K., *Harvest of Barren Regrets: The Army Career of Frederick William Benteen.* Glendale, CA: Arthur H. Clark Co., 1985
Philbrick, Nathaniel, *The Last Stand*

Thomas Custer
Day, Carl F., *Tom Custer: Ride to Glory.* Norman, OK: University of Oklahoma Press, 2002.
Donovan, James, *A Terrible Glory: Custer and the Little Bighorn*
Philbrick, Nathaniel, *The Last Stand*
The Medal of Honor of the United States Army, Washington, D.C.: Government Printing Office, 1948

Myles Keogh
Convis, Charles L., *The Honor of Arms: A Biography of Miles Keogh.* Tucson, AZ: Westernlore Press, 2010
Donovan, James, *A Terrible Glory: Custer and the Little Bighorn*
Longellier, John R., Kurt Hamilton Cox, Brian C. Pohanka, *Myles Keogh: The Life and Legend of an "Irish Dragoon" in the Seventh Cavalry.* El Segundo, CA: Upton & Sons, 1998

Marcus Reno
Connell, Evan S., *Son of the Morning Star: Custer and the Little Bighorn*
Donovan, James, *A Terrible Glory: Custer and the Little Bighorn*
Hammer, Kenneth, *Men with Custer: Biographies of the 7th Cavalry June 25 1876.* Hardin, MT: Custer Battlefield Historical and Museum Association, 2000
Hutton, Paul Andrew, *The Custer Reader.* Lincoln, NE: The University of Nebraska Press, 1993
Philbrick, Nathaniel, *The Last Stand*

George Yates
Donovan, James, *A Terrible Glory: Custer and the Little Bighorn*
Panzieri, Peter, *Classic Battles: The Little Bighorn 1876.* Oxford, UK: Osprey Publishing, 1995
Philbrick, Nathaniel, *The Last Stand*
Utley, Robert M., *Cavalier in Buckskin.* Norman, OK: University of Oklahoma Press, 2001

Grenville M. Dodge
Ambrose, Stephen E., *Nothing Like it in the World: The Men Who Built the Transcontinental Railroad 1863-1869.* New York: Simon & Schuster, 2000
Becher, Ronald, *Massacre Along the Medicine Road.*
"Grenville Dodge." http://www.linecamp.com/museaums/americanwest/western_names/
dodge/grenville_mellen.html Extracted September 13, 2013
Hixshon, Stanley P., *Grenville Dodge: Soldier, Politician, Railroad Pioneer.* Bloomington, IN: Indiana University Press, 1967
McDermott, John D., *Circle of Fire: The Indian War of 1865*
Potter, James B., *Standing Firmly by the Flag: Nebraska Territory and the Civil War, 1861-1867*

John O. Gibbon
Donovan, James A., *A Terrible Glory: Custer and the Little Bighorn*
Gibbon, John, and Alan D. Gaff and Maureen Gaff (eds.), *Adventures on the Western Frontier.* Bloomington, IN: Indiana University Press, 1994
Gibbon, John, *Gibbon on the Sioux Campaign of 1876.* Bellevue, NV: The Old Army Press, 1970
Lavery, Dennis S., "John Gibbon," *Encyclopedia of the American Civil War: A Political, Social, and Military History.* New York: W.W. Norton & Company, 2000
Warner, Ezra J., *Generals in Blue: Lives of the Union Commanders.* Baton Rouge, LA: Louisiana State University Press, 1964
West, Elliott, *The Last Indian War: The Nez Perce Story.* New York: Oxford University Press, 2011

John I. Gregg
Eicher, John H. and David J. Eicher, *Civil War High Commands*
"John Irvin Gregg," http://en.wikipedia.org/wiki/John_Irvin_Gregg. Extracted June 14, 2013
"John Irvin Gregg, Major General, United States Army," http://www.arlingtoncemetery.net/jigregg.htm. Extracted June 14, 2013
O'Connor, Eugene M. "The Eighth Regiment of Cavalry" http://www.history.army.mil/books/R&H-8CV.htm. Extracted June 14, 2013
"8th Cavalry Regiment (United States)" http://en.wikipedia.org/wiki/8th_Cavalry_Regiment_United_States Extracted June 14, 2013

Benjamin H. Grierson
Dinges, Bruce J., "Benjamin H. Grierson" in *Soldiers West: Biographies of the Military Frontier*
Dinges, Bruce J. and Shirley A. Leckie, *A Just and Righteous Cause: Benjamin H. Grierson's Civil War Memoir.* Carbondale, IL: Southern Illinois University Press, 2008
Leckie, Shirley A. and William A. Leckie, *Unlikely Warrior: General Benjamin H. Grierson and His Family.* Norman, OK: University of Oklahoma Press, 1984
Temple, Frank, "Colonel Grierson in the Southwest." *Panhandle Plains Historical Review* 30, 1957

Warner, Ezra J., *Generals in Blue: Lives of the Union Army Commanders*
Wellman, Paul I., *The Indian Wars of the West.*

Winfield Scott Hancock
Chalfont, William Y., *Hancock's War: Conflict on the Southern Plains.* Norman, OK:
Arthur H. Clark Company, 2010
Guelzo, Allen C., *Gettysburg: The Last Invasion.* New York: Alfred A. Knopf, 2013
Jordan, David M., *Winfield Scott Hancock: A Soldier's Life.* Bloomington, IN:
Indiana University Press, 1996
Tucker, Glen, *Hancock the Superb.* Dayton, OH: Morningside Books, 1980
Wellman, Paul I., *Indian Wars of the West*

William S. Harney
Adams, George Rollie, *General William S. Harney: Prince of Dragoons.* Lincoln,
NE: University of Nebraska Press, 2001
Archer, Jules, *Indian Foe, Indian Friend: The Story of William S. Harney.* New
York: Atheneum, 1970
Phillips, Thomas D., *Battlefields of Nebraska.*
Werner, Fred H., *With Harney on the Blue Water: Battle of Ash Hollow, September
3, 1855.* Greeley, CO: Werner Publications, 1988

Oliver O. Howard
Beal, Merrill D., *I Will Fight No More Forever: Chief Joseph and the Nez Perce
War.* Seattle, WA: University of Washington Press, 1963
Eicher, John H. and David J. Eicher, *Civil War High Commands*
Howard, Oliver O., *Autobiography of Oliver Otis Howard.* Sligo, Ireland: HardPress
Publishing, 2008
Howard, Oliver O., *In Pursuit of the Nez Perces: The Nez Perce War of 1877.*
Missoula, MT: Mountain Meadows Press, 1993
Howard, Oliver O., *My Life and Experiences Among Our Hostile Indians: A Record
of Personal Observations, Adventures, and Campaigns.* Sligo, Ireland: HardPress
Publishing, 2013
Weland, Gerald, *Of Vision and Valor: General Oliver O. Howard, a Biography.*
Canton, OH: Daring Publishing Group, 1991
West, Elliott, *The Last Indian War: The Nez Perce Story.* New York: Oxford
University Press, 2011
Utley, Robert F., *Indian Wars*

Stephen W. Kearny
Bauer, Jack K., *The Mexican War: 1846-1848.* Lincoln, NE: University of Nebraska
Press, 1974
Clark, Dwight L,. *Stephen Watts Kearny: Soldier of the West.* Norman, OK:
University of Oklahoma Press, 1968
Dagard, Martin, *The Training Ground.* New York: Little, Brown, and Company,
2008
Groom, Winston, *Kearny's March: The Epic Creation of the American West, 1846-
47.* Alfred A. Knopf, 2011

Hutton, Paul Andrew and Durwood Ball, *Soldiers West: Biographies from the Military Frontier.*
Thrapp, Dan L., *Encyclopedia of Frontier Biography.* Lincoln, NE: University of Nebraska Press, 1991

Robert R. Livingston
Andreas, A.T., *History of the State of Nebraska, Vol I.* Chicago, IL: The Western Historical Company, 1882
Becher, Ronald, *Massacre Along the Medicine Road*
Morton, J. Sterling and Albert Watkius (eds.), *Illustrated History of Nebraska, Vol II.* Lincoln, NE: Jacob North and Company, 1906
Potter, James E., *Standing Firmly by the Flag: Nebraska Territory and the Civil War, 1861-1867*
Scherneckau, Albert, *Marching with the First Nebraska.* Norman, OK: University of Oklahoma Press, 2007

Ranald Mackenzie
Bourke, John Gregory, *Mackenzie's Last Fight with the Cheyennes: A Winter Campaign in Wyoming and Montana.* London: Argonaut Press, 1966
Buecker, Thomas R., *Fort Robinson and the American West: 1874-1899.* Norman, OK: University of Oklahoma Press, 1999
Moore, Fred H. and Ella Mae Moore, *On the Border with Mackenzie; or, Winning West Texas from the Comanches.* Texas State Historical Association, 2007
Pierce, Michael D., *The Most Promising Young Officer: A Life of Ranald Slidell Mackenzie.* Norman, OK: University of Oklahoma Press, 1993
Robinson, Charles M. III, *Bad Hand: A Biography of General Ranald S. Mackenzie.* Buffalo Gap, TX: State House Press, 1993
Thompson, Richard A., *Crossing the Border with the 4th Cavalry: Mackenzie's Raid into Mexico 1873.* Waco, TX: Texian Press, 1986
Wallace, Ernest, *Ranald S. Mackenzie on the Texas Frontier.* West Texas Museum Association, 1964

Wesley Merritt
Alberts, Don E., *General Wesley Merritt: Brandy Station to Manila Bay.* General's Books, 2001
Greene, Jerome A., *Battles and Skirmishes of the Great Sioux War, 1876-1877*
Eicher, John H. and David J. Eicher, *Civil War High Commands*
Hedron, Paul, *First Scalp for Custer: The Skirmish at Warbonnet Creek, Nebraska, July 17, 1876.* Lincoln, NE: University of Nebraska Press, 1980
Phillips, Thomas D., *Battlefields of Nebraska*
Robinson, Charles M. III, *A Good Year to Die: The Story of the Great Sioux War, 1876-77*
Werner, Fred H., *The Slim Buttes Battle.* San Luis Obispo, CA: Werner Press, 1981

Nelson Miles
Demontravel, Peter R., *A Hero to his Fighting Men: Nelson A. Miles, 1839-1925.* Kent, OH: Kent State University Press, 1998

Greene, Jerome A., *Yellowstone Command: Colonel Nelson A. Miles in the Great Sioux War, 1876-1877.* Norman, OK: University of Oklahoma Press, 2006
Hedron, Paul, *Great Sioux War Order of Battle: How the United States Army Waged War on the Northern Plains, 1876-1877.* Norman, OK: The Arthur H. Clarke Company, 2011
Hutton, Paul Andrew and Durwood Ball, *Soldiers West: Biographies from the Military Frontier*
Wooster, Robert, *Nelson A. Miles and the Twilight of the Frontier Army.* Lincoln, NE: University of Nebraska Press, 1996

Robert B. Mitchell
Becher, Ronald, *Massacre Along the Medicine Road*
Josephy, Alvin M., Jr., *Civil War in the American West*
McDermott, John D., *Circle of Fire: The Indian War of 1865*
"Robert Byington Mitchell" Arlington Cemetery Website, http://www.arlington.cemetery.net/rbmitchell.htp Extracted September 17, 2013
Ware, Eugene F., *The Indian War of 1864.* Topeka, KS: Crane & Co., 1911
Scherneckau, Albert, *Marching with the First Nebraska*

Thomas Moonlight
Becher, Ronald, *Massacre Along the Medicine Road*
Blackmer, Frank W., *Kansas: a cyclopedia of state history, embracing events, industries, counties, cities, towns, prominent persons, etc.,* Chicago: Standard Publishing Co., 1912
Eicher, John H., and David J. Eicher, *Civil War High Commands*
McDermott, John D., *Circle of Fire: The Indian War of 1865*
"Thomas Moonlight," Wyoming State Archives http://www.wyohistory.org/encyclopedia/thomas-moonlight. Extracted September 17,2013

Frank J. North
Buechler, Ronald, *Massacre Along the Medicine Road*
Grinnell, George Bird, *Two Great Scouts in the Pawnee Battalion: The Experiences of Frank J. North and Luther H. North, Pioneers in the Great West 1856-1882.* Lincoln, NE: University of Nebraska Press, 1973
McDermott, John D., *Circle of Fire: The Indian War of 1865*
North, Frank J. and Donald F. Danken (ed.), *The Journal of an Indian Fighter: The 1869 Diary of Frank J. North, Leader of the Pawnee Scouts.* Literary Licensing, 2011
(Reprinted from Nebraska History, V39, No. 2, June 1958)
Wellman, Paul I., *Indian Wars of the American West*
Van de Lugt, Mark, and Walter R. Echo-Hawk, *War Party in Blue: Pawnee Scouts in the U.S. Army.* Norman, OK: University of Oklahoma Press, 2010
Wilson, Ruby E., *Frank J. North: Pawnee Scout Commander and Pioneer.* Athens, OH: Swallow Press, 1984

Edward O.C. Ord
Denger, Mark J. and Charles R. Cresap, *Californians and the Military: Major General Edward Otho Cresap Ord.* California State Museum
http://www.militarymuseum.org/Ord.html Extracted September 26, 2012
Eicher, John H. and David J. Eicher, *Civil War High Commands*
Handbook of Texas Online
http://www.tshaonline.org/handbook/online/articles/OO/for1.html Extracted
September 26, 2012
History of the Department of the Platte
http://www.rootsweb.com/~nerresour/andreas/military/military-p8.html#deplatte.
Extracted August 4, 2013
Wellman, Paul I., *The Indian Wars of the American West*

John Pope
Carley, Kenneth, *The Sioux Uprising of 1862.* St. Paul, MN: The Minnesota
Historical Society, 1976
Cozzens, Peter, *General John Pope: A Life for the Nation.* Champaign-Urbana, IL:
University of Illinois Press, 2000
Ellis, Richard M., *General Pope and U.S. Indian Policy.* Albuquerque, NM:
University of New Mexico Press, 1978
Jones, Robert Huhn, *The Civil War in the Northwest.* Norman, OK: University of
Oklahoma Press, 1960
Warner, Ezra J., *Generals in Blue: Lives of the Union Army Commanders*

Joseph J. Reynolds
Greene, Jerome A., *Battles and Skirmishes of the Great Sioux War, 1876-1877*
Greene, Jerome A., *Lakota and Cheyenne: Indian Views of the Great Sioux War,
1876-1877.* Norman, OK: University of Oklahoma Press, 1994
Hedegaard, Michael L., *Colonel Joseph J. Reynolds and the Saint Patrick's Day
celebration on the Powder River; Battle of Powder River(Montana, 17 March
1876).* BiblioScholar, 2012
Warner, Ezra J., *Generals in Blue: Lives of the Union Commanders*

Philip Sheridan
Drake, William F., *Little Phil: The Story of General Philip Henry Sheridan.*
Prospect, CT: Biographical Publishing Company, 2005.
Keim, DeBenneville Randolph and Paul Andrew Hutton, *Sheridan's Troopers on the
Borders: A Winter Campaign on the Plains.* Lincoln, NE: University of Nebraska
Press, 1985
Morris, Roy, Jr., *Sheridan, The Life and Wars of General Phil Sheridan.* New York:
Vintage, 1997.
Rister, Carl Coke, *Border Command: General Phil Sheridan in the West.* London:
Greenwood Press, 1974

Henry H. Sibley
Carley, Kenneth, *The Sioux Uprising of 1862*
Christgau, John, *Birch Coulee: The Epic Battle of the Dakota War.* Lincoln, NE:
Bison Books, 2012

Jones, Robert Huhn, *The Civil War in the Northwest*
Sibley, Henry Hastings, *Biographical Data of the United States Congress.*
http:bioguide.congress.gov/scripts/biodisplay.p1?index=S000396 Extracted July 21, 2013
Wellman, Paul I., *The Indian Wars of the West*

David S. Stanley
Athearn, Robert G., *Forts of the Upper Missouri.* Lincoln, NE: University of Nebraska Press, 1967
Philbrick, Nathaniel, *The Last Stand*
Stanley, David S., *Personal Memoirs of Major-General D.S. Stanley, USA.* Lake Monticello, VA: Olde Soldiers Books, 1987
Stanley, David S., *Report on the Yellowstone Expedition.* Washington, D.C.: Library of Congress, 1874
Warner, Ezra J., *Generals in Blue: Lives of the Union Commanders*

Samuel D. Sturgis
Brown, Mark H., *The Flight of the Nez Perce.* New York: G.P. Putnam's Sons, 1967
Eicher, John H. and David J. Eicher, *Civil War High Commands*
Greene, Jerome A., *The Nez Perce Summer, 1877.* Helena, MT: Montana Historical Society Press, 2010
National Archives Letter, RDTR1-13-05462-EHH, Archives 1. Reference Section, Archival Operations, Washington, D.C. July 12, 2013
"Sturgis, Samuel Davis", *American National Biography.*
http://www.anb.org/articles/05/05-00756.html Extracted July 21, 2013
West, Eliot, *The Last Indian War: The Nez Perce Story*

Alfred H. Sully
Carley, Kenneth, *The Sioux Uprising of 1862*
Clodfelter, Michael, *The Dakota War: The United States Army versus the Sioux, 1862-65.* Jefferson, NC: McFarland & Co. Publishers, 1998
Finerty, John B., *War-Path and Bivouac: The Big Horn and Yellowstone Expedition.* Lincoln, NE: University of Nebraska Press, 1966
Jones, Robert Huhn, *Civil War in the Northwest*
Kennan, Jerry, "The Battle of Whitestone Hill." *Wild West,* June 2008, pp. 44-49
Sully, Langdon, *No Tears for the General: The Life of Alfred Sully 1821-1879.* Palo Alto, CA: American West Publishing Company, 1974
"The U.S. Army and the Sioux – Part 2: Battle of the Badlands"
http://www.nps.gov/thro/historyculture/the-us-army-and-the-sioux-part-2.htm
National Park Service. Extracted July 17, 2013

Edwin V. Sumner
Becher, Ronald, *Massacre along the Medicine Road*
Boatner, Mark M. III, *The Civil War Dictionary.* New York: Crown Publishing, 1988
Etcheson, Nichole, *Bleeding Kansas: Contested Liberty in the Civil War Era.* Lawrence, KS: University Press of Kansas, 2004
Mullis, Tony R., "The Dispersal of the Topeka Legislature," *Kansas History: A Journal of the Plains.* Spring-Summer 2004

Tate, Thomas K., *General Edwin Vose Sumner, USA: A Civil War Biography.* Jefferson, NC: McFarland, 2013
Claiborne, Thomas, *The Warrior Generals: Combat Leadership in the Civil War.* New York: Crown Publishers, 1997

Alfred H. Terry
Bailey, John W., *Pacifying the Plains: General Alfred Terry and the Decline of the Sioux, 1866-1890.* Westport, CT: Greenwood Press, 1979
Brady, Cyrus Townsend, *The Sioux Indian Wars: From the Powder River to the Little Big Horn.* New York: Barnes & Noble, 1992
Donovan, James, *A Terrible Glory: Custer and the Little Bighorn*
Finerty, John F., *War-Path and Bivouac: The Big Horn and Yellowstone Expedition*
"Terry, Alfred Howe," *The New Student's Reference Book.* Chicago: F.E. Compton and Co., 1914
Philbrick, Nathaniel, *The Last Stand*
Wagner, Margaret E., Gary W. Gallagher, Paul Finkelmann (eds.), *The Library of Congress Civil War Desk Reference.* New York: Simon & Schuster, 2002

George Wright
Cutler, Don, "Your Nations Shall Be Exterminated," *Military History Quarterly.* March 24, 2011
Fuller, George W., *A History of the Pacific Northwest.* New York: Alfred A. Knopf, 1948
Hemphill, Major General John A. and Robert C. Cumbow, *West Pointers and Early Washington: The Contributions of U.S. Military Academy Graduates to the Development of Washington Territory, from the Oregon Trail to the Civil War 1834-1862.* Seattle, WA: The West Point Society of Puget Sound, Inc., 1992
Hubbell, John T. and James W. Geary (eds.), *Biographical Dictionary of the Union: Northern Leaders of the Civil War.* Westport, CT: Greenwood Press, 1995
Pollard, Lancaster, *A History of the State of Washington.* New York: The American Historical Society, 1937
Schlicke, Carl P., *General George Wright: Guardian of the Pacific Coast.* Baton Rouge, LA: Louisiana State University Press, 1964

THE AUTHOR

THOMAS D. PHILLIPS

During a 36-year military career, Tom Phillips led an isolated
unit through a terrorist episode, ran a think tank for the Commander-
in-Chief Strategic Air Command, served as director of the Air Force
Personnel Readiness Center during Operation Desert Storm, and led
some of the first American troops into Sarajevo, Bosnia-Herzegovina.
Following his military service, Phillips worked as a university
administer before beginning a writing career. His published works
include poetry, fiction, and non-fiction articles and books on defense
issues, military history, and baseball. He also teaches courses on
Americana and military history for the Osher Lifelong Learning
Institute at the University of Nebraska.

INDEX

1st Colorado Volunteers 19
1st Minnesota 273, 335
1st Nebraska Infantry 282
1st United States Dragoons 170
2nd California Cavalry 4
2nd Cavalry Division 31
2nd Kansas Infantry 286
2nd Missouri Light Artillery 218, 219
2nd New Mexico Infantry 20
3rd Infantry 276
3rd U.S. Artillery 4
4th Cavalry 9, 112, 118, 291, 326, 377
5th U.S. Cavalry 11
6th California Infantry 4
6th Illinois Cavalry 257
6th Michigan Cavalry 219
6th Ohio Volunteer Cavalry 204
7th Cavalry ix, 11, 26, 35, 40, 41, 48, 49, 51, 52,
    53, 54, 55, 58, 59, 61, 62, 63, 64, 69, 70, 71, 72,
    73, 74, 76, 77, 104, 118, 140, 141, 161, 164, 165,
    166, 248, 267, 269, 325, 327, 329, 331, 348, 350,
    351, 352, 361, 374
7th Iowa Cavalry 206, 211, 283
8th Infantry 3, 353
9th Cavalry 76, 122, 260
11th Ohio Volunteer Cavalry 204, 288
12th Missouri Cavalry 149, 218, 219
16th Kansas Cavalry 218, 283
36th Ohio Volunteer Infantry 31

A

Adobe Walls xix, 7, 8, 113, 202, 203
Susanna Alderdice 15
Grand Duke Alexis 58
American Fur Company 91, 317
Scott J. Anthony 22
Antietam 31, 50, 71, 72, 73, 96, 110, 131, 182, 187,
    244, 252, 273, 330, 335, 345
Apache Canyon 19, 20
Apache Indians xvii, xix, 3, 5, 6, 7, 8, 16, 17, 19,
    20, 30, 33, 34, 44, 45, 46, 55, 97, 98, 119, 142,
    143, 171, 172, 175, 178, 196, 197, 200, 202, 233,
    263, 300, 371
Apache Pass xix, 5
Appaloosa horses 99
Appomattox 8, 32, 49, 50, 70, 110, 122, 131, 160,
    243, 245, 253, 298
Arapaho Indians 21, 23, 55, 62, 89, 113, 148, 161,
    189, 196, 197, 219, 220, 221, 235, 241, 269,
    278, 348
Arikara Indians 63, 65, 270, 276
Arkansas River 161, 225, 226, 235, 258, 268, 277,
    278
Czar Alexander II 58
Arlington National Cemetery 46, 77, 94, 144, 168,
    176, 182, 251, 255, 300, 316, 333, 367, 369

Army of the Cumberland 97, 286, 310, 326
Army of the Potomac 32, 49, 96, 97, 121, 131, 159,
    230, 252, 273, 330, 335, 344, 345, 373
Army of the Tennessee 97, 238, 257, 297
Aroostook War 1
The Artillest's Manual 244
Ash Hollow 80, 83, 89, 90, 228, 288, 365, 376
Assiniboine Indians 270
Henry Atkinson 79, 275, 276
Christopher C. Auger 13, 149
Lucien Auguste 81
"Autie" Custer nickname 48

B

John B. Babcock 15, 16
Badlands xix, 61, 91, 305, 328, 338, 339, 340, 380
Eugene S. Baker 3, 164, 271, 327
Frank Baldwin 134, 343
Bannock Indians 95, 102, 104, 105, 106, 107, 170,
    172, 173, 176, 369
Bannock Pass 102
Bannock War in 1878 105
George N. Bascom xvii, 54, 162, 171, 202
Battle Butte 135, 136, 137, 138
Battle of the Badlands 305, 340, 380
Battle Ridge 68, 71
Battle of Bear Paw xix, 105, 140, 142, 250, 333,
    352
Bear River xix, 214, 216, 372
Bear River Massacre 216
Beaver Creek 12, 13, 53
William W. Belknap xvii, 48, 60, 272
Frederick Benteen v, 47, 64, 66, 67, 68, 69, 71, 72,
    73, 74, 75, 76, 77, 248, 332, 351, 374
Bent's Fort 197, 198, 199, 203, 278, 279
William Bent 196, 197
Reuben F. Bernard v, 106, 107, 108, 109, 170, 171,
    172, 173, 174, 175, 176, 180, 183, 369
Bernicia Barracks 254
Big Camas Prairie 106, 173
Big Crow 137, 217
Battle of the Big Hole xix, 102, 249, 250, 352
Bighorn Mountains 117, 139, 191, 218, 219
Big Mound xix, 304, 322
Big Piney Creek 191
Big Sandy Creek 27
Bijou Basin 23
Birch Coulee xix, 319, 320, 379
Bitterroot Mountains 99
"Black-bearded Cossack" 10
Blackfeet Indians 236, 270
Black Hawk War 78, 225, 342
Black Hills (Paha Sapa) 34, 42, 59, 60, 70, 71,
    116, 123, 126, 153, 154, 165, 166, 194, 218, 236,
    241, 251, 270, 271, 298, 347, 348
Black Hills Expedition 60, 298

383

INDEX

Chief Red Cloud 35, 40, 58, 85, 89, 122, 140
Red Cloud Agency 42, 116, 123, 124, 127, 153, 166
Red Cloud's War 36, 186, 188, 341, 347
Chief Red Leaf 42, 116, 153, 166
Red River xix, 2, 54, 112, 113, 114, 115, 132, 156, 163, 164, 179, 265, 276, 303, 320
Red River War 113, 114, 115, 156, 163, 164
Chief Red Warbonnet 114
Red Willow Creek 58
Autie Reed 68
Reno Hill 66, 67, 69, 72, 73, 75, 76, 351, 361
Marcus Reno v, xvii, 61, 62, 63, 64, 65, 66, 67, 68, 69, 72, 73, 74, 75, 76, 190, 191, 247, 248, 349, 350, 351, 361, 374
Republican River 10, 11, 12, 13, 15, 51, 53, 132, 149, 152, 162, 234, 269, 283, 289, 329, 344, 363, 371
Republican River Expedition 13, 15, 363, 371
Joseph J. Reynolds vi, 34, 35, 97, 165, 273, 281, 309, 310, 311, 312, 313, 314, 315, 316, 379
Rio Grande River 5, 6, 116, 158, 178, 227, 228, 244, 259, 260, 261, 262, 279, 300, 310
Thomas L. Roberts 5
Chief Rock Forehead 58
Rocky Mountains 13, 14, 21, 226
Rogue River 31, 158, 297, 354
Rogue River Wars 158, 354
Laura Roper 293
Rosebud Creek xix, 35, 36, 38, 39, 43, 60, 62, 122, 133, 139, 166, 246, 247, 316, 349, 350, 351
Rush Creek xix, 24, 204, 210, 212, 213, 235, 284, 290, 367, 372
Almira "Allie" Russell 272

S

Sac Indians 225, 226, 277
Sage Creek 124, 126
Saline River xix, 13
Salmon River 99, 100, 108, 174
San Carlos Agency 44
San Carlos Reservation 142, 263
Sand Creek viii, xix, 18, 20, 22, 24, 25, 26, 27, 56, 89, 140, 203, 206, 217, 234, 235, 236, 241, 267, 284, 292, 361, 364, 372
Sangre de Cristo Mountains 19
Sans Arcs Sioux 236
Santa Fe Trail 2, 6, 196, 233
Santa Maria River 254
Santee Sioux 336, 339
Sappa Creek 12
James Sawyers 223
Winfield Scott 82, 93
William Scurry 19, 20
John Sedgwick xvii, 52, 53, 96, 269, 344
Seminole War 79, 178, 184, 214, 277, 291, 296, 353
Sergeant Major Creek 55
Wilson Shannon 343, 344, 371

Sheepeater Indians 95, 106, 107, 109, 170, 172, 174, 175
Sheepeater War of 1879 106, 107
Philip H. Sheridan v, ix, x, xii, xiii, 12, 30, 31, 35, 39, 44, 45, 48, 49, 50, 51, 54, 57, 58, 60, 61, 91, 92, 104, 115, 121, 122, 123, 124, 128, 139, 153, 156, 157, 158, 159, 160, 161, 162, 163, 164, 165, 166, 167, 168, 182, 195, 214, 246, 258, 263, 271, 298, 299, 310, 316, 327, 348, 349, 352, 359, 366, 379
"Sheridan's Ride," 160
Sheridan, Wyoming 195
William T. Sherman xii, 48, 49, 51, 53, 56, 57, 61, 71, 97, 99, 102, 128, 132, 142, 152, 156, 157, 163, 167, 182, 185, 238, 239, 240, 257, 259, 266, 267, 269, 296, 297, 298, 330, 348, 349, 370
Samuel Shore 343
Shoshoni Indians 31, 36, 37, 38, 107, 196, 216
Henry H. Sibley vi, 4, 19, 20, 201, 236, 304, 305, 308, 317, 318, 319, 320, 321, 322, 323, 324, 336, 338, 341, 379
Sierra Diablo Mountains 10
Franz Sigel 96
Singing Grass 197
Sioux Indians viii, xiv, 10, 12, 13, 16, 18, 21, 24, 25, 34, 35, 36, 37, 38, 40, 41, 42, 43, 46, 51, 52, 58, 59, 60, 62, 63, 67, 78, 80, 82, 86, 89, 90, 91, 92, 99, 116, 118, 121, 124, 128, 129, 133, 134, 139, 140, 143, 144, 145, 147, 148, 149, 151, 153, 154, 155, 156, 162, 163, 165, 166, 167, 186, 189, 190, 193, 194, 204, 205, 206, 210, 212, 213, 222, 223, 225, 229, 233, 235, 236, 239, 248, 269, 270, 271, 276, 277, 278, 282, 283, 284, 288, 292, 293, 294, 295, 298, 299, 303, 304, 305, 311, 314, 317, 318, 319, 320, 321, 322, 323, 325, 327, 328, 335, 336, 337, 338, 339, 340, 344, 347, 348, 352, 369, 371, 373, 375, 377, 379, 380, 381
Sitting Bull 99, 116, 121, 133, 134, 144, 155, 166, 340, 352
"Slaughter Slough" 318
Slim Buttes xix, 16, 41, 71, 123, 129, 352, 377
Edmund Kirby Smith 179
Smoky Hill River 287
Jacob Snively 226, 227
Solomon River 12, 146, 161, 234, 283, 288
Silas Soule 23, 24
Southern Cheyenne Indians 18, 21, 113, 114, 162
South Mountain 31, 106, 244, 330
South Pass 2, 196, 198, 205, 227
Spokane Indians 297
Battle of Spokane Plains 357
Chief Spotted Tail 35, 40, 58, 85, 89, 122, 140
Spring Creek 15
"Staked Plains" 164
Chief Standing Bear x, 43, 44, 363, 364
David S. Stanley vi, 59, 164, 325, 326, 327, 328, 368, 375, 380
Edwin Stanton xvii, 201, 234, 260, 294
Steens Mountain 106
Edward Steptoe 355, 358, 359

OTHER TITLES ABOUT
THE WEST
FROM
CAXTON PRESS

The Pony Express Trail
Yesterday and Today
by William Hill
ISBN 978-0-87004-476-2, 302 pages, paper, $18.95

Battlefields of Nebraska
by Thomas D. Phillips
ISBN 978-0-87004-4717, 300 pages, paper, $18.95

A Fate Worse Than Death
Indian Captivities in the West
by William Hill
ISBN 0-87004-xxx-x, xxx pages, paper, $18.95

The Deadliest Indian War in the West
The Snake Conflict 1864-1868
by Gregory Michno
ISBN 978-0-87004-460-1, 450 pages, paper, $18.95

Massacre Along the Medicine Road
The Indian War of 1864 in Nebraska
by Ronald Becher
ISBN 0-87004-289-7, 500 pages, cloth, $32.95
ISBN 0-87004-387-0, 500 pages, paper, $22.95

For a free catalog of Caxton titles write to:

CAXTON PRESS
312 Main Street
Caldwell, Idaho 83605-3299

or

Visit our Internet web site:

www.caxtonpress.com

Caxton Press is a division of THE CAXTON PRINTERS, Ltd.